The Reign of the
Ayatollahs

THE REIGN
OF THE
AYATOLLAHS

Iran and the
Islamic Revolution

Revised Edition

SHAUL BAKHASH

Basic Books, Inc., Publishers   New York

Library of Congress Cataloging-in-Publication Data

Bakhash, Shaul.
    The reign of the ayatollahs.

    Includes bibliographical references and index.
    1. Iran—History—1979–   . I. Title.
DS318.8.B34 1984   955′.054   83–46078
ISBN   0–465–06887–1 (cloth)
ISBN   0–465–06889–8 (paper)
ISBN   0–465–06890–1 (revised paper)

To Roy,

who made this book possible,

and to my Iranian friends,

who loved the revolution,

not knowing it would not love them back

CONTENTS

PREFACE TO THE REVISED EDITION

IN February 1989, Iran marked the tenth anniversary of the Islamic Revolution. Ayatollah Khomaini, the towering figure of the Iranian revolution, died in June, bringing to an end the Khomaini decade. Two other events in 1988–89 also neatly demarcated the end of the first decade of the Islamic Republic. In July 1988, the eight-year-old war between Iran and Iraq came to an end, allowing Iran's leaders to address long-neglected social, economic, and foreign policy problems. In July 1989, Iranians approved far-reaching amendments to the constitution, which altered in important ways the structure of the state and set the stage for the post-Khomaini era. The constitutional amendments reflected yet another attempt to come to grips with the problems Iran's leaders have encountered in attempting to establish an Islamic state based on Islamic law and governed by the clerics.

The Reign of the Ayatollahs was first published in 1984; the paperback edition with a new epilogue appeared in 1986. Reader interest in the book has remained gratifying. However, it seemed desirable to publish a new edition that incorporated recent major developments, and the tenth anniversary seemed an opportune time to take stock of the Iranian revolutionary state.

The revised edition of *The Reign of the Ayatollahs* contains three new chapters (10, 11, and 12). Some of the material in the epilogue to the first paperback edition has been incorporated in chapters 9 and 10, but most of the material in both these chapters, and all of chapter 12, is new. The conclusion has been recast in the light of the larger perspective that is now possible on the significance of the Iranian revolution.

In addition, I have corrected typographical errors, slightly altered the spelling of some Iranian names for the sake of consistency, and made a few small changes in wording in the interest of greater precision. But I have made no major alterations to the body of the book.

A sabbatical from my home institution, George Mason University, and a fellowship at the Woodrow Wilson International Center for Scholars permitted me to undertake the research and to write the new material for this edition. My thanks to both institutions. I am also grateful to my energetic and indefatigable research assistants, Hooman Bakhtiar and Patricia Mann, for their help, and to C. J. Wigginton for his careful reading of the first edition and for his helpful suggestions.

PREFACE

ON 16 January 1979, one of the landmark days of the Iranian revolution, I was walking down Fisherabad Avenue, toward Ferdowsi Square, in Tehran. The debris of a year of rioting and political turmoil was everywhere: burnt-out tires, shattered glass, shuttered shops, strewn leaflets, graffiti-covered walls. The unusual afternoon silence was suddenly shattered by the cacophony of car horns, cheers of demonstrators, and a growing, almost palpable, excitement among the afternoon crowds. A car came careening up the avenue. A young man, body thrust half out of the window, triumphantly held aloft the front page of the afternoon paper, *Kayhan*. The bold, black headline told its own story: *Shah Raft*, "The Shah Is Gone."

Mohammad Reza Pahlavi, King of Kings, had quit the country. Within two weeks, Ayatollah Ruhollah Khomaini would return from fifteen years of exile, to be greeted by delirious millions. Within four weeks, his revolutionary followers would be masters of the country. As I picked my way through the euphoric crowds that January afternoon, one image stuck in my mind. From opposite ends of a side street, two cars, each packed with celebrants, came at great speed toward the crossing. The driver of the first car was driving on his extreme right; the driver of the second car on his extreme left. The predictable happened. The two vehicles collided head on at the crossroads. It appeared to be an ironic foretaste of the many collisions that lay ahead.

During the previous summer and fall, I had watched as the revolutionary movement gained momentum and the Shah stumbled toward his Armageddon. For nearly a year after Khomaini's return to Tehran, I was able to observe firsthand the great events of the revolution: the seizure of power, the debates over the new constitution of the Islamic Republic, the taking of the American embassy, the unraveling of the revolutionary coalition, and the violent struggle for control of the revolution. These events were the stuff of newspaper headlines; but they were rooted deep in recent Iranian history. As a journalist and a historian, I felt impelled to write a book that would capture both the immediacy and historical significance of these momentous events. The present work, the product of both direct experience and later study, is the result.

Thanks are due to a large number of friends and colleagues who assisted in the completion of this book. Patrick Seale first encouraged me to undertake a book on the Iranian revolution. Andrew Knight, the editor of the *Economist,* commissioned a long article that became the kernel of the present work. Valuable support was given by Clifford Geertz, Albert Hirschman, Albert Hourani, J. C. Hurewitz, Bernard Lewis, Roy Mottahedeh, and Avrom Udovitch. Charles Issawi and A. K. S. Lambton read one or more chapters of the manuscript. A. Aghassipour, Ahmad Ashraf, Mansur Farhang, Farhad Hakimzadeh, Rahim Iravani, Hasan Khosrowshahi, Hamid Lajvardi, and Ahmad Salamatian shared with me their knowledge of Iranian events.

My wife, Haleh, undertook much of the research, read drafts, corrected copy, and provided sound advice. The book could not have been completed without her.

Steve Fraser of Basic Books displayed the patience of Job while this book was being completed, and Sheila Friedling saw the manuscript through the press. The Near Eastern Studies Department at Princeton University, the Institute for Advanced Study at Princeton, and the National Humanities Center in North Carolina provided me with a home where parts of this book were written; and gracious ladies at all three institutions typed the many drafts of the manuscript.

The Reign of the Ayatollahs

Introduction

IN FEBRUARY 1979, the fifty-year-old Pahlavi monarchy collapsed in a brief two-day popular uprising. The uprising delivered the coup de grâce to a regime that had already been battered and broken by a year of street clashes, strikes, and demonstrations. The Shah had already left the country. His leading courtiers and officials were abroad. His generals were no longer at their posts. The writ of the government he had left behind barely extended beyond the building housing the office of the prime minister. The revolutionaries were in control of the streets, and strike committees of the instruments of administration. On 10 and 11 February, the people of Tehran took over the physical symbols of government: the military barracks, the police stations, the government buildings. Bearded revolutionaries sat in the offices of ministers; turbaned mollahs occupied the palaces of kings.

This is a book about the course and consequences of the revolution that has convulsed Iran over the past five years. In writing it, I have sought to provide a political history of the revolution, to trace the emerging institutional structure of the Islamic Republic, and to describe the ideology and aims that actuate Iran's new rulers.

In Iran, the revolution has been a cataclysmic event which has resulted in an extensive transformation of the country's political, social, and economic structure. The centuries-old monarchy has been abolished and replaced by a republic; a secular state has given way to a quasi-theocracy. Islamic law codes have replaced secular statutes. A large part of the economy has passed from private into government hands. The former ruling strata of courtiers, high-ranking civil servants, military officers, and court-related businessmen have been replaced by a new administrative and military elite. The revolution has led to internal rebellion and foreign war.

Some measure of the depth of the upheaval wrought by the revolution can be read from the raw figures of casualties and shifts of population. Half-a-million Iranians, primarily from the middle and professional classes, quit the country to live as emigrés and exiles abroad. Some 10,000 were executed in waves of revolutionary terror. Thousands more lost their lives in the Kurdish rebellion. Nearly 100,000 were killed and 300,000 wounded in the war with Iraq. The war created 2 million refugees.

The revolution has had repercussions extending beyond Iran's borders. Major shifts have taken place in Iran's system of alliances, foreign policy, and military capability. This has disturbed the strategic balance in the region. As a result of the revolution, the dominant American position in Iran has come to an end, and the skein of military, intelligence, and economic relations linking Iran and the United States has been ruptured. Iran, considered under the monarchy as a guarantor of stability in the Persian Gulf, under the Islamic Republic is in the business of exporting revolution. The power vacuum created by the collapse of the monarchy facilitated the Soviet invasion of Afghanistan. The Iran–Iraq war was a direct outcome of the Iranian revolution.

Due to its specifically Islamic character, the Iranian revolution has also galvanized Islamic communities in the Persian Gulf and the Middle East. The revolution appeared to provide evidence of the ability of Islam to mobilize millions, to overthrow an autocratic government, to humiliate the United States, to defend the national frontiers, to wage foreign war, and to begin the task of realizing the ideal of an Islamic state.

Fears that the Iranian revolution presaged a wave of similar upheavals in other countries in the region have proved excessively alarmist. The Iranian revolution derives from specifically Iranian conditions and Iranian historical, cultural, and religious traditions. It is not a "model" which other countries can follow or a blueprint of the direction other Islamic societies will take. There are limits to its "exportability."

Iran is predominantly Shi'a*; the Arab states are predominantly Sunni. The Sunni clerics have not normally assumed the oppositional and political role played by Iran's Shi'a clerics. Age-old Arab–Iranian and Sunni–Shi'a animosities persist. Turmoil, political division, and revolutionary violence have somewhat dimmed the early attraction of the Iranian revolution to many Muslims in the Arab world.

Nevertheless, Khomaini remains a magnetic figure. There are large Shi'a communities in Iraq and Lebanon, and smaller communities in Saudi Arabia and the Gulf states, to whom the Iranian example seems pertinent. The Shi'as tend to come from the poorer classes and thus find Khomaini's vision of Islam as a religion of the deprived classes particularly attractive. Khomaini's militancy and anti-imperialism appeal to Sunnis as well as Shi'as. Iran has supported its revolutionary propaganda with contingents of the Revolutionary Guard, as in Lebanon; with subversion, as in Bahrain; and with money, as in a number of Persian Gulf states.

Developments in Iran bear watching for one further reason. In the current Islamic revival, a number of Islamic countries, notably Pakistan, Egypt, and Saudi Arabia, are experimenting with Islamic legal codes, "Islamic banking," and Islamic economic and governmental organizations. It is in Iran, however, that the most comprehensive effort to forge Islamic legal and economic institutions and to establish an Islamic state is under way. Difficult doctrinal and practical problems are involved. Iran's success or failure in resolving these problems is bound to influence similar attempts elsewhere in the Islamic world. A close examination of the issues and problems posed by the process of establishing an Islamic state in Iran will help us better to comprehend the nature of these problems as they arise in other Islamic countries.

This book deals first with the background and causes of the revolution. Chapter 1 locates the roots of the revolution in a complex interplay of social, economic, and political discontent, the existence of a religious and mosque organization capable of mobilizing the masses for opposition, the powerful pull of Islamic ideology, the charismatic leadership of Ayatollah Ruhollah Khomaini, and the faltering response of the Shah to the rising challenge to his rule.

Second, this book understandably devotes considerable attention to

---

*The turned comma has been used to indicate both the letter *'ayn* and the *hamzeh*.

Khomaini himself. Chapter 2 examines his early political activities and his ideas, while subsequent chapters attest to his continuing importance to the course of the revolution. Khomaini emerged early as the undisputed leader of the opposition movement. He provided the umbrella under which the disparate opposition forces could unite against the Shah. He articulated many of the themes that were used so effectively against the Pahlavis. When, during the protests of 1978, other opposition leaders were inclined to a compromise solution, he remained steadfast in demanding the Shah be overthrown. He formulated the concepts on which Iran's Islamic Republic is founded. In the postrevolutionary period he remained the final arbiter between the conflicting groups and on the critical issues.

This is not to suggest that Khomaini predetermined the course of the revolution, or that he and his lieutenants were invariably in control of events. On the contrary, a third point this account emphasizes is the degree to which postrevolutionary developments escaped central control and direction. The revolution released powerful and disruptive aspirations. It spawned a plethora of political parties, interest groups, and ideological schools driven by conflicting aims and programs. It lit a blaze of revolutionary ferment that could not be easily extinguished. Moreover, tens of thousands of weapons fell into the hands of the citizenry. The revolutionary committees emerged as pockets of fragmented power throughout the country and challenged the central authority. Political and religious leaders deployed the street crowd, inflammatory rhetoric, the club, and the gun to advance political ends.

Chapter 3 describes these postrevolutionary conditions and their contribution to the fall of the Bazargan government. Subsequent chapters deal with the repeated failure of attempts to curb the revolutionary organizations, their emergence as the vehicles for the advancement of upwardly mobile groups, and their contribution to the radicalization of the revolution. The radical clerics around Khomaini, however, learned to ride this revolutionary tiger. They gained the support of the revolutionary organizations by bending to their will and refusing to join in efforts to curb them. They eventually used the revolutionary organizations to eliminate their rivals and to impose their version of the revolution on the country. Khomaini, too, unwilling to risk his popularity with the urban masses, seemed often to be led by rather than to be leading public opinion. However, he used each crisis further to consolidate his hold on the country and to pursue, single-mindedly, his aim of establishing an Islamic state.

A fourth concern of this book has been to describe the character of the Islamic state which has been taking shape in postrevolutionary Iran. The Islamic Republic was inspired in the first instance by the ideas of Ruhollah Khomaini; but its leaders also drew on the concepts articulated by other writers on Islamic government and economics. These ideas, as chapter 4 suggests, were considerably elaborated during the great constitutional debates that took place in the summer of 1979. They were enshrined in the new constitution. They were given institutional expression in the constitutionally mandated primacy of Islamic law and doctrine over all aspects of Iranian life; in the powers vested in Khomaini as *faqih,* or Islamic jurist, and the authority vested in the Council of Guardians; in the elaboration of a corpus of Islamic laws and rules of social behavior; and in the clerical domination of Parliament, the judiciary, and other key areas of administration.

The passage from a secular to an Islamic state, however, has been a stormy one. Insofar as the creation of an Islamic government was believed to require the complete transformation of political, legal, economic, and cultural institutions, the process of Islamization constituted a great upheaval in Iranian life. At the same time, the imposition of certain Islamic principles, such as the ban on interest, proved impractical and had to be abandoned. Considerable resistance to the imposition of Islamic government developed among secular groups. The struggle between the proponents and the opponents of a theocratic state, which dominated the first four years following the revolution, is described in chapters 3, 5, and 6.

There was also little agreement among leading Islamic jurists on such crucial issues as sovereignty, property, or even the role of the religious classes and of Islamic law in an Islamic state. These disagreements were expressed most forcefully in the disputes over land and economic policy, which are examined in chapters 7 and 8. The doctrinal disputes, as this examination shows, were important in themselves, served as a vehicle for political and bureaucratic rivalries, and reflected an underlying conflict between competing social and political groups. The upshot was an uneasy impasse rather than the resolution of prickly doctrinal issues and deeply rooted social conflicts.

The results of the Iranian experience in creating an Islamic state have therefore been mixed. Islam has provided a powerful vehicle for mass mobilization, the advancement of upwardly mobile groups, the institution of rule by the clerics. On the other hand, the attempt to impose one version of Islam on a country that, like other Middle Eastern states, is a mosaic of Islamic sects, ethnic and language groups, and social classes and communities with sharply differing cultural orientations and values, has proved to be divisive and disruptive. The Islamic revolution has enjoyed mass support; the religious leaders, as recounted in chapter 9, have succeeded in consolidating their rule. But Islamization has been achieved, and then only imperfectly, at the price of coercion and repression.

Moreover, the impossibility of achieving the Islamic ideal, implementing Islamic law in all its particulars, or even agreeing on the specifics of the law, has led to a series of thinly disguised compromises. Five years after the revolution, the Islamic Republic appears to be firmly entrenched. Yet the gap between the ideal and the reality gnaws at the legitimacy and credibility of the state. A concluding chapter examines the elements of stability and the sources of conflict and weakness in the Islamic Republic.

Chapter 1

The Collapse of
the Old Order

THE IRANIAN REVOLUTION in 1979 astonished the world because an opposition armed only with slogans and leaflets overthrew a ruler with formidable assets at his disposal. The Shah commanded an army of 400,000, a large police force, and a fearsome secret police, Savak, with 4,000 full-time agents and scores of part-time informers. The government controlled the mass media and kept a tight rein on the press. There was only one officially sanctioned political party, and it was subservient to the monarch.

Moreover, the revolution took place against the background of nearly two decades of impressive economic growth. Using a steady flow of oil revenues, the Shah had built roads, dams, railroads, and ports; he had established steel and petrochemical industries; he had helped an entrepreneurial private sector develop a range of consumer industries.

A slight downturn in oil income in 1977 did not alter the fact that the country had strong foreign exchange reserves, investments abroad, few foreign debts, and an inflow of oil revenues that, compared to the Iranian situation only four years earlier, still constituted a cornucopia of plenty. In addition, Iran's borders were secure and it dominated the region. Until nearly the very end, the Shah had the support of both great powers, the western European states, his immediate neighbors, and the Arab states of the Persian Gulf.

Roots

Recent studies have emphasized the complex nature of the background to the Iranian revolution.[1] The Pahlavi dynasty, established in 1925, did not have deep roots in the country, and the Shah almost lost his throne in 1953. At that time, he was restored to power by an army coup, engineered with the assistance of the CIA. In 1963 widespread riots again shook the country. They were inspired by Ruhollah Khomaini, a religious leader who was just rising to preeminence, and they were put down with great severity. The Shah gained support in the 1960s, thanks to a program of land distribution, a number of other reforms, and a decade of sustained economic growth. By the eve of the revolution, however, this credit had been dissipated by the Shah's autocratic tendencies, the dislocations caused by a reckless economic program, and policies that alienated important sectors of the community.

But between 1963 and 1977, even as he carried out reforms, the Shah steadily reinforced the foundations of a royal autocracy. He suppressed the independent political parties and founded court-sponsored political movements. He packed Parliament with yes-men and he muzzled the press. He extended government control over such organizations as labor unions and trade guilds. He avoided the older, independently minded officials of his youth—men like Ali Amini, Abol Hasan Ebtehaj, and Abdollah Entezam—and surrounded himself either with sycophants or with technocrats who were competent but who lacked an independent political base of their own.

One result of these developments was to push elements of the opposition toward an increasingly radical position. The suppression of the 1963 protest movement persuaded young men of the National Front that constitutional methods of opposition against the Shah were ineffective. The National Front (NF), a coalition of parties headed by the nationalist prime minister, Mohammad Mossadegh, during the oil nationalization movement of 1950–53, was in 1963 still the major opposition political party. Two groups broke away to form what later became the Mojahedin-e Khalq and the Fadayan-e Khalq guerrilla movements, both dedicated to the violent overthrow of the regime. Secret movements emerged among the seminary students and younger clerics of Qom, a major religious center, also dedicated to overthrowing the regime.

The propensity of Savak to extend its operations, the desire of the Shah and his bureaucracy to impose state control over universities, private schools, business groups, religious endowments, and numerous other private organizations, meant that citizens who would not normally concern themselves with politics found the bureaucracy increasingly involved in their lives. In 1975, the Shah abolished political parties, including the Iran Novin which he had himself sponsored, and announced the establishment of a single party, Rastakhiz (Resurgence), for all Iranians. Those who did not wish to be part of the political order, he remarked, could take their passports and leave the country. Civil servants, university professors, and ordinary citizens were pressed to join the party. For the first time, nonpolitical individuals were being required to declare themselves and publicly identify with a royal political party.

Moreover, the Shah's rule appeared increasingly arbitrary. Although Parliament was a rubber stamp, he preferred to rule by imperial decree, in direct contravention of the constitution. He personally announced the nationalization of the secondary schools and he ordered industrialists to sell 49 percent of their shares to their workers. In both cases, implementation began long before the proper legislation was approved by Parliament. The leading officers of the government took their cue from the ruler. In order to make way for new streets and avenues, the mayor of Tehran sent bulldozers to demolish private homes and working-class districts, and in 1977 riots occurred as a result of this policy. To create agroindustries, the government forced villagers to sell their farmland and often razed entire villages. The minister of agriculture, intent on creating agricultural "poles" where rural populations could be concentrated and agricultural services more efficiently delivered, secured approval from Parliament for a law which permitted him to transfer the population of whole villages from one district to another.

A dimension of lawlessness was added to this arbitrary system of rule in 1977, when the first public protests in many years began to be voiced against the regime. A woman university professor who had participated at politically charged poetry-reading sessions in November 1977 was taken to an empty lot by agents of the police and beaten. Bombs, too small to cause great damage, but large enough to serve as a warning, were placed in the homes and offices of several of the lawyers active in the Iranian Committee for the Defense of Freedom and Human Rights. When members of opposition groups met for discussions in a private garden outside Tehran, "workers" showed up and beat up the participants, many of whom were middle-aged. One analyst of the Iranian revolution has noted that the Shah generated in Iranians a sense of humiliation and ultimately rage; ". . . the behavior of the Shah increasingly came to be experienced as an insult—a narcissistic injury to his own people. . . . He showed the Iranians no compassion and no empathy."[2]

Economic grievances fed the unrest. The period between 1963 and 1973 was a decade of rapid economic growth, which led to expanding job and education opportunities, improved standards of living, and rising patterns of consumption. More Iranians were able to buy radios, cars, refrigerators, or shoes, but the benefits of the economic boom were not evenly spread. People in some social strata did far better than those in other strata; the urban centers benefited more than the countryside. Government credit policy tended to favor the large industrialist and farmer as against the workshop owner or small cultivator. Housing conditions in large urban centers declined for the lower income groups. However, as long as the majority saw a chance to improve their condition at a reasonable pace, these problems did not seem likely to generate insuperable political problems. It was the explosion in oil prices in 1974 that severely dislocated both economic and social life.

Virtually overnight, Iran's oil revenues quadrupled, from under $5 billion to nearly $20 billion a year. The Shah believed that this money would enable him at last to carry the country to his long promised "Great Civilization" and within a decade, turn Iran into one of the world's five leading industrial countries. He plunged into a reckless spending program.

The results were predictable: the economy overheated, prices of housing, food, and basic necessities soared. Rural migrants drained the countryside of agricultural labor and swelled the shantytowns and the urban underclass of the large cities. Bottlenecks developed in all sectors of the economy. Ships waited months for their turn to unload cargo at Iranian ports; there were shortages of cement and steel for home construction.

The shortage of skilled labor necessitated the bringing in of tens of thousands of foreign workers. There were massive electricity shortages. Iranians remarked that the power failures and blackouts marked the arrival of the Great Civilization.

Moreover, if real incomes for workers and the white-collar salaried employees steadily improved in the 1963–73 period, after 1974 the economic position of these groups deteriorated. Resentment was intensified by the widening gap in incomes, by the ability of the privileged few to make fortunes by dealing in land, scarce commodities, and goods and through commissions on large and questionable government contracts.

To bring down prices, the government launched a campaign against the business community. Established industrialists were hauled off to jail or sent into exile. Some 10,000 inexperienced students were recruited to check on prices in shops and the bazaar. Some 250,000 shopkeepers were fined, 23,000 traders banned from their home towns, and 8,000 shopkeepers were jailed.

The government decided to deflate the economy by cutting back on investment, curtailing projects, and stopping new hiring in the civil service. The sudden about-face, after a period of uncontrolled spending, led to a business downturn and reduced employment and business opportunities. It also burst the balloon of inflated expectations. The purchase of a house, or even a car, was suddenly beyond the reach of middle-class families; bazaar merchants were faced with dwindling business opportunities; clerical staff on fixed salaries felt bitterly resentful and betrayed. The pressure of frustrated aspirations triggered the political crisis that followed.

The economic crisis coincided with pressure on the Shah from such organizations as Amnesty International and the International Commission of Jurists on the condition of prisons and treatment of political prisoners in Iran. More important was the pressure for human rights reforms emanating from the Carter Administration. The Shah was sensitive to such pressure, particularly from a Democratic administration. In 1961–62, during another period of internal crisis, he had been persuaded by the Kennedy Administration to appoint a reformist prime minister and to implement land reform. It was an experience the Shah did not soon forget. In 1977, he saw the Carter human rights campaign as a repeat performance of his experience with Kennedy. This time, he took the initial measures on his own initiative. For example, he introduced new regulations that permitted civilian defendants brought before military tribunals to be represented by civilian lawyers and to enjoy open trials. The Shah also slightly eased press controls.

Protests

Members of the intelligentsia, professional groups, and leaders of the middle-class opposition parties were quick to take advantage of this slight opening. In May 1977, fifty-three lawyers addressed a letter to the imperial court, demanding an independent judiciary. In June, three leaders of the National Front wrote directly to the Shah asking for a restoration of press freedoms, the implementation of the constitution, and the freeing of political prisoners. A group of forty writers and intellectuals wrote to the prime minister, Amir-Abbas Hoveyda, to protest censorship and the suppression of intellectual freedom. Ninety-eight intellectuals signed a second letter to the prime minister in the same vein.

Several professional organizations were formed to work for constitutional liberties. A group of sixty-four lawyers established a watch-dog committee to defend the constitutional laws and the independence of the judiciary. Political leaders, intellectuals, and lawyers joined hands to establish the Iranian Committee for the Defense of Human Rights and Freedoms. A group of lawyers and judges formed the Association of Iranian Jurists to look after the interests of prisoners. The Writer's Association was reactivated and university faculty members formed a National Organization of University Teachers. In November, ten evenings of poetry readings at the Goethe Institute and Arya Mehr University in Tehran were turned into a forum for the denunciation of the government's repressive practices.

Protests entered a new phase in January 1978, when seminary students in the holy city of Qom took to the streets to object to a government-inspired article in the newspaper, *Ettelaat*, that cast aspersions on the character of Ayatollah Ruhollah Khomaini. Khomaini, who had a large following among the seminarians, had been expelled from Iran in 1964 for his attacks on the Shah and was living in exile in Iraq (see chapter 2). A confrontation with the authorities during the Qom demonstrations led to a number of deaths.

The Qom clashes sparked a series of mourning ceremonies, processions, and riots that over the next twelve months shook dozens of towns and cities. In February 1978, mourning ceremonies for the Qom dead were observed in half-a-dozen cities. But in Tabriz, a young man was shot and there were severe riots. In March, mosque services and processions were organized in fifty-five urban centers; in half-a-dozen towns the ceremonies turned violent. In May, there were more demonstrations and riots.

This new phase of the opposition movement differed significantly from what had come before. The earlier protests were led by the intelligentsia and the middle classes, took the form of written declarations, and were organized around professional groups and universities. The new protests were led by clerics, were organized around mosques and religious events, and drew for support on the urban masses. While the earlier protests were concentrated in Tehran, this new phase spread the protests to the entire country. The earlier protests were generally reformist in content, seeking a redress of grievances and the implementation of the constitution. The mosque-led demonstrations were more radical, even revolutionary in intent. It has been alleged that it was only in the later stages of the protest movement that the Shah was personally denounced, demands made for his overthrow and for the establishment of an Islamic form of government, and Khomaini treated as the leader of the opposition forces. In fact, these themes appear in the pamphleteering literature of the mosque-led protests as early as February 1978. During the year of protests in 1978, it was adherents of Khomaini, and the proponents of a radical solution, who rapidly gained the upper hand.

The clerics displayed their ability to mobilize the people on 4 September, when they organized mass prayers to mark *id-e fetr* (the end of the Ramadan fasting period). In Tehran, almost 100,000 came together for the communal prayer, then marched to Shahyad Square, shouting pro-Khomaini slogans. For the next three days demonstrations continued, growing larger in size and more radical in their slogans. On 7 September, demonstrators openly called for an Islamic government, denounced the Shah, and repeated the slogan, "Khomaini is our leader." The government, alarmed by the size and the radical temper of the demonstrations, and by indications that the demonstrators were attempting to subvert the troops, declared martial law on the night of 7–8 September. The next day, at Jaleh Square in the working-class district of Tehran, demonstrators, unaware of the martial law regulations, refused to disperse; troops opened fire, and large numbers of demonstrators were killed.

The Jaleh Square massacre, which became known as "Black Friday" in the folklore of the revolution, was a turning point in the protest movement. Compromise with the Shah became extremely difficult if not impossible after this date, and the moderates found themselves forced to take a more radical, uncompromising stand.

Demonstrations continued after 8 September. In October, the first of the strikes in the public sector occurred, and they spread quickly. By November, workers in the oil industry, the customs department, the post office, government factories, banks, and newspapers were on strike. These strikes crippled and finally paralyzed the economy.

The Royal Response

The Shah's response to these developments was uncertain and erratic. He alternated between concession and clampdown; but neither the periods of clampdown nor the concessions he made were effective, given the crisis in the country and the demands of the opposition. In response to the initial riots, he dismissed unpopular officials, released political prisoners, announced free elections, and promised a Western-style democracy.

In August 1978, following a fire at the Rex Cinema at Abadan in which 477 people lost their lives, he removed Jamshid Amuzegar and appointed Ja'far Sharif-Emami as prime minister. Sharif-Emami made several concessions to the clerics. He set aside the "monarchic" calendar, imposed two years earlier and based on the date Cyrus founded the Persian empire; he closed down gambling casinos and nightclubs, abolished the post of minister of state for women's affairs, set up a ministry for religious affairs, released jailed clerics from prison, and permitted the great prayer meeting on *id-e fetr*. He made concessions to the secular opposition by lifting press censorship, permitting freer debate in Parliament, and allowing renewed activity by political parties.

However, Sharif-Emami proved unable to restore order or to quell demands for more radical change, and in November 1978 the Shah replaced him with a military man, General Gholam-Reza Azhari. The new prime minister, in turn, announced tougher measures against rioters, strikers, and violators of marital law regulations. On the other hand, the Shah went on national television, referred to himself as *padishah* (king) rather than the title he always demanded, *shahanshah* (king of kings), told the people he had heard their "revolutionary message," and promised to correct past mistakes. Presumably to placate public opinion, he allowed the arrest of 132 government leaders, including the former prime minister, Amir Abbas Hoveyda, and the former Savak chief, General Ne'matollah Nasiri.

The Shah's uncertain response to the crisis is attributable to a number of factors, including the fact that he had never been decisive under pressure, and the situation was inherently difficult. By September 1978, it was unclear whether even a massive crackdown could end the protests; and in any case the Shah was reluctant to use greater force and cause more bloodshed. Moreover, he was receiving conflicting advice both from his own advisers and from Washington.

Throughout the crisis, he waited for the United States to tell him what to do. But in Washington counsels were divided: the State Department, under Cyrus Vance, believed the Shah should negotiate with the opposition. The National Security Adviser, Zbigniew Brzezinski, believed that the Shah should be told he would have U.S. support for whatever measures he thought necessary to restore order. The message the Shah received, through his own ambassador to Washington, Ardeshir Zahedi, and through the American ambassador in Tehran, William Sullivan, was thus conflicting, and this added to the ruler's paralysis and indecision.

In December, the Shah finally decided to deal with the opposition. He invited the National Front leader, Karim Sanjabi, to the palace with a view to offering him the government. But Sanjabi was already bound by an agreement with Khomaini which did not recognize the Pahlavi monarch as the legitimate ruler of the country. The National Front leader wanted the Shah to leave the country, but the Shah refused.

By the end of December, however, the Shah's position had become untenable, and the British and American ambassadors were urging him to go abroad. The Shah now turned to another member of the National Front, Shapour Bakhtiar. Bakhtiar was committed to a constitutional transfer of power; he had little use for clerical rule. He agreed to accept the prime ministership from the Shah and to remain loyal to the constitution, on condition the Shah handed over authority to a Regency Council and left the country on a "vacation" of undetermined length. The Shah left Iran on 16 January 1979.

Bakhtiar acted with energy. He dissolved Savak, gave freedom to the press, and announced he would sever diplomatic relations with Israel and South Africa. He sought desperately to maintain calm on the streets. Fearing an army coup, he begged Khomaini not to return to Iran yet (even closing the airport to prevent Khomaini's return), and offered to go to Paris himself to talk to the Imam.

However, Bakhtiar lacked power on the streets. Three days after the Shah's departure, a million people marched in Tehran demanding Bakhtiar's resignation. At Khomaini's instruction, employees in ministries refused to let Bakhtiar's ministers into their offices. When he arrived back in Tehran on 1 February 1979, Khomaini appointed his own prime minister, Mehdi Bazargan. It was only a matter of time before the government of Bakhtiar would collapse, and the end came on 11 February. The revolutionary forces took control, and Khomaini triumphantly announced the establishment of the Islamic state.

Chapter 2

Khomaini:

The "Idol Smasher"

THE UNCHALLENGED LEADERSHIP of the revolutionary movement that gathered force in Iran in 1978 fell to a seventy-six-year-old religious leader, Ruhollah Khomaini, who had been living in exile in Iraq since 1965. Khomaini became the symbol of the revolutionary movement for a number of reasons. For nearly two decades, he had remained steadfast in his opposition to the Shah. In exile abroad, he was able to be more uncompromising than religious or political leaders at home. His sensitive antennae carefully attuned to the public temper, he was able to articulate themes and touch on issues that powerfully roused the mass of the people. He managed to be all things to all people. Islamic fundamentalists and westernized intellectuals, bazaar merchants and the urban masses, came to see in his vision of an Islamic state the chance to realize their very disparate aspirations. Moreover, he had in Iran a network of clerical leaders, religious students, and young political activists devoted to his cause and determined to keep his name at the forefront of the revolutionary agitation. To millions of Iranians he came to be seen, like the Old Testament prophets, as the *bot-shekan*, the idol-smasher, and as *the* Imam, the religious and political leader of the community.

Ruhollah Khomaini was born in Khomain, a village some 180 miles south of of Tehran, in 1902.[1] Both his father and his grandfather were religious scholars. His grandfather, Seyyed Ahmad Musavi al-Hindi had settled in Kashmir, India, thus acquiring the descriptive "al-Hindi" that was sometimes attached to the family name. Seyyed Ahmad returned to Iran eventually and settled in Khomain. Khomaini's father, Seyyed Mostafa, a local religious figure, was killed, possibly in a dispute over land or water rights, when Ruhollah was five months old. The young boy was brought up by an uncle, Seyyed Allameh Morteza Musavi Parvaresh. The family owned land and appears to have been reasonably comfortable. Several of the male members of the family, viewed in traditional terms, were well educated.

Qom: 1921–1961

Khomaini received a largely religious primary education in Khomain. At the age of fifteen or sixteen, he was sent to Arak, a provincial center, to continue his religious studies. At the time, the seminary at Arak was under the direction of Abdol-Karim Ha'eri-Yazdi, one of the leading Shi'a teachers and theologians of the interwar period. In 1922, when Ha'eri accepted an invitation to undertake the revival of Qom as a center of Islamic studies, Khomaini followed him. At Qom, he underwent the traditional course of studies in the Islamic sciences, jurisprudence, Koranic exegesis, scholastic philosophy, and ethics. He also studied *erfan*, or gnosticism.[2] The course was valued for providing an insight into the inner logic of Islamic jurisprudence and therefore giving the initiate a certain leeway in the interpretation of Islamic law. The study of *erfan* was also valued for developing strength of character and courage in adversity, qualities which Khomaini in later years urged on his students. He was by all accounts an able student, asking probing questions, and skilled in the give and take of argument and debate that was used as a teaching tool in the classroom. After he received his diploma, he became an instructor at Qom.

As a teacher, he lectured on subjects and texts that were a part of the seminary curriculum. He taught jurisprudence and also philosophy, a subject which the more orthodox religious scholars regard with slight condescension. But it was his lectures on ethics that attracted the largest following. He used these lectures to urge his students to develop character and moral fiber; he interpreted Islam as a commitment to social and political causes. "The discussion would go on for hours," Ayatollah Mohammad-Javad Bahonar, a former student and a later colleague, remembered. "The two issues he emphasized were the necessity for Islam and Iran to be independent of both Eastern and Western colonialism and the need to get the clerics out of the mold of an academic straightjacket. He said the clergy had a responsibility for humanity not only in Iran but wherever people were hungry and oppressed."[3]

The powerful magnetism was already evident in the young Khomaini. Mehdi Ha'eri, another former student recalled: "You felt the immanence of God; God was ever-present with Khomaini."[4] The lectures on ethics, delivered twice each week, grew in popularity and drew hundreds of listeners, both students and townspeople from Qom. The government eventually brought pressure to bear on the religious authorities in Qom, and the lectures had to be suspended.

Khomaini's residence in Qom, both as a student and a young teacher, coincided with the rise to power of Reza Khan, the later Reza Shah and founder of the Pahlavi dynasty. Reza Shah was determined to establish a strong central government and, in the style of Kemal Ataturk in neighboring Turkey, to modernize and westernize Iran. The religious classes appeared to him to constitute a barrier to the achievement of these goals, and he set about eroding their power and standing.

His reign was marked by deep inroads into those areas where clerical influence was especially marked. He secularized and codified the laws, adopted European-style law codes, and established a system of secular courts that greatly reduced the judicial functions of the ulama (men learned in Islamic religion and law—the community of clerics). By requiring judges to hold a law degree from the newly established Tehran University, he effectively prevented the graduates of the religious seminaries from becoming judges. He withdrew from the clerics the authority to notarize and register documents, thus denying them both important functions and important sources of revenue.

The network of schools and colleges Reza Shah established broke the near monopoly the religious classes had exercised over education. By establishing a rival center of Islamic studies at Tehran University, he challenged the ulama even on their home ground of religious education. Under his direction, the government began to interfere in the certification of seminary students and graduates, and in the curriculum of the religious schools, ostensibly in an effort to "modernize" them.

The government went far in extending its jurisdiction over the administration of religious endowments, a step which the ulama could only regard as an attempt to tamper with the financial independence of the religious classes and to make religion subject to the direction of the state. Clerics were harassed in a multitude of petty ways: the government interfered in matters of religious dress; restrictions were placed on the holding of religious mourning services and prayer meetings; and religious students were in certain instances made subject to military service. Reza Shah's commitment to secularization and Westernization was offensive to religious sensibilities; and his dictatorial and arbitrary methods seemed to the ulama to exceed the bounds of what was tolerable.

Clerical dissatisfaction with these developments manifested itself in an undercurrent of passive resistance that occasionally broke out into active opposition. In 1927, Hajj Aqa Nurollah, a religious leader in Isfahan, led a mass protest march from Isfahan to the shrine at Qom, where he and his followers took *bast*, or sanctuary. For three months, the bazaars of Isfahan remained closed as a mark of support, before the protestors could be dispersed. In the following year, in another incident, Ayatollah Mohammad-Taqi Bafqi was forcibly dragged out of the shrine at Qom and beaten by Reza Shah himself for having questioned the appropriateness of the dress worn by female members of the royal family when they entered the shrine. Repeatedly, clerical leaders were imprisoned or exiled. The most dramatic confrontation occurred in June 1935, when troops entered the shrine of Imam Reza at Mashad, one of Shi'ism's holiest religious centers, to break up prayer meetings under way to protest Reza Shah's measures. The troops opened fire and dozens were killed, hundreds injured.

These events left a deep and lasting mark on Khomaini. His speeches and declarations in the 1960s and 1970s are sprinkled with references to the humiliation suffered by the ulama and the willful denigration to which Islam was subjected under Reza Shah. This partly explains Khomaini's sensitivity and opposition to the measures which Reza Shah's successor, Mohammad Reza Shah, began to introduce in 1962, under the general rubric of his "White Revolution." Khomaini saw these measures as a reenactment of the Reza Shah experience, a renewed attempt to extend arbitrarily the power of the state, and to erode the place of religion in society.

Shortly after Reza Shah's abdication in 1941, Khomaini gave vent to his feelings about the Shah in a book entitled *Kashf ol-Asrar* (The Unveiling of Secrets).[5] The book is interesting as an early exposition of Khomaini's ideas on the relationship between religion and the state. Khomaini treated Reza Shah as a usurper, the parliaments of the period as lacking in legitimacy, the laws they had approved as harmful, the ministries as corrupt, the police cruel, and officials as lacking in concern for the poor and the downtrodden. He attributed this condition in large part to Reza Shah's deliberate policy of ignoring Islamic precepts and undermining the religious community. As in later years, he was critical of the tendency to adopt Western law codes and employ Western advisers, and the extension of various freedoms to women.

But Khomaini did not in this early book declare monarchy to be by its nature illegitimate. While stressing the desirability of permitting the ulama a large measure of supervision over governmental affairs, he did not claim for them the right to rule, or require the ulama to refrain from all forms of cooperation with the government. On the contrary, he indicated the readiness of the ulama to accept a far more limited role and to cooperate even with bad governments in upholding the state because "they consider even this rotten administration better than none at all."[6]

The ulama, he pointed out, served as a pillar of the state. They helped to ensure internal order, suppress insurrection, and protect the country against foreign interference and influence. But by the same token, he noted that the government must protect and uphold the religious classes. This point of view helps explain Khomaini's hostility to Reza Shah who not only directly attacked the privileges and standing of the ulama, but by weakening the religious leaders and Islam, in Khomaini's view, also endangered the independence of the state itself.

Khomaini shunned political involvement in the 1940s and early 1950s, even during the tumultuous years of the oil nationalization movement and the prime ministership of Mohammad Mossadegh in 1951–53. Mossadegh and his National Front may have been too secular in temper for Khomaini's taste. He may have been reluctant to offend the leading religious figure of the day, Ayatollah Mohammad Hosain Borujerdi, who pursued a policy of quietism and disapproved of clerical involvement in political affairs. Significantly, Khomaini's own period of active political involvement dates from the death of Borujerdi in 1961. Borujerdi's death also coincided with the Shah's new activist phase as he attempted to blunt domestic unrest and American pressure for reform by a series of measures, the linchpin of which was land reform.

It was the n   nner of their enforce-
ment, the in   ..... puncy by the government that they implied,
and the Shah's increasingly authoritarian manner of rule that brought
Khomaini into conflict with the authorities. But the first clash occurred
over a matter which, on the surface at least, appeared to be of relatively
minor importance.

The Local Councils Law: 1962

In October 1962, the government of Asadollah Alam approved by cabinet decree a law which provided for the election of representative local
councils throughout the country. The religious leaders found the law
objectionable on three grounds. It allowed women to vote for the first
time; it did not require adherence to Islam as a necessary qualification
for either voters or candidates; it specified that elected councillors would
take their oath of office, not on the Koran, but on "the holy book," a
wording that permitted the swearing in of councillors belonging to
non-Muslim religious denominations. In parliamentary elections, members of the recognized minority faiths—Christians, Jews, and Zoroastri-
ans—voted separately as distinct groups and elected their own representatives to the Majles (the lower house); but the law made no special
provision for members of minority religions in local elections. The government no doubt intended the local councils law as the thin end of a
wedge for a more extensive reform.

But what the government regarded as progressive, the religious leaders viewed as an attack on the integrity of the Islamic community. They
treated the extension of the vote to women as a violation of Islamic
principles. Khomaini later described the measure as an attempt "to
corrupt our chaste women."[7] They saw the substitution of "the holy
book" for the Koran as a sinister attempt to remove religion from its
central place in national life. Moreover, they believed the wording of
the local councils law was designed to open a back door to elective office
to the Baha'is. Because the Baha'is broke with Islam in the nineteenth
century to found their own religion, they are regarded as apostates by
orthodox Muslims. They were denied the recognition extended to the
other minority religions, and any attempt to permit Baha'is to hold
public office was regarded with suspicion by the ulama.

Larger issues were involved. Earlier in the year the government had begun a program of land distribution. It had also established the Literacy Corps, under which young men were conscripted into the army and sent as teachers into the rural areas to teach village children to read and write. From the point of view of the ulama, the Literacy Corps threatened to spread the seeds of secularism from the cities to the villages and challenged the role of the mollas, or clerics, as village teachers. Land reform was viewed as a violation of the sanctity of private property. Applied to the religious endowments, it threatened the financial independence of the mosques, religious seminaries, and the clerical community. Parliament, moreover, had been dissolved and the government, since May 1961, had been ruling by cabinet decree. Iranians other than the ulama regarded this situation with misgivings. The country was in the throes of an economic recession, and unemployment and economic hardship were widespread. This was a situation to which the clerical classes, with their links to the bazaar and the common people, were especially sensitive.

The ulama of Qom sent telegrams to the Shah and the prime minister protesting the local councils law. Preachers and instructors began to preach and teach against the new measure in mosques and seminaries, and similar agitation was started in other cities. Signatures, sometimes numbering several thousand, were collected on petitions protesting the measure.[8] Prime Minister Alam sought to defuse the crisis first by ignoring it, then by seeking to explain away the offending clauses, and finally by offering to postpone the local council elections. None of these measures succeeded in placating the ulama, who called for nationwide meetings of protest and prayer for 1 November. In a session on 31 October that continued well past midnight, the cabinet decided to avoid a confrontation. In the early hours of 1 November, Alam sent telegrams to the religious leaders in Qom and letters to those in Tehran informing them that the local councils law had been suspended.

Early in the crisis, Khomaini joined other clerical leaders in protesting the local councils measure. He sent a telegram under his own signature to Alam; and when Alam did not reply, he addressed the prime minister again and also sent a separate telegram to the Shah. In these communications, he was careful not to implicate the Shah directly; it was the prime minister he treated as the official responsible for the measure. Alam, he argued, was violating the constitution and Islamic law, and was erring in his refusal to heed the advice of the religious community and the wishes of the nation. He not only demanded that Alam correct the offending paragraphs of the law, he also peremptorily told the prime minister to "take care that such things do not happen again."[9]

Khomaini, moreover, chose from the beginning to widen the issue. He criticized the government not only for the councils law but also for the general state of the country and the economic hardships of the people. He insisted that the law was part of a wider plot hatched by foreign elements and aimed at Islam and therefore at the independence of the country. The local councils law, he said:

> . . . was perhaps drawn up by the spies of the Jews and the Zionists. . . . The Koran and Islam are in danger. The independence of the state and the economy are threatened by a takeover by the Zionists, who in Iran have appeared in the guise of Baha'is.[10]

The idea that the Baha'is in Iran acted as the agents of the Jews and Israel remained a persistent theme in Khomaini's declarations.

Already on the local councils issue, Khomaini also displayed both his intransigence and his ability to take a position independent from that of his colleagues among the ulama. When Alam sought to give assurance that he would interpret the law in a manner acceptable to the ulama, Khomaini insisted that such personal assurances had no legal force and that the cabinet must take legislative action to undo what it had done. When Alam tried to explain away the objectionable clauses, Khomaini labeled these explanations as "pure deception." Although he worked with the other religious leaders, he consistently took a more uncompromising stand. Even after Alam gave ground, Khomaini refused to cease speaking against the law, insisting that the cabinet decision, privately communicated to the ulama, must be made public. It was not until 1 December, when Alam, at a press conference, announced the cabinet decision to suspend the local councils law, that Khomaini was finally satisfied.

Other features of Khomaini's tactics during the crisis are noteworthy. If at the beginning of the agitation he was careful not to criticize the Shah directly, by the end of the crisis he had abandoned such caution and even seemed to take relish in taunting the Shah. "He [the Shah] says, 'I have no business with the clerics. Sir. The clerics have business with you.' "[11] Although he and other religious leaders justified their opposition to the local councils law on the basis of the constitution, Khomaini made clear that the constitution was important to the ulama only because of its provisions prohibiting any legislation in conflict with Islamic principles. "Otherwise," he said, "for us the constitution is not the last word. We will oppose whatever is contrary to the Koran, even the constitution."[12]

Finally, Khomaini appears to have been deeply impressed by the alacrity with which large numbers of people responded to clerical direction and their avowed readiness, expressed in letters, telegrams, and petitions, often addressed to Khomaini himself, to lay down their lives in defense of Islam. It gave him a sense of the power the ulama could wield in a confrontation with the government. "If one word had been said," he remarked later, "there would have been an explosion."[13] This was a lesson Khomaini did not forget.

The Collision of Moharram: 1963

Although the local councils issue had been laid to rest momentarily, Khomaini continued to speak out against the government. It was in his nature to exploit an opponent's weakness and to press his advantage. For him, the issues were now much broader, involving the very nature of the government's intentions and the role of religion in the direction of affairs. He believed, not without cause, that the government had merely decided on a tactical retreat, not the fundamental change of course desired by the clerical leaders. The government, despite clerical opposition and the tenor of its promises to leading religious figures, was pushing ahead in any case with its various programs.

In January 1963, the land reform law was revised and given wider application. The upper limit on land holdings was drastically reduced and the law's provisions were extended to cover religious and other endowment properties. The prime minister refused a last-minute request from the prominent clerical leader, Ayatollah Mohammad Behbahani, that the government exempt the religious endowments. On 26 January, the Shah submitted land reform and five other measures, including the Literacy Corps plan and measures for the nationalization of forests and pastureland, to a national referendum.

The 99.9 percent "yes" vote was a figment of the government's imagination. But the land reform was highly popular in the villages; and this helps explain why the leading ulama, despite their opposition to the land distribution, refrained from issuing *fatvas*, or religious decrees, against it. However, the possibility that the government might gain support in the villages strengthened Khomaini's resolve to discredit the administration. The Shah, moreover, added insult to injury by appearing in Qom during the week of the referendum to denounce the religious classes as elements of "black reaction" and by making references elsewhere to "the lice-ridden mollas." In February, the Shah, claiming powers he alleged were vested in him by the constitution, personally extended the right to vote to women. Other bills under preparation, including a judicial measure where reference was made to the swearing-in of judges, again sought to substitute the term "the holy book" for the Koran.

Khomaini did not remain passive in the face of these developments. Mossadegh's old National Front, which had for years called for land reform and could not very well oppose the Shah's other reform measures, adopted the slogan, "reform yes, dictatorship no." But Khomaini condemned the whole reform program as a fraud and forbade his followers to participate in the referendum on the "White Revolution." On the eve of the Iranian New Year *(Now Ruz)* on 21 March, he issued a declaration describing the New Year as "a time for mourning, not celebration." He called attention to the poverty and suffering of the poorer classes. He made the assertion again that the government was acting in the interests of foreign forces to destroy Islam and the religious classes. "In the interests of the Jews, America and Israel," he said, "we must be jailed and killed; we must be sacrificed to the evil intentions of foreigners."[14] In sermons to the large numbers of pilgrims who had come to Qom for the New Year, Khomaini stressed these same themes.

March 22 coincided that year with mourning to commemorate the death of the sixth Shi'a Imam, Ja'far Sadeq. Feeling against the government was high among the seminary students, and this manifested itself in antigovernment statements, prayers, and protests. On 22 March, the government struck back. Army commandos, dressed as civilians, attacked the Faiziyyeh seminary, beat up the students, and pushed some of them off balconies, terraces, and rooftops. One young student was killed, scores were injured. Roving remnants of these commando units continued to harass seminary students over the next couple of days.

Khomaini reacted by describing the attack as "no cause for anxiety, and even beneficial" because it sharply galvanized feeling against the authorities. He sent a telegram to the ulama of Tehran and a protest to Prime Minister Alam. In a sermon delivered during mourning ceremonies held forty days after the attack on Faiziyyeh, he described the government as a "usurper," called for its removal, and accused it of renewing "the crimes of the Mongols and Tatars." He played skilfully on the fact that the attackers on the Faiziyyeh had been shouting pro-Shah slogans. "Love of the Shah means rapine, violation of the rights of Muslims and violation of the commandments of Islam," he said. He again sought to depict the government as the agent of Israel and said the Iranian army "is not prepared to see the country crushed beneath the Jewish boot." Addressing the prime minister, he stated, "I have bared my breast to your bayonets . . . I will never bow my head to your tyranny." When Ayatollah Mohsen Hakim, the senior Shi'a cleric in Iraq, invited the ulama of Qom to move to Najaf in Iraq as a mark of protest against the destruction of the Faiziyyeh, Khomaini refused, saying Qom could not be abandoned to "unbelievers and infidels."[15]

The end of May and early June coincided with the mourning month of *Moharram,* during which the passion and martyrdom of Imam Hosain, reenacted in villages and towns across the country, revives in dramatic form the themes of resistance to tyranny and of martyrdom in the name of Islam and justice. Feelings run particularly high on *tasu'a* and *ashura,* the ninth and tenth days of the month, which mark the passion and death of Imam Hosain, son of the first Imam, Ali, on the plains of Karbala in an unsuccessful bid to realize his claim to the Caliphate.

Khomaini was scheduled to deliver a sermon on *ashura,* 3 June. His pictures had already appeared in the bazaar and in shops and on walls throughout Qom. On the day of the sermon, the crowd filled the school, its balconies, rooftops, and terraces and spilled out into the great town square and the side streets beyond. Khomaini stressed three themes in his address on this highly emotional day. He was at pains to defend the religious classes against charges of being reactionary. He strongly attacked the Shah himself and accused the Pahlavis of aiming to destroy Islam. He renewed his charges against Israel. And he wove together the themes of the Shah's alleged designs against Islam and Israel's alleged designs against the country together. "Israel," he said, "does not want the Koran to survive in this country. Israel, through its black agents, crushed the Faiziyyeh seminary. It crushes us. It crushes you, the nation. It desires to take over the economy. It desires to destroy our commerce and agriculture. It desires to seize the country's wealth."[16]

He addressed the Shah contemptuously as "you unfortunate wretch," and warned him to heed the advice of the ulama. Noting that Savak had demanded of the ulama that they refrain from criticizing the Shah, mentioning Israel, or warning of dangers to Islam in their sermons, he remarked: "What connection is there between the Shah and Israel? . . . Mr. Shah! Perhaps they want to depict you as a Jew, so that I should declare you an infidel, and they [the people] should throw you out of Iran."[17]

Khomaini's address aroused powerful antigovernment currents, not only in Qom but in Tehran and other cities as well. In the early hours of the morning of 5 June, security officers entered Khomaini's home, placed him under arrest, and drove him immediately to Tehran where he was incarcerated in a room at the Eshratabad military barracks. News of his arrest spread rapidly. Violent demonstrations exploded in the Tehran bazaar and moved rapidly uptown. Rioting spread to Qom, Shiraz, Isfahan, and Mashad. At Varamin, near the capital, several hundred men, wearing death shrouds as a symbol of their readiness for martyrdom, marched toward the capital. The demonstrations continued on 6 June, and as the intensity of the rioting mounted, the Shah ordered the army to put them down by force. The collision between the Shah's forces and the opposition was the bloodiest since the overthrow of Mossadegh ten years earlier. Rioting continued into the next day, and martial law had to be imposed on Tehran, Mashad, Isfahan, Shiraz, and other cities before order could be restored. The number left dead was certainly higher than the figure of 200 cited by the government; and the bloodshed of Moharram in 1963 sowed the seeds of a bitterness whose harvest would be reaped in the revolution fifteen years later.

Along with Khomaini, a large number of religious figures were arrested on 5–7 June. All except three—Khomaini, Ayatollah Baha ad-Din Mahallati, and Ayatollah Hasan Qomi-Tabataba'i—were soon released. Reports circulated that Khomaini would be tried; the prime minister, Alam, was said to favor having him executed. Ayatollah Kazem Shariatmadari, Ayatollah Hadi Milani, also a senior *marj'a-e taqlid* or source of emulation for Shi'as, other prominent religious leaders, and provincial ulama gathered in Tehran and made representations to the government. Khomaini, they argued, was a *marja'* in his own right, and it was hardly fitting to try him.[18] The government relented, and a trial was not held.

A group of younger, middle-rank clerics, many of them Khomaini's former students, also worked assiduously to secure Khomaini's release. They issued a declaration protesting the continued detention of Khomaini and his two colleagues in July and circulated a second protest in August. The instructors at the Qom seminary issued a similar declaration in March 1964. They criticized the regime for muzzling the press, assuming arbitrary powers, and attempting to "turn constitutional government into one-man rule." In addition, they forcefully asserted the claim of the religious leadership to a voice in political affairs, and of the duty of the believers to follow their guidance; they claimed for Khomaini an authority at least equal to that of the other leading religious figures.[19]

The activities of these signatories were an early indication of Khomaini's growing following among a significant segment of the middle ranks of the ulama. Clerical opposition to the local councils law marked the first serious involvement of the religious community in national politics for nearly a decade. The experience had a galvanizing effect on many of the younger clerics, serving as an initiation into opposition activity, demonstrating the political power of Islam in the hands of committed religious leaders, and casting Khomaini in the role of model and leader. Ali-Akbar Hashemi-Rafsanjani, a Khomaini devotee who after the revolution became speaker of the Iranian Parliament, was a young student in Qom at the time. He later described the impact on his generation of Khomaini's political militancy in 1962:

> Mr. Khomaini was in the vanguard, and struggled more firmly than many others in this cause. I, who was with him, was his student and found his approach more to my liking, drew closer to him. That year, for the first time, I began political activity.[20]

Many of the signatories of these declarations, little known at the time, continued to preach and to participate in clandestine political activity in the 1960s and 1970s, played a critical role in the 1978 agitation leading to the overthrow of the Pahlavis, and assumed important positions in postrevolution Iran. Among the signatories,[21] for example, Ayatollahs Hosain-Ali Montazeri and Mohammad Sadduqi in 1978 led the revolutionary agitation, respectively, in Najafabad and Yazd. After the revolution, Montazeri became Friday prayer leader in Tehran and, later, Qom and was widely regarded as Khomaini's heir-apparent. Sadduqi became Friday prayer leader in Yazd. Hashemi-Rafsanjani was a founding member of the Islamic Republic Party (IRP). Ali Qoddusi became the revolutionary public prosecutor, and Ahmad Azari-Qomi the Tehran revolutionary prosecutor. Mohammad-Ali Andalibi became the chief judge of the revolutionary courts in Shiraz, Ayatollah Abdol-Rahim Rabbani-Shirazi a member of the Guardianship Council, and Mohammad Yazdi a prominent member of the IRP and of Parliament. While still under arrest, Khomaini was visited by a number of emissaries from the Shah, including the chief of Savak, General Hasan Pakravan. These visits were aimed at persuading Khomaini to refrain from further interference in politics. One of the visitors (Pakravan), Khomaini later recounted, told him, "Politics is lies, deception, shame and meanness. Leave politics to us." Khomaini, recalling the incident, remarked: "All of Islam is politics."[22]

Khomaini was finally released and allowed to return to Qom early in April 1964, or some ten months after his initial arrest. The government claimed Khomaini won his freedom by agreeing to stay out of politics. But Khomaini denied giving such an undertaking. Ten days after his return, he addressed a large congregation at Qom's A'zam mosque. He was both defiant and conciliatory, both militant and seemingly accommodating. He maintained this tone of defiance and seeming moderation in a sermon delivered in June to mark the death of antigovernment demonstrators in the previous year, and also in an address to students from Tehran University in September.

In all three addresses Khomaini continued his harsh castigation of the government. He described the Shah as a lackey of foreign powers, he proclaimed his determination to continue to resist. "We remain in the same trench where we stood before," he said. "We oppose all cabinet decrees that are contrary to Islam. We oppose all the bullying. We oppose the pressures being brought on the nation. We oppose the imprisonment of the innocent."[23]

Yet Khomaini also seemed to hold out the hand of compromise. He invited the government to send representatives to Qom for talks. "Do we say the government should go?" he asked. "We say the government should stay. But it should respect the laws of Islam, or at least the constitution." He seemed to suggest there would be grounds for a reconciliation if the government broke relations with Israel, enforced the constitution, accepted the guidance of the religious community, and allowed the ulama a share in administration. The government, he said, should at least hand over responsibility for the administration of education and the religious endowments to the ulama and allow them "a few hours of radio time."[24]

Behind this seemingly conciliatory approach lay Khomaini's concept of the interdependence of religion and government—but government guided by what Khomaini believed to be Islamic principles—and also a great deal of calculation. His request for a "modest" share for the ulama in administration was rooted in his belief that the clerical class would set such an exemplary model in their limited sphere that all would recognize the superiority of religious administration. At the same time he understood very well the powerful weapon "a few hours of radio time" would constitute in the ulama's hands. If he urged the government to implement the constitution, it was because the constitution provided the ulama with a veto power over legislation considered contrary to Islamic precepts.

There was, however, little chance his offer of accommodation would be accepted. His criticisms of the Shah and the government had already gone too far. The Shah was not about to make concessions which were so at variance with his other policies and whose implications were momentous. Events were, in any case, moving toward another confrontation between Khomaini and the state.

The Status of Forces Law: 1964

After two years of rule by cabinet decree, elections had been held and Parliament reconvened in the fall of 1963. In July 1964, in one of its last sessions before the summer recess, the Senate, or upper house, was presented with and quickly approved a bill that extended diplomatic immunity to the personnel of American military advisory missions in Iran, to their staffs, and their families. The effect of the status of forces law, as it was called, was to make such Americans resident in Iran subject to the jurisdiction of American and not Iranian courts. The bill aroused memories among Iranians of the humiliating capitulatory rights imposed on Iran by the great powers in the nineteenth century. Despite the government's haste in pushing the bill almost secretively through a pliant Senate, news of the measure spread rapidly in Tehran and then in other cities during the summer and early fall. Tracts appeared against the measure, and Khomaini raised his voice against it; news spread even to distant villages.

In October, when Parliament returned from its summer recess, the bill was presented to the Majles, or lower house. Even in the hand-picked Majles, the measure aroused considerable opposition. For the first time in many years, several deputies spoke against a government-sponsored piece of legislation, an act of considerable courage given the atmosphere of the times. When the vote was taken, the measure passed by a majority of only thirteen votes. Not only had sixty-one deputies voted against the bill; some sixty-five had deliberately absented themselves during the balloting. Moreover, because the Majles approved a $200 million American loan for arms purchases immediately after passage of the status of the forces act, it was widely assumed that the two measures were connected: the government had made humiliating concessions to the United States for money.

Shortly after the Majles vote, Khomaini issued a declaration and also preached a sermon denouncing the status of forces law as "a document for the enslavement of Iran."[25] The Parliament, he said, had by its vote "acknowledged that Iran is a colony; it has given America a document attesting that the nation of Muslims is barbarous." He construed the measure as further evidence of the threat posed to national independence when Islam was weakened. "If the men of religion had influence," he said, "it would not be possible for the nation to be at one moment the prisoner of England, at the next, the prisoner of America. . . . If the men of religion had influence, governments could not do whatever they pleased, totally to the detriment of the nation."

He alleged that America desired to exploit Iran and thus sought to destroy Islam and the Koran as the barriers in its path. He called on the ulama to speak out and agitate against the measure, on the people to oppose it, and on the army "not to permit such scandalous events to occur in Iran . . . to demand of their superiors that they bring down this government."

Khomaini's declaration attracted widespread attention. A clandestine leaflet reproducing his remarks was extensively distributed. Tape recordings of his sermon were sold in the bazaars. His remarks were further publicized by word of mouth. Within days of his declaration Khomaini was arrested and quietly banished to Turkey, going first to Ankara and subsequently to Bursa. The following year, in October 1965, he was permitted to change his place of exile to the Shi'a shrine city of Najaf, in Iraq, where he was to spend the next thirteen years.

In contrast to his arrest in June 1963, Khomaini's arrest and exile in November 1964 did not spark off demonstrations and riots. The bloody outcome of the fearful clash in 1963 was still fresh in the public mind and land reform had won the government a degree of credit. Nevertheless, Khomaini's outspoken criticism of the status of forces law, and his subsequent arrest and exile, greatly enhanced his standing. In the confrontation with the government in *Moharram* in 1963, he was able to draw on the support of the working classes and the urban poor, but only to a very limited extent on the support of the middle classes. In his criticism of the status of forces law in 1964, however, he was echoing sentiments widely shared among the educated and middle classes. Moreover, his stand on the status of forces measure consolidated his position among the clerical class and reinforced his claim to primacy among the religious leaders. Many mollas in Tehran and the provinces refused to preach in their mosques following his exile. Within weeks of his banishment, tapes of his declarations began to be smuggled from Turkey into Iran.

Khomaini in Exile: 1964–1978

In exile in Iraq, Khomaini directed his efforts into the type of activity that during his Qom period he had described as incumbent on a religious leader: teaching, writing, speaking, and issuing declarations, all aimed at exposing the "crimes" of the Iranian government, warning of the threat posed to Islam and Iran by a regime of "tyranny and unbelief," using Islam as an instrument for mobilizing and forging a united opposition, and teaching his followers to gird themselves for resistance to a ruler who had turned himself into "a servant of the dollar."

His circle of students in Najaf grew. He remained in touch with his supporters in Iran whose oppositional activities he encouraged. He established contact with Iranian student organizations in Europe and the United States. He made it a point to comment publicly on major events in Iran, such as the Shah's coronation in 1967, the twenty-fifth centennial celebrations of the Iranian monarchy in 1971, and the establishment of the single-party state in 1975. He condemned acts of official suppression and applauded signs of public resistance. The arrest, and subsequent death in prison, of Ayatollah Sa'idi in 1970; the use of troops to crush student demonstrations at Tehran's Arya Mehr University the following year; and the indifference with which Iranians greeted the Shah's call to join the single party, Rastakhiz, were all marked by declarations from Khomaini.

His themes in these statements remained consistent.[26] He continued to condemn the imprisonment of religious figures, university students, and other opposition elements, the practice of "medieval torture" and execution, and the suppression of basic freedoms. He protested that the regime was violating not only Islamic law but also the constitution. He spoke repeatedly of the condition of the poor and downtrodden, and occasionally of the ill-effects of government policy on shopkeepers and bazaar merchants. He condemned the life-style of the ruling classes and the royal family as "corrupt, the pursuit of animal pleasures."

He also denigrated various aspects of the Shah's reform policies, criticizing the Literacy Corps on one occasion, the extension of voting rights to women, or some aspect of the Shah's programs on another. Such criticism appeared at times to stem from general hostility to the regime and suspicion of its intentions, rather than from antagonism to specific measures. (Khomaini, for example, made no attempt to dismantle the Literacy Corps after the revolution.) He wished to retain the initiative, not to permit the government to gain credit through "enlightened" acts.

But Khomaini was also actuated by specific dangers he perceived in government measures. He was deeply disturbed by attempts of the state to secure control over the religious establishment and direction of spiritual affairs. He condemned a measure announced by the Shah in 1971 to send government-recruited religious teachers into the villages. When the government in 1973 renewed attempts to extend supervision by the state-controlled Endowments Organization over mosques, seminaries, and religious centers, he was reminded of similar efforts under Reza Shah. The measure was an attempt, he charged, "to install turbaned mercenaries in place of the preachers and the ulama . . . to transform all ulama and preachers into government employees . . . and destroy the spiritual integrity of Islam."[27]

The perceived threat to Islam and the independence of the country remained the basic theme of all Khomaini's statements during his exile in Iraq. The Shah, he reasoned, was a foreign lackey; he was "selling" the country to foreigners. He was permitting the exploitation of Iran's valuable oil resources and exchanging the revenues for expensive American weapons, which were as useless to Iran as "scrap metal." He was allowing Europeans and Americans vastly to expand their presence in the country. While patriotic Iranians were subjected to "beatings, torture, disrespect, and savage and inhuman treatment," Americans enjoyed immunity from prosecution by Iranian courts. Foreign businesses, he believed, were plundering the country. When American capitalists met in Iran in 1970 to consider further investment in the Iranian economy, Khomaini declared that the Shah "will place the agriculture, industry, mines, forests, even food distribution and tourism throughout the country in their hands; and for the Iranian nation nothing will remain except hardship and toil for the capitalists, humiliation and poverty."[28]

Khomaini believed that the Shah attacked the clerical classes because they stood in the way of his intention to deliver the country to the great powers. The ulama were "the difficult class," the only group determined to resist the foreign domination and plunder of the country. In later years, there were those who would argue that Khomaini was concerned with the integrity of Islam, not of Iran, and that his Islamic concerns overrode his national ones. After the revolution, as the dispute between the Islamic and the secular, nationalist elements grew more bitter, he too tended to stress an opposition between Islam and nationalism. But in these earlier years, Khomaini most often mentioned state and religion, Iran and Islam, in the same breath. Throughout, he reacted powerfully both to what he regarded as threats to Islam and what he deemed as threats to the integrity of Iran. For him, the two were interdependent. He regarded the independence of the state as an essential condition for the establishment of an Islamic community; and he saw adherence to Islam as essential to the preservation of this independence.

During his exile, Khomaini also frequently commented on wider issues concerning the Islamic world, particularly the Arab–Israeli conflict. He received delegations from the Palestine Liberation Organization (PLO) and issued *fatvas* describing it as incumbent on Muslims to support the Palestinian cause. His deep hostility to the state of Israel was reflected in references to the need to "uproot this germ of corruption" from the Islamic world and his references to the "gang of Jews" who run the Jewish state.[29] But the Arab–Israeli problem was, for him, also the national problem writ large.

In the same way the imperialist powers sought to dominate and exploit Iran, he believed, they also sought to dominate and plunder the Islamic world. In order to do so, they aimed at the destruction of Islam; and Israel was the instrument of this policy. Rulers and governments that facilitated great-power influence in the Islamic world, like the Shah, were by definition agents of the great powers. Disunity among the Islamic states and indifference to Islam among their peoples would lead to a weakness that could invite foreign interference. Thus Khomaini's prescription for the Islamic states, as for Iran, was a return to the Koran, commitment to a society based on Islamic rule, and unity of all Muslims.

Khomaini's opposition activities in Iraq virtually ensured his primacy as leader of the religious community in Iran, and earned him respect as an unflinching critic of the Shah among opponents of the Pahlavi regime. But the period of exile, particularly after 1970, was noteworthy for two specific developments. First, Khomaini's ideas underwent a sharp transformation. He began to direct his attacks not only at the person of the Shah, but at the institution of monarchy itself; to urge not only adherence to Islamic law, but the establishment of an Islamic state. He began to preach not only radical change, but revolution. Second, economic, social, and political dislocations in Iran created a fertile ground for Khomaini's radical ideas. For large numbers of Iranians, conditions in Iran came increasingly to mirror Khomaini's depiction of them, once considered to be an exaggeration.

Velayat-e Faqih: Government of the Islamic Jurist

Khomaini's implacable hostility to the Pahlavis and his basically revolutionary concept of the Islamic state were expressed in a series of lectures he gave to his students in Najaf around 1969. These lectures were published as a book under the title of *Velayat-e Faqih*. [30] The term implies the vice-regency, or the government of the Islamic jurists, the men learned in Islamic law. *Velayat-e Faqih* articulates Khomaini's essential ideas about the state and also the goals he was to pursue over the next decade. It is a blueprint for the reorganization of society. It is a handbook for revolution.

Four essential themes emerge from the book. First, it comprises a condemnation of the institution of monarchy as alien to Islam, abhorrent to the Prophet, and the source of all of Iran's misfortunes over 2,500 years of history. Second, it presents the Islamic state, based on the Koran and modeled after the Islamic community governed by the Prophet in the seventh century, not as an ideal achievable only in some distant future, but as a practical form of government realizable in the lifetime of the present generation.

Third, it is a forceful assertion of the claim of the clerical class, as heirs to the mantle of the Prophet, to the leadership of the community. The two qualities essential to the ruler or governor, according to *Velayat-e Faqih,* are justice and expertise in Islamic law. So overriding is the importance of this knowledge of the law that "the real governors are the Islamic jurists themselves," Khomaini wrote. [31] It is they who must exercise supervision over all the executive, administrative, and planning affairs of the country. Moreover, while the ulama might exercise leadership over the community collectively, in consultation with one another, leadership may be vested in a single, outstanding religious figure.

> If a deserving jurist is endowed with these two qualities [justice and knowledge of Islamic law], then his regency will be the same as enjoyed by the Prophet in the governing of the Islamic community, and it is incumbent on all Moslems to obey him.[32]

Finally, *Velayat-e Faqih* describes it as incumbent on all believers to work actively for the overthrow of the non-Islamic state: "We have no choice," Khomaini wrote, "but to shun wicked governments, or governments that give rise to wickedness, and to overthrow governors who are traitorous, wicked, cruel and tyrannical."[33] His book also lays down the steps by which the Pahlavis are to be overthrown. It is thus a manual for revolution—but not violent revolution. Khomaini urged religious students and clerics, teachers, university professors, and all Iranians to work for the realization of the Islamic state by speaking out, teaching, and actively organizing. "When they oppress you," he stated, "cry out, protest, deny, uncover falsehood."[34]

At the same time, he urged his followers to deny the existing government and its institutions legitimacy by refusing them recognition and directing their loyalty to other, Islamic institutions. The people should take their lawsuits not to the state courts but to their own Islamic judges, he said. They should pay taxes not to the government but to their Islamic leaders. They should, in short, create a kind of parallel government. Such activity, accompanied by outspoken opposition, will gradually mobilize the population:

> . . . the people will awaken and grow active . . . A wave . . . an opposition movement will be created in which all men of religion and honor will participate . . . In the end, they will as a force penetrate a great government, or they will fight and overthrow it.[35]

Khomaini in these years also began to attract the attention of Iranian opposition elements abroad. Among these were Ebrahim Yazdi, Mostafa Chamran, Sadeq Qotbzadeh, and Abol-Hasan Bani-Sadr, all of whom were to hold high official positions in postrevolutionary Iran. Yazdi and Chamran, both products of Bazargan's Iran Freedom Movement, had for many years been active in organizing Islamic associations among Iranian student and opposition groups in the United

States. Yazdi visited Khomaini on a number of occasions in Iraq; in 1972 he was appointed Khomaini's unofficial representative in the United States.

Bani-Sadr, a supporter of the National Front and active in opposition politics during his student days at Tehran University in the early 1960s, had come to Paris in the midsixties. Both he and Qotbzadeh were active among opposition groups in Paris.

Beginning in 1970, Khomaini also began to exchange messages with Iranian student associations in Europe and the United States, in which he urged Iranian students to shun secular ideologies and to devote themselves to the promotion of an Islamic government for Iran. These student associations and other Iranian activists did not always take seriously Khomaini's theocratic ideas. But they saw in him a possible leader in their common cause against the Shah. They had contacts among the American and European press, among parliamentarians in various European countries, and with international human rights organizations; and they were able to call attention to human rights violations and other negative aspects of the Shah's regime.

The Khomaini "Network"

When he went into exile in 1964, Khomaini left behind clerics in Tehran, Qom, and other provincial cities who were either committed to him personally or who broadly shared his political aims. Some of these, like Montazeri and Hashemi-Rafsanjani, remained in touch with Khomaini, handled funds on his behalf, and consulted him regarding their political activities. Khomaini loyalists found their way into a network of mosques in Tehran and other cities. After Khomaini's arrival in Iraq, substantial amounts of money were contributed in the form of charitable dues (the *sahm-e imam*) in Khomaini's name. Religious figures in towns and villages across the country collected these contributions as Khomaini's representatives, and transmitted them to Khomaini's brother, Morteza Pasandideh, in Qom. The funds constituted a source of considerable influence and were used not only to support clerics, mosques, seminary students, and Islamic cultural activities, but also to fund opposition political movements. In the 1960s and early 1970s this network did not yet add up to an elaborate organization. Many clerics and numerous Islamic associations operated independently and were linked to Khomaini only through an informal skein of personal contacts, mosques, and study groups.

Not all the clerics who achieved prominence after the revolution were militant Khomaini advocates during the years of exile. Morteza Motahhari, Mohammad Beheshti, Mohammad-Javad Bahonar, and Mohammad Mofatteh managed to retain discreet links with Khomaini even while accommodating themselves to the Shah's regime.[36] All four had been Khomaini's students. Motahhari was a distinguished professor of Islamic philosophy at Tehran University's Faculty of Theology. His interest in philosophy and his association with Tehran University set him somewhat apart from the more traditionally minded ulama of Qom, where jurisprudence remained the queen of the Islamic sciences. However, his personal relations with Khomaini remained close. When he was killed by an assassin in May 1979, Khomaini remarked: "I have lost a dearly beloved son . . . one I considered among the fruits of my life."

Beheshti, Bahonar, and Motahhari had undergone the traditional training at the Qom seminary. The first two had also taken the trouble to acquire degrees at Tehran University's Faculty of Theology. They were thus regarded as "modernists." They sought to move both in the world of traditional Islamic learning represented by Qom and the world of modern, secular learning represented by Tehran University. Along with Motahhari, Bahonar and Beheshti were involved in a wide range of cultural and educational activities designed to give Islamic teaching and doctrines relevance in terms of contemporary social, economic, and political problems.

Motahhari and Beheshti were contributors to two publications, *Maktab-e Eslam* (The School of Islam) and *Maktab-e Tashayyo'* (The School of Shi'ism) dedicated to examining the role of Islam in the contemporary world. Motahhari was an organizer and Beheshti a participant in the *Goftar-e Mah* (Talk of the Month) lecture series in which Mahmud Taleqani, Mehdi Bazargan, and others took part and which were devoted to similar problems. Motahhari, Beheshti, Taleqani, and Bazargan contributed papers to a discussion organized after the death of Ayatollah Borujerdi in 1961 to consider the role of the *marja'-e taqlid* and of the religious establishment in contemporary Iran. Most of the contributors emphasized the need for a reform of the religious establishment and for efforts to awaken in the ulama a concern for the pressing social issues of the day. In the 1970s Motahhari led a discussion group on Islam in his home, which was attended by many lay intellectuals. Beheshti, who had spent the 1965–71 period as head of the Shiʻa mosque in Hamburg, returned to Iran in 1971 where he led a class in Koranic exegesis, often attended by several hundred young students. One of the participants was a one-time Tehran street peddler, Mohammad-Ali Rajaʻi, who in 1980 became the second prime minister of the Islamic Republic.

Although these educational activities, like those of more militant clerics, were important over the long run in gaining adherents and shaping attitudes, Motahhari, Beheshti, and Bahonar remained on good terms with the authorities. The highly respected Motahhari was on the board of the Imperial Academy of Philosophy, whose patron was Empress Farah. Beheshti and Bahonar worked for the ministry of education in preparing the textbooks on Islam for the school curriculum. Beheshti's appointment to the Hamburg mosque would not have been possible without official acquiescence. Bahonar had been arrested briefly in 1963; but he appears to have kept his political activism within acceptable bounds after this date. Beheshti's contributions to the symposium held after the death of Borujerdi suggest a certain radical view of Islamic government; but if he entertained strongly radical views, Beheshti managed to keep them well in the background. This group of Khomaini's associates, moderate in their public positions until the eve of the revolution, avoided serious difficulties with the authorities during the years of Khomaini's exile.

This was not the case with a second group of Khomaini's adherents, who were in these years repeatedly sentenced to prison and internal exile due to the militant content of their sermons and of the religious classes they conducted. There was a spate of arrests of such clerics in 1962–65, during the protests against the local councils legislation, the referendum on the "White Revolution," and the status of forces law; another round of arrests in 1965, after the assassination of Prime Minister Hasan-Ali Mansur; more arrests in 1967, around the time of the Shah's coronation; and widespread arrests after 1971, when there was a resurgence of clerical opposition activity.

For example, Ali Khameneʻi,[37] one of Khomaini's former students who in 1981 became the third President of the Islamic Republic, was in the 1960s and 1970s preaching in Mashad. He served as one of Khomaini's representatives in the city and was repeatedly arrested. One of his duties was to collect the charitable dues paid in Khomaini's name for transmission to Khomaini's brother Morteza Pasandideh.

In Tehran, Mohammad-Reza Mahdavi-Kani,[38] who was appointed minister of the interior after the revolution, led congregational prayers at the Jalili mosque. He also headed discussion groups on Islamic economics and other subjects for young students, and worked closely in such cultural activities with Motahhari, Mofattah, and Hashemi-Rafsanjani. He was working on a book on the Koran with Beheshti, Moffateh, and Musavi-Ardabili when he was rearrested in 1974 and sentenced to three years exile in Bukan, Kurdistan. Musavi-Ardabili, who served as prosecutor-general after the revolution, headed another important Tehran mosque in the Amirabad district. Reza Sa'idi,[39] a former student of Khomaini's and a devoted Khomaini follower, was arrested in 1970 for preaching against American investment in Iran. His case received wide publicity when he died under interrogation. Hosain Ghaffari,[40] who led congregational prayers at the Khatam al-Owsya and the al-Hadi mosques in Tehran, had been arrested briefly during the 1962 and 1963 protests. He was arrested again in 1965 because of his links with Khomaini and in 1974 for comparing the Shah to pharaoh and to Mu'awiyya, the seventh-century caliph regarded by the Shi'as as a tyrant. He too died in prison.

Ironically, exile to isolated provincial towns only allowed these clerics to spread their teaching further afield. The 1970s found Mahdavi-Kani teaching and preaching in Bukan; Ali Khamene'i in Iranshahr; Montazeri in Tabas, Khalkhal, and Saqqez; Ali Tehrani in Saqqez; and Mohammad-Mehdi Rabbani (a member of the Assembly of Experts that, after the revolution, wrote the new constitution) in Shahr-e Babak.

A third group, drawn from these militant preachers, also engaged in clandestine political activites. By the mid-1960s there was a proliferation of Islamic associations, most of them devoted to teaching and cultural activities, some using such activities as a cover for organizing opposition to the regime. Several of these groups formed an umbrella organization, the *Jam'iyyat-e Hay'at ha-ye Mo'talefeh* (Association of United Societies). In around 1964, at the association's request, Khomaini named Motahhari, Beheshti, and two others to serve as a political–religious coordinating council for the organization.[41] Members of the association planned and carried out the assassination of Premier Mansur in January 1965. Four of the participants in the plot were subsequently sentenced to death, and nine others were sentenced to various prison terms. One of the men sentenced to life imprisonment, Habibollah Asgar-Owladi, became minister of commerce in the postrevolution Raja'i government.

Although the Association of the United Societies did not survive the post-Mansur assassination crackdown, militants among the clerics soon regrouped. In the early 1970s, Khomaini lieutenants in Iran decided to fund the Mojahedin-e Khalq guerrilla organization, which had begun armed operations against the Shah's government. The intermediary between the clerics and the Mojahedin was Hashemi-Rafsanjani, at that time responsible for the relations of the clerical opposition with other clandestine opposition groups. As Rafsanjani later explained, the opposition forces at the time were so few, "we considered any form of struggle against Savak a blessing."[42] Rafsanjani himself had been imprisoned briefly after the assassination of Mansur in 1965, and on the eve of the Shah's coronation in 1967. In 1971 he was arrested again, but the authorities were unable to prove he was the author of a letter to Khomaini urging support for the Mojahedin.

In 1975, Rafsanjani secretly went to Lebanon to meet with members of the Islamic opposition working abroad, a number of whom were training with the PLO. During his absence, Savak had arrested Vahid Afrakhteh, a member of the Mojahedin. Under interrogation, Afrakhteh had revealed his contacts with Rafsanjani, times and places of meetings, and even the amount of money that passed from the clerics to the Mojahedin. Rafsanjani was arrested on his return to Iran and this time badly treated. A large number of other clerics who were believed to be implicated were rounded up. Both Montazeri and Mahdavi-Kani were taken from their places of exile to Savak prisons. Montazeri was sentenced to ten years in prison, Rafsanjani to six, Mahdavi-Kani to four. Mahdavi-Kani was released in 1977; most of the others were released in 1978 on the eve of the revolution.

When the first protests against the Shah's regime broke out in January 1978, there was, therefore, the nucleus of a Khomaini organization in place, a more elaborate network of mosques, Islamic associations, and clerics sympathetic to Khomaini, large numbers of young men who had learned at Islamic discussion groups to regard Islam as a dynamic force for change and opposition, and a vast reservoir of dissatisfaction with the regime which the opposition could tap. In the course of 1978, the clerical opposition itself coalesced and strengthened its organizational structure; it exploited the weaknesses of an increasingly vulnerable, wavering, and disoriented administration; and it found in Khomaini a leader who could give the movement leadership, direction, and concrete goals. Nevertheless, the clerics and the network of mosques and Islamic associations dedicated to Khomaini's cause remained only loosely integrated. This helps explain the fragmentation of power, once the monarchy was overthrown.

The Revolutionary Year, 1978

Khomaini, like many others both in the government and the opposition, was surprised by the breadth and intensity of the antiregime demonstrations which erupted in the early months of 1978. He expressed astonishment that the people, for so long quiescent, had at last found their voice. However, he understood very early that the opportunity for which he had worked and hoped for a decade was at hand. "The Shah," he announced, "stands on the edge of the precipice."[43] He marked each of the mass demonstrations, clashes, the drumbeat of mourning days, with proclamations and messages to the Iranian people. As in the past, these were generally condemnatory of the regime. But in both his public declarations and his private exchanges with his lieutenants, Khomaini now set himself four goals: to maintain the momentum of the protests, to use the movement to overthrow the Shah and the Pahlavi dynasty, to block all attempts at compromise, and to make the establishment of an "Islamic government" the goal of the entire movement.

By the early spring, the protest movement had assumed a powerful momentum of its own. Yet Khomaini feared that the protests would falter and that the Shah, "this wounded snake," would recover and crush the opposition. "If this fire in the hearts of the people is extinguished," he warned in one of his proclamations, "it cannot be ignited again."[44] He therefore called on the religious leaders and the people in general to demonstrate in larger numbers, to speak out, issue leaflets, and use the religious mourning days "like a sword in the hands of the soldiers of Islam" to arouse the population and expose the crimes of the regime. "Maintain this movement," he urged, "don't let this movement die."[45] Even in September when an earthquake took hundreds of lives in Tabas and left the ancient caravan city on the edge of the Kavir desert in ruins, he did not lose sight of his priorities. "Be awake!" he said. "Do not let them divert you from your path by earthquakes, floods and other problems. . . . Until the foundations of bullying and autocracy are uprooted, do not desist from your uprising."[46]

Khomaini also took care to ensure that the Shah remained the central issue. "The Iranian nation will not be fooled," he declared when the Shah began to dismiss his ministers and to imprison a number of them. "It will not overlook the real criminal."[47] He built up his case against the Shah carefully, often appealing to constitutional and legal arguments. The Shah's rule was not legitimate, he said, because his father had established the dynasty at the point of the bayonet. The Shah himself had been imposed on the country, and would not have survived without American backing. The Shah had personally ordered the killing of demonstrators, the repression of rights, the insults to Islam. He had destroyed the country's culture, corrupted its youth, and "with his own hands has presented to foreigners the riches and resources of this oppressed nation." The Shah was therefore "a traitor and a rebel." Moreover, even if the Shah had come by his throne legitimately, the people no longer wanted him. The entire nation, he said, "from east to west, from north to south, abhors the Shah."[48]

Khomaini was also greatly concerned to crush the impulse toward a resolution of the crisis by any arrangement short of the destruction of the Pahlavis and the abolition of the monarchy. The possibility of some kind of a compromise appeared to loom large as late as November 1978. The Shah, as already noted, had made concessions to the opposition in August. In November, he went on television, admitted to past mistakes, pledged to adhere to the constitution, and urged national reconciliation. He promised free elections. All this did not carry much conviction; but important secular and religious personalities were prepared to accept an arrangement under which the Shah would reign and not rule, as provided by the constitution. The U.S. embassy in Tehran was exploring such a possibility with Bazargan and other moderate opposition leaders. Elder statesmen, led by Amini, were making similar proposals. Several ideas were being canvassed, including the Shah's abdication in favor of his young son, who would rule under the supervision of a Regency Council.

Khomaini moved determinedly to discredit the idea of compromise. He denounced the change in prime ministers as "exchanging one checker-piece for another," the promise of free elections as a diversionary tactic, the Shah's "repentance speech" in November as untrustworthy. He was especially harsh on those who advocated a return to constitutional rule, because that implied retaining the Shah, or at least the monarchy. He ruled out the succession of the Crown Prince ("he is the son of that same father"), and he rejected any form of regency. Any arrangement that permitted the preservation of the Pahlavis or the monarchy, he said, "is treason to Islam and the nation."

Khomaini's public statements on this issue were the outward manifestation of the views he was expressing in discussions with representatives of various Iranian political groups. In a pattern that would be repeated after the revolution, these factions were already lobbying intensely to win him over to their point of view. Khomaini's public declarations and sermons during this entire year can be read as a response to political developments in Iran and the debate on tactics and ultimate goals that was taking place within his own camp.

One of those urging moderation on Khomaini was Mehdi Bazargan, the leader of the Iran Freedom Movement. Bazargan was concerned by the lack of any clearly defined channels through which Khomaini's instructions could be transmitted to the opposition in Tehran and the views of the moderate elements in the opposition movement transmitted to Khomaini. He found some of Khomaini's proclamations "unsuitable." In July 1978, he sent Khomaini a lengthy memorandum. It was carried by a prominent bazaar merchant who met secretly with the Ayatollah while on a pilgrimage to the holy places in Najaf.

In this memorandum Bazargan urged Khomaini not to denounce the constitution which, he said, provided the opposition with the only legal basis for making a case against the Shah. He agreed that the Shah should go, but he urged that Khomaini leave open the question of the nature of a successor regime. He agreed that the establishment of an Islamic government should be the "ultimate" goal; but he urged that such a government first be defined more precisely. He advised against "a clerical monopoly of the leadership of the movement"; the religious leaders lacked sufficient experience and technical expertise, he said, and such exclusivity had not yielded good results in the past. Bazargan also told Khomaini that "the sharp edge of the attack should be aimed at absolutism, not imperialism," in other words at the Shah, not at the United States, because the opposition needed American and European goodwill. Finally, he said the opposition should welcome the Shah's promise of free elections, test the Shah's sincerity, and participate in elections. Bazargan thus opted for a gradualist approach that kept the existing constitution and provided for participation by the opposition in the political process. He did not rule out retaining the institution of monarchy and expressed cautious misgivings both about an Islamic state and clerical leadership.[49]

Khomaini rejected virtually all of Bazargan's advice. He continued to denounce the monarchy, the constitution, and the United States. Moreover, he stressed the centrality of Islam to the whole opposition movement, warned against "groups with non-Islamic tendencies" who wished to join it, and insisted that only under the banner of Islam could the opposition mobilize and unify the people, and achieve ultimate victory. In a proclamation issued on July 27, perhaps in direct response to Bazargan's plea, Khomaini claimed for the religious establishment the exclusive leadership of the antiregime campaign:

> Iran's recent, sacred movement . . . is one hundred percent Islamic. It was founded by the able hand of the clerics alone, and with the support of the great, Islamic nation. It was and is directed, individually or jointly, by the leadership of the clerical community. Since this 15-year-old movement is Islamic, it continues and shall continue without the interference of others in the leadership, which belongs to the clerical community.[50]

Khomaini addressed the question of establishing an Islamic Republic with increasing frequency after he arrived in Paris in October. He was under greater pressure by the international press to define his position, victory appeared nearer, and the debate among the Iranian opposition about the government in postrevolution Iran had grown more urgent. At times, Khomaini suggested that an Islamic Republic could be established after a revision (rather than a total rejection) of the existing constitution. But he left little doubt about the ultimate goal or the nature of such a regime:

> There can be no return [to monarchy], and individuals who say they want such a return are in the minority. The whole nation, throughout Iran, cries out: "We want an Islamic Republic." An Islamic regime and an Islamic Republic rests on the general will and a general referendum. Its constitution is the law of Islam and must be in accordance with the laws of Islam. The law of Islam is the most progressive of laws. That part of the constitution that is in accordance with this progressive law will remain in place, and that part which is contrary to this law is not binding.[51]

Khomaini took the view that the public referendum had already been held. The people, through their mass demonstrations and declarations, had already voted for an Islamic Republic, he said. At the same time, he studiously avoided defining such a state, finding refuge in vague formulations. This exchange with an Arab journalist was not untypical:

> *Khomaini:* You think there is no program? Not at all. There is a program. Islam has a program. We also have a program. But the program is Islam and it is better and more progressive than the program implemented by the colonialists . . .
> *Interviewer:* May we know the main guidelines?
> *Khomaini:* Not yet. You must go, study and then grasp the main outlines. We will in the future announce all our political, economic and cultural policies.[52]

Paris: October 1978–February 1979

The Iraqi government, probably at Iran's request, was in the meantime pressuring Khomaini to desist from political activities and inflammatory statements. When he refused, he was asked to leave the country. Khomaini tried to cross over into Kuwait, but was refused entry. Khomaini next considered trying to enter Syria. But Ebrahim Yazdi, who had hurried to Khomaini's side, urged him to come to Paris rather than to try and settle in another Arab country.

The transfer of Khomaini to Paris in October contributed to the consolidation of the revolutionary movement in two ways. First, it gave Khomaini and the Iranian opposition worldwide exposure. Journalists from the world's leading newspapers, magazines, and radio and television networks beat a path to Neuphle-le-Château. Khomaini gave over 120 interviews during his four months in Paris, sometimes at the rate of 5 or 6 a day. This exposure gained the Iranian opposition sympathy and acceptance abroad, reinforced Khomaini's position at home by reassuring the wavering middle classes, and further eroded the self-confidence of the Shah's government. Second, given the excellent air and telecommunications links with Tehran, Paris permitted much closer coordination between Khomaini and the leaders of the revolutionary movement in Iran than had been possible at Najaf. It was in the Paris period that Khomaini's domination of the opposition movement came to be acknowledged by key Iranian political leaders and that the groundwork was laid for the postmonarchy revolutionary government.

Very quickly, a simple but highly effective telephone link was established between Khomaini's headquarters in Neauphlé-le-Château and Tehran. Each day, Khomaini's declarations were transmitted by telephone to Iran, taped, transcribed, and xeroxed in hundreds of thousands of copies. Telephone and personal contact between Khomaini and his aides in Iran, and between Khomaini and other political leaders, became simple. Among the stream of Iranian personalities who flew to Paris to meet with Khomaini were his own aides, Motahhari, Beheshti, and Montazeri; the leader of the Iran Freedom Movement, Mehdi Bazargan; the leader of the National Front, Karim Sanjabi; the leader of the Iranian Nation party, Daryush Foruhar; and eventually, an emissary from Shapour Bakhtiar, the Shah's last prime minister.

A number of these meetings had important consequences. Sanjabi's discussions with Khomaini early in November resulted in a carefully worded, three-point declaration, issued under Sanjabi's name alone. Khomaini was by now considered too powerful and too important to attach his name to that of another political leader in a joint declaration. Sanjabi declared that the Shah, by violating the constitution, had lost his right to the throne, that the "illegal monarchical regime" itself should be abolished, and that the future form of government in Iran, based on "Islamic and democratic" principles, should be determined by a national referendum.[53] The National Front, as it turned out, did not control large numbers of organized troops to deliver to Khomaini. But the Sanjabi declaration was nevertheless of considerable symbolic significance. For two-and-a-half decades the National Front had by general consent represented the broad coalition of the center—of the bazaar, the middle classes, and the lay intelligentsia—forged under Mossadegh. Moreover, the National Front had always stood solidly behind the constitution; for twenty-five years, the Front had demanded of the Shah a return to constitutional rule and a constitutional monarchy. The careful wording of the Sanjabi memorandum could not disguise the fact that the National Front and its middle-class constituency had little leverage with Khomaini. The declaration meant that the traditional party of the constitution had gone over to the Khomaini camp, had opted for the abolition of the monarchy, and had agreed to the revolutionary, rather than the constitutional, transfer of power to a successor regime.

Bazargan, along with Yazdi, had met with Khomaini on October 20, about a week before the Sanjabi meeting. It was Bazargan's first encounter with Khomaini in sixteen years. Bazargan again urged a policy of gradualism on Khomaini and again advised working toward a transfer of power based on the constitution. He believed the opposition should take part in the free elections that the Shah had promised and should use Parliament to bring about the changes it desired. "The Shah," he told Khomaini, "can be thrown out step by step and the regime changed by legal means, through a constituent assembly." He spoke of his fears of what America might do to protect its interests in Iran and urged Khomaini not to alienate the United States. "The world of diplomacy and the international arena," he told him, "are not the seminaries of Najaf and Qom." Although forewarned by Beheshti, Bazargan later wrote that he was nevertheless "astonished and frightened" by Khomaini's lack of interest in the views of others, his unawareness of the immense problems Iran faced, his calm certainty of victory, his confidence that the path would be smooth once the Shah was overthrown.[54] Unlike Sanjabi, Bazargan did not issue a statement of position after his meeting with Khomaini; he rejected Yazdi's advice that he acknowledge Khomaini's leadership publicly before returning to Tehran. Bazargan perhaps hoped in this way to maintain a certain distance from Khomaini; but his silence signified at least an acquiescence to the revolutionary path Khomaini had determined for Iran.

Khomaini had already designated a small nucleus of clerical leaders, Motahhari, Beheshti, Hashemi-Rafsanjani, Musavi-Ardabili, and Bahonar, to act on his behalf in Tehran.[55] At his meeting with Bazargan, explaining that he "did not know anyone," Khomaini asked Bazargan and Yazdi to suggest a group of men to act as his consultants. The task of these advisers would be to propose men suitable for cabinet office and also individuals whom Khomaini could later recommend as parliamentary deputies. Bazargan sent a list of seventeen individuals to Khomaini, which was transmitted to Motahhari for final approval. Motahhari added only one name, Javad Bahonar, to the list. These eighteen individuals came to constitute the Khomaini transitional team in Tehran.[56] Six, of them, Motahhari, Beheshti, Hashemi-Rafsanjani, Mahdavi-Kani, Bahonar, and Abolfazl Zanjani, were clerical leaders. The first five were Khomaini's own men. Zanjani, a liberal religious leader, had been associated with Bazargan and his Iran Freedom Movement (IFM). Four were from the IFM: Bazargan himself, Yazdi, Yadollah Sahabi, and Ahmad Sadr Hajj Seyyed Javadi. Four others, Kazem Sami, Ezzatollah Sahabi, Mostafa Katira'i, and Naser Minachi, were described by Bazargan as representing the "combatant and Muslim masses." All four were in fact close Bazargan associates. Ezzatollah Sahabi, the son of Yadollah, was a socialist. Sami headed JAMA (acronym for the Revolutionary Movement of Iranian Muslims) which also advocated socialist economic policies. Minachi and Katira'i, like Bazargan, were moderates. Two other members, Aali Nasab and Hajj Kazem Hajji Tarkhani, were bazaar merchants. The last two members, Lieutenant General Ali-Asghar Mas'ud and Lieutenant General Valiollah Gharani, were, respectively, a police officer and an army officer who had fallen foul of the Shah because of their political views. The core group in this transitional team remained the clerical leaders, who were closest to Khomaini. The team, virtually unchanged, was reconstituted as the Revolutionary Council in January 1979.

Khomaini himself returned in triumph to Tehran on 31 January. A few days later, even before the Bakhtiar government had fallen, he named Bazargan as his prime minister and asked him to form a cabinet. When the monarchy fell on 11 February, it was the seventy-two-year-old Bazargan who led the first Islamic government.

Chapter 3

Bazargan: A Knife Without the Blade

MEHDI BAZARGAN[1] was a moderate who found himself heading a revolutionary government, a gradualist in a country clamoring for radical change. Educated as an engineer in France, he had developed a lasting admiration for democracy and constitutional rule. Personally devout, he was persuaded that Iran's political salvation lay in welding religious faith to political activism, Islam to nationalism. At the age of seventy-two, he had already spent over thirty years in politics, mostly in the opposition, first in the National Front, then in the 1950s and 1960s in the National Resistance Movement (*Nehzat-e Moqavemat-e Melli*) and the Iran Freedom Movement (*Nehzat-e Azadi-ye Iran* [IFM]). His political activities had earned him several periods in jail.

An organizer, he had participated in and helped establish a large number of associations and movements designed to promote the idea of Islam as a force for social and political change and to bring together clerics and lay intellectuals. As a young professor at Tehran University he had formed the Islamic Students Society and later the Society of Engineers. He had worked closely with Mahmud Taleqani, a politically active cleric, in organizing Islamic discussion groups. The Iran Freedom Movement, which he helped establish, itself represented the religiously oriented wing of the National Front. In the 1960s he worked with Motahhari and Beheshti in organizing the Islamic lecture series of the *Goftar-e Mah* group. He thus had friends and associates both among the clerics and the secular politicians.

Ironically, the eight-month period of his prime ministership served to emphasize the gap rather than the community of interests between the secular and the clerical forces, the moderates and the radicals who had made the revolution. It was also a period when the revolutionaries shaped the institutions of the new order, reformed old and established new political movements, and defined the issues which would excite and agitate the country over the next several years.

"A Passenger Car, Not a Bulldozer"

As head of the provisional government, Bazargan saw himself as the prime minister of the transition from the old order to new, with a strictly limited mandate. His task, as defined by the decree of appointment drawn up (with his approval) by the Revolutionary Council and signed by Khomaini, was twofold: to get the government administration and the economy, paralyzed by a year of strikes and disorder, moving again, and to prepare the ground for the Islamic Republic that would follow. In pursuit of the first goal, he emphasized normalization and business as usual. In pursuit of the second, as set out in his instructions, he was to consult the people in a referendum on Iran's future form of government, draft a new constitution, submit it for approval to a constituent assembly, and hold elections for a new parliament. That done, he said, he would hand over the reins to the new government and resign. Bazargan named a minister of state for "revolutionary projects," responsible for drawing up long-term plans for changes in government administration, the military, and the economy. But such sweeping changes, he said, were for the future. He would begin with small changes. Until the new order was in place and the laws changed, the existing constitution (minus the monarchy) and the existing laws would remain in force; the existing administrative system would be retained. "Do not undermine the present order for the sake of an order that has not yet taken its place and has not yet been constructed," he advised the people.[2]

In a country seething with revolutionary turmoil, Bazargan made little effort to disguise his commitment to moderation, method, and the rule of law. Before accepting his mandate from the Revolutionary Council, he reminded his colleagues that he was "a stickler" for order and regulations. "I avoid haste and extremes," he said. "I am given to careful study and gradualism. I was this way in the past and will not change my approach in the future."[3] A few days later, he took the same message to the public. Speaking to a huge crowd at Tehran University, he remarked:

> Don't expect me to act in the manner of [Khomaini] who, head down, moves ahead like a bulldozer, crushing rocks, roots and stones in his path. I am a delicate passenger car and must ride on a smooth, asphalted road.[4]

He set four criteria in selecting his ministers: that they should be believing and practicing Muslims, with a record of active opposition to the former regime, of good repute, and competent and experienced in their areas of responsibility. Bazargan presented his cabinet as a coalition government. In fact, the ministers were virtually without exception close political and professional colleagues. Four of the seventeen ministers (Yadollah Sahabi, Ahmad Sadr Hajj Seyyed Javadi, Reza Sadr, and Mahmud Ahmadzadeh) were from his own Iran Freedom Movement (IFM). Four others (Mostafa Katira'i, Abbas Taj, Yusef Taheri, Ali-Akbar Mo'infar) were members of the Islamic Society of Engineers, an organization with which Bazargan had long been associated. Six others (Karim Sanjabi, Daryush Foruhar, Ali Ardalan, Mohammad Izadi, Admiral Ahmad Madani, and Asadollah Mobasheri) were colleagues from the National Front days. Naser Minachi, an "independent" without party affiliation, had worked closely with Bazargan on the eve of the revolution in the Iranian Committee for Human Rights and in the negotiations Bazargan and his colleagues conducted with American diplomats in Tehran.[5]

It was a cabinet of engineers, lawyers, educators, doctors, and former civil servants, men drawn from the professional middle class and the broad center of Iranian politics. The majority had pursued successful professional careers. A number headed prosperous engineering or business firms. Almost all had been active in opposition politics, primarily with an Islamic orientation; but only Kazem Sami, the new minister of health, had a "radical" past; a founder of the Revolutionary Movement of Iranian Muslims (JAMA), he was an advocate of Islamic socialism and administration based on popularly elected councils and was sympathetic to the left-wing guerrilla organizations. At a moment when a beard and army fatigues or an open-necked shirt were the necessary symbols of revolutionary zeal, Bazargan's ministers were for the most part clean shaven and dressed in business suits and neckties.

Later, the appointment of Ebrahim Yazdi as foreign minister and Mostafa Chamran as defense minister introduced into the cabinet men sympathetic to paramilitary organizations and "revolutionary" justice and given to radical rhetoric. But both men were members of the Iran Freedom Movement. In fact, ministerial changes up to July tended to strengthen the Bazargan component in the cabinet. Two groups were conspicuous by their absence from the list of ministers. Bazargan, as expected, included no representatives from the radical left-wing parties. Moreover, although he took care to secure approval for his ministerial appointments from the *Showra-ye Enqelab* (Revolutionary Council), only Gholam-Hosain Shokuhi, the minister of education, had been proposed by the clerics on the council. Otherwise, the clerics and their protégés had no share of cabinet seats. For the rest, Bazargan named governors to the provinces, officers to military commands, and directors to state-owned companies. "Those who imagine the revolution still continues are mistaken," Bazargan's press spokesman, Abbas Amir-Entezam, announced. "The revolution is over. The era of reconstruction has begun."

A City with a Hundred Sheriffs

Bazargan's authority and his vision of a rapid return to normalcy were challenged from several directions: by the spirit of revolution abroad in the streets; by the rapidly developing "parallel government" of revolutionary committees, courts, and guards backed by the Revolutionary Council; by a plethora of political parties and movements advocating various radical policies; and by ethnic uprisings.

The victory of the revolution and the collapse of the old regime had released powerful forces and aspirations. Security had collapsed. The officers and the rank and file in the army, national police, and gendarmerie in major towns and centers had abandoned their barracks, police stations, and posts. The citizenry was in control of barracks and police stations, palaces, and ministries. In government offices, private companies, factories, and universities, employees, in a riot of participatory democracy, were demanding to be consulted on policies and appointments. Army units refused to accept commanders appointed by the provisional government; newly appointed police chiefs were arrested by citizen's committees; governors found the way to their offices barred by revolutionary youths. More serious from the government's point of view was the emergence of the revolutionary committees, courts, and guards. Gradually earning the grudging support of the clerics on the Revolutionary Council, these organizations came to exercise a powerful influence on the course of the revolution.

THE REVOLUTIONARY COMMITTEES

The *komitehs,* or local revolutionary committees, sprang up in cities, towns, and districts throughout the country on the morning after the revolution. Many of these *komitehs* were extensions of the neighborhood committees formed around mosques during the revolutionary year of 1978 to mobilize the inhabitants, organize strikes and demonstrations, and distribute scarce items like kerosene. The postrevolution committees, however, were far greater in number, less disciplined, vastly more powerful, and fully armed. Most of the 300,000 rifles, submachine guns, and light arms seized from military arsenals on 10 and 11 February fell into the hands of the young revolutionaries who found their way into the local *komitehs.*

The revolutionary committees served both as local security forces in the immediate aftermath of the revolution and as the agents of the revolutionary authorities against the members of the old regime. On the one hand, they policed their districts, guarded government buildings and palaces, searched cars on the streets at night, and intervened in labor disputes. On the other hand, they took it upon themselves to make arrests, confiscate property, and cart people off to prisons. Many of those arrested were obvious targets for the revolutionaries: agents of the Shah's secret police, Savak, army officers responsible for the administration of martial law in the months leading up to the revolution, or high-ranking officials of the former regime. Others were arrested simply because they were prominent businessmen, were wealthy, or had fallen foul of their employees; and still others because of unfounded accusations, a tendency to see "collaborators" everywhere, and because personal scores were being settled.

Some of the armed retainers of the revolutionary committees were attached to official organizations. The revolutionary prosecutor-general, *(Dadsetan-e Enqelab)*, Mehdi Hadavi, for example, ensconced in the former offices of the military prosecutor of the imperial army, was assisted by a team of armed guards who served warrants, made arrests, and guarded prisoners. Armed men were attached to the Tehran and provincial revolutionary courts, where they served as prison guards and executioners. Officials and powerful clerics had their own armed retainers. Mostafa Chamran, who served as an assistant to Bazargan in charge of security affairs before he became minister of defense, established a revolutionary committee at Tehran airport, whose members arrested at will passengers leaving the country. In the provinces, revolutionary committees tended to be attached to powerful local clerics. For example, in Isfahan, the two influential religious figures in the city, Ayatollah Jalal ad-Din Taheri and Ayatollah Hosain Khademi, each ran a string of committees. In Tabriz, the revolutionary committees owed allegiance to half-a-dozen clerical and local leaders.

"The committees are everywhere," Bazargan remarked, "and no one knows how many exist, not even the Imam himself."[6] In Tehran alone, there were 1,500 committees. When in the early summer a purge of the committees was undertaken, 40,000 to 50,000 members were sent home; but thousands still remained to man the *komitehs*.[7] Bazargan made hardly a speech during his eight months as prime minister in which he did not complain of the revolutionary committees. He criticized them for unauthorized arrests and confiscations of property, unauthorized dismissal and appointment of officials, interference in the government's work and, along with the revolutionary courts, creation of an atmosphere of "instability, terror, uneasiness and fear." The committees, he said, "turn our day into night. They upset our applecart."[8]

Bazargan was not alone in attempting to curb the *komitehs*. Revolutionary prosecutor-general Hadavi on 14 April issued an order canceling all warrants for arrest and property confiscation issued by the revolutionary committees throughout the country.[9] On 23 May, he prohibited the arrest of military personnel without authorization. On 30 May, the Tehran revolutionary prosecutor issued yet another ban on unauthorized arrests. Such orders would be repeatedly issued over the next two years, and would be repeatedly ignored. Many others tended to see the committees as a temporary phenomenon. Ali-Akbar Hashemi-Rafsanjani, a member of the Revolutionary Council and not an advocate of moderation, said early in the summer that "the committees will not remain forever and must soon be dissolved."[10] Mohammad-Reza Mahdavi-Kani, another of the clerics on the Revolutionary Council, took the same view.

In late February, Mahdavi-Kani was charged by Khomaini with responsibility for imposing order on the revolutionary committees and coordinating their work. As the head of the central Tehran revolutionary committee, he was to supervise the other *komitehs* in the capital and in the provinces. The instructions he issued to the committees on 7 March reflect the equivocation with which he approached his task. On the one hand, he instructed the committees to refrain from entering homes, making arrests, or confiscating property without proper authorization; told them to cooperate closely with the police and the judicial authorities; and ordered them to work toward "the transfer of duties to the responsible government authorities, the full establishment of the authority of the provisional government of the Islamic Republic over affairs and the eventual dissolution of the *komitehs*."[11] On the other hand he retained for his own central committee the power to issue arrest and confiscation warrants, and he accorded the *komitehs* a wide range of responsibilities, including the arrest of political and ordinary criminals, members of the former regime and counterrevolutionaries, the resolution of neighborhood disputes, and the identification of profiteers.

In Tehran, Mahdavi-Kani dissolved many of the local committees, consolidated others, and established fourteen major district committees, each headed by a cleric, to supervise the work of numerous subcommittees. He also ordered a purge from the committees of undesirable personnel. He was able to extend his writ to the provinces only gradually, and only to a limited degree. While Mahdavi-Kani would again touch on the desirability of dissolving the revolutionary committees, ironically his work of consolidation and centralization contributed to the permanence of the *komitehs*. It conferred on the revolutionary committees a measure of formal recognition, a niche as one of the much-honored revolutionary organizations, and eventually, a permanent place in the state budget. In April 1979, the Bazargan government made its own attempt to absorb and dissolve the revolutionary committees. The police chief, Naser Mojallali, announced that the national police were ready to assume their official duties, thus implying that the *komitehs* were no longer needed, and offered to hire 4,000 committee members and other volunteers as auxiliary police. Not surprisingly, the members of the *komitehs,* who were already well paid and enjoyed considerable freedom and authority, did not find this offer tempting.

The *komitehs* probably never faced a serious threat of dissolution. They were armed, and the government never had a viable force to deploy against them. They quickly became a powerful lobby in their own right. In the provinces, they served to enhance the authority of the clerics to whom they were attached. They provided the radicals among the clerical party with an instrument of coercion and, along with the revolutionary courts, the means by which the members of the former regime could be eliminated. For the clerics, the revolutionary committees, and later the Revolutionary Guard, assumed greater importance as a counterweight to the growing influence of the left-wing parties. Moreover, Khomaini stood behind the committees. He noted in April that "in some towns there are as many committees as there are influential individuals, and they differ among themselves and commit acts that violate Islam." But he said that "the committees need purging, not dissolution. . . . As long as corrupt individuals exist, there is need for committees."[12]

THE REVOLUTIONARY TRIBUNALS

If the revolutionary committees were the unintended offspring of the revolutionary turmoil, the revolutionary courts *(Dadgah-ha-ye Enqelab)* were born out of a premeditated act of policy. While he was in Paris Khomaini had warned that officials of the Shah's regime would stand trial. Because many of the revolutionaries had suffered personally or had lost family and friends at the hands of Savak, and because many had been killed and injured during the demonstrations and street clashes in 1978, the punishment of high-ranking Savak, army, and police officials and lower-rank officers was virtually a foregone conclusion. The revolutionaries had alleged so insistently that the Shah's ministers had sold the country to foreigners and wrecked the economy that the trial of high-ranking civil servants seemed inevitable after they fell into the hands of the revolutionaries. Moreover, the pervasive fear of counterrevolution led to a deliberate attempt to eliminate the military and civilian leaders of the former regime. The revolution produced its share of judges and prosecutors who derived a perverse satisfaction from harsh punishments. Once the executions began, they fed public excitement and the taste for vengeance and violence.

The first of the revolutionary tribunals convened secretly in Tehran in the school where Khomaini had set up his headquarters. The first four death sentences were pronounced by Hojjat ol-Eslam Sadeq Khalkhali, a middle-rank cleric and a long-time follower of Khomaini's, were approved by Khomaini and were carried out in the early hours of the morning of 16 February, only five days after the victory of the revolutionary forces, on the roof of the building where Khomaini held court. All four were high-ranking commanders. Other death sentences quickly followed. By 14 March, when there was a brief hiatus in the work of the revolutionary courts, 70 persons had been put to death. The revolutionary courts resumed their work on 6 April. By the time the Bazargan government resigned in early November, over 550 persons had faced the firing squads.[13] The example of the tribunal in Tehran was quickly emulated by the provincial revolutionary courts. In the major provincial cities, the first execution took place in Abadan on 1 March, in Shiraz and Rasht on 5 March, in Qom and Yazd later that month, and in Isfahan, Tabriz, and Mashad in April. Initially, most of the executions were concentrated at the capital. By November, however, about twice as many executions had taken place in the provinces as in Tehran.

By far the largest number of those executed were members of Savak and the army, and to a lesser extent of the national police and gendarmerie. Virtually all of the leading military commanders who fell into the hands of the revolutionaries were put to death, both in Tehran and in major cities. But in smaller localities, large numbers of junior officers and even constables, personally known to the inhabitants, were executed for having fired at demonstrators. Some twenty of those executed were ministers, high-ranking government officials, or members of Parliament under the old regime. One was a prominent Jewish businessman. Later in the summer the revolutionary tribunals turned their attention to those charged with "counterrevolutionary" activities and to ordinary criminals. Several Khuzestan Arab-speaking inhabitants were executed in August, some for confrontations with the authorities, others on charges of sabotage. Some seventy-two persons were executed in a three-week period in August and September for participation in the Kurdish uprising. One of these, a physician named Rashvand-Sardari, was put to death for treating a wounded Kurdish rebel. A number of those executed elsewhere were charged with narcotics smuggling, prostitution, and sexual crimes.

Protests against the revolutionary tribunals were lodged by lawyers' groups, by prominent religious leaders, including Ayatollah Shariatmadari and Ayatollah Hasan Qomi-Tabataba'i, and by the civil judiciary. In the prevailing atmosphere, few were willing to question the fairness of the death sentences passed by the tribunals. Critics focused instead on the procedures of the revolutionary tribunals: their secrecy, the midnight sessions, the vagueness of the charges, the absence of defense lawyers or juries, and the failure to give the accused an opportunity to defend themselves. Bazargan, who described the trials as "shameful," attempted to bring an end to or at least to limit the jurisdiction of the revolutionary courts by appealing to Khomaini and securing from him general amnesties for those charged with lesser crimes, by seeking to regulate the revolutionary tribunals, and by establishing a parallel court system under the government's own jurisdiction. The revolutionary tribunals emerged from each of these attempts stronger and more firmly entrenched.

In March, after the trial of the former prime minister, Amir Abbas Hoveyda, had opened before the Tehran revolutionary tribunal, Bazargan prevailed on Khomaini to suspend the work of the courts until regulations governing their operations could be drawn up. The new regulations were promulgated on 5 April.[14] They provided for revolutionary tribunals to be established in Tehran and provincial centers at the discretion of the Revolutionary Council and with the approval of Khomaini. They gave the tribunals jurisdiction over a number of vaguely defined activities, including "crimes against the people," "crimes against the revolution," "ruining the economy," and "violation of the people's honor." The regulations authorized the courts to sit until persons accused of such crimes had been tried, and gave very limited rights to defendants. The trials and executions resumed the next day. On 7 April, Hoveyda was tried and executed all within a few hours, apparently in disregard of even these regulations. Hoveyda's judge, Sadeq Khalkhali, later related that, fearing lest an international protest lead to a lighter punishment for Hoveyda, he had hurried to Qasr prison. He had ordered all the doors to be locked and the telephones disconnected. He judged Hoveyda and had him immediately executed.[15]

In July, Bazargan attempted to outflank the revolutionary tribunals by securing approval from the Revolutionary Council for a bill to establish special courts to deal with "counterrevolutionary" crimes. Two aspects of the bill were particularly significant. The "counterrevolutionary" courts, which were granted wide powers, were to be established under the jurisdiction of the ministry of justice rather than the revolutionary judicial authorities; and the new courts were to take over the duties of the revolutionary tribunals, which would be dissolved.[16] The measure, however, was stillborn. The revolutionary tribunals insisted that they could be dissolved only by Khomaini himself; and Khomaini did not move against them.

Bazargan had secured from Khomaini an amnesty for personnel of the army, gendarmerie, and police charged with "minor crimes." On 13 May, Khomaini issued an order permitting the execution only of persons directly involved in killing, those who had issued orders leading to massacres, and those guilty of torture leading to death. Finally on 10 July, in what was at the time considered an important victory for the prime minister, Khomaini issued a general amnesty for all members of the former regime, except those directly or indirectly involved in killing or torture, and persons guilty of plundering the public treasury.[17] These amnesties were ignored both in the spirit and in the letter. Few persons were released from prisons as a result. The courts continued to sentence members of the former regime, guilty of crimes other than those specified by Khomaini, to death and to prison terms.

The revolutionary courts survived and expanded their jurisdiction because they had supporters as well as critics. In the early months of the revolution, the left-wing parties, including the Fadayan, the Mojahedin-e Khalq, and the Moscow-oriented Tudeh party applauded the exercise of "revolutionary justice" by the tribunals and were sharply critical of any indication of leniency on the part of the courts. There was powerful resistance to leniency as well within the revolutionary courts themselves, among prosecutors, judges, and Revolutionary Guard. In mid-March, when the work of the courts was suspended pending the drawing up of new regulations, a delegation consisting of the Tehran revolutionary prosecutor and representatives of the revolutionary courts and guards went to Qom to ask Khomaini to permit the executions to continue. "If you don't do it, we will kill all the prisoners without any form of trial,"[18] they said. Following Khomaini's general amnesty in July, both Khakhali and the Tehran revolutionary prosecutor, Azari-Qomi, asserted that the ban on death sentences did not apply to persons found guilty of "sowing corruption on earth"; such persons could still be executed.[19]

Khomaini took the view that the insistence on open trials, defense lawyers, and proper procedures was a reflection of "the Western sickness among us," that those on trial were criminals, and "criminals should not be tried; they should be killed." He also believed that trials were an expression of the popular will. "If the revolutionary courts did not prosecute them," he said of those brought to trial, "the people would have gone on a rampage and killed them all."[20] Radical clerics around Khomaini encouraged this view: "The revolutionary courts were born out of the anger of the Iranian people," said Sadeq Khalkhali, "and these people will not accept any principles outside Islamic principles."[21]

THE REVOLUTIONARY GUARD

The *Pasdaran-e Enqelab,* or the Revolutionary Guard, was formally established under a decree issued by Khomaini on 5 May. The organization was shaped by two conflicting motives. On the one hand, the formation of the guards reflected yet another attempt to impose some discipline on the armed retainers of the revolutionary committees; it was an alternative to the abortive plan to merge the committees into the national police. On the other hand, the formation of the guards reflected the desire of the radical clerics to have their own organized armed force, as a counterweight both to the regular army and to the parties of the left, who were suspected of creating their own armed units. Among the early promoters of the Revolutionary Guard proposal were Hadi Ghaffari and Jalal ad-Din Farsi, a radical Islamic ideologue who, like Ghaffari, had trained with the Palestine Liberation Organization (PLO). Some 6,000 persons were initially enlisted to undergo training.

The guards were regarded as a prize from the beginning. Among Bazargan's colleagues, both Yazdi and Chamran vied for influence with the unit, as did Farsi and Mohammad Montazeri, a young cleric, son of Ayatollah Montazeri and another product of the PLO training camps. Supervision of the guards was initially entrusted by Khomaini to a moderate religious leader from the Caspian region, Ayatollah Hasan Lahuti. When the guards held their first public parade and marched in Tehran in the summer, they were still a bedraggled lot. But the guards gained valuable experience in August and September, when they were deployed against the rebels in Kurdistan, and they gained influential support when they came under the wing of the clerics of the Revolutionary Council and the Islamic Republic Party. Lahuti was replaced as the senior cleric responsible for the guards first by Hashemi-Rafsanjani, who was then replaced by Ali Khamene'i. For the Bazargan government, the guards became another center of independent power in a country the prime minister described as "a city with one hundred sheriffs." Like the revolutionary committees, the guards made arrests, ran prisons, interfered with the work of government officials, and played an important role in exacerbating the crisis in Kurdistan. Curbing the Revolutionary Guard, courts, and committees became, in time, a central point at issue between the government and the Revolutionary Council.

Council and Government

The Revolutionary Council that Khomaini established in January, on the eve of the fall of the monarchy, was in membership a slightly altered version of the transition team formed in Tehran the previous October. In the transformation of the transition team into the Revolutionary Council, Ayatollah Abolfazl Zanjani was dropped, but Taleqani and Musavi-Ardabili were added to the clerics' group. Among the secular members, Sami and Minachi were not carried over; but Ezzatollah Sahabi and Abbas Shaybani, both Bazargan's political colleagues, were included. The two bazaar merchants of the transition team were not named to the council. The Revolutionary Council, nevertheless, like the transition team, consisted of a core of seven religious figures associated with Khomaini, Bazargan and six secular opposition figures associated with him, and the two representatives of the security forces, General Valiollah Gharani and General Ali-Asghar Mas'ud.

With the formation of the provisional government, the Revolutionary Council underwent a significant change in composition; and with the fall of the monarchy on 11 February, the council acquired extensive new powers. Bazargan and his six colleagues left the council to constitute the cabinet. To replace them, Khomaini named Mir-Hosain Musavi, Habibollah Payman, Abol-Hasan Bani-Sadr, Sadeq Qotbzadeh, and Jalali.[22] Musavi was a young engineer and a Beheshti protégé. Payman, a dentist by profession, was a proponent of Islamic socialism. The political group he had formed, *Jonbesh-e Mosalmanan-e Mobarez* (Movement of Combatant Muslims) was small. But his journal, *Ommat* (The Community), with its advocacy of socialist policies, Islam, and anti-imperialism, was highly influential among the young. Bani-Sadr was at this time also preaching radical economic and political change. Qotbzadeh, a one-time Bazargan associate and now director of the radio and television network, tended to tack his sails to the wind; and he would, in time, turn against his old mentor, Bazargan. The overall effect of these changes was, therefore, to strengthen the weight of the clerical and radical elements on the Revolutionary Council and to weaken the influence of Bazargan and the moderates. The assassination of Morteza Motahhari in May, moreover, removed a cleric who might have played a moderating and mediating role between the council and the provisional government and between the moderates and the increasingly radical clerical members of the revolutionary body.

The Revolutionary Council was at the same time designated as the supreme decision-making and legislative authority in the country. It was the Revolutionary Council that, sitting in Khomaini's presence, proposed and approved Bazargan's appointment as prime minister and confirmed his ministerial choices. Bazargan took care to consult with the council on his major domestic and foreign policy decisions. Over the next few months, there issued from the council hundreds of rulings and laws, dealing with everything from bank nationalization to nurses' salaries. Both Bani-Sadr and Bazargan, writing much later and from different perspectives, agree that initially the clerics on the Revolutionary Council were in agreement with the government and its secular members on the need to curb the revolutionary committees and courts and to impose a degree of central control. The friction that rapidly developed between the provisional government and the council, between the secular and the clerical elements in the revolutionary coalition, was rooted in a number of issues.

With the formation of the Islamic Republic Party (IRP) by Beheshti and the other clerics of the Revolutionary Council, the clerical party became a contender for power against the provisional government. The exclusion by Bazargan of the clerics and their protégés from the cabinet became a source of resentment. The clerics and the provisional government spoke for different constituencies. The one objection to the criteria set by Bazargan for the selection of cabinet ministers was voiced by Beheshti. He argued that moral character and reputation, not experience and expertise, should constitute the primary criteria for selecting ministers. Those who lacked experience and technical training, he said, could be assisted by qualified undersecretaries.[23] This was an early indication of the struggle for power that would erupt in the following year between the Westernized technocrats and the new claimants to office. Many of the clerics initially may have hesitated to assume office because of an overwhelming sense of lack of experience and training. As Ali Khamene'i, the later president of the Islamic Republic put it, Bazargan was made prime minister "because we had no one else, and at that time we ourselves lacked the ability."[24] The clerical leaders, however, soon lost this diffidence.

Moreover, the political strength of the clerics lay in the urban work-ing-class neighborhoods and the mosque network. The clerics were sensitive to the aspirations and radical temperament of the working-class youths who manned the revolutionary committees, guards, and courts. They feared the pull of the radical left on the young and saw the Westernized, technocratic elite as rivals for power. The clerics desired office for themselves and their many protégés. More ready and more adept at deploying street crowds and the revolutionary organizations to achieve their ends, they were unwilling to risk popularity by calling the revolutionary organizations to heel. The clerics of the Revolutionary Council thus began to champion the cause of these revolutionary bod-ies, exacerbating relations with the Bazargan government.

Bazargan continued to seek an accommodation with the Revolution-ary Council and also to enlist Khomaini's support. Khomaini had left Tehran for Qom. Once a week, the prime minister took a large part of the cabinet to the holy city for consultations with the Imam. Occasion-ally, he arranged for joint sessions of the cabinet and the Revolutionary Council in Khomaini's presence. In July, at Bazargan's insistence, a much closer integration between the cabinet and the council took place. Mohammad-Reza Mahdavi-Kani, the head of the Tehran central revo-lutionary committee, was named as minister of the interior. Three oth-ers, Hashemi-Rafsanjani, Khamene'i, and Javad Bahonar, joined the government as undersecretaries, respectively, in the ministries of inte-rior, defense, and education. In turn, Bazargan and three ministers, Katira'i, Mo'infar, and Reza Sadr, joined the Revolutionary Council. This arrangement resulted in greater coordination between the council and the government. But it signaled a formal recognition of the new realities of power. It gave the clerics a first taste of cabinet office, minis-terial experience, and greater confidence, and it proved a first step to-ward a full assumption of power by the clerics.

Political Movements

The revolution gave rise to a welter of political parties and movements ranging across the political spectrum, from Islamic-fundamentalist to Islamic-radical, from liberal to conservative, from socialist to Marxist-Leninist and Maoist. The plethora of groups reflected the pent-up polit-ical energies of many years of tight controls and the heady sense of freedom and experimentation released by the revolution. Most of these parties fell into three broad groupings: the Islamic parties linked to religious figures, the parties of the center and the center-left, including the liberals and the socialists, and the parties of the radical left.

Among the Islamic parties, two stood out: The IRP and the Islamic People's Republican Party (IPRP). Five of the six founders of the IRP, Beheshti, Musavi-Ardabili, Hashemi-Rafsanjani, Bahonar, and Khamene'i, were clerics closely associated with Khomaini and already close to the centers of power. The sixth, Hasan Ayat, had been associated in the 1950s with Mozaffar Baqa'i's Iran Toilers' Party, had gravitated in the 1960s toward Islamic political groupings and conceived himself as the ideologue of the IRP. The party was distinguished by its strong clerical component, its loyalty to Khomaini, its strong animosity to the liberal political movements, and its tendency to support the revolutionary organizations. The IRP called for state takeover of large and "dependent" capital enterprises, for the establishment of an Islamic cultural and university system, and for programs to assist the deprived classes.

The party could count on the support of many of the provincial ulama and also contained a radical nucleus, including Ayat, Hadi Ghaffari, Jalal ad-Din Farsi, and Behzad Nabavi. Ghaffari and Nabavi provided the party with its storm troops. Ghaffari headed the *hezbollahis*, the "partisans of the party of God," so called because of their rallying cry: "Only one party—of Allah; only one leader—Ruhollah." Ruhollah was, of course, Khomaini's first name. The *hezbollahis* were popularly known as *chomaqdars*, "the club wielders," because of the clubs they used to break up rival political gatherings. Behzad Nabavi was the head of the *Mojahedin-e Enqelab-e Eslami* (the Mojahedin of the Islamic Revolution, not to be confused with the Mojahedin-e Khalq), a movement formed by the merger of five small Islamic guerrilla groups and also given to attacking the rallies of political opponents.

The IPRP was founded by a group of bazaar merchants, middle-class politicians, and clerics associated with Khomaini's chief rival in Qom, Ayatollah Shariatmadari. The IPRP declared itself an Islamic party dedicated to the broad goals of the Islamic Republic, but it differed from the IRP in many important respects. The IRP emphasized the role of Khomaini as leader, refrained from criticizing the revolutionary courts and committees, harshly attacked the liberal and secular parties, and envisioned restrictions on political groups considered as un-Islamic. The IPRP emphasized collective religious leadership, criticized the unruly behavior of the revolutionary committees and the harsh judgments of the revolutionary courts, was ready to cooperate with the secular parties, and demanded free access for all to the broadcast media. The IPRP was established as a counterpoise to the IRP and immediately came under attack from the rival party. Khalkhali criticized Shariatmadari personally for sponsoring the party, and IPRP offices in Karaj, Arak, Saveh, Ardabil, and Khalkhal were attacked.

Of the three major movements of the political center, two—the National Front and the Iran Freedom Movement—predated the revolution. The Freedom Movement had been more outspoken against the Shah, and its enthusiasm for Islam was not shared by the more secular National Front. Both groups, however, were dedicated to constitutionalism and the parliamentary system; both were fully represented in the provisional government. The third group—the National Democratic Front (NDF)—was new. It was founded by Hedayatollah Matin-Daftari, a grandson of Mossadegh and a lawyer who had been active in human rights causes. Matin-Daftari had been a member of the National Front; he now hoped to draw on the Mossadegh heritage to reestablish a coalition of the middle classes and the intelligentsia, but somewhat to the left of the National Front. The NDF emphasized political freedoms, guarantees for individual rights, access for all political groups to the broadcast media, the curbing of the revolutionary guards, courts, and committees, economic programs favoring the mass of the people, and a decentralized system of administration based on popularly elected local councils.

On the extreme left were three groups: the Moscow-oriented Iranian communist party, the Tudeh, and the two major anti-Shah guerrilla organizations—the Fadayan-e Khalq and the Mojahedin-e Khalq. The Tudeh initially guaranteed itself a relatively unhampered political existence under the Islamic Republic by throwing its full support behind Khomaini, putting up with restrictions on freedoms by declaring the struggle against American imperialism to be the most important post-revolution task, pressing gently for more radical economic measures, such as expropriations, and joining the IRP in criticizing the liberal parties.

The Fadayan-e Khalq and the Mojahedin-e Khalq, acting separately, posted similar programs. Both demanded the cancelation of all security arrangements with the United States, expropriation of multinational companies, nationalization of agricultural and urban land, banks, and large industries, administration of the army and other institutions by people's councils, creation of a "people's army," regional autonomy for Iran's ethnic minorities, and a host of measures to benefit the workers and the peasants. The two movements, however, adopted different tactics. The Mojahedin channeled their efforts into winning adherents and developing their party network. The Fadayan threw their efforts into revolutionary action. Party workers fanned out into the countryside, particularly in the Turkoman regions along the Caspian, encouraging peasants to seize land and to take over farms. The Fadayan played an important role in instigating the violent clashes that broke out in the Turkoman areas in the summer and were active alongside the Kurds in the fall.

The sudden emergence of a range of political parties with little tolerance for one another proved divisive and further hampered the work of the government. By the summer, Bazargan felt hemmed in from all sides. He had no control over the Revolutionary Guards, courts, or committees. He could not prevent arrests, confiscations, executions, the suppression of the press, or the disruption of political meetings by the *hezbollahis*. Lawyers groups, judges, professional associations, and university professors were demanding from him guarantees for individual rights he was powerless to give. The left-wing parties were pressing for radical measures he believed would only further disrupt the economy. His influence with Khomaini was not equal to the influence exerted by the revolutionary organizations or Khomaini's clerical associates. His government, he said, was powerless, "a knife without the blade." He had already submitted his resignation to Khomaini on several occasions. But it was ostensibly an issue of foreign not domestic politics that brought about the fall of his government.

Dealing with the Great Satan

Contacts had been established between Bazargan, his aides in the IFM, and American diplomats in Tehran before the fall of the Shah. Bazargan himself met with the American ambassador, William Sullivan. His aides, Abbas Amir-Entezam and Mohammad Tavassoli, and his associate, Naser Minachi, had met on several occasions with members of the embassy staff. Bazargan's purpose in these meetings was to persuade American officials to end their support for the Shah, to assure them of the reasonableness of the opposition, and to use them as a channel to dissuade the Iranian armed forces from staging a coup. He kept the Khomaini camp informed of these discussions.

As prime minister of the provisional government, he resumed such contracts, primarily through his aides. There were a large number of bilateral issues that required discussion: Bazargan desired an early normalization of relations with the United States, the Iranian army needed delivery of military spare parts, and, moreover, Bazargan was suspicious of Russian intentions toward Iran. He also feared that the Soviet Union and Iraq were assisting the rebel Kurds in Iran. He hoped the American government might be able to assist Iran with intelligence information on Soviet involvement. Beginning in the early summer, Amir-Entezam on several occasions asked embassy officials if Washington would share with Tehran data on activities both within Iran and in neighboring countries of importance to Iran's security.

Bazargan believed he had the Revolutionary Council's mandate to pursue normalization of relations with the United States. Khomaini had approved a circumscribed program to purchase military spare parts. Yet anti-American feeling in the country ran high. Washington was seen as the Shah's friend and supporter. American imperialism was depicted as the cause of many of Iran's difficulties. The left-wing parties and Khomaini himself engaged in strong anti-American rhetoric. Within the IRP and the Islamic movement there were groups strongly opposed to a rapprochement with the United States and hostile to the Bazargan government as well.

In the fall, Bazargan arranged to meet with the National Security adviser, Zbigniew Brzezinski, in Algiers, where both men were attending independence day celebrations. The meeting took place on 1 November, with Bazargan, Yazdi, and Chamran taking part on the Iranian side. Meantime, against the advice of the Iranian government, Washington had permitted the Shah, ailing with cancer, to enter the United States for medical treatment. The two events—the Shah's admission to the United States and the Bazargan–Brzezinski meeting—allowed the opponents of the government and of the United States in Tehran to kill two birds with one stone. On 4 November, the American embassy in Tehran was occupied by revolutionary youths calling themselves "students following the Imam's line." Huge demonstrations denounced both the United States and Bazargan. On 6 November, Bazargan submitted his resignation.

Bazargan's fall was a setback for the moderates in the revolutionary coalition, strengthened the hand of the clerical party, and exacerbated divisions in the country. Even before the prime minister's resignation, a bitter battle was already under way between the various parties over the new constitution and the structure of the Islamic Republic.

Chapter 4

The Debate on

the Constitution

ON THE EVE of Khomaini's return to Tehran from Paris, the newspaper *Ayandegan* published an article by Mostafa Rahimi, a Tehran writer and lawyer, entitled "Why I Am Against the Islamic Republic." Casting his essay in the form of an open letter to Khomaini, Rahimi argued that Islamic principles formulated in the seventh century were not relevant to the complex problems of the modern world, that history did not support the view that Islam could serve as a barrier to tyranny, and that entrusting government to the religious classes would lead to dictatorship. Rahimi urged Khomaini to eschew the idea of an Islamic republic and to permit instead, "a republic pure and simple," as the best guarantee for liberty and national unity.[1]

A riposte from Abdol-Reza Hejazi, a cleric, appeared in *Ayandegan* the following day. "Why, when you speak so much of the Iranian people," Hejazi taunted Rahimi, "do you resist the idea of an Islamic government. The near-unanimous majority of the people are Muslims—and not Christians or Jews, capitalists or communists or, like you, socialists floundering in the ditch of contradiction."[2] *Ayandegan* published the views of another religious leader, Ayatollah Allameh Nuri. A liberal among his colleagues, Nuri nevertheless insisted that Iran must have an Islamic government, based on Islamic law, and led by the pious and the religiously knowledgeable.[3]

These exchanges served to highlight the contrast between the secular and the Islamic interpretations of the revolution and were the opening shots in a debate that was to engage the attention of Iranians over the next ten months. Postrevolution Iran was to have a new constitution; and the realization that the constitution would define the new political order lent urgency and intensity to the debate.

Early Skirmishes

The initial confrontation took place over the referendum to decide the general form of the post-Pahlavi state. Such a referendum had been foreshadowed in statements by Khomaini during his stay in Paris and in a number of semiofficial documents of the revolutionary movement. The revolutionary authorities intended to give the people the choice of a yes or no vote on the proposal to establish an Islamic republic. Most of the secular parties, supported by Ayatollah Shariatmadari, called for an open referendum, a wider choice of options, or, at the very least, a choice between an "Islamic" or a "democratic" republic, an Islamic republic or a republic plain and simple.

Later opposition claims notwithstanding, Khomaini in Paris had not pledged to permit the people a free choice on the form of government that would replace the monarchy. He took the position, rather, that the people had already voted in a "referendum" for an Islamic republic by taking part in the great anti-Shah demonstrations, or that a referendum would be held, but only to confirm a choice already made. He agreed during his meeting with Karim Sanjabi in Paris in November 1978 that the future government of Iran would be "democratic and Islamic," but his published views hardly suggested he understood the word *democratic* to mean a Western parliamentary democracy. The decree he issued in January 1979 appointing Bazargan head of the provisional government charged the prime minister with arranging for a referendum "to alter the political system of the country to that of an Islamic republic."

Faced with an opposition determined to establish a secular state,

Khomaini grew more insistent on establishing an Islamic one. By the end of February, he was no longer willing, as he had been earlier, to countenance the coupling of the terms *Islamic* and *democratic* to describe the government of the revolutionary republic. The two terms had become code words, resonant with mutually exclusive meanings. Khomaini addressed this issue before a great crowd on his return to Qom on March 1. "What the nation wants," he said, "is an Islamic republic: not just a republic, not a democratic republic, not a democratic Islamic republic. Do not use this term, 'democratic.' That is the Western style."[4]

On 30 and 31 March, the voters were therefore asked to approve a single proposal, to replace the monarchy with an Islamic republic. The potential opposition was split. The National Democratic Front (NDF), the Fadayan, and seven Kurdish groups boycotted the referendum. The Mojahedin declared their "conditional" approval. Bazargan's Iran Freedom Movement (IFM), Sanjabi's National Front (NF), and Shariat-madari's Islamic People's Republican Party (IPRP) joined the Tudeh and the Islamic Republican Party (IRP) in urging a yes vote. The voting age was lowered to sixteen to swell the electorate. Khomaini and clerics across the country called for massive turnout. Measures were taken to discourage negative votes. Even without these measures a respectable majority would have voted for an Islamic republic. As it was, the government announced a 98.2 percent majority in favor of an Islamic state.

With the referendum out of the way, the contending parties focused their attention on the draft constitution. Khomaini and his corevolutionaries had come to power determined to transform Iranian society. But they had only a vague notion of the government they would create for this purpose. Khomaini's important book on Islamic government had established that the Islamic state would be led by the clerical classes and would be modeled on the community the Prophet founded in seventh-century Arabia. But his treatise was singularly lacking in any discussion of the institutions of the Islamic state. Khomaini merely assigned to the government the traditional duties of protecting Islam, defending the frontiers, administering justice, and collecting taxes; and he appeared to assume a simple administration would be adequate to fulfill these tasks.

A legislature would not be needed, he noted, since all the necessary laws were laid down by the Koran and Islamic traditions. Islamic tribunals, unencumbered by appeals courts, bureaucracy, and Western law, would settle in days cases that languished for years in the Shah's courts. Islamic charitable dues and taxes collected from the bazaars of Tehran and other great cities would be sufficient to meet the expenses of the state and to provide for public welfare.

Other writers on Islamic government, though confident that the Islamic state would be a model of justice, equity, and liberty were equally vague on the institutions and workings of the new order. A similar vagueness characterized the pronouncements of the parties on the left. The problem was discussed only in general terms in the Khomaini camp in Paris. It was only after they had seized power that the revolutionaries confronted the problem of creating the Islamic, socialist, Marxist, or democratic state they had been advocating.

The task of drawing up the new constitution fell to the provisional government and primarily to Mehdi Bazargan's minister of state for revolutionary affairs, Yadollah Sahabi. Sahabi and his colleagues drew on a partial draft constitution hastily put together in Paris and based on the Iranian constitution of 1906 and the constitution of France's Fifth Republic; they consulted Bani-Sadr, Sanjabi, and members of the cabinet and Revolutionary Council; they showed drafts of the constitution to Ayatollah Shariatmadari and others.

The constitution the government unveiled on 18 June reflected its eclectic origins. The abolition of the monarchy aside, its most prominent feature was a strong presidency, based on the Gaullist model. The articles on social welfare and private property did not depart dramatically from actual practice under the monarchy. Like the 1906 constitution, the draft provided for limited individual rights and freedoms. It also paid lip service to the idea of an Islamic state. But it reserved no special authority for the religious classes; it made no mention of the doctrine of the vice-regency of the *faqih*. A Council of Guardians to ensure the laws were in keeping with Islam was given only limited veto powers; the majority of its members were to be lay judges, not Islamic jurists. The draft constitution was hardly "revolutionary"; but it hardly bore out the worst expectations of the secular parties.

The draft was approved by the cabinet and the Revolutionary Council. Khomaini made only two small changes (in part to bar women from the presidency and judgeships) when Beheshti and Bani-Sadr presented it to him, but he raised no objections to the rest of the document.[5] Khomaini, in fact, proposed to bypass the promised constituent assembly and to submit the draft directly to a referendum. Bani-Sadr and Bazargan objected to this procedure in a private meeting with Khomaini. With the exception of the IRP, other political parties condemned the idea when it became public.

A proposal to submit the draft to a forty-man, appointed and advisory Assembly of Experts failed to quell the protests. The opposition demanded an elected constituent assembly of up to 500 members, with power to revise the draft. Shariatmadari, supporting the movement, announced he would not vote in a referendum to approve a constitution that had not been reviewed by the representatives of the people.

A compromise was struck with Shariatmadari. The authorities announced revised plans for an Assembly of Experts of seventy-three rather than forty members, to be elected rather than appointed, and empowered to amend and redraft the constitution. Shariatmadari announced himself satisfied with these arrangements and the other opposition parties had to go along. Elections were set for 3 August. The secular parties achieved partial satisfaction of their demand for a full review of the draft constitution. They did not foresee that in doing so they would open the door to Islamic radicals who were equally committed to a revision of the constitution. Hashemi-Rafsanjani, himself a cleric, was more prescient. "Who do you think will be elected to a constituent assembly?" he said to Bani-Sadr. "A fistful of ignorant and fanatic fundamentalists who will do such damage that you will regret ever having convened them."[6]

The Draft Constitution

The draft constitution had meantime sparked off a widespread debate. The major parties commented on the draft in detail, as did a clutch of minor parties claiming to speak for "combatant socialists," "militant workers," and "united Muslims"; Kurd, Arab, and Baluchi ethnic movements; organizations of lawyers, engineers, book dealers, newspapermen, and judges; human rights and women's groups; and such bodies as the Syndicate of Theater Artists and Employees, which wanted the constitution to pay more attention to the rights of artists. Newspapers filled pages with articles and letters from readers. Organizations and members of the public submitted sixty-two draft constitutions and over four thousand proposals to Sahabi's office. Several seminars were convened to discuss the government's constitutional proposals.

Two of these seminars were particularly important. The first, the Seminar on the People's Expectations from the Constitution, was organized by the Iranian Lawyers Association. The second, the Congress of Muslim Critics of the Constitution, was organized by clerics and organizations with an Islamic orientation. The two conferences met, almost simultaneously, in separate buildings at Tehran University. The few hundred yards that separated the two groups only served to emphasize the divisions in the revolutionary alliance. Few participants crossed over from one conference to another and there was little inclination on either side to seek out areas of agreement.

The variety of views expressed during the preliminary discussion of the draft constitution tended, broadly, to fall into three categories. A minority was prepared to accept the draft constitution with some revision but without major redrafting. These might be described as the "moderately satisfied" parties. Two other groups were bent on a thorough recasting of the constitution, one from an Islamic perspective, the other from the perspective of the secular parties on the left.

The National Front (NF) was the most important of the "moderately satisfied" parties. The NF leader, Karim Sanjabi, described the draft as "progressive, based on Islam, on national sovereignty and on individual and social freedoms."[7] The NF recommended reducing the powers of the president in favor of Parliament and the cabinet. It introduced mechanisms to guard against cabinet instability or paralysis of the work of the legislature by a minority. It spelled out in detail the manner in which authority over local affairs was to devolve to the provincial councils. The NF also recommended changes in wording so as to give weight in the constitution to common law as well as Islamic law, and to Iranian culture as well as to Islamic culture. It strengthened articles referring to property rights.

The National Front, however, did not basically challenge the concept of a strong executive, the limited provision for individual freedoms, the articles which relegated women primarily to the home, or the mild Islamic provisions of the draft constitution. The NF, Shariatmadari, and a few others were restrained in their criticism by temperament, because they feared the Islamic radicals would subject the draft to a thorough revision if the constitutional question were reopened, and because they looked to a workable rather than to an ideal constitution. Naser Katuzian, a Tehran university professor and human rights activist, voiced the attitude of the "moderately satisfied" parties. The draft constitution, he noted, could be much improved. But he would vote for it even in unamended form because more important than a "deluxe constitution" was a constitution that the people understood and which could be implemented.[8]

The most important critique of the constitution from the perspective of the secular left was made at the Seminar on the People's Expectations from the Constitution. The seminar's final declaration reflected the views of the Iranian Lawyers Association, the Iranian Committee for the Defense of Freedom and Human Rights, and the National Democratic Front. The centerpiece of the critique was the notion that the people are sovereign and that "the legislative branch is the sole expression of national sovereignty."[9]

The seminar thus proposed to limit the president to a ceremonial role and to deny him the power to veto laws, dissolve Parliament, approve cabinet appointments, or serve as commander-in-chief of the armed forces. Rather, the seminar proposed to make Parliament supreme and to vest in the legislature the authority to supervise the work of the government, the judiciary, the military, and the broadcast media.

It sought to ensure an independent judiciary through legal provisions, elected judges, and budgetary autonomy, laid great stress on individual rights and equal rights for women, proposed to make the Universal Declaration of Human Rights part of the Iranian constitution, and to give international human rights organizations and lawyers the legal authority to defend Iranian nationals before Iranian courts.

The lawyers' seminar also emphasized the transfer of authority for local affairs to provincial councils, the rights of ethnic minorities, the "democratization" of the army through provisions permitting army personnel to participate in politics, and the nationalization of land, banks, large industry, and foreign trade.

Further to the left stood the two guerrilla movements and a collection of socialist, Marxist, and self-proclaimed workers' parties. The Mojahedin offered a more radical version of the policies embraced at the lawyers' seminar. The Fadayan and various workers' parties viewed the constitution merely as an instrument for advancing capitalist interests, and the projected elections for the Assembly of Experts as a sham.[10] "The bourgeoisie want with this constitution to put an official seal on their anti-revolutionary intentions and activities," a coalition of six radical workers' parties declared.[11] Since they considered the election results a foregone conclusion, the extreme left-wing groups explained their participation in the election campaign as a means not of achieving office but of awakening the people to the conservative, capitalist nature of the regime.

Among the ethnic movements, Mohammad Taher Al-e Shubayr al-Khaqani, the spiritual leader of the Khuzestan Arabs, was cautious in pressing his claims for local autonomy. But Ezzed-Din Hosaini, the spiritual leader of the Kurds, took the view that Iran was a "multinational" society. He therefore argued for a constitution based on the rights of the "nations" of Iran, on "autonomous provincial, administrative, security, cultural and economic institutions" for the ethnic minorities, and on a redrawing of the provincial frontiers to include large chunks of other provinces in Kurdistan.[12] The United Muslims of Kurdistan, meantime, threatened to take up arms if the constitution was not revised to satisfy their demands, while the *Ettehad-e Moslemin* (Union of Muslims) party of Baluchistan demanded the right to revise any national law not in keeping with local requirements before application to their province.

The assault on the draft constitution by the secular parties led Khomaini to spur the Islamic groups to a counterattack. In remarks to a delegation of preachers from Mashad at the end of June, he said clerics and Islamic groups must review the draft "from an Islamic perspective and for an Islamic constitution," rather than allowing "others" to correct the document.

> This right belongs to you. It is those knowledgeable in Islam who may express an opinion on the law of Islam. The constitution of the Islamic Republic means the constitution of Islam. Don't sit back while foreignized intellectuals, who have no faith in Islam, give their views and write the things they write. Pick up your pens and in the mosques, from the altars, in the streets and bazaars, speak of the things that in your view should be included in the constitution.[13]

The Islamic parties were quick to take up Khomaini's advice. The critique of the draft constitution from the Islamic perspective was articulated at the Congress of Muslim Critics of the Constitution in a detailed commentary and alternate draft distributed by Ayatollah Hosain-Ali Montazeri, in sermons, and in articles and remarks by clerics published in the press.[14] These groups and individuals sought to enshrine Islam as the basis of the constitution, the institutions of the state, its economic and judicial system, and even the institution of the family.

They insisted that twelver Shi'ism (professed by a majority of Iranians) and not just Islam be specified as the official religion of the state, that the president and prime minister be practicing Shi'as, knowledgeable in Islamic law, and that a religious test be applied to the commanders of the army. They desired to give a right of veto over all laws to the Council of Guardians, to empower the Islamic jurists to appoint judges, supervise the judiciary, and approve presidential candidates. They rejected the idea of equality of men and women and noted specifically that under Islam women could not serve as judges or governors.

They noted that sovereignty belongs only to God and through him to the Prophet, the imams, and the jurists and thus challenged the idea of popular sovereignty. "In Islam," said one speaker at the Congress of Muslim Critics of the Constitution, "sovereignty does not belong to the people. . . . This is not a general right. Rather, to be governed by God's law and to be the subject of government is the general condition."[15]

They also injected into the debate over the constitution the concept of government by the Islamic jurist. "If the *velayat-e faqih* [the vice-regency of the Islamic jurist] is not specified," said one contributor to the debate, "the constitution will not be Islamic."[16] Some wished to see Khomaini assume the presidency for life; others, arguing that the *faqih* was superior in authority even to the president, asserted that Khomaini should exercise supervision over all three branches of government and be vested with specific executive powers.

A number of the Islamic critics of the draft constitution, like the secular critics, advocated nationalization of land and other forms of wealth, limits on property, and common ownership of the tools of production. There were also advocates of "Islamic internationalism." Hasan Ayat, arguing that "Islam recognizes no borders," wanted the constitution to provide for the eventual adherence of other Islamic states to Iran's Islamic Republic, and the creation of a unified state of all the Muslim nations.[17] Another contributor to the debate ridiculed the article in the draft stating that Iran would neither permit itself to be dominated nor seek to dominate others. Islamic governments, he suggested, had a duty to spread Islam. "Islamic culture and knowledge," he added, "are by nature domineering."[18]

The debate on the constitution revealed a deep cleavage, but also a broader universe of shared ideas among competing and politically vocal groups than is generally assumed. With few exceptions, groups across the political spectrum opposed a strong president, fearing the office would serve as a springboard to dictatorship. Most groups favored generous programs for social welfare, egalitarian economic policies, and, with the exception of the National Front, sweeping nationalization. If the bazaar merchants, the propertied classes, the IPRP, and conservative clerical leaders favored greater protection for private property and more moderate economic policies, they found it impolitic to press their views.

All groups favored extensive decentralization, although none, with the possible exception of the NF, appear to have given serious thought to the mechanics of power sharing between the center and the provinces. Almost all favored an explicitly anti-imperialist, neutralist foreign policy and a commitment to oppressed people everywhere.

The basic split centered not on economic, foreign, or even social policy but on political arrangements and on the role of Islam in the republic. The secular parties, the left, and the liberals looked to a secular state, governed by secular law, in which power would lie with what they considered to be the elected representatives of the people. The Islamic parties looked to a state governed by Islamic law, in which power would lie with Islamic jurists qualified to interpret this law. Sharply conflicting interpretations regarding political authority, popular sovereignty, individual rights, and judicial independence flowed from these divergent perspectives.

While secular and left-wing parties continued to emphasize the sovereignty of the popular will, these groups also began to voice muffled doubts about the reliability of popular opinion. The Seminar on the People's Expectations from the Constitution urged that the constitution be approved by a constituent assembly alone, without reference to a referendum. The Fadayan and various socialist parties blamed their inability to mobilize mass support on the lack of political sophistication among the working class, the relatively brief life of the revolutionary movement, and the success of the authorities in buying off the workers. The Mojahedin began to stress the role of the vanguard, the "informed elements," in the leadership of the people. An editorial in the party newspaper *Mojahed* noted that "With all its greatness, the worth of the spontaneous movement of the masses must not be regarded as absolute."[19]

On the eve of the election for the Assembly of Experts, the secular parties concluded that they could exert little influence over the mass of voters. The National Front and the National Democratic Front, expressing concern over the freedom of elections and government control over the broadcast media, announced they would boycott the voting. Several parties representing Arab and Kurdish ethnic movements joined the boycott. The IPRP called on the government to postpone the election for ten days to permit more time for campaigning. Ayatollah Shariatmadari urged a reversion to the 1906 constitution, minus the monarchy, until a broader consensus on a new constitution could be achieved.

The seventy-three seats on the Assembly of Experts (four of which were assigned to the Armenian, Assyrian, Jewish, and Zoroastrian minorities) were nevertheless contested by over 1,000 candidates from a wide spectrum of parties, often linked together in a complex maze of alliances. The largest was a coalition of ten Islamic organizations led by the IRP. Many prominent candidates were supported by several parties, and sometimes by groups with widely divergent ideologies.

The results of the voting, however, were hardly in doubt. Some fifty-five of those elected were clerics. Over fifty were candidates directly sponsored by the IRP coalition; several others tended in practice to vote with the IRP group. The IPRP, along with the closely affiliated Radical Movement, led by Rahmatollah Moghaddam-Maraghe'i, made a strong showing only in East Azarbaijan, where it won some four seats. Other potential dissenters, representing the NF and the IFM, liberal clerics like Ali Golzadeh-Ghafuri and Mohammad-Javad Hojjati-Kermani, provincial representatives without party affililation, and freefloaters like Bani-Sadr took barely ten more seats. The dominance of the Islamic coalition was later evident in voting patterns. The controversial articles of the constitution were invariably carried by between fifty and sixty votes, with perhaps a dozen candidates abstaining or casting negative ballots.

The Assembly of Experts

The Assembly of Experts convened on 18 August. In an inaugural message, Khomaini told the delegates that the constitution must be "one hundred per cent Islamic," that "discussion of proposals contrary to Islam lies outside the scope of [its] mandate," and that determining whether articles of the constitution met Islamic criteria "lies within the exclusive jurisdiction of the leading Islamic jurists." Delegates lacking the necessary expertise and authority, he said, should not interfere in the Islamic provisions of the constitution.[20]

Once in session, the members elected Montazeri as chairman and Beheshti as deputy chairman. It was Beheshti, however, who chaired the assembly and directed its work. The members ignored Khomaini's directive to leave judgment on the Islamic nature of the constitution to the jurists and agreed that a two-thirds majority of all members would be required for the approval of constitutional articles. They decided to use the government's draft constitution as the basis for their deliberations and to consider, and vote on, the constitution article by article.

To facilitate the debate, they established seven committees. Draft articles were debated first in committee, then before the full house. When members of the committees could not agree, two differently worded drafts might be presented to the assembly. The assembly met six days a week; and when the originally mandated one-month time limit ended and the assembly found itself only halfway through the drafting of the constitution, members simply voted to extend their sittings for a further period. The minority of liberal and secularly minded delegates to the assembly complained that their views were not receiving adequate coverage on radio and television. But newspaper coverage of the deliberations was adequate. On the floor of the assembly the discussion was open and often vigorous.

The problem for the secularly minded members was precisely that they constituted a minority in an assembly dominated by clerics and laymen determined to draft an Islamic constitution. Moreover, by the time the Assembly of Experts convened, the Islamic groups and their leaders had a much clearer idea of the shape and institutions of the Islamic state they wished to establish. The draft constitution had made no mention of the doctrine of the vice-regency of the Islamic jurist, a central idea in Khomaini's book on Islamic government. Beheshti and Hosain-Ali Montazeri, who later led the campaign to invest the *faqih* with extensive powers, did not touch on the idea in their early comments on the draft.

The demand that Khomaini, as *faqih,* should be entrusted with supreme authority under the constitution was initially espoused by middle-rank and provincial clerics and quickly taken up by other Islamic groups. During two months of public debate and discussion of the draft constitution the idea was further elaborated, the powers of the *faqih* were specified, and the *faqih's* constitutional role was more precisely defined. It quickly became clear to Khomaini and his lieutenants that there existed considerable support and no mass opposition to the doctrine and that the constitution could serve to institutionalize both the supremacy of the *faqih* and clerical rule. As Ezzatollah Sahabi noted when the Assembly of Experts convened, the clerical party was in the majority and also had a clearly defined program.[21]

This program was facilitated by Beheshti's deft handling of the Assembly of Experts. Beheshti did not always have his way. But aware of Khomaini's wishes and the general sense of the assembly, he concentrated on the essentials and kept the discussions in a chamber of prickly and senior clerics on course. He used his position as chairman to cut off debate when necessary, to interpret the gist of the discussions as he saw fit, and to present the "official" view of critical articles of the constitution. At one point, a frustrated Moghaddam-Maraghe'i stormed out of the chamber shouting at Beheshti: "The microphone sits before you and you speak whenever you wish. You are like the teacher, while we sit here and listen like pupils."[22] Along with a number of colleagues, Beheshti planned and drafted the revised constitution, even as the members of the assembly were painfully debating the draft article by article. He was active behind the scenes and in the committees in preparing key articles.

As a result, by the time the Assembly completed its deliberations on 15 November, it had thoroughly revamped the draft constitution and laid the foundation for a theocratic state. The new constitution made the *faqih* the central figure in the political order, enshrined the dominance of the clerical community over the institutions of the state, entrenched Islamic jurisprudence as the foundation for the country's laws and legal system, and limited individual freedoms to what was considered permissible under Islam. The constitution provided for a twelve-man Council of Guardians empowered to veto all legislation in violation of Islamic or constitutional principles and reserved to the six Islamic jurists on the council the power to declare laws in conflict with Islam. "All civil, penal, financial, economic, administrative, cultural, military, political and other laws and regulations," article 4 of the constitution stated, "must be based on Islamic criteria."[23]

The revised constitution provided for a president who had lost the bulk of his powers to the *faqih,* however; for a cabinet headed by a prime minister who would be appointed by the president and confirmed by Parliament; and for a single-chamber legislature (Majles) whose legislative authority was considerable but subject to the control of the Guardianship Council. The constitution also gave a permanent place in the new order to the Revolutionary Guard, which the Islamic parties regarded as a counter to the regular army. It provided, at least on paper, for certain limitations on property, for economic justice for the masses, and for devolution of authority to provincial councils.

During the debate on the revision of the draft constitution, it was the role of the *faqih* that aroused the most heated controversy. On the day the authority of the *faqih* was debated, over thirty members of the assembly signed up to speak. The debate spilled out of the assembly floor into the newspapers and was pursued in interviews, round-table discussions, and public speeches.

The operative clauses of the constitution were article 5 which conferred "the vice-regency and the leadership of the nation" on a just, pious, courageous, and capable jurist possessing administrative ability, acquainted with the circumstances of the time, and recognized as leader by the majority of the people; and articles 107–112, which spelled out the powers and mode of selection of the *faqih*. The constitution authorized the leader to appoint the jurists on the Council of Guardians, the chief officials of the judiciary branch, the chief of staff of the armed forces, the commander of the Revolutionary Guard, the majority of the members of the Supreme Defense Council, and also the commanders of the three branches of the armed forces, at the recommendation of the Supreme Defense Council. The *faqih* was also authorized to approve candidates running for the office of president and to dismiss the president after he had been declared incompetent to serve by Parliament or found negligent in his duties by the Supreme Court. The constitution conferred the vice-regency on Khomaini for life and provided for him to be succeeded either by an equally qualified jurist or in the absence of such a candidate, by a council of three or five jurists to be elected by yet another Assembly of Experts.

Only a handful of members of the assembly, with considerable courage, opposed this interpretation of the role of the *faqih*. The most outspoken were Moghaddam-Maraghe'i and Ezzatollah Sahabi, with occasional support from Bani-Sadr, and three clerics, Ali Golzadeh-Ghafuri, Mohammad-Javad Hojjati-Kermani, and Naser Makarem-Shirazi. These men tried to argue from religious doctrine, the principle of constitutional consistency, and practical politics. They asserted, variously, that true vice-regency belongs only to the *ma'sum*, one free from sin, or at the very least, one who was expert not only in Islamic law but also in administration, politics, economics, and everyday affairs. "It may be possible to find a *faqih* with these characteristics and qualities," Sahabi noted, "but the channels through which a *faqih* is trained are not designed to cultivate such knowledge and qualities."[24]

Moghaddam-Maraghe'i and Makarem-Shirazi contended that while a problem would not arise during Khomaini's lifetime, there was no guarantee that his successor would have similar leadership qualities. "In 1,400 years, Khomaini is an exception," Moghaddam-Maraghe'i said.[25] "Several centuries may pass before a man with his superior qualities and characteristics and [similar] conditions of time and place, arise again," Makarem-Shirazi added.[26]

On the day the powers of the *faqih* were approved, Makarem-Shirazi made an impassioned plea for reconsideration. The role of the *faqih*, he said, conflicted with the principle of popular sovereignty already approved in earlier clauses of the constitution. Critics abroad would say that "all the strings are in our hands . . . that the clerics have established their own government." The people, "say nothing. But tomorrow they will put this law aside."[27] Hojjati-Kermani warned that insistence on the *faqih* clauses had created division in society. "Today there is anticlerical propaganda everywhere. We should beware lest the fire burn us all."[28] Sahabi, in a speech outside Parliament that earned him a reprimand from Beheshti and the IRP, went further and remarked that making religious authority vulnerable to the criticism normally directed at political authority would spell "the beginning of the decline of Islam." The doctrine of the *faqih,* he said, creates "a sovereignty and a guardianship without parallel, an authority to rival the authority of the government that is unacceptable in today's world."[29]

The majority, however, defended the doctrine of the *faqih* as essential for realizing the Islamic state, guaranteeing the Islamic nature of the laws, and lending legitimacy to the acts of the president, the prime minister, and the legislature. The government will not be Islamic, Hosain-Ali Montazeri said, unless the president, the prime minister, and the chief justice are jurists or confirmed and supervised by the *faqih.* "If the entire nation votes for the president, and the *vali-ye faqih* and *mojtahed* [jurist] does not confirm him," Mohammad Yazdi, another cleric said, "this has no effect, and the government will be usurped."[30] Abdol-Rahim Rabbani-Shirazi argued that the separation of powers does not apply in Islam. "In Islam, the vice-regent constitutes the executive power, the legislative power and the judicial power."[31]

Many delegates viewed the *faqih* as a barrier to the reemergence of a dictator or absolute ruler, a neutral figure who would order relations between different classes, resolve conflicts, and ensure the good order of society. Fatehi regarded it unjust to couple the *faqih* with dictatorship. "The *faqih,* like the Prophet, brings mercy, kindness and justice to the people, not absolutism."[32] Hasan Ayat, citing Rousseau's social contract and the idea that people give up certain freedoms for a general good, noted: "If the social contract were once in reality realized, it was in relation to Islam."[33]

The arguments for the *faqih* were summarized by another clerical member of the assembly, Hasan Taheri-Khorramabadi:

> We entrusted the vice-regency to a just *faqih* in order that our government be an Islamic government, in keeping with the conditions that Islam designates for the governor; so that Muslims regard themselves as responsible to

the government and consider its commands to be God's commands and its dispositions legal and binding; and so that a duly qualified authority prevent dictatorship and colonialism.[34]

Two efforts were made to head off the Assembly of Experts from the direction it was taking. Hojjati-Kermani suggested that the assembly approve the clauses related to Parliament, the president, and the Guardianship Council, and leave it to Khomaini to draft the rest of the constitution with the assistance of a committee of lawyers, men of letters, and other specialists. The Assembly of Experts would then reconvene and be given a week to approve the final draft. The members proved unenthusiastic about the proposal.

In mid-October, just as the Assembly of Experts was debating the powers of the *faqih*, Bazargan's personal aide Abbas Amir-Entezam and a group of his associates agreed to seek the support of the prime minister and the cabinet for an appeal to Khomaini to halt the work of the assembly altogether. They would argue that the assembly had exceeded its mandate by revising the draft constitution beyond recognition and by extending its deliberations beyond the originally agreed one-month time limit.[35]

While the details of what followed are not entirely clear, it appears that a reluctant Bazargan was persuaded to support the initiative. A sufficient number of cabinet ministers agreed to go along for a memorandum to be presented to Khomaini asking for the dissolution of the Assembly of Experts. Khomaini rejected the proposal. Details of the initiative were not made public at the time. But Khomaini indirectly referred to the initiative in remarks to a group of clerics on 22 October. He warned against "deviationists" who were plotting the dissolution of the assembly, denied that the vice-regency of the *faqih* would lead to "bullying and dictatorship," and added: "The *velayet-e faqih* is not something created by the Assembly of Experts. It is something that God has ordained."[36]

Articles of the constitution providing for freedom of speech, assembly, and association, for habeas corpus and protection against torture also proved controversial.[37] Clerical members of the assembly seemed at once persuaded that Islam provided for basic freedoms and concerned lest these freedoms be used to undermine Islam, create disorder, spread undesirable doctrines, and protect those who deserved punishment. Several members appeared uncertain whether the mass of the people, "illiterate, poor and envious," as one delegate put it, would be able to resist the blandishments of rival religions and ideologies.[38]

Hosain-Ali Montazeri thought freedom of association should be denied to the Baha'is, Abdol-Rahim Rabbani-Shirazi to the communists. Ayatollah Ali Meshgini said Islam permitted freedom of speech to the extent that individuals might argue Islamic precepts before experts and receive their answer, "not that someone should go to some village and speak against Islam. This, Islam does not permit."[39] Another delegate, Ja'far Sobhani, noted that freedom of press was desirable. "But should we permit a book that denies Islam and the *khatamiyyat* [the finality of Mohammad's prophetic mission]? On the assumption that the people are free, would it be wise to let them read it?"[40]

Ayatollah Jalal ad-Din Taheri found even the article banning torture problematic. "Tomorrow they will form a gang and, based on the constitutional ban on torture, they will commit every kind of crime. Take this article out of the constitution."[41] Ayatollah Meshgini, also expressing reservations about the article, noted that, "say, important personages are kidnapped, and we know a couple of people who have information; if [these persons] are arrested and given a couple of slaps, they might confess."[42]

Bani-Sadr appealed to the delegates to reconsider and to think of their own interests. "We are drafting these articles in a manner that, step-by-step we introduce a kind of absolutism in the constitution," he said. "Tomorrow, a military man might come and use these articles against you."[43] But Mohammad Karami, a clerical member of the assembly, was not moved by these arguments. "If a principle violates the framework of Islam, we will not approve it. Beware that we will not countenance these freedoms under whose cloak you want to introduce apostasy."[44] As a result, the final draft of the constitution provided for basic freedoms, but only to the extent permitted by law and by Islam.

Articles of the constitution providing for the establishment of provincial and local councils were approved quickly. The provincial councils remained a dead letter, however, and the demand for regional autonomy by the Kurds, Baluch, and other ethnic minorities were not satisfied. The implications had been only hazily considered. The prevailing disorder put a premium on reasserting governmental authority, not on transferring a nonexistent authority to the provinces. The uprising in Kurdistan, and ethnic unrest in Khuzestan, Gorgan, and Baluchistan fed fears that the provinces would slip out of control altogether.

The economic clauses of the constitution, though liable to a radically egalitarian interpretation, also proved less controversial than might have been expected. Some members were concerned that the articles on property and economic justice were so worded as to lead inevitably to state ownership of the means of production. Others feared that industrial workers, taking literally a constitutional provision guaranteeing each the tools of his own labor, would demand the dismantling of the factories. Nevertheless, the articles of the constitution referring to economic policy were not seriously contested; and they were later utilized by one IRP faction to press for radical economic policies.

Many members considered article 6, which treated sovereignty as stemming from the popular will, to be in conflict with the vice-regency of the *faqih*. The constitution, however, left these two concepts of sovereignty standing side by side in uneasy or—given a different perspective—creative symbiosis. The 1906 constitution, at an earlier time and in similar fashion, had declared sovereignty to be a divine gift bestowed by the people on the monarch. The 1979 constitution was a reminder that seventy years after the Constitutional Revolution, Iranians were still uncertain whether it was the people or God and the clerics who ruled.

The Presidential Elections

The constitution was a product of Khomaini's concept of Islamic government and reflected the clerical domination of the Assembly of Experts and the levers of power. In its final form, it left unrealized the aspirations of various groups: the ethnic minorities, the secular parties of the center and the left, and the moderate and conservative elements in the religious establishment. These dissatisfied elements voiced their opposition through newspapers, protest marches, and, finally, a major uprising in Tabriz. The clerical party responded with further acts of repression.

Within days of the election of the Assembly of Experts, on 8 August the revolutionary prosecutor-general banned *Ayandegan*, a popular newspaper with left-wing, but by no means extremist, leanings. *Ayandegan's* offices and printing works, seized in the name of the Foundation for the Disinherited, were subsequently used to publish a new newspaper *Sobh-e Azadegan*, the organ of the Islamic radicals in the IRP camp. Nine other publications were subsequently shut down.

Protest demonstrations, organized by the NDF on 13 August, were disrupted by the stick-wielding *hezbollahis*. The NDF was proscribed and a warrant was issued for the arrest of the NDF leader, Hedayatollah Matin-Daftari, ostensibly for disrupting public order. The next day, the *hezbollahis*, urged on by Hadi Ghaffari, attacked the headquarters of the Fadayan guerrilla organization and expelled the members from their headquarters. The Mojahedin decided to evacuate their headquarters rather than to wait for the attack of the menacing bands of *hezbollahis* that had collected outside their offices.

In December, after the referendum on the constitution, it was the turn of the IPRP and Shariatmadari to come under attack. Shariatmadari had continued to criticize the new constitution, the doctrine of the vice-regency of the *faqih* which it articulated, and the excesses of the revolution. He did not discourage the many political groups who, alarmed at the drift of events, looked to him to articulate their grievances and sought to build around his person a focus of loyalty to rival Khomaini's. He earned Khomaini's indirect but harsh reprimand when he received a delegation of university professors and acknowledged the justice of their concern over public whippings, executions "possibly even of pregnant women, 12-year-old children and 90-year-old men," and purges of university faculty.

Meantime, discontent was growing in Azarbaijan, Shariatmadari's native province. It came to a boil over the new constitution. In early December, members of the IPRP and Shariatmadari's followers in the provincial capital, Tabriz, took to the streets, seized the television station, and began to broadcast demands and grievances. For a moment, it appeared that the opposition had found a powerful base from which to check the spreading power of the IRP and the Khomaini party. Tabriz was Iran's second largest city; it was here that the first massive riots had taken place that eventually toppled the Shah. The Azarbaijans were numerous and influential in the Tehran bazaar and in the capital's retail trade. In Azarbaijan, the opposition had a geographical base, strongly committed to Shariatmadari; and in Shariatmadari it had a religious leader who might give legitimacy to the movement.

The revolutionary authorities, however, responded by ordering the Revolutionary Guard to retake the broadcasting station by force of arms. They sent a delegation of mediators to Tabriz, which managed to blunt the fervor of some of the local leaders. They contrived to stage massive pro-Khomaini counterdemonstrations in Tabriz, thus indicating that the Shariatmadari monopoly over the city no longer obtained.

Much more seriously, Shariatmadari wavered. At one moment, he appeared ready to support and encourage his followers. At another he seemed inclined to wash his hands of the movement, the IPRP, and its leaders. Shariatmadari's hesitation proved fatal to the Tabriz movement. The minirevolt in Tabriz faltered. The IRP organized a massive campaign to demand the dissolution of the IPRP. The party, launched nine months earlier with Shariatmadari's blessings, obliged. It announced it was suspending activities.

The presidential elections, the first step in putting in place the institutions foreseen in the constitution, took place in January. The field of candidates was gradually whittled down. Bazargan, who aspired to the presidency, chose not to run. The "students of the Imam's line" had begun to use the documents discovered at the American embassy to cast aspersions on moderate secular leaders. Bazargan knew better then to expose himself to their mercies. The candidacy of the Mojahedin leader, Mas'ud Rajavi, was vetoed by Khomaini, ostensibly because the Mojahedin had boycotted the referendum on the new constitution. Beheshti hoped to be president and would have been a formidable candidate for the IRP; but Khomaini banned clerics from running for office.

The candidate the IRP announced, Jalal ad-Din Farsi, ran into difficulty. The constitution required the president to be Iranian by birth. Farsi had an Afghan father. He was disqualified a few days before the balloting. The IRP's substitute candidate, Hasan Habibi, was unknown and the party had no time to organize a campaign on his behalf. This left Bani-Sadr and Admiral Ahmad Madani as the only two serious candidates. Madani, a naval officer and governor-general of Khuzestan province, was the law-and-order candidate and the favorite of the upper-middle classes. On the eve of the elections, the "students of the Imam's line" published documents damaging to Madani; nevertheless, he secured over a million votes.

Madani, however, could not have beaten Bani-Sadr, for Bani-Sadr was popular. Unencumbered by government office for most of the eight months since the revolution, he had become widely known, traveling around the country making speeches. His books on Islamic government, oil, and Islamic economics had earned him a following among the young. He polled 75 percent of the vote, far out-distancing his two nearest rivals. His victory was a personal triumph and an indication of the strength of the secular and left-of-center sentiment among certain sectors of the electorate. But the message of the election was a mixed one. Bani-Sadr had run against a diminished field of candidates. The IRP had been caught off guard and had not organized for the election. In the mind of the mass of the voters, Bani-Sadr was closely identified with Khomaini. He exuded an aura of both radicalism and Islam. The ballot could not be interpreted as a vote against the clerics; it did not prove that revolutionary fervor had died down; and it was not a true test of the organizing abilities of the IRP.

Chapter 5

Bani-Sadr: The "Devoted Son" as President

THE FIRST PRESIDENT of the Islamic Republic was the product of a clerical home and a secular education, the provincial middle class and Paris, Islam and the political currents fashionable among the French left. Abol-Hasan Bani-Sadr was born in Hamadan in 1933 to a moderately prosperous landowning family. His father, Nasrollah, was a middle-rank cleric. Bani-Sadr received some religious training at home and attended secular schools in Hamadan. His father wished him to train to become a cleric at the great Faiziyyeh seminary in Qom. But he acceded to his son's desire to attend Tehran University instead, where a more "modern" theological training was available, and where Bani-Sadr ended up studying at both the faculty of theology and the faculty of law. At the university, he was a student political leader active in the university branch of the National Front (NF) and inclined toward the movement's Islamic elements. At the same time, he worked on various projects at the newly established and university-affiliated School for Social Research, which had become a magnet for younger scholars interested in Iranian social problems. There he became acquainted with the

French Marxist sociologist, Paul Vieille, who was considerably to influence Bani-Sadr's intellectual formation.

After some difficulty with the authorities over his political activities, Bani-Sadr went to Paris in the early 1960s to continue his studies. He worked with Vieille, began a never-completed doctoral thesis on the destruction of Iranian society under the impact of the Shah's absolutism and Western domination, and continued his political activities. He also wrote extensively: on Shi'a Islam as a force against despotism and on Islamic government and economics; on his heroes, the nationalist leader Mohammad Mossadegh and the early twentieth century religious leader Hasan Modarress; on the dangers of the cult of the personality, and on current Iranian politics. His books were at once a critique of the Shah's system of rule and an elaboration of an alternative form of government based on Islamic principles, under which freedom, national independence, social justice, and prosperity would be realized. He remained an ardent nationalist in these years; he became a self-proclaimed revolutionary, committed to the overthrow of the Shah; and he grew stronger in the conviction that the answer to Iran's political and economic problems lay in a return to a (reformed) Islamic ideology.

But his writings in Paris also reflect new influences. He espoused critiques of Western capitalism and imperialism that stressed the "dependent" economic and political relationship between third world and industrialized countries. The theme of Western, and particularly American "domination," and of third world and Iranian "dependence," is prominent in many of his books and essays. Bani-Sadr's imagination was also captured by the Paris student movement of 1968 and its apparent spontaneity. When Iranians began to march and demonstrate against the Shah in 1978, Bani-Sadr viewed the protest movement as a similar manifestation of "popular effervescence," in which the nation was united, "class values effaced themselves," and the people "spontaneously" reached out toward a higher stage of development.[1] As president, Bani-Sadr would continue to aspire to a politics based on the unstructured and spontaneous action of the mass of the people.

In his critique of the Iranian regime, Bani-Sadr charged the Shah with suppressing freedoms, crushing individual talent, and creating a cult of personality around himself; with inculcating Western values, fostering a consumer society, and thus threatening the integrity of Iranian culture and identity; and with allowing the country to be plundered by the United States and the industrialized nations. In his view, the Shah and his ministers were agents of American policy. The Iranian army, closely linked to the United States military, had no independent will of its own. The Iranian economy, totally dependent on imported machinery and raw materials, boasting no real industry or productivity, was "a sucking machine," designed to funnel Iranian wealth and resources to foreign pockets. The Shah must therefore be overthrown, independence from foreign domination asserted, and a state based on Islamic economic and political principles established.

Bani-Sadr's ideas on Islamic government stemmed from an extreme reaction to all forms of authority, authoritarian figures, and restraints on the individual. His ideal Islamic state is characterized by the absence of formal structures and considerable diffusion of power. In such a state, he wrote, there will be no concentration of economic, political, or intellectual power, no classes and no dominant ideology, because "any ideology that becomes official becomes an instrument of power, the opium of the masses; because authority, in using belief to legitimize itself, will use it as a club." This stricture applies to Islam itself, for "will Islam not become an opiate if you turn it into an instrument of administration?"[2]

In its foreign policy, an Islamic government will not seek to dominate others, base relations on power, or use the army for offensive purposes. Since the entire community will be engaged in a continuous holy war to achieve a society of divine unity, all the citizenry will be armed, leading to the disappearance of the military as an instrument of class domination and "the dissolution of the army in the society." Even clothing will reflect the absence of power relations and serve only a pragmatic function, since "Islam forbids to the individual dress that distinguishes him from others."

The people will exercise supervision over their leaders through their network of mosques where "the Government of God" will be realized, "for the mosque is a place where no one has the right to give orders to anyone; only God has sovereignty." The community will have an imam, or leader; but he will not represent any special class or interest, be idolized, or become the focus of a cult of the personality: "good and beloved men must be cherished, but not made absolute." Rather, leadership itself will become diffused, and each member of the community, through piety and self-discipline, will become an imam. The imamate will thus be "generalized," all will share in the leadership, "all will become *mojtaheds* [jurists] and no one will need to ask his duty from another. . . . Otherwise, religious tyranny will result."[3]

Bani-Sadr's concept of the "generalized imamate" *(ta'mim-e imamat)* was thus a far cry from Khomaini's concept of the vice-regency of the jurist *(velayat-e faqih)*. To Khomaini, sovereignty belongs collectively to the religious leaders, or individually to the outstanding jurist of his time, as heirs to the mantle of the Prophet. The *faqih* is supremely qualified to lead the community and to serve as a *marja'-e taqlid,* a source of emulation, because of his long and arduous training in Islamic jurisprudence and his expertise in Islamic law. To Bani-Sadr, on the other hand, each member of the community, through personal striving, achieves the qualities of jurist and leader. He has no need for *taqlid,* or emulation. In Bani-Sadr's version of Islamic government, the individual citizen appears to appropriate for himself the right to interpret the divine sources of the law. In a sense, therefore, there are no followers or leaders, no emulators or sources of emulation.

These strikingly different approaches to Islamic government did not prevent the two men from coming together against the Iranian regime. Bani-Sadr was first drawn to Khomaini in 1962–63, when the religious leader launched his campaign against the Shah's policies. "When Mr. Khomaini dared to oppose the Shah," Bani-Sadr later wrote, "it was as if the world had opened up"; and when Khomaini's criticism of the status of forces law and the American role in Iran led to his exile in 1964, Bani-Sadr was elated. "At last, we had found a cleric conforming to our own views: a man capable of rising up against domestic despotism and foreign domination."[4] Bani-Sadr met Khomaini in 1972, when in Iraq for his father's funeral. His admiration grew. He saw in Khomaini a spiritual leader devoid of personal ambition and the means through which the Shah could be overthrown. He came to regard himself as Khomaini's disciple, his "devoted son." He sent copies of his writings to Khomaini, urged him to speak out more openly, and to make known his views on Islamic government. He worked to promote Khomaini's reputation abroad and to buttress his position as the leading religious authority at home.

Khomaini appears to have reciprocated this affection, perhaps viewing the younger man as a "spiritual son." Bani-Sadr served as a link to the Iranian opposition movement abroad and to Iran's Westernized intelligentsia. He was an adept propagandist. He provided Khomaini with "evidence" that the Shah was wrecking the economy, selling Iran's resources to the imperialists, and turning Iran into an instrument of American policy. He continued to assure Khomaini of the imminent collapse of the Pahlavi regime. Moreover, though Bani-Sadr was the son of a cleric, he had received a Westernized education but had remained committed to Islam. He seemed versed in the Western sciences of economics and politics, yet he worked these into an Islamic mold. "You are a cleric like us," Khomaini once said to him, "you are one of us."[5] When Khomaini was expelled from Iraq in October 1978 and came to Paris, he initially stayed at the apartment of Bani-Sadr's friend, Ahmad Ghazanfarpour.

Along with Ebrahim Yazdi and Sadeq Qotbzadeh, Bani-Sadr made the arrangements for Khomaini's stay in the French capital. The three men acted as interpreters, dealt with the press and the occasional diplomat, coached Khomaini to make suitable remarks on such questions as women's rights and civil liberties, and took quiet satisfaction when Khomaini echoed one of their pet phrases, for example that "sovereignty must revert to the people." They helped produce the bland responses that persuaded a host of foreign journalists, unfamiliar with Khomaini's own writings, that once in power in Tehran, the Ayatollah would withdraw from affairs and preside as the benign father of a liberal democracy. Along with a small group of other Iranian advisers, all three were consulted on critical decisions. Bani-Sadr no doubt gained standing with Khomaini by firmly opposing compromise with either the Shah or later with the liberal prime minister, Shapour Bakhtiar.

Bani-Sadr was one of the favored passengers on the chartered jet that flew Khomaini from Paris to Tehran in January 1979. Khomaini pressed Bazargan to include him in his first cabinet, but Bazargan refused. Bani-Sadr, he said, regarded everyone else with contempt, refused to work as part of a team, and had no previous administrative experience, "not even in running a Koran grade school."[6] Soon after the revolution, however, Bani-Sadr became a member of the Revolutionary Council, Khomaini named him to various investigatory commissions, and he played an important role in the decision to nationalize the banks and major industries. As a member of the Assembly of Experts he unsuccessfully sought to strengthen the constitutional guarantees for individual rights. He opposed, but with circumspection, the provisions on the sovereignty of the *faqih;* on the day the vote was taken on this critical article, he chose to absent himself from the assembly. Nevertheless, even in its final form, the constitution and its preamble reflected many of his ideas. In November, following the seizure of the American hostages, Bani-Sadr served briefly as foreign minister and then as minister of finance, becoming president in January 1980.

As an exile and revolutionary, Bani-Sadr had been primarily a man of books, a pamphleteer and a popularizer of ideas. His strong rejection of any form of authority and power, his admiration for the "spontaneous effervescence" of the masses, lent to his ideas a populist, even an anarchist streak. He himself cited approvingly a friend's observation that he was "the first anarchist, in the philosophical sense of the term, to have achieved the presidency of a republic."[7] At the same time, like many other revolutionary figures, he was attracted by the idea of social engineering. He too wished to eradicate the Pahlavi system and its values, to transform society and its institutions root and branch, and to create a new, revolutionary man.

"A Fistful of Fascist Clerics"

The huge majority by which Bani-Sadr was elected president did not reflect the real distribution of power in the country. Yet the new president came to office believing he had won a sweeping mandate to "redress" the revolution and to rescue it from "a fistful of fascist clerics."[8] He interpreted the election results as a rejection of the Islamic Republic Party (IRP) and its leaders and concluded he could now make a clean sweep of his opponents. Although when out of government he had advocated populist ideas (which he did not now abandon), and had played a role in undermining the Bazargan government, as president he became almost overnight an advocate of central authority. To reassert the authority of the government and its formal institutions was, in fact, the key element in his program.

He intended, he said, to reorganize and revive the army, police force, and gendarmerie. He wanted to see the judiciary once again playing its proper role. He intended to do away with the revolutionary organizations and what he described as "multiple centers of authority." The clerics must be subject to the state. The militant students holding American hostages, he wryly remarked, could continue to follow the Imam's line, "but in their respective colleges." The Revolutionary Guard would be absorbed into the regular army, the revolutionary courts would give way to the regular court system, and the revolutionary committees would be dissolved. Even Bani-Sadr's economic policies sounded more orthodox. Although exercised to refute charges that he would discontinue radical economic measures, including expropriations, he nevertheless said the emphasis would now be given to economic development.

Bani-Sadr was also determined to end Iran's dependence on outside powers and to begin the task of transforming Iranian society. The army, he said, had five types of "dependent" relations with America; he had counted fifty-seven types of "dependent" relations in the country as a whole. "We must break those to be free." The center of decision making on Iran, he asserted, "must no longer be in Washington, Moscow, London and elsewhere. The fate of Iran must be determined by the Iranian nation." Moreover, while the former regime had been overthrown, the military, bureaucratic, economic, social, and cultural order and institutions bequeathed by the Pahlavis remained standing. "We must overturn this structure from its foundations so that the establishment of the Islamic Republic becomes possible."[9] While denying any desire to export revolution, Bani-Sadr nevertheless argued that Iran would be secure against great-power domination only when similar revolutions had occurred elsewhere; he promised assistance to other Islamic and liberation movements, and invited Europe to join hands with Iran in throwing off American hegemony.

To carry out this program, Bani-Sadr's strategy was to secure control of the legislative, executive, and judicial branches of the government. He was convinced his overwhelming electoral majority would carry over into the forthcoming parliamentary elections and give him control over the new Majles, or Parliament. A parliamentary majority, he believed, would give him control of the executive branch, since the new constitution empowered the president both to appoint the prime minister and to approve the premier's choice of cabinet ministers, subject to confirmation by Parliament. The minister of justice, according to the constitution, was to be appointed by a somewhat different process; but he too would be a member of the cabinet and serve as the link between the judicial, legislative, and executive branches. Control of the other department important to Bani-Sadr, the state-operated radio and television network, would presumably automatically follow, since the three branches of government were jointly responsible to oversee the activities of the broadcasting services.

Bani-Sadr could also count on Khomaini's backing. On 29 January Khomaini described support for Bani-Sadr as incumbent on the people; and following Khomaini's lead, other clerics pronounced in Bani-Sadr's favor. Ayatollah Khamene'i, the leader of Friday prayers in Tehran, told the people to "respect him, follow him, support him in the field, cooperate with him, do not undermine him." The influential Society of Seminary Teachers at Qom indicated its support; and as a result of mediation of the Association of the Combatant Clerics of Tehran, Bani-Sadr and several of the leading figures of the IRP agreed to work together for national unity.

But the IRP leader, Ayatollah Beheshti, gave early warning of what was to come in interviews and public comments which indicated that IRP support for Bani-Sadr was provisional and conditional. Bani-Sadr, he suggested, like Bazargan, was incapable of leading a country in a state of revolution; his presidency posed "the same danger" of liberalism, which many millions continued to prefer to Islam. The IRP, he said, had its differences with Bani-Sadr and reserved its position on various questions. It would support the president as long as he pursued a militant Islamic path. "Whenever he strays," Beheshti added, "we will warn, we will criticize; if he persists, we will oppose him." Besides, he remarked, according to the constitution, "the president counts for nothing."[10]

The first issue between Bani-Sadr and the IRP centered on the swearing-in of the president. Bani-Sadr, hoping to name the prime minister and cabinet and to have the new government in place before the parliamentary elections, argued that in the absence of the Majles, he should be sworn in before Khomaini. This was an exceptional moment in the country's history and required exceptional measures, he said, and the constitution did not provide the relevant guidelines for the distribution of authority. The members of the IRP, not normally sticklers for constitutional niceties, stood four-square on the constitution, insisting that the president take his oath of office before Parliament, whose election was at least two months away. "The president," suggested Ali-Akbar Hashemi-Rafsanjani, a founding member of the IRP, "should in the meantime devote himself to study and to preparing for the presidency."[11]

However, through the agency of Khomaini's son Ahmad, Bani-Sadr was able to persuade the Imam to adminster the oath of office himself. Khomaini did so in a hastily arranged ceremony in a room at the Reza'i Hospital, where he was recovering from a heart attack. The decree of appointment was written out in longhand on a sheet of paper bearing the hospital letterhead.

Bani-Sadr was in business.

Initially, the president seemed to notch up several victories against his opponents. When the students at the American embassy produced documents allegedly compromising the minister of information, Naser Minachi, and arranged for his arrest, Bani-Sadr was able to intervene and secure Minachi's release within twenty-four hours. The students were forced to postpone a march they had called so that it would not conflict with the president's swearing-in ceremony. Bani-Sadr criticized them as "children" and for trying to form "a government within a government"; and he secured the agreement of the Revolutionary Council to deny the students free access to radio and television.

On 7 February, Khomaini appointed him chairman of the Revolutionary Council. He did not permit Bani-Sadr to name a prime minister, but he agreed that until Parliament convened, the president should be able to propose new ministerial appointments and new legislation to the Revolutionary Council. On 19 February, Khomaini delegated to Bani-Sadr his powers as commander-in-chief of the armed forces. Moreover, he permitted Bani-Sadr to name his own appointees to run the state radio and television stations and to command the Revolutionary Guard. At Bani-Sadr's suggestion, the Revolutionary Council approved a general code of conduct for state radio and television, which on paper would have made the broadcasting networks more objective in their reporting and more accessible to voices other than those of the IRP and its allies. As part of this policy, he secured for Mehdi Bazargan an hour of television time—virtually the first opportunity given him to appear on television since his resignation. Bazargan issued a general appeal for moderation and defended his own record.

In March, Khomaini issued a new general amnesty for persons charged with crimes under the old regime or with compromising relationships with the Pahlavis. Like earlier amnesties, this one excluded those directly involved in or responsible for ordering killings and torture and those guilty of plundering the national wealth. But the amnesty nevertheless reflected a desire to rein in the excesses of the revolutionary courts and committees and to restore a semblance of security to the country.

The Year of Order and Security

Bani-Sadr's desire for a return to normalcy was elaborated more fully in the message that Khomaini issued on 20 March, on the eve of the Iranian New Year. The message bore the firm imprint of Bani-Sadr's ideas and even his language. It was read publicly by the Ayatollah's son, Ahmad Khomaini, who was then cooperating closely with the president. Clearly an attempt to reassert the authority of the central government, the message urged Iranians to make the coming year "the year for a restoration of order and security."[12]

In the message, Khomaini condemned indiscipline in the army, police, and Revolutionary Guards, in the civil service, factories, and places of work. He called for a ban on factory strikes and described striking workers as counterrevolutionaries. He urged the revolutionary courts to act within the framework of the constitution, forbade them to maintain their own armed retainers, and banned unauthorized seizures of property. He said the revolutionary courts must be gradually merged into the regular judicial system. He called for an investigation of the Foundation for the Disinherited, whose handling of confiscated and nationalized property had been criticized by Bani-Sadr and others, and he stressed the need for economic development, another favorite Bani-Sadr theme.

Khomaini also used his New Year message once more to attack liberal and left-wing political groups. Without mentioning the two former guerrilla organizations by name, he accused the Fadayan of fomenting strikes in factories and the Mojahedin of "corrupting Islam with Marxism." He accused journalists of "plotting." He called for the Islamization of education and described the intellectuals as "the source of all our misfortunes." Bani-Sadr too had accused the Mojahedin of mixing Mohammad with Marx, and the Fadayan of encouraging industrial unrest. But Khomaini's broad attack on the liberals and the left, the universities and the press, went beyond what Bani-Sadr himself might have wished. Bani-Sadr's hand, however, was evident in Khomaini's condemnation of Russia's "brutal aggression" in Afghanistan and his indirect condemnation of Soviet as well as American imperialism. "We are as much at war with international communism as with the world-devourers of the West," Khomaini said.

Over the next few months, Bani-Sadr sought to use Khomaini's call for a return to order as the vehicle through which to assert central authority. He was not alone. Other revolutionary officials, more often associated with hard-line views, also attempted on the strength of Khomaini's directives, to curb the revolutionary organizations. Ayatollah Ali Qoddusi, the revolutionary prosecutor-general, and Ayatollah Mohammad Mohammadi-Gilani, chief of the capital's revolutionary courts, moved to subject the provincial revolutionary tribunals to Tehran's supervision. Ayatollah Mohammad Beheshti, appointed chief justice of the Supreme Court, and Ayatollah Musavi-Ardabili, the prosecutor-general (*Dadsetan-e Kol*, not to be confused with the prosecutor-general of the revolutionary courts) spoke hopefully of integrating the revolutionary tribunals into the regular court system. Ayatollah Mahdavi-Kani, the interior minister, revived the idea of merging the armed retainers of the revolutionary committees into the national police and assigning them to other duties, for example, he suggested ingenuously, "to guarding electric power stations." An investigation was opened up into alleged corruption at the Foundation for the Disinherited.

The most ambitious effort was directed at the judiciary. The revolutionary courts and related institutions had come under increasing criticism. Ayatollah Qomi-Tabataba'i, of Mashad, who had stayed aloof from the revolutionary regime, told *Bamdad* in early March that many of the proceedings and judgments of the revolutionary courts violated Islamic principles and constituted "unwarranted expropriations, unwarranted jailings, unwarranted judicial decisions, unwarranted killings, unwarranted whippings." He criticized the property seizures by the Foundation for the Disinherited and said "the oppression and cruelty perpetrated in the name of the Crusade for Reconstruction has exceeded all bounds."[13] Clerics in the government also desired to control the revolutionary tribunals. The chain of authority by which judges in provincial revolutionary tribunals had been appointed was often confused. Judgments were inconsistent; a similar "antirevolutionary" crime might earn a short prison term in one court and the death sentence in another. Mounting arrests meant the prisons were overflowing. At the Evin prison, where those accused of association with the former regime or crimes against the revolution were kept, over 7,200 cases were pending, while the revolutionary tribunals were handling only 20 cases a day. "We have no prosecutors, we have no judges," Ayatollah Qoddusi said, "and our only two judges have become candidates for Parliament, said goodbye and left."[14] There was little coordination between revolutionary judges, magistrates, and prosecutors, the tribunals, and the Revolutionary Guard; excesses were everywhere pervasive. Qoddusi, soon after taking office, said none of the revolutionary tribunals had "the least resemblance" to Islamic courts. He attributed property confiscations to avariciousness, likened those carrying them out to "people in a famine attacking a bakery where they hear there is bread," and labeled the action "looting in the name of confiscation."[15]

The measures initiated in the spring arose from these conditions. In line with Khomaini's amnesty decree, his 20 March message, and instructions issued to Ayatollah Montazeri and Ayatollah Ali Meshgini, a special committee, the Council for the Appointment of Judges, was established in Qom. The council was charged with assigning judges to the revolutionary tribunals and given extensive authority to review court procedures and court decisions, hear complaints against the tribunals, and ensure that Khomaini's amnesty decree was being carried out. The council dispatched ten committees to the provinces to inspect the work of the revolutionary tribunals and hear grievances; it warned that the amnesty order "must be implemented precisely and hair by hair"; and it ordered the revolutionary tribunals to send copies of all court cases and judgments to Qom for review. Montazeri and Meshgini issued instructions against unnecessarily harsh judgments and unauthorized arrests and confiscations. "The revolutionary character of organizations," they said, "does not justify anarchy, disorder and indiscipline." In the capital, Qoddusi and Mohammadi-Gilani ruled that all important cases before the provincial revolutionary tribunals must be referred to Tehran for judgment. Qoddusi, in an additional circular similar to several issued by his predecessor, Mehdi Hadavi, said that no summons, or court order for arrest or the confiscation or freezing of property and bank accounts served in Tehran, and no court order served on members of the armed forces anywhere in the country, would be valid without his personal signature.[16]

All these projects came to nothing, or very little. Mahdavi-Kani abandoned the project to merge the revolutionary committees into the national police. Beheshti did not tamper with the revolutionary courts. The investigation into the finances of the Foundation for the Disinherited provided tantalizing glimpses into possible gross corruption (some 800 complaints were submitted to the investigating committee), and then petered out. The appointments to the revolutionary courts were to a large degree regularized; but the appointees were often men with local sources of power and in any case not subject to regulation once appointed. The amnesty decree led to the release from prison of some 650 persons guilty of minor crimes, and then, like its earlier incarnations, was forgotten. Although to a certain degree death sentences had to be approved in Tehran or Qom (a Qom cleric, Mohammad Mo'men, was the official responsible), this did not long halt executions, which began again in the spring.

The reasons were numerous. Powerful clerics like Montazeri and Meshgini, Mohammadi-Gilani, and Qoddusi were exercised to regulate the revolutionary courts; but they were not prepared to see the courts dissolved altogether, to surrender the immense power the revolutionary tribunals conferred on the clerics, or to yield primacy in the direction of the judicial apparatus to the advocates of a secular judicial order like Bani-Sadr. Khomaini himself, deeply committed to the revolutionary tribunals, ruled that they must continue as long as they were needed and until such time as the entire judicial system was Islamized. Taking his cue from Khomaini, Beheshti set committees to work drawing up new civil, criminal, and procedural codes based on Islamic law. Officials of the revolutionary tribunals in the provinces, supported by their armed retainers and other revolutionary bodies, deliberately set about destroying the apparatus of the old judiciary. At the very time when Beheshti and Musavi-Ardabili were assuring members of the civil courts that there would be a place for them in the new judiciary system, in towns like Nahavand, Langarud, Lahijan, and Amol in the north, Malayer in the west, and Bushehr in the south, revolutionary judges, prosecutors, and guards joined hands to purge and sometimes to imprison officials of the civil courts.

Moreover, the rank and file of the revolutionary courts, guards, and committees, encouraged by radical political groups, were opposed to any leniency in the courts. When Qoddusi returned confiscated property to the owners in two minor cases and blocked the confiscation of property of thirty-two others, cases he considered unjustified, staff at the revolutionary prosecutor's office and at Evin prison went on strike. Qoddusi's files were rifled, documents attesting to his wrongdoing were given to the newspapers, and the revolutionary prosecutor-general was even accused of corruption. Qoddusi did not soon forget this experience. It was to his own radicals that Qoddusi referred when, responding to Amnesty International criticism of the revolutionary tribunals, he remarked: "Should we dance to the tune of Amnesty International, that asks why we kill and do not grant amnesty, or to the tune of these gentlemen, who ask why we grant amnesty?"[17] Such was the uproar when the prison sentence of the former military commander of Qom was reduced from ten to five years that on appeal, the presiding judge, Mohammad Mo'men, sentenced the officer to death and had him executed. In Shiraz, members of the Revolutionary Guard, considering the Islamic judge, Ayatollah Mohammad-Ali Andalibi, too lenient toward landowners and the rich, refused to enforce his decisions and denied him and his officials access to the court.

Bani-Sadr's Plan Unravels

Bani-Sadr's own grand plan began quickly to unravel. Khomaini's appointment of Beheshti as chief justice effectively took any control of the judicial apparatus out of the president's hands. Bani-Sadr also failed to win a majority in Parliament. The elections for the 270-seat Majles were held in two stages, the first round in March and the second round in May. The IRP had learned the lesson of its setback on the presidential ballot. The party insisted on a two-stage vote, which meant many of the smaller parties would be knocked out in the second round. It fielded the most candidates, forged strategic alliances, claimed the blanket endorsement of groups such as the Combatant Clerics of Tehran which it did not have, and used its network of clerics, mosques, party workers, and affiliated organizations to pull out the vote. At the end of the first round, the Mojahedin, the NF, and several other parties charged election fraud. Khomaini's brother, Morteza Pasandideh, claimed the IRP had tampered with the vote in the family hometown of Khomain. But Bani-Sadr's attempt to have these complaints investigated proved abortive; Khomaini declared the elections fair. When the balloting was over, the IRP confirmed trends evident in the first round by sweeping the election.

Of the 241 seats decided, IRP candidates won 85 seats and IRP affiliates perhaps another 45. In practice, an even larger number of deputies, many unaffiliated representatives from small provincial constituencies, tended to vote with the IRP on critical issues. Bani-Sadr's own supporters won only a handful of seats. Also elected were a number of the moderates affiliated with Mehdi Bazargan's Iran Freedom Movement (IFM), including Bazargan himself, Ebrahim Yazdi, Yadollah Sahabi, Ezzatollah Sahabi, Ahmad Sadr Hajj Seyyed Javadi, Hashem Sabaghian, and Ali-Akbar Mo'infar. For a party that ran candidates only in the Tehran area, this was an impressive performance. A few of the candidates of the center and left-of-center parties, such as Karim Sanjabi of the NF, Abolfazl Qasemi of the Iran Party, and Kazem Sami of the Revolutionary Movement of Iranian Muslims (JAMA) also won seats, as did a handful of moderate clerics, including Ayatollah Hasan Lahuti, Mohammad-Javad Hojjati-Kermani, and Ali Golzadeh-Ghafuri, who would later make common cause with Bani-Sadr. But the IRP dominated the Majles and moved to consolidate its authority.

Hashemi-Rafsanjani was elected speaker of the Majles. The credentials of several of the moderates were rejected. The NF leader, Karim Sanjabi, and the leader of the Iran Party, Abolfazl Qasemi, were not seated. Admiral Ahmad Madani, who only a few weeks earlier had been received by Khomaini as a candidate for the prime ministership, was accused of antirevolutionary activities. Fearing arrest, he refused to appear before the credentials committee of Parliament and fled the country. Khosrow Qashqa'i, a leader of the Qashqa'i tribe, was arrested on vague charges and not seated once released. Elections were not held in most of the Kurdish-dominated areas, and those Kurdish representatives elected feared to take up their seats. Not a single member of the Mojahedin won a seat.

Bani-Sadr also failed to gain control over the cabinet. With an IRP majority virtually certain on the eve of the second round of the Majles elections in May, Bani-Sadr maneuvered to ward off the inevitable. He once again proposed to Khomaini that he be permitted to appoint the prime minister before Parliament convened; but Khomaini did not give the president's proposal unqualified support; a majority on the Revolutionary Council would not acquiesce in it; Beheshti and other IRP leaders opposed it; and men like Admiral Madani, whom Bani-Sadr proposed for the post, realized no prime minister could survive without Khomaini's unequivocal endorsement or IRP and parliamentary backing. Bani-Sadr suggested Ahmad Khomaini as prime minister; but Khomaini refused to allow his son to accept the post. When Parliament convened, Bani-Sadr selected the name of Mostafa Mir-Salim from a list of "approved" prime ministerial possibilities drawn up by the IRP.

Mir-Salim, commander of the national police and deputy minister of interior, was a member of the central committee of the IRP. He was a moderate, an advocate of law and order with little enthusiasm for the excesses of the revolutionary organizations. He had risen in Bani-Sadr's estimation by forthrightly condemning a violent attack by the *hezbollahi* club wielders on a mass Mojahedin rally at Amjadieh stadium in June. But it was precisely this position that made Mir-Salim unacceptable to the IRP rank and file, the revolutionary committees, and the Revolutionary Guard. These elements forced the IRP to shift position. The Majles leadership rejected Mir-Salim even before his candidacy could be considered by the full house, and the president withdrew his name. The struggle over the appointment of the prime minister continued through June and July. Finally, in early August, Bani-Sadr was forced to yield to the inevitable and accept as prime minister the IRP candidate, Mohammad-Ali Raja'i.

Raja'i, born in 1933, was a relative unknown even among the obscure figures who rose to prominence through the IRP. His father, a shopkeeper in the Qazvin bazaar, died when Raja'i was only four, leaving the family destitute. As a boy, Raja'i worked in Tehran as a shop assistant and street vendor, selling cheap meals to poor brick kiln workers in south Tehran. He signed up as a low-rank technician in the air force, where he spent five years. He finished high school, taught primary classes in the provinces, and then managed to enter and graduate from the Tehran Teachers Training College to qualify as a mathematics instructor. During his years as a street vendor, he was attracted to the fundamentalist Fadayan-e Eslam, attended Islamic discussion groups, and sat in on Ayatollah Mahmud Taleqani's classes in Islamic exegesis. In the 1960s he joined Bazargan's Iran Freedom Movement (IFM) and in 1963 was jailed for two months. It was in prison that he became acquainted with Ayatollah Mohammad-Javad Bahonar, a cleric who involved himself in educational affairs and who was later one of the founding members of the IRP.

Out of prison, he became a Bahonar protégé, assisted him in various activities, and joined in forming one of a proliferating number of Islamic welfare associations, which carried out ideological and quasi-political activities under the cover of welfare associations. He was sentenced to a five-year prison term in November 1974 and this time brutally treated. When he was released in 1978, Bahonar arranged for him to be appointed principal of the Refah School, an Islamic high school for girls which Bahonar had helped establish. It was at the Refah School that Khomaini established his headquarters on his return to Iran on the eve of the revolution. Raja'i served as Khomaini's host. In the governmental reorganization of July 1979, he was appointed deputy minister, then minister of education and caused the Bazargan government much consternation by announcing, without consulting the prime minister, the nationalization of the private schools.

Under IRP auspices, he was elected as a deputy from Tehran to Parliament in 1980. When he became prime minister, he was without previous administrative experience or independent political power. He was the creature of Bahonar and of Beheshti, to whom he looked for direction. A diminutive, soft-spoken, self-effacing man, his demeanor disguised a dogged determination. It was this quality, and his loyalty, that recommended him to Bahonar and Beheshti. Backed by them and the IRP, he was more than a match for the president.

Bani-Sadr could barely contain his contempt for Raja'i, whom he declared incompetent and lacking sufficient knowledge of Iran and international affairs to be prime minister. At one of their early meetings, he told Raja'i, "you have been talking for an hour and have lied twelve times," a remark that promptly found its way into the press. He sent him letters declaring that a man of his ignorance should honor the office of the prime minister by resigning the post.

The two men clashed over the appointment of cabinet ministers.

Bani-Sadr argued that the ministers should constitute "a cabinet of talents." Raja'i, citing Khomaini's instructions that the ministers should be "one hundred percent Islamic and revolutionary," took the view that piety and revolutionary credentials were more important qualifications for office than education and expertise. Bani-Sadr favored associates and technocrats educated at Western universities who in training, social background, and attitude differed little from the technocrats who had staffed the Shah's bureaucracy. Many of Raja'i's nominees had also trained at American or European universities: but most had received all or the bulk of their training in Iran, came from somewhat less privileged backgrounds, politically had attached themselves to the Islamic rather than the secular opposition movements, and, most important, owed their loyalty to the IRP leadership. Raja'i's associates belittled government based on a "Westernized" technocracy precisely because, as under the Shah, this offered them little chance for advancement.

The deadlock between Raja'i and Bani-Sadr was finally and partially resolved by Khomaini who suggested that the two men at least fill the cabinet posts on which they could agree. In September, Raja'i presented the president with a twenty-one-man cabinet. Only Mahdavi-Kani, the minister of interior, was a cleric, and at fifty-eight he was a member of the older generation and a major holdover from the previous cabinet. The remaining nominees were younger newcomers, technocratic and bureaucratic types who were rising to prominence as a result of the revolution. By age, the proposed ministers were in their thirties or early forties. Half-a-dozen of them had studied at American or British universities, the rest entirely in Iran, in such fields as civil engineering, electronics, economics, and medicine.

A number, as students, had been active in university Islamic societies, several had spent short spells in prison for political activities, but only five were involved in radical opposition politics under the Shah or had suffered long prison terms. By occupation they had worked in the lower ranks of the bureaucracy, as school or university instructors, one or two in the private sector. Most had already served the revolutionary government in some capacity: three had been appointed as provincial governors, three had headed academic institutions, one was Khomaini's personal physician, a number had staffed IRP party headquarters. Most were younger protégés of Beheshti, Bahonar, or other party officials. Mir-Hosain Musavi, for example, a Beheshti protégé, had edited the party newspaper *Jomhuri-ye Eslami*, and was a member of the IRP central committee.

Bani-Sadr rejected seven of Raja'i's candidates and approved fourteen. Even these he termed "barely acceptable." Parliament approved this rump cabinet on 10 September, but several key ministries, including education, foreign affairs, finance, commerce, labor, and justice were left vacant. The struggle between Raja'i and Bani-Sadr over these ministries continued week after week and month after month. Bani-Sadr rejected at least six different candidates Raja'i proposed as minister for foreign affairs. It was not until November that Bani-Sadr approved Raja'i's choices for the ministries of labor and justice; December when the minister of education was named; and March of the following year when the two men could finally agree on the ministers of commerce and finance. Parliament eventually passed a special measure permitting the prime minister to name caretakers to departments still without ministers, paving the way for the appointment of an acting foreign minister; but Bani-Sadr refused to sign the bill. The issue was still unresolved when Bani-Sadr was deposed in June 1981.

Bani-Sadr was exercising his constitutional rights in insisting that ministerial appointments meet with his approval. But his long, rearguard action over the selection of the cabinet served little purpose. It paralyzed the work of ministries which Raja'i and the IRP came to control anyway through Islamic committees, loyal undersecretaries, or other key officials. It provided the IRP with one more reason to seek Bani-Sadr's removal from office; and in the end it helped persuade Khomaini that the president was obstructing the work of the government.

Bani-Sadr's inability to exercise his authority was reflected elsewhere. In May 1980, in his capacity as commander-in-chief of the armed forces, the president officially named Abbas Zamani, better known as Abu-Sharif, as commander of the Revolutionary Guard. Abu-Sharif, a colorful individual, had undergone guerrilla training in Palestinian camps, fought in the Lebanese civil war, and participated in armed underground groups active against the Shah's government. By May 1980, he had already been acting as the Revolutionary Guard commander for several months, and thus Bani-Sadr merely confirmed him in his existing post. But Bani-Sadr's action proved to be the kiss of death. Within a month, Abu-Sharif resigned, citing his inability to administer his command. He was replaced by an IRP loyalist, Morteza Reza'i, and the Revolutionary Guard too slipped permanently out of Bani-Sadr's hands.

Abu-Sharif's resignation was followed within a few days by the resignation of Taqi Farrahi, whom Bani-Sadr had appointed six weeks earlier to run the state broadcasting services. Farrahi soon discovered that real influence in the Voice and Vision of the Islamic Republic, as the broadcasting services came to be called, was wielded by Islamic committees and IRP appointees, headed by Mohammad Musavi-Khoeniha, the mentor of the "students of the Imam's line" at the American embassy. In November, armed revolutionary guardsmen forcibly evicted Ahmad Salamatian and Ahmad Ghazanfarpour, two Bani-Sadr appointees responsible for television news, from their offices and physically took over the offices of the second television channel, which had remained sympathetic to the president. Bani-Sadr had charged that the broadcast media acted as an IRP monopoly, distorted the news, and censored the president; by the fall, radio and particularly television were fully living up to that description.

"Purification" by Purge and Firing Squad

In addition to direct confrontation with the IRP, Bani-Sadr also sought to secure allies among the hard-line clerics, to seize the initiative on some popular issue, and thus to win over part of the IRP's mass following. In April, he sought to capture leadership of what was dubbed the "cultural revolution" and which led to an attack on the universities and their subsequent closure. His initiative, however, earned him no support among the followers of the IRP and cost him heavily among his liberal constituency. In May he appointed Sadeq Khalkhali to head an antinarcotics campaign. Due to the breakdown of control over frontier smuggling and domestic opium cultivation, and perhaps because of the ban on alcohol and mass unemployment, drug use had spread at an alarming rate following the revolution. Bani-Sadr estimated that one Iranian in ten was a drug user. Khalkhali, as an Islamic judge, had already sent hundreds of Iranians before the firing squad. But he had been generally supportive of Bani-Sadr; and he was popular with the urban masses, who applauded his "revolutionary decisiveness."

On 20 May, within days of his appointment, Khalkhali ordered the execution of twenty persons found guilty of trafficking in drugs. Over the next several weeks, he sent scores of alleged drug smugglers, peddlers, users, and others to their death, often on the flimsiest evidence. By the end of August, some two hundred persons had been executed on Khalkhali's orders. This figure rose considerably before Bani-Sadr, and Beheshti, working behind the scenes and for his own reasons, secured Khalkhali's resignation in December. Ironically, Khalkhali was forced to resign not for his conduct as an Islamic judge but primarily because he was unable to account in detail for the equivalent of nearly $14 million seized through drug raids, confiscations, and fines. Khomaini had in the 1970s described as "inhuman" the execution of drug traffickers on a far more limited scale under the Shah. Yet he voiced no objection to the executions carried out by Khalkhali and made no move to stop him.

Khalkhali's antinarcotics campaign had other consequences. Aside from scattered executions in April and early May, death sentences had not been carried out for several months when Khalkhali received his new assignment. But like a great wound that, once opened, begins to hemorrhage uncontrollably, Khalkhali's executions seemed to feed a new flood of bloodletting. At least 582 persons had been executed between February 1979 and January 1980, a period which included the extensive, immediate postrevolution trials of the members of the former regime. Between January 1980 and June 1981, when Bani-Sadr was overthrown, at least 906 executions took place, primarily after 20 May 1980.[18] Men and women were killed for everything from drug and sexual offenses to "corruption on earth," from plotting counter-revolution and spying for Israel to membership in opposition groups.

Farrokhru Parsa, a leading figure in Iranian women's movements and former minister of education, became the first woman to be executed by the revolutionary government for alleged "crimes" committed under the former regime. Yusef Khoshkish, governor of the Bank Melli, the national bank, under the Shah, sentenced earlier to life imprisonment, was taken out of his cell and shot. In Tabriz, two members of the Islamic Republic People's Party were put to death for having organized antigovernment rallies. In Shiraz, a physician, Isma'il Narisima, was executed for siding with protestors during demonstrations at Shiraz University.

It was a period of particularly grizzly sentences. On 3 July in Kerman, two middle-aged women found guilty of prostitution and two men charged with sexual offenses were dressed in white robes, buried up to their chests in the ground, and stoned to death. The judge of the Islamic court who passed these sentences threw the first stone. Khalkhali defended this method of execution for sex-related crimes: "We approve of anything in the Koran," he said. On 8 July, Khalkhali ordered seven alleged drug offenders shot by firing squad in full public view on a Tehran street. A week later, he had another seven persons shot on the same thoroughfare. That same month, a gallows was raised on a Tehran street on Khalkhali's orders and eight persons found guilty of drug and sex offenses were made to stand on discarded Coke and Pepsi-Cola cartons, with nooses around their necks. The cartons were then kicked away. When the makeshift gallows collapsed, Khalkhali had the eight men and women shot.

In September, the Supreme Judicial Council, headed by Ayatollah Beheshti, sent a circular to the revolutionary courts forbidding further executions (and confiscations of property) without the council's written permission.[19] But by then the fever chart of death sentences had abated somewhat; and the judicial order did not, in any case, stand in the way of further court-ordered death sentences in subsequent months or the renewed wave of executions in the following year.

The tendency for events to spin out of the control of Bani-Sadr and the moderates, and the determination of new claimants to office to replace the old bureaucracy, were evident also in the purges that started up again in the summer. At the time, the head of the civil service, Mostafa Katira'i, was planning to submit to the Revolutionary Council new legislation that would establish stricter criteria for the "purification," as the purges were called, of government departments and to permit those already expelled to appeal their cases and receive part of their pensions. In June, in the course of remarks berating the president and the ministers for not doing enough for the mass of the people, however, Khomaini also attacked the ministries for continuing to use letterheads bearing the royal insignia and postage stamps bearing the ex-Shah's (suitably canceled) picture. He concluded that the civil service was still overrun by royalists. "We are still plagued by monarchists," he said. "Our country is still a royalist country."[20]

Khomaini's remarks became the excuse for a new wave of purges in government. Within a few days of Khomaini's statement, 150 purge committees were operating throughout the country and 1,400 officials had been purged. The foreign minister, Sadeq Qotbzadeh, boasted that out of 2,000 people working in the foreign ministry, 800 had been purged: "No other ministry has purged as much as five percent," he said. Raja'i recalled that during his tenure at the ministry of education 20,000 teachers had been expelled. Only four months earlier, the minister of defense had declared the purge in the army completed. By then, nearly 8,000 officers had been purged or slated for dismissal and retirement. But the chief of staff, Valiollah Fallahi, now announced a new purge committee had been established and was dismissing army officers at the rate of 100 a day.[21]

The purge was turned into the occasion for a broader attack on the center forces and moderate policies. On 4 July, tens of thousands of representatives of the IRP, the Mojahedin of the Islamic Revolution, the Revolutionary Guard, the Crusade for Reconstruction, the "students of the Imam's line," the Seminary Teachers of Qom, the Combatant Clerics of Tehran, and others staged a rally in support of Khomaini's call for a new bureaucratic order. As expected, the demonstrators adopted resolutions that called for a thorough purge from the civil service of all elements of the former regime and "agents of East and West." The demonstrators also demanded the dissolution of all "godless and eclectic groups" (a reference to the Fadayan and the Mojahedin-e Khalq) and the trial of their members, the Islamization of the broadcast media and the universities, the condemnation of all groups critical of the religious leaders, and the end to official efforts to limit the budgets of such revolutionary organizations as the Crusade for Reconstruction.[22]

Eventually, Ayatollah Montazeri, one of the initiators of the rally, and Sadeq Tabataba'i, another man close to Khomaini, found it necessary to suggest that the purge committees had perhaps acted with excessive zeal and that the purges should stop. By then, according to an incomplete tally, 4,000 civil servants had lost their jobs,[23] some because of their liberal views, most because they held posts others wanted. Several hundred, and perhaps as many as 2,000 to 4,000 officers had been dismissed from the armed forces.[24] During the purge, Islamic dress was finally imposed on all women working in government offices. The purge marked another setback for Bani-Sadr, strengthened the hand of the IRP and the Islamic groups in the bureaucracy, and further cowed those who might have supported the president. In December, the prime minister presented to the Majles a bill, euphemistically entitled "the Law for the Renewal of Manpower Resources in the Ministries and Government Offices," that was approved in the following year. Harsh on the Baha'is and members of "antirevolutionary" organizations, the law nevertheless represented a considerable limitation of grounds for dismissal from the civil service. However, as the struggle between Bani-Sadr and the IRP alliance grew more intense in the spring of 1981, purges were resumed and again became widespread following the president's fall from power.

"I Have Wasted My Best Hours"

The American hostage crisis was another issue that served to erode the authority of the president. By the time Bani-Sadr took office in January 1980, public excitement, Khomaini's own uncompromising stand, and domestic rivalries had moved the issue of the hostages to the center of Iranian domestic politics; and the position in both Tehran and Washington had hardened. Iran's demands for the Shah's extradition and the return of his wealth, and the admission by the United States to "crimes" it had allegedly committed against the Iranian people were unacceptable to Washington. President Carter, on 14 November 1979, had frozen over $11 billion in Iranian assets held by American entities, banks, and their overseas branches, and had banned further imports of Iranian oil. In Tehran the students at the American embassy were threatening to try the hostages as spies.

Bani-Sadr, as finance minister, was the first ranking Iranian to declare the taking of the hostages unlawful and unwise. Once elected president, and in the face of the galvanizing effect on the public of the embassy seizure, he was forced to modify his views. He acknowledged the justice of the students' cause. He too began to insist on conditions for the hostages' release. Yet Bani-Sadr had reason to wish the hostage crisis out of his way.

He blamed the crisis for Iran's diplomatic isolation and economic difficulties. He believed the United States to be behind Iran's ethnic unrest. He feared Washington would resort to more direct means to punish Iran. Moreover, the "students of the Imam's line" were a standing challenge to his authority. They turned the embassy compound, with its chained gates and ragtag revolutionary guards, virtually into an independently administered enclave. Government officials and foreign mediators could visit the hostages only with the students' permission. Billions of dollars in Iranian assets had been tied up as a result of the students' action. On a critical issue of foreign policy, the government had lost its freedom of action. Factory workers and civil servants, Bani-Sadr believed, were being encouraged by the students' example to strike, hold their superiors hostage, and to disregard with impunity the authority of the central government.

The students, under the direction of their mentor, Mohammad Musavi-Khoeniha, a religious leader and member of the radical wing of the IRP, were using carefully selected diplomatic dispatches and reports discovered at the embassy against moderate politicians and public figures. The documents often recorded meetings between embassy officials and Iranians, usually on official business. Iranians at these meetings not infrequently expressed a desire for improved relations with the United States or, indiscreetly, expressed dissatisfaction with clerical rule. In the charged atmosphere of the time, these views were made to appear tantamount to treason.

On the basis of the embassy documents, Abbas Amir-Entezam, a deputy to prime minister Bazargan and ambassador to Scandinavia, was recalled and arrested as a CIA spy. The minister of information, also a member of Bazargan's IFM, was arrested. Rahmatollah Moghaddam-Maraghe'i, the moderate politician from East Azarbaijan, first governor-general of the province after the revolution, head of the Radical Movement, and a close associate of Ayatollah Shariatmadari, fled the country to avoid a similar fate. Simon Farzami, a retired Jewish journalist, was arrested and put to death. The embassy documents were used to influence the presidential elections and later to deny Admiral Madani and Khosrow Qashqa'i their seats in Parliament. Documents the student militants retained in their possession hovered like the sword of Damocles above the heads of other politicians who might have been mentioned in embassy dispatches.

For the IRP and its allies, the attacks on these individuals served as the cutting edge of a wider effort to discredit the moderates both inside and outside the government. If the embassy documents revealed American diplomats to be unfavorably disposed toward the revolutionary courts and committees, it followed that Iranian critics of the revolutionary organizations were "adherents of the American line." If an embassy dispatch contained praise of the moderation of a Western-educated Iranian minister or official, it followed that he and his like were American agents or, at best, unwitting tools of American policy.

The Tudeh Party, the Fadayan, the Mojahedin, and other left-wing groups also saw in the hostage crisis a means for discrediting the liberals and the United States. The Mojahedin, for example, renewed their call for nationalization of all American and "dependent" economic enterprises, the renunciation of remaining treaties between Iran and the United States, and the break of all links between the Iranian and the American military. They were convinced that there were American agents everywhere. Their editorial on Amir Entezam in their newspaper, *Mojahed,* was entitled "A Snake in the Sleeve of the Revolution." In other articles, they insisted on the full publication of the embassy documents and the identification of other Iranian "CIA agents." The Tudeh sought as usual to destroy the reputations of all those they considered anti-Soviet and pro-American, including Bazargan, the NF, and Bani-Sadr. The Fadayan treated every attempt at settlement as an unacceptable compromise with the Great Satan. The Islamic radicals adopted a similar attitude. It was not the first time that a volatile issue found the extreme left and the extreme right in the same camp.[25]

In these circumstances, Bani-Sadr and the foreign minister, Sadeq Qotbzadeh, sought to redefine Iran's demands in a manner that would satisfy Khomaini and Iranian public opinion yet be acceptable to the United States, that would result in the release of the hostages, yet not leave them vulnerable to charges of a sellout to the Great Satan. Thus, the president and the foreign minister labored week after week on imprecise, vaguely worded formulations that would satisfy these conflicting ends.

In late February and early March, Bani-Sadr and Qotbzadeh believed that they had reached such an understanding through Olaf Palme, the mediator appointed by the U.N. Secretary-General, Kurt Waldheim. Washington would agree to the formation of a commission to investigate Iranian grievances against the United States, while Iran would arrange for the transfer of the hostages from the students to the Revolutionary Council, as a first step toward their eventual release. This plan, however, quickly collapsed. On the eve of the arrival of the U.N. commission in Tehran, on 23 February, Khomaini declared that only Parliament, whose election was still several weeks away, could decide the fate of the hostages. The "students of the Imam's line," encouraged by Khomaini, balked at handing over the hostages to the Revolutionary Council, and the council, in any event, voted not to take charge of the Americans. On 11 March, the U.N. commission left Iran empty handed.

Bani-Sadr and Qotbzadeh next attempted to have the Shah arrested in Panama, where he had taken up residence after leaving the United States in December, and have him extradited to Iran. Working through the unlikely agency of a French lawyer identified with left-wing causes,

Christian Bourget, and an Argentine businessman–adventurer, Hector Villalon, the two Iranians believed they had reached an understanding with the Panamanian president, Omar Torijjos, for the Shah's extradiction to Iran. But the Shah, understandably refusing to play his assigned role in this scenario, abruptly left Panama for Egypt on 23 March, just before Iran's request for his extradition was presented to the Panamanian authorities. Another scheme to resolve the hostage deadlock failed. In early April, Bani-Sadr attempted to interpret a communication from Washington as the long-awaited American apology from President Carter. But Washington poured cold water on this attempt by denying that any letter had been sent or apology proffered.

With the failure of these initiatives, Bani-Sadr decided that Washington was deliberately blocking a resolution of the crisis as part of a plot to undermine the Iranian revolution and "aimed at me personally." He would wash his hands of the hostage crisis, he said; he would no longer waste the better part of his time on it. But Bani-Sadr's problem lay in the skillful manner in which the embassy takeover had been used against him at home. He could not leave the hostage issue alone, and the more he unprofitably addressed it, the more his authority leaked away. Nor did the hostages leave him alone. In April, American aircraft and helicopters landed in the Iranian desert west of Tabas on a secret mission to rescue the hostages. The mission proved a disaster. Two helicopters failed to function. When the commander decided to abort the mission, a helicopter and a C-130 aircraft crashed and eight American airmen were burned to death in the flames. The next day, viewing the dead bodies and the wreckage on their television screens, Iranians were certain that a miracle, God himself, had interceded to defend their cause and their revolution. Heavenly intercession, however, did little to improve Bani-Sadr's position.

The July Plot and Other Conspiracies

The rescue mission had far-reaching domestic repercussions. It provided proof of America's perfidy and further undermined the position of those who advocated a settlement with the United States. It left the Westernized liberals more vulnerable to attack by the Islamic parties. The failure of the mission did nothing to bolster the self-confidence of the revolutionary government. On the contrary, it revived fears, never far from the minds of the revolutionary leaders, of an American or royalist-inspired attempt at the overthrow of the government. The ease with which Iranian airspace had been penetrated, and Iranian radar bypassed, was frightening. It was assumed, with reason, that the United States had agents in Iran set to move once the rescue mission arrived in Tehran. Orders by the air force commander, General Bahman Amir-Baqeri, to bomb the aircraft abandoned in the desert stoked suspicions that elements in the Iranian army were part of the conspiracy and had acted to destroy valuable evidence.

These suspicions led to a shake-up in the armed forces. Baqeri was removed as air force commander and later arrested. General Hadi Shad-mehr, the chief of staff, lost his post, although Bani-Sadr was able to retain him as a personal military adviser. However, rumors of an impending army coup swept the country. On 14 May, Bani-Sadr announced that ninety-six Americans had landed in the Bakhtiari mountains in western Iran and were about to launch a campaign of sabotage and assassination. A few days later, the Mojahedin of the Islamic Revolution warned of a plot being hatched in the army. The Fadayan and the Mojahedin-e Khalq insisted elements in the army were implicated in the American rescue mission. On 24 May, a call from a clandestine radio based in Iraq for an army coup caused a brief panic.

It was in this paranoid atmosphere that the chief judge of the military revolutionary tribunal, Mohammadi-Rayshahri, announced in quick succession the discovery of two plots in the armed forces. The first, announced in June and code-named "Operation Overthrow," was centered on the military base in Piranshahr in Kurdistan. Some twenty-seven junior and warrant officers were arrested in the plot; it appeared to be a minor affair, primarily related to the Kurdish rebellion, although Rayshahri treated it as an attempt at a full-scale coup to return the Shah and Shapour Bakhtiar to power. The second conspiracy, announced by Rayshahri, Bani-Sadr, and other government officials in July, code-named "Red Alert" and centered on the Hor air force base in Hamadan, was a far more serious affair. Two generals, Sa'id Mahdiyun, former commander of the air force, and Ahmad Mohaqqeqi, a former gendarmerie commander, and some 300 others were arrested. Another 300 were sought. Some 10 of the conspirators were killed when the Revolutionary Guard broke into their headquarters. The government alleged that the plotters planned to seize strategic points in Tehran, to round up some 700 revolutionary leaders, to utilize 17 aircraft from the Hor base to bomb the home of Khomaini and other targets, and to restore Bakhtiar to power.

The sweeping executions and the broader attack on the entire officer corps that followed owed something both to the seriousness of the conspiracy and the pervasive fear of a military coup. But four other factors also played a role: Khomaini's attitude, the rivalry between the army and the Revolutionary Guard, the rivalry between Bani-Sadr and the IRP, and the IRP's desire to place its own loyalists at the head of the armed forces. Although Khomaini had condemned calls by the left for a dissolution of the imperial army, he too remained suspicious of the officer corps. "The military," he told Bani-Sadr, "have the Shah in their blood."[26] He rejected Bani-Sadr's plea for clemency and said all those involved in the conspiracy must be killed. When Mohammadi-Rayshahri's military tribunal had completed its work, over 100 and as many as 140 officers had been executed for involvement in the plots.[27] The trials were held in camera; and although "Operation Red Alert" was itself no fabrication, the objectivity of court proceedings remained in doubt.

The plot brought into the open the up-to-then barely disguised struggle for control of armed force in the Islamic Republic. Bani-Sadr emerged as a champion of the military. He opposed calls for further purges, protected, insofar as he was able, men like Baqeri and Shadmehr from retribution, and called for a strengthening of the army. Radicals in the IRP alliance, like their counterparts in the left-wing political movements, distrusted the army and desired a sweeping purge of the officer corps. They supported the aspirations of the Revolutionary Guard, which perceived the army as a hindrance to the expansion of its own role and importance. Clerics in the government, unable to win the trust of the higher-ranking officers, sought leverage with the rank and file and supported the army Islamic societies which the officers often could not control. Clerics of the Ideological-Political Bureau in the military garrisons, Khomaini appointees, competed with the officers for the loyalty of the rank and file.

The IRP and its allies thus played up the plot as proof of the unreliability of the army, with which Bani-Sadr was now associated. "They talked as if I were one of the plotters—against myself," the president remarked. He urged the people to ignore propaganda directed at the army: "They desire the collapse of the armed forces," he said.[28] The IRP, Behzad Nabavi's Mojahedin of the Islamic Revolution, and Habibollah Payman's Jonbesh-e Mosalman-e Mobarez issued separate but similar declarations that clearly indicated their wider purpose. They called for an extensive purge of suspect officers, the arrest of all antirevolutionary elements in the army, the execution of all the plotters, and the end to Bani-Sadr's support for "corrupt" officers like Baqeri and General Vali-ollah Fallahi, the acting chief of staff. "The majority of the high-ranking officers are America's mercenaries," Nabavi's group said. They demanded heavy weapons for the Revolutionary Guard and expansion of the force, support for the army's Islamic societies and the appointment of their favorite as the commander of the air force.[29] The July plot and its repercussions once again played havoc with the army. The extent of the damage was to become obvious when the Iraqi forces invaded Iran on 22 September.

The National Front, of which Bakhtiar had been a member, was another casualty of the July plot. The speaker of the Majles, Hashemi-Rafsanjani, announced that the Front was implicated in the conspiracy. On 21 July, Hadi Ghaffari's *hezbollahis* attacked and occupied the National Front's headquarters. The party newspaper was closed down. The Iran Party leader, Abolfazl Qasemi, was arrested. For good measure, the Tudeh party headquarters were also attacked; but unlike the NF, the Tudeh was soon permitted to resume operations.

By the end of the summer, Bani-Sadr's position appeared decidedly less secure than at his accession to office in January. He had been unable to turn to advantage an impressive popular vote, to organize the forces of the center, or to translate into effective power Khomaini's verbal support and considerable delegation of authority. On the contrary, he had lost to the IRP and the clerical parties control over Parliament, the cabinet, much of the bureaucracy, the judiciary, and the broadcast media. The revolutionary committees, the Revolutionary Guards, the Foundation for the Disinherited, and other powerful revolutionary organizations were out of his hands. He did not control the streets. Potential supporters had been purged from the bureaucracy; sympathetic parties of the center had been proscribed or were under pressure. The economy appeared to be in shambles, the Kurdish rebellion had not been settled, the tribesmen along the entire Soviet frontier from Azarbaijan to Baluchestan had been roused because the Revolutionary Guard, without consulting the government, had arrested their khans. "He is a president," said one of his aides, "who can give orders only to himself."

Meantime, it was not only Bani-Sadr and the center parties who were under attack. The parties of the left were also waging a struggle for survival.

The Left: "Kill Them . . . Throw Them into the Sea"

In addition to the two main guerrilla movements the revolution spawned a plethora of left-wing organizations—Marxist, Leninist, Maoist, Trotskyite, and socialist. These parties exerted a significant influence on the course of postrevolution developments. They were active in factories and workshops. They tried to mobilize the urban poor; they instigated some of the land seizures that occurred soon after the revolution; and they encouraged movements for autonomy among Baluch, Turkoman, and Kurdish ethnic minorities.

Moreover, they exerted a continuous pressure for radical measures, first on Bazargan, then on Bani-Sadr, with persistent demands for sweeping nationalization, distributive justice, transfer of power to popular bodies, dissolution of the army, cancelation of "imperialist" agreements, and rejection of anyone connected with the former regime. Bazargan blamed the Marxist left and the Mojahedin-e Khalq for feeding the revolutionary turmoil and undermining his government.[30] A year later, Bani-Sadr was making similar charges against the radical left.[31]

The clerics around Khomaini also eyed the left-wing parties with animosity. On a number of issues, such as the role of the clerics and autonomy for the ethnic minorities, the radical left and the radical right were at daggers drawn. But on many other questions, the two extremes came full circle to meet in unacknowledged agreement. Nevertheless, the clerics, as always, feared the pull of Marxist and radical, secular ideologies on the country's youth. They too believed that the left-wing parties were creating mischief in the factories, villages, and areas inhabited by the Turkoman, Kurd, and Baluch minorities. The left-wing organizations were armed.

They were attracting a large following among the young, a constituency whose support the clerics also sought. Thousands turned up each week at one of Tehran's universities to hear Mas'ud Rajavi, the Mojahedin leader, deliver his series of lectures on Mojahedin ideology. Applying the style he had learned at Taleqani's classes in Koranic exegesis and drawing on Islam, social Darwinism, Marxism, and critiques of capitalism, he told his young audience that history was moving inexorably toward a classless society and that the future belonged to those who adapted themselves to this process. "The struggle is over two kinds of Islam," he said, "One, an Islam of class, which ultimately protects the exploiter; and a pure, authentic and popular Islam, which is against classes and exploitation."[32]

When the Fadayan called a May Day rally in 1980, tens of thousands showed up. When Rajavi addressed a meeting at Amjadieh in June, the stadium was filled to overflowing. The IRP acted to squelch this movement. It used legislation to shut down left-wing newspapers and close left-wing organizations. It used force to browbeat the rank and file of these movements; and it deployed preachers to denounce the left as unIslamic and as enemies of religion.

The universities were major centers of left-wing political activity. Many left-wing organizations had taken over rooms in university buildings and had set up kiosks on the campuses where they sold their books and ideological tracts. On most days the campus of Tehran University was a huge center for political debate. Members of the IRP viewed the universities as hotbeds of left-wing agitation and as recruiting centers for the Kurdish and Turkoman rebellions. The "students of the Imam's line" pressed for a closure of the universities. The issue was taken up at the 18 April meeting of the Revolutionary Council. It was agreed not to shut the universities but to give the left-wing political organizations three days to vacate university buildings and grounds. Evacuation was set for 22 April.

However, after Friday prayers on 18 April, Khomaini harshly attacked the universities. "We are not afraid of economic sanctions or military intervention," he said. "What we are afraid of is Western universities and the training of our youth in the interests of West or East."[33] His remarks served as a signal for an attack that evening on the Tehran Teachers Training College. One student was reportedly lynched, and according to a British correspondent, the campus was left looking like "a combat zone." The next day, *hezbollahis* ransacked left-wing student offices at Shiraz University. Some 300 students required hospital treatment. Attacks on student groups also took place at Mashad and Isfahan Universities.

Attempts by Bani-Sadr to arrange a peaceful evacuation of the Tehran University campus broke down, and bloody clashes broke out on 21 April. Clashes continued the next day at the universities at Ahwaz and Rasht. Over twenty people lost their lives in these university confrontations. On 22 April, Bani-Sadr led a large crowd of people into the Tehran University campus, now free of left-wing groups, to proclaim the start of a "cultural revolution" to Islamize the institutions of higher education. By identifying himself with the attack on the universities, Bani-Sadr embittered the left and secured no credit with the clerical party. The universities closed soon after the April confrontation for "Islamization." They were not to open for another two years.

The left-wing parties were harassed in other ways. Newspaper sellers were attacked, kiosks smashed, bookstores looted. The Mojahedin, as the largest of the left-wing groups, became the prime target of the IRP. In February 1980, 60,000 copies of *Mojahed* were seized and burned. In Mashad, Shiraz, Qa'emshahr, Sari, and dozens of small towns, club wielders attacked and looted Mojahedin headquarters, student societies, and meetings. Since the Mojahedin meetings were often large, these attacks turned into huge melees. Some 700 were injured in the attack on the Mojahedin headquarters at Qa'emshahr in April, 400 in Mashad. Ten members of the organization lost their lives in clashes between February and June 1980.

Preachers were often the instigators of these attacks. In Qom, anti-Mojahedin marches took place after sermons by Mohammad Taqi Falsafi and Mohammad-Javad Bahonar. In Behshahr, the Mojahedin were attacked after a sermon by Fakhr ad-Din Hejazi. Hojjat ol-Eslam Khaz'ali moved from town to town to preach against the Mojahedin. "If they do not repent," he told a crowd in Shahrud, "take them and throw them in the Caspian Sea." He accused the Mojahedin of being communists, taking part in the Kurdish uprising, killing Revolutionary Guardsmen, and misleading young girls. "Even if they hide in a mousehole," he told a Mashad congregation, "we will drag them out and kill them. . . . We are thirsty for their blood. We must close off their jugular."[34]

The Mojahedin grew increasingly critical of the "monopolists" of the IRP. But they continued to seek Khomaini's good will. They addressed him respectfully as "honorable father," pledged him their support, and attempted to show there existed basic agreement between their views and those of the Imam. In December 1979, they urged Khomaini to accept the presidency of the Islamic Republic, as the leader best suited to the task and most likely to ensure the success of the revolution.

Khomaini did not reciprocate these gestures. He was suspicious of the Mojahedin's growing strength and disapproved of their attempts, as laymen, to appropriate to themselves the authority to interpret Islamic doctrine. In June 1980, Khomaini publicly denounced the Mojahedin as polytheists and hypocrites and contemptuously referred to Rajavi as "this lad who calls himself the leader."[35] The Mojahedin responded by quietly closing all their branch offices and retreating further underground.

Other left-wing groups followed suit. The Tudeh, however, continued to enjoy limited immunity from attack because of their support for the regime. In mid-1980, the Fadayan, riven by doctrinal differences, split. A "minority" faction remained in opposition. The "majority" faction accepted the Tudeh thesis that the Khomaini regime deserved support for its uncompromising stand against U.S. imperialism and its concern for the disinherited. By the fall, the government had thus gained another adherent among the left-wing groups, while most of the left-wing organizations were under severe pressure. In the meantime, foreign war intervened to alter the political landscape.

Chapter 6

The Destruction
of Bani-Sadr

ON 22 SEPTEMBER, Iraqi aircraft struck at ten Iranian airfields and bombed targets deep in Iranian territory, Iraqi guns shelled Iranian cities, and Iraqi troops invaded Iran at several points in the southern end of the 300-mile common frontier. In invading Iran, the Iraqi president, Saddam Hussein, hoped to achieve three aims: to inflict a humiliating and perhaps decisive defeat on the Iranian revolution, which he found troublesome; to secure from Iran territorial and strategic concessions; and to realize his ambition to emerge as the leading figure in the Arab world.[1] The Iraqi president failed to achieve any of these aims. The war he launched, on the other hand, inflicted severe physical damage both on Iran and his own country, led to tens of thousands of casualties, influenced the alignment of forces in the Persian Gulf and the Arab world, and accelerated the revolutionary process in Iran itself.

War

Saddam Hussein harbored two grievances against Iran. The first originated with the Shah's government and centered on the Shatt al-Arab, the 120-mile frontier waterway on which are located Iraq's main commercial and oil terminals around Basra, and Iran's major port and refinery facilities, at Khorramshahr and Abadan. Until 1975, navigation on the Shatt was regulated by an agreement concluded between the two countries in 1937. The agreement gave sovereignty over virtually the entire waterway to Iraq. In 1975, however, under an agreement signed in Algiers, Iran was able to correct what it always regarded as a one-sided arrangement. Iraq recognized the thalweg, or deep-water line, running roughly midway down the river, as the frontier between the two countries. In exchange, the Shah agreed to make some land frontier rectifications in Iraq's favor and to drop his assistance to Iraq's Kurdish rebellion. The rebellion collapsed a few weeks after the withdrawal of Iranian support. Saddam Hussein, then deputy chairman of Iraq's Revolutionary Council, signed the agreement for Iraq. He regarded the treaty as a humiliation and a strategic setback that he would attempt to undo.

Saddam's second grievance arose from the Iranian revolution, which he regarded as a destabilizing force in the region and in Iraq itself. Iraq had a large Shi'a population, centered on the shrine cities of Najaf and Karbala. There was a tradition of political militancy in these shrine cities which in the 1970s came to be expressed partly through an underground movement, *al-Da'wa al-Islamiyya*. Al-Da'wa itself came to be associated with a popular Shi'a religious teacher and writer, Mohammad-Baqer Sadr, who sought to combine militant Shi'ism with socialism and political activism (see chapter 7). The Iranian revolution greatly excited Iraq's Shi'as; and Sadr began to write and teach about the positive aspects of the Islamic state.

At the same time, while the Bazargan government denied any desire to export revolution, many revolutionary leaders spoke of the desirability and even the necessity of doing so: to spread "authentic" Islam, to liberate other Muslim peoples, to protect Iran's own revolution from the great powers and hostile neighbors. Iranian propagandists traveled in the Persian Gulf carrying the message of the Iranian revolution to the Gulf emirates. Iranian diplomatic representatives in the region often acted as spokesmen for Khomaini's brand of militant Islam. One clerical leader, Ayatollah Sadeq Ruhani, advised the ruler of Bahrain to treat his people with more consideration; otherwise, he said, he would call on the inhabitants to overthrow him. Ayatollah Montazeri, Bani-Sadr, and others harshly criticized Persian Gulf leaders and encouraged Arab states to follow the Iranian revolutionary example.

Saddam Hussein viewed these developments with some anxiety. He appears to have encouraged members of the Arab-speaking population in Iran's oil province of Khuzestan, who had organized political and cultural societies and were agitating for local administrative and cultural autonomy. He dealt ruthlessly with unrest among the Shi'a population in Iraq. When an attempt was made on the life of the Iraqi deputy prime minister, Tarik Aziz, in April 1980, he arrested the leaders of al-Da'wa and hundreds of Shi'a activists. He rounded up over 25,000 Iranians resident in Iraq and unceremoniously dumped them on the Iranian border. In June, he secretly put to death Sadr and his sister.

The Iraqi president also viewed the Iranian revolution as an opportunity. He believed that the country and the army had been gravely weakened by revolution, purges, internal rivalries, and ethnic uprisings. He concluded that by inflicting a severe military defeat on Iran he could undo the Algiers agreement, discredit the revolutionary regime, and perhaps even establish a client government in Tehran. As early as October 1979, the Baghdad government began to demand a revision of the Algiers treaty. In April 1980, serious border clashes occurred between the two countries. On 17 September, Saddam Hussein announced Iraq was unilaterally abrogating the Algiers agreement. Five days later, Iraqi divisions crossed into Iran.

The Iranian situation appeared desperate. The army had lost thousands of officers to purges and dismissals. Arms purchase orders had been canceled by the revolutionary government, maintenance of equipment neglected. The computerized system for keeping stock of spare parts had broken down. As late as January of 1980, many units were only 25 percent operational. The best units were either tied down in Kurdistan or stationed along the frontier with the Soviet Union. Along the entire border with Iraq there were only 120 tanks; only two divisions were in position to meet the brunt of the Iraqi attack. Defense was complicated by the large number of paramilitary and volunteer units that poured into the war zone. Eleven different paramilitary groups joined the fighting in Khorramshahr. Some of the commanders believed that the Iraqi advance could be resisted, at a maximum, for four days.

Iraq aimed at the key port of Khorramshahr and at the heart of the Iranian oil industry, centered on Abadan and Ahwaz. Cut off from access to its oil resources and revenues, the Iranian economy would die. Iraqi troops made steady, if slow, progress against stiff Iranian resistance. Khorramshahr fell at the end of October. Abadan, then Susangerd, were besieged; at the end of November, the Iraqis opened a second front farther north, around Iranian Kurdistan. But the drive had already been halted. The Iranian defense held. Iraqi troops were unable to push out of Khorramshahr, to take Abadan, or capture Ahwaz. Both sides settled down to a long war of attrition.

The war had both regional and domestic consequences. It influenced the shifting alliances in the Persian Gulf and the Arab world, and brought about changes in Iran's own foreign policy posture. Syria, Iraq's perennial rival, along with Libya, supported Iran in the war, while Jordan, at loggerheads with Syria, supported Iraq and placed its port and overland trade routes at Baghdad's disposal. Iran, as a result, patched up its quarrels with Libya and drew closer to Damascus. Iranian hostility toward Saudi Arabia and Kuwait was exacerbated because these countries provided Iraq with port and overland facilities and, in time, with substantial financial assistance. Iran grew more inclined to make common cause with Algeria and Libya against Saudi Arabia in the Organization of Petroleum Exporting Countries (OPEC) and to challenge the Saudi leadership in the organization.

The loss of Khorramshahr, Iran's largest port, forced the government to divert imports to overland routes through Turkey and the Soviet Union. Shortage of foreign exchange inclined the government to favor barter trade arrangements; the Soviet bloc countries and neighboring states like Turkey, Pakistan, and India began to account for a larger share of Iran's foreign trade. Unable to purchase arms in sufficient quantities in Western Europe, Iran looked to other sources of supply. North Korea, no doubt with Soviet approval, became an important arms supplier.

The financial costs and domestic repercussions of the war were also significant. Iraqi bombing and shelling destroyed 65 percent of Iranian refinery capacity, severely damaged the port of Khorramshahr and the Iran–Japan petrochemical complex at Bandar Mahshahr, left the city of Khorramshahr itself in ruins, and reduced to rubble residential and commercial areas in Abadan, Susangerd, Dezful, and smaller border towns. Some two million refugees eventually fled the war zone and had to be housed elsewhere. Heavy arms purchases became necessary. The government estimated the cost of war matériel, import of refined products, and refugee relief at $2.6 billion for the first six months of the war alone, and allocated $4.2 billion over and above the regular defense budget in 1981–82 to cover the prosecution of the war, oil product imports, and refugee relief.

The war permitted the armed forces to regain credibility and standing in the eyes of the Iranian public, to rebuild their shattered command structure, and to revitalize such neglected areas as logistics, maintenance, the organization of spare parts stocks, and arms purchases. The war also accelerated the rise of the Revolutionary Guard. Numbers were expanded, recruitment regularized, training improved, command structure strengthened, war experience acquired. The Revolutionary Guard secured more sophisticated weapons, gained in self-confidence, and reinforced its claim as the true guardian of the revolution. The war also permitted the revolutionary committees to reassert themselves as they took on the duties of enforcing blackouts and curfews, conducted car searches, and watched out for "subversives."

Rationing was imposed on gasoline, fuel, and essential foods. The rationing system accelerated government involvement in foreign trade and the domestic distribution of goods. Ration cards were distributed through local mosques, providing the authorities with another means for ensuring political conformity. The sense of national unity apparent in the early weeks of the war was quickly dissipated, however. Within weeks, representatives of left-wing political movements, who had joined the irregular fighting units, were warned to leave the war zone. The rivalry between Bani-Sadr and the IRP was, if anything, aggravated by the invasion.

The President's Diary

With the outbreak of hostilities, Bani-Sadr once again secured the trappings of authority and once again proved unable to control the course of events. On 12 October, Khomaini named the president chairman of the Supreme Defense Council and granted the council wide powers in prosecuting the war, conducting war-related foreign relations, and overseeing the press and broadcast media during the war emergency. Bani-Sadr, however, was unable to turn the Supreme Defense Council, where he was outvoted and outmaneuvered, into an instrument through which to reassert his authority. War propaganda was entrusted to the government news agency, which Bani-Sadr did not control. Numerous difficulties were raised for the president over the command of the armed forces. Moreover, Prime Minister Raja'i blocked Bani-Sadr at every turn.

In a circular, he instructed government departments to deal with the president only through the office of the prime minister. He implemented cabinet decrees without securing the president's approval. In control of the passport office and the airport, he prevented the governor of the Central Bank, Ali-Reza Nobari, a Bani-Sadr appointee, from attending the annual International Monetary Fund conference in Washington and other presidential aides from leaving on foreign missions. Increasingly, the prime minister seized the initiative on foreign policy. He represented Iran at the United Nations Security Council session on the Iran–Iraq war himself, preventing Bani-Sadr from doing so or sending an aide. When the negotiations over the release of the hostages began in earnest through Algerian intermediaries, Raja'i named his own negotiator and took the matter out of Bani-Sadr's hands. Through an interim finance minister, Raja'i encroached on the making of economic policy, which the president considered his domain. This put the prime minister and the governor of the Central Bank on a collision course; and Raja'i and the Islamic Republic Party (IRP) worked assiduously to replace Nobari with their own appointee.

In late October, in a confidential letter to Khomaini, Bani-Sadr sought to enlist the Imam's support in ridding himself of the Raja'i government altogether. He urged Khomaini to dismiss the cabinet, which he described as "a greater calamity for the country than the war with Iraq." The government, he said, was incompetent, lacked public support, and had declared war on the president. Its propaganda incited the people against him. Its policies would lead the revolution to ruin and the country to "the greatest abyss in its history." Comparing himself with the great British wartime leader, Winston Churchill, Bani-Sadr suggested that in the same way Chamberlain had stepped aside for Churchill on the eve of World War II, Raja'i should now step aside for him.[2] Khomaini did not act on Bani-Sadr's suggestion.

Soon after the start of hostilities Bani-Sadr began to spend more time on the front in Khuzestan than in his presidential office in Tehran. The front provided an escape from the frictions and frustrations, from "that poisoned atmosphere and those barren conflicts," of the capital. It allowed Bani-Sadr to give priority to the war effort and to build up his base of support inside the army. It also made for excellent public relations. Newspaper photographs often depicted the president in army fatigues, peering down gunsights, sharing a humble tray of rice with the troops, or touring the battle zone from the rumble seat of a motorcycle, his arms wrapped tightly around the waist of the driver and, except for a bristling black mustache, his face lost beneath a fierce-looking pith helmet.

Bani-Sadr would later claim he was able single-handedly to "remake" an Iranian army, "lacking organization, lacking spirit, lacking hope." In fact, Iranian resistance and the setbacks the Iranian forces were eventually able to inflict on the Iraqis were due in large part to the training hundreds of officers had received while the Shah was still on the throne, the skill of Iranian pilots, the spirited defense of Iranian cities by the irregular militia and Revolutionary Guard, the huge arsenal of weapons and spare parts stockpiled under the old regime, and what survived, despite purges and upheaval, of the imperial army's organizational structure. The revival of Iranian nationalism, a determination to defend the revolution, and dedication to Khomaini also played a role. Nevertheless, Bani-Sadr kept alive the flame of resistance in the early weeks of the war when an Iranian collapse seemed imminent. He championed the cause of the army and nurtured its fighting spirit when others, for political reasons, were busy denigrating the armed forces and instigating disaffection within the ranks. He strove for unity between the armed forces and the Revolutionary Guard when others were bent on sharpening the friction between them. The pilots whose release he secured from prison helped to inflict severe damage on key Iraqi installations and to cripple Iraq's port and oil-exporting facilities. At a moment of severe trial for the country he refused to take a defeatist attitude. All this was no mean accomplishment.

From his base in Khuzestan, Bani-Sadr continued to engage in Tehran's politics. His very absence from Tehran was meant as an eloquent rebuke to the IRP hard-liners, who made it impossible for the president to discharge his duties at the capital. He returned to Tehran regularly, generally once every week, and he used these visits to renew political contacts, to visit with Khomaini and press his case on the Imam, and to try and resolve his differences with the Raja'i government, the Parliament, and the IRP. From the war zone, he made side trips to provincial towns where, ostensibly on presidential business, he found occasion to make speeches attacking his political rivals. For his newspaper, *Enqelab-e Eslami* (Islamic Revolution), he wrote a regular column entitled "The President's Diary."[3]

The diary remains unique in a revolution that has led to the publication of numerous unusual documents. Each day, Bani-Sadr gave readers an account of his comings and goings and his meetings with foreign diplomats and Iranian officials and military men. Often, he provided detailed accounts of his political and diplomatic discussions, openly described his war plans, and virtually gave forewarning of coming military offensives. He acquainted readers with his visits to his aging mother, the state of his health, and the rise and fall of his blood pressure. He provided column upon column of his "philosophy" of government, his views on leadership, Islam, liberty, administration, and the like. He reproduced in excruciating detail his lengthy exhortations to the military commanders on these and other subjects and reported his discussion on the nature of Satan with the Guinean president, Sekou Touré, in Iran as part of an Islamic peace mission. He listed his bedtime reading and treated his readers to pertinent summaries of everything from Karl Popper to Erich Fromm.

The diary had a political purpose. Bani-Sadr used it to build up his image as the beleaguered defender of freedom and the national cause, to air his differences with his rivals, and to subject his opponents to a barrage of criticism. He accused the IRP and their men in Parliament of undermining the war effort, breaking the spirit of the army, and acting as "a poisoned dagger that strikes at our heart from behind." His critics, he said, had allowed themselves to become the tools of Iraq and America, who also sought to destroy the president and the army. He compared the IRP to the Shah's unpopular single party, Rastakhiz, and to the Umayyads, the early Islamic dynasty execrated by the Shi'a. His opponents, he said, forced Iran's experts to leave the country, closed the universities, and attacked knowledge and expertise because they had none. In a lengthy diary entry under the title, "What Is Stalinism?" he left little doubt that he was describing the tactics utilized by the IRP. The only methods his rivals knew, he said, were "harshness, killing and vengeance."

Bani-Sadr's diary was sufficiently discomfiting to the IRP for sixty-seven deputies, led by Hasan Ayat, to sponsor a motion in Parliament to have the president brought to trial for revealing "state secrets" in his column. In December, when an attempt was made through the agency of the Combatant Clerics of Tehran to patch up the differences between Bani-Sadr and the IRP, a condition posed by the IRP was that the president cease to air his differences with the party in public. Bani-Sadr, however, continued to do so until his newspaper was finally shut down on 7 June 1981. Bani-Sadr also sought to rally mass support through a series of public speeches, and it was at these large meetings that he first touched on two themes that would later assume considerable importance. Speaking to a huge meeting in Tehran on 19 November 1980, to mark *ashura*, the height of the religious mourning period, Bani-Sadr charged that torture continued in Iranian prisons:

> How is it that today every person and organization has its own prison? ... Why is a commission not set up to investigate these various prisons? Why do they not investigate whether there is torture? How is it that in the Islamic regime, it is possible to condemn a man to death as easily as one takes a drink of water, and before anyone knows of it, everything is over?[4]

In Jiroft, in southeastern Iran, two months later, he called on the people to join him in "resisting" the drift toward dictatorship.

The issue of torture, to which Bani-Sadr repeatedly returned, was emotionally charged. Many of the revolutionary leaders had suffered torture in the Shah's prisons. Tens of Savak agents had been executed after the revolution for practicing or ordering torture. The Islamic revolution was supposed to bring an end to the evil practice. Bani-Sadr's call on the people to resist, also repeated over the next four months, gradually shaded, at least in Khomaini's view, into a call by Bani-Sadr for open rebellion.

In his confrontation with the IRP, Bani-Sadr was not alone. As the president continued to address the issues of freedom of speech and press, the lawlessness of the revolutionary institutions, and the attempt of the IRP to monopolize power, his own followers rallied. Moreover, other individuals and political groups, both of the center and the left, sensing at last the possibility of breaking the IRP's growing grip on the country, also joined in the assault. The awkwardly named Office for the Coordination of the People's Cooperation with the President, established by Bani-Sadr immediately after his election and by now defunct, was revived. The office organized a series of pro-Bani-Sadr rallies in Tehran, Mashad, Isfahan, Kerman, Jiroft, Hamadan, Lorestan, Khorramabad, and towns of the Caspian coast, anywhere the president was thought to enjoy some support. In Parliament, Ahmad Salamatian, deputy from Isfahan and a member of one of the leading merchant families of the city, led a small nucleus of left-of-center Bani-Sadr loyalists. Among Bani-Sadr's supporters in Parliament were three moderate clerics: Ayatollah Hasan Lahuti, deputy from Kuchesfahan on the Caspian, whose liberal views had cost him his early close association with Khomaini, and two Tehran deputies, Ali Golzadeh-Ghafuri and Mohammad-Javad Hojjati-Kermani.

In the Majles, Bazargan and the four or five other deputies from the Iran Freedom Movement (IFM), Kazem Sami of JAMA, and a few others also joined in more vocal criticism of the ruling party. Bazaar merchants, lawyers and professional groups, university professors, and intellectuals organized public protests. The Mojahedin-e Khalq edged closer to Bani-Sadr and, along with the "minority" Fadayan (the "majority" faction of the Fadayan, having thrown in its lot with the Tudeh, supported the government) began sending its supporters into the streets against the *hezbollahis*. Members of Khomaini's household, Ahmad Khomaini, Morteza Pasandideh, and Shahab ad-Din Eshraqi, again and again spoke in Bani-Sadr's favor. A number of clerics outside Parliament issued declarations sharply critical of the IRP and, by implication, of Khomaini himself. Among these was Ayatollah Abolfazl Zanjani, a respected elder religious figure who had long been associated with the NF and with Mehdi Bazargan; the two leading religious leaders of Mashad, Ayatollah Hasan Qomi-Tabataba'i and Ayatollah Abdollah Shirazi; and a younger religious teacher and propagandist based in Mashad, Shaikh Ali Tehrani.

Mashad for a brief period appeared to constitute a base for opposition to the ruling party. A center of pilgrimage, Mashad was the country's foremost shrine city and second only to Qom as a teaching and seminary center, although more traditional and conservative in its approach. In 1978, it had been a city of fierce anti-Shah demonstrations. It had served as the home base of the much-loved "ideologue" of the revolution, Ali Shariati. His father, Mohammad-Taqi Shariati, continued to run the Islamic Learning Publications Center in the city, dedicated to the propagation of Shariati's own works and other Islamic literature. Mashad's two leading clerics, Qomi and Shirazi, however, had been among the early critics of the revolution. Disturbed at the excesses of the revolutionary organizations, out of sympathy with the political involvement of the clerics and the role evisaged for the *faqih* under the constitution, resentful perhaps of the prominence of Khomaini and of Qom as a result of the revolution, Qomi and Shirazi had remained aloof from the revolutionary government. Khomaini in turn favored other clerics in the city and moved to silence these two when they grew too critical and outspoken.

The IRP and its allies, for their part, sought to denigrate Bani-Sadr's record as president and war leader, to cast doubt on his revolutionary credentials and loyalty to Khomaini, and to identify him with the liberals, America, the extreme left, and other real or imagined enemies of the Islamic Republic. They used their control over radio and television to deny Bani-Sadr and their other opponents access to the broadcast media, their club wielders to break up opposition meetings, and their courts and Revolutionary Guard to arrest, imprison, and intimidate opposition elements. They mobilized their considerable administrative and financial resources to organize huge counter-rallies and demonstrations. They also deliberately worked to sharpen the dispute and turn it into a struggle between Islam and secularism, the clerics and the Westernized intellectuals, revolutionary steadfastness and compromise, and ultimately, loyalty and disloyalty to the person of Khomaini. They hoped in this way to draw to their side the wavering clerics, the urban masses, and those who, whatever their political inclinations, felt an instinctive loyalty to Khomaini.

The seven-month period from November 1980 to the overthrow of Bani-Sadr in June 1981 was thus a time of intense political activity and lobbying for Khomaini's support. Political, professional, and interest groups marshaled their forces and followers, staked out their positions, and formed informal alliances. They engaged in pamphleteering and debate, rallies and demonstrations, and fought over the control of the levers of power and for the loyalty of various sectors of the population. It was a period when the strength of the various parties was tested not only in offices and factories, in mosques and political rallies, but also with rocks and clubs in the city streets.

Bonaparte on a Tank

The role of the army and of Bani-Sadr in the war became an early issue of contention. The war permitted the army to restore its shattered reputation, cast Bani-Sadr in the role of military leader, and gave the president a potentially powerful base of support. This development was worrisome to the IRP, to its allies on the left, the Tudeh and the majority faction of the Fadayan, and to the Revolutionary Guard. The left-wing parties charged that by championing the cause of the army the president was reviving Bonapartism. IRP clerics suggested to Khomaini that in either victory or defeat Bani-Sadr would ride to

Tehran atop a tank and seize power. "I have heard them say," Khomaini's grandson, Hosain, later remarked, "that it is preferable to lose half of Iran than for Bani-Sadr to become the ruler."[5] Prime Minister Raja'i took the president to task for not going on the offensive. Ayatollah Montazeri said excessive caution was costing Iranian lives. Montazeri attempted to instigate the recruits against their officers, citing complaints by conscripts that their views on strategy were not being heard. He arranged for soldiers to be brought to the Majles to provide suggestions on the conduct of the war. Khomaini himself began to press Bani-Sadr to take the offensive.

While the president credited resistance to the Iraqi invasion to the regular army, the IRP attributed Iranian successes to the irregular forces. Bani-Sadr stressed the importance of professionalism in prosecuting the war, Raja'i the importance of piety, of being a *maktabi*—a doctrinaire Muslim. "A *maktabi* army," he said, "is preferable to a victorious army."[6] The IRP's supporters charged that the army was deliberately remaining in the background and leaving the Revolutionary Guard to shoulder the brunt of the fighting. A bill was introduced in Parliament requiring the Revolutionary Guard to be equipped with heavy weapons and be given first choice of army recruits. So deep was the animosity between the paramilitary units and the regular army that when Bani-Sadr toured the war zone in November, a guardsman caustically asked him whether, from one end of the front to the other, the regular army was anywhere in evidence. At Friday prayers in Tehran, a petition was circulated demanding the dismissal of the president as commander-in-chief. Some eighty deputies sponsored a similar motion in Parliament. Beheshti argued that Khomaini had delegated his powers as military commander to Bani-Sadr when ill; and that the president's commission had automatically lapsed now that Khomaini was in good health. These pressures finally forced Bani-Sadr to launch an offensive in January, before the army was ready; it proved a military disaster.

The debate over the relative merits of "professionalism" and "piety" was a throwback to the earlier argument between Bani-Sadr and Raja'i over the qualities desirable in appointees to cabinet office. It reflected once again a struggle between different political and social groups for office, privilege, and power. The IRP on this occasion turned the debate into a broad attack on the "liberals." It included among the liberals Bani-Sadr and his followers, the IFM, and political groups of the center, the secular intelligentsia, the Western-educated technocrats, and all those who preferred a secular to a clerical government. IRP spokesmen identified the "liberals" with America, bourgeois capitalism, the narrow interests of the "technocratic-bureaucratic elite," and opposition to the principle of *velayat-e faqih.* "The opportunists who stress excessively specialization and technique," said Abdol-Majid Ma'adikhah, a member of Parliament and of the IRP central committee, "follow the American line."[7] The IRP newspaper, *Jomhuri-ye Eslami,* described liberalism as "the bulldozer of colonialism and the steamroller of imperialism."[8]

Bazargan complained of this tendency to turn liberalism and nationalism into pejorative terms and to treat "education, specialization and reason a crime and a link to imperialism."[9] Support for the professionals came from Khomaini's son-in-law, Eshraqi, who, with a dig at the clerics, said war cannot be fought "with sandals and prayer beads, cane and staff, fist and slogan. . . . We cannot go to war on donkeys and frighten those armed with MiGs and Mirages."[10] IRP spokesmen, on the other hand, retorted that "training" and "specialization" were being utilized by the technocrats to secure their own interests, to deny pious Muslims jobs and office. Among the leadership, the division in this debate was not clearly along "class" lines. There were clerics on both sides of the argument. Many of the secular leaders of the IRP, including Ayat, Ali-Akbar Parvaresh, and Behzad Nabavi, emerged from social and political backgrounds similar to those of the "liberals," frequently former political colleagues, whom they now so fiercely attacked. Yet these two groups appealed to and spoke for different constituencies; here class differences were more evident. The "liberals" were primarily secular in orientation, drew their support from the middle and better-educated classes, slid more easily into the bureaucracy and technocracy inherited from the Pahlavis, placed their faith in a system based on law, and despite their denials, wished to see the clerics largely excluded from politics and Khomaini's constitutional authority diminished. The IRP was dominated by clerics, "Islamic" in orientation, and drew support from the urban masses, the upwardly mobile, and largely uneducated young men moving up through the Revolutionary Guard, committees, organizations, and the lumpen elements of the *hezbollahi* street gangs; it sought power and advancement through the link with Khomaini, the mosque network, and the uninhibited freedom of action provided by revolutionary turmoil and the freewheeling revolutionary organizations. Not surprisingly, debate often gave way to less gentle forms of persuasion.

The Opposition Rallies

On 7 November, the former foreign minister, Sadeq Qotbzadeh, was arrested in his home on orders of the revolutionary prosecutor's office. A day earlier, in an interview on television's channel 2, Qotbzadeh had accused the IRP of monopolizing power and the broadcast media of feeding lies to the people. The revolutionary prosecutor also issued a warrant for the arrest of Mohammad Moballeghi-Eslami, the director of channel 2 and a Bani-Sadr man, who had conducted the interview. The offices of the second television channel were taken over by armed guards, and the prosecutor-general, Musavi-Ardabili, appointed new directors for broadcasting services and channel 2, although he had no legal authority to do so.

Qotbzadeh's arrest became a rallying point for the opposition. Bazargan denounced the arrest from the floor of Parliament. Several clerics criticized the action, including Khomaini's brother, Morteza Pasandideh, the parliamentary deputy, Ayatollah Hasan Lahuti, and Ayatollah Allameh Nuri, whose mosque near Jaleh Square in Tehran had served as the headquarters for major anti-Shah demonstrations in 1978. More significantly, merchants in the bazaar organized protests in Qotbzadeh's favor and secured 30,000 signatures on a petition demanding his release. Qotbzadeh was set free three days after his arrest through the personal intervention of Ahmad Khomaini.

Two weeks after the Qotbzadeh affair, however, masked men smashed up the editorial offices of *Mizan*, Bazargan's newspaper. A few days later, thugs broke into the Shariati Islamic Learning Publication Center in Mashad and destroyed thousands of books and pamphlets. When the Office for the Cooperation of the People with the President organized a rally in Mashad that Lahuti, Salamatian, Mohammad-Taqi Shariati, and Shaikh Ali Tehrani were to address on four successive nights, Salamatian's speech, at which he condemned repression, was interrupted by hecklers and rowdies. The pro-Bani-Sadr crowd, which was large, responded with slogans condemning "the corrupt three: Khamene'i, Rafsanjani and Beheshti," called on the clerics to stop interfering in politics, and attacked the IRP headquarters in Mashad.

The IRP interpreted the Mashad rally as an attack on the clerical community as a whole and Salamatian's speech as an insult to Khomaini himself. The day following Salamatian's address, the IRP closed down parts of the Tehran and Qom bazaars and organized demonstrations in favor of Khomaini and the clerical involvement in politics in half-a-dozen other cities. In Isfahan, Salamatian's home constituency, a rally organized by Ayatollah Jalal ad-Din Taheri, the leader of Friday prayers and Khomaini's personal representative, approved resolutions supporting the principle of clerical sovereignty and calling for Salamatian's dismissal from Parliament. On 8 December, bazaar merchants and other inhabitants rallied in Salamatian's support. But a young man, in full view of the television cameras and in what appeared to be a staged incident, tore up a picture of Khomaini. National television repeatedly broadcast film of this "insult" to the leader of the revolution, and Ayatollah Taheri took the grave step of quitting Isfahan in protest, nominally leaving the city without a Friday prayer leader. He also pointedly made Islam and Khomaini's leadership the basic issue between the IRP and its opponents: "I fear that tomorrow, in the name of freedom, they will also raise the cry of death to Islam and death to the Koran," he said. "Today, they insult the *vali-ye amr* [Khomaini]. God knows what plans they have laid for tomorrow."[11]

As the moderate opposition attempted to rally its forces over the next few weeks, meetings continued to be disrupted by the *hezbollahi* club wielders. Thugs broke mosque windows and interrupted the sermon when Shaikh Ali Tehrani attempted to speak to a congregation at the Ark mosque in Tehran. In Isfahan, where Tehrani was to address a rally at the Takhti stadium, club wielders first forced the crowd into the adjacent playing field and then interrupted the talk by cutting off the microphones. In February, Ayatollah Lahuti's sermon at the China-Sellers' mosque in Rasht was disrupted. When Lahuti tried to preach at the Friday mosque in Kuchesfahan, his home constituency, a few days later, rowdies broke windows, mobbed his car, and shot his bodyguard in the leg. Clashes between the *hezbollahis* and left-wing political groups occurred in the Caspian province towns of Babol, Amol, Sari, Qa'emshahr, Ramsar, and Enzeli, as well as in Kerman and Kermanshah.

These developments led bazaar, academic, and political groups and individuals to make a stand. In December 1980, merchants of the Tehran bazaar associated with the NF issued a declaration calling for the resignation of the Raja'i cabinet and warning that the government's incompetence was leading to "the complete annihilation" of the country.[12] The spokesman for the signatories, Abol-Hasan Lebaschi, head of the Union of Merchants and Shopkeepers, had helped organize and finance anti-Shah protests and bazaar strikes under the old regime. The Lahuti affair elicited protests from several clerics and members of

Khomaini's household, including Eshraqi, Pasandideh, and Ahmad Khomaini. Forty Majles deputies signed a declaration calling on the government to prevent the violent disruption of public meetings.[13] Mehdi Bazargan, one of the signatories of this declaration, was especially active. In an open letter addressed to Khomaini, he said the Imam was depending on limited and biased sources of information and was kept ignorant of dissatisfaction in the country. The situation, he said, could have "extensive and serious repercussions for the revolution, the nation and for [Khomaini] himself."[14] In February, in a major speech in Parliament, and as usual seeking to strike a balance between the contending factions, Bazargan took Bani-Sadr to task for claiming powers not vested in the president and for his excessive polemics and pamphleteering. He criticized the prime minister for obstructing the president and violating the constitution; but he reserved his sharpest criticism for the chief justice, Ayatollah Beheshti, whose extensive powers and activities he aptly described:

> The honorable chief justice of the Supreme Court, while actively leading his party and taking non-neutral political positions, devotes much time to interviews and press conferences. . . . Few of the country's affairs are not officially or unofficially under his influence and direction. He receives the ambassadors and ministers of foreign governments. He visits and supervises the battlefront and government offices. He expresses views about, and exerts his influence over, economic and labor affairs, the policies of the state and the formation and confirmation of the cabinet. In short, he extends his great weight and dominance over all the branches of the Islamic Republic.[15]

In February, Bazargan and three other colleagues from the Iran Freedom Movement also addressed a large rally in Tehran. For once the rally was not disrupted; Ebrahim Yazdi criticized the ruling party for its "Stalinist and un-Islamic" methods.

That same month, 133 writers, academics, journalists, and intellectuals issued an open letter, without reference to Bani-Sadr to protest illegal trials, suppression of basic freedoms, the muzzling of the press, burning of books and bookstores, and other violations of the constitution.[16] The well-known writer and essayist, Ali-Asghar Hajj Seyyed Javadi, an outspoken critic of constitutional violations under the Shah, issued a separate declaration decrying the "Islam of the stick and the club," and the corruption and absolutist tendencies of the ruling party. "The monster of fascism," he said, "has been let out of the bottle."[17] IRP rule was also criticized by a number of religious leaders. Shaikh Ali

Tehrani went on a speaking tour, wrote a series of articles for *Enqelab-e Eslami*, gave interviews, and issued an open letter to Khomaini. He compared the IRP to the Shah's secret police and described it as "a new Savak." He alleged that the party enjoyed the support of only a minority of the clerics. In his open letter, he charged Khomaini himself with violating Islamic principles: "It appears as if, in order to retain power, you act contrary to your own religious decrees and Islamic principles. Many come to us and say the statements and attitude of Ayatollah Khomaini are causing our wives and children to turn against religion."[18]

Senior religious leaders joined in the criticism. Ayatollah Zanjani decried the excesses of the revolutionary tribunals and purge committees. Ayatollah Qomi-Tabataba'i described the majority of the revolutionary courts as "corrupt and cruel" and said that "trials, tortures, judgments and confiscations of property perpetrated by the present leaders are all contrary to Islamic principles and rules." Ayatollah Shirazi remarked that the activities of the ruling party had created a situation in which "an explosion threatens Iran."[19] More seriously for the IRP and for Khomaini, these senior clerics questioned on doctrinal grounds the legitimacy of the institutions of the state, including Khomaini's own supreme position in the constitutional order. Qomi and Zanjani both questioned the legitimacy of the revolutionary tribunals and argued that the clerics appointed to the courts lacked the competence to be Islamic judges. Both, moreover, questioned the validity of the wide and exclusive powers conferred under the constitution on Khomaini; both argued that the authority to interpret the laws and issue *fatvas*, or religious decrees, devolved on any qualified jurist and must be shared more widely. Qomi questioned even the involvement of the religious leaders in politics. In a barely veiled reference to Khomaini and the clerics around him, he said:

> Real clerics do not seek power. . . . Real clerics do not support those among the religious leaders who govern over us. The real task of the clerics is to enjoin the good and to enlighten the people.[20]

By the early spring, the alignment of forces on both sides of this struggle had become more distinct. At the center of the groups ranged against the ruling party were some merchants and bazaar elements in a number of major cities. Their strength derived from their roots in the propertied and middle classes, traditional links to the clerical community, financial power, and the ability to shut down the bazaar. Informally associated with them were moderate religious leaders, including Ayatollahs Zanjani and Shariatmadari, and political groups such as the Iran Freedom Movement, the remnants of the National Front, and the Iran Party. To their right were a number of conservative religious leaders in Mashad, Qom, Tehran, Isfahan, and other cities. Among these, Ayatollahs Qomi and Shirazi of Mashad were outspoken; the majority had been cowed into silence. To the left were the somewhat more radical political groups represented by JAMA, Bani-Sadr's followers, the now-underground National Democratic Front, and a clutch of other small organizations. Despite many differences, they shared a common commitment to egalitarian economic policies, a vague notion of a political order founded on popularly elected councils, and in foreign policy, sympathy for third world causes. Also to the left stood a number of professional and lawyers' bodies and loose associations of university professors and intellectuals, many of whom identified with radical causes.

Much further left stood the Mojahedin-e Khalq, whose association with Bani-Sadr tended to grow as the president came under increasing pressure from the IRP. The Mojahedin appear to have seen in Bani-Sadr a potential ally because he defended a number of causes, such as freedom of association and speech, they considered important for political survival and because association with him might allow them to shed a part of their radical image and gain acceptability among the middle classes. The Mojahedin assisted Bani-Sadr by providing him with information, political support, organizational skills, and eventually, physical backing in the streets. The Mojahedin had sought an understanding with Bani-Sadr on the eve of the attack on the universities in April 1980, and they supplied the president with material on the mistreatment of political prisoners to use against the IRP. After Bani-Sadr began publicly to attack the ruling party, they mobilized their supporters to swell the audiences at his rallies and promoted his newspaper. They were to play a key role in rounding up the hecklers at his 5 March rally at Tehran University. Mojahedin sympathizers began to serve in information gathering, public relations, and propaganda in the Office for Cooperation of the People with the President.

The Mojahedin, as well as the minority Fadayan, also sent their supporters into the streets. In February, some 5,000 followers of the Fadayan and Paykar, a Marxist group that had split off from the Mojahedin-e Khalq, clashed with the Revolutionary Guard in Tehran; they carried banners with the legend "we want jobs, freedom, and independence." Some forty people were treated for bullet and stab wounds. In April, there were further confrontations between Fadayan demonstrators and guards. That same month, and in early May, Mojahedin supporters and guards fought with sticks and rocks near Tehran University. Confrontations in provincial towns involved primarily left-wing groups.

The moderate opposition enjoyed a number of advantages. There were among their leaders men of political and regional influence. Through these leaders, the opposition could hope to tap regional bases of support in Mashad, Tabriz, Hamadan, Rasht, Isfahan, and Tehran. There was a reservoir of middle-class support for the IRP's opponents. Despite the atmosphere of fear and intimidation, Bazargan and Yazdi, Bani-Sadr, Salamatian, and their colleagues, the Mojahedin, and clerics not associated with the IRP could still draw large and sometimes huge crowds to their political rallies. When Bazargan called for private contributions for a $70,000 fund for the defense of the arrested editor of *Mizan,* the fund was quickly oversubscribed. *Enqelab-e Eslami* gained in circulation as the paper's criticism of the ruling party gained in cutting edge.

But the opposition was also beset by numerous weaknesses. The different parties shared a common desire to curb the power of the IRP and secure for themselves the opportunity to compete freely in the political arena. But the opposition was not homogeneous. Instances of cooperation between Bani-Sadr and the Mojahedin, the Bazargan group, and the bazaar aside, there were virtually no formal ties between its various elements. On the contrary, the economic views of the Mojahedin were hardly acceptable to the bazaar or the conservative religious leaders. The religious leaders did not share the desire for a secularization of society. The intellectuals issued declarations on themes emphasized by the president, but they kept their distance from Bani-Sadr whose long association with Khomaini and role in the closure of the universities they could not yet forgive. A number of the president's colleagues found the Mojahedin too radical, feared they might end up taking over Bani-Sadr's organization, and advised against collaboration with them.

Bani-Sadr gained in standing as he began forthrightly to attack censorship, the suppression of freedoms, arbitrary arrest, and executions. But many were put off by what they saw as his self-importance and his lack of consideration for others. The president's style, moreover, seemed often an exercise in organized chaos. Believing in the "effervescent spontaneity" of the masses, he showed little patience for building up organizational support. He remained, in many ways, the revolutionary exile of Paris. Even as president, pamphleteering, political journalism, debating, and polemics excited his interest far more than the pedestrian tasks of administration.

The IRP Responds

Between January and June 1981, the IRP was able to check this challenge to its hegemony and then to overwhelm its opponents because of these weaknesses and because of the strength it derived from its domination of the institutions of the state and the broadcast media, the collaboration of the revolutionary courts, guards, and committees, the network of mosques and clerics at its disposal across the country, a near-monopoly over the instruments of coercion, the prestige gained through close identification with Khomaini and, ultimately, sheer brutality. IRP loyalists were in key positions not only in the ministries in Tehran but in provincial administration, often down to the township and district level. Control of the government and revolutionary organizations such as the Foundation for the Disinherited and the Crusade for Reconstruction placed considerable funds and patronage at the disposal of the party and its friends and made opposition activity, particularly in the provinces, more difficult.

Clerics throughout the country, whether out of conviction or calculation, continued to cooperate with the IRP. The mosques distributed food coupons, issued permits for the purchase of scarce but much sought-after items like refrigerators, and testified to the good standing of local inhabitants seeking jobs for themselves or schools for their children. Patronage, coercion, and appeal to religion permitted the IRP to counter the rallies of the opposition with huge rallies of its own. Moreover, in many towns and cities, the IRP managed to retain an image as the champion of the disinherited against the privileged, and to serve as the vehicle for advancement of the upwardly mobile young men and recent migrants of the urban slums. In the same way that new aspirants to jobs and privileges were rising through the revolutionary committees and the Revolutionary Guard, the bureaucracy and the Crusade for Reconstruction, to push aside established members of the technocracy and civil service, in centers like Isfahan, Mashad, and Tabriz, lesser clerics were utilizing the revolution, the IRP, and populist themes to challenge the older, established clerical leaders who refused to move with the revolutionary tide. In the Isfahan area, Ayatollahs Taheri and Montazeri were relative newcomers to the ranks of the leading clerical families. But they were able to mobilize support in the surrounding villages and to capitalize on public resentment against the old merchant families with whom the traditional religious leaders were often associated. In Mashad, Ayatollahs Qomi and Shirazi, despite their prestige, failed to shake the hold of the IRP and Khomaini's representative on the city and its mosques. In Tabriz, religious figures loyal to Ayatollah Shariatmadari were outflanked by Khomaini appointees.

The IRP utilized the media and increasing coordination among Friday prayer leaders to swamp the opposition with adverse propaganda and to advance its own point of view. The ideological-political bureaus in the army, national police, and gendarmerie indoctrinated the rank and file and guarded against ideological deviation. Islamic committees fulfilled similar functions in government offices and on the factory floor. The Revolutionary Guard, courts, and committees were not necessarily in the government's or the party's control; but they collaborated with the IRP against the opposition. In many provincial centers, party, revolutionary organization, and the mosque were inextricably intertwined. The IRP and the local revolutionary committee shared the same offices. The cleric who was Friday prayer leader was also a member of the party and the head of the revolutionary tribunal. Few among the opposition were immune from the retribution of the revolutionary courts. Several months after the demonstrations in favor of Qotbzadeh, two prominent Tehran merchants were executed. One of the merchants, Dastmalchi, had supported Khomaini against the Shah. Another merchant and erstwhile Khomaini supporter, Abol-Hasan Lebaschi, who had helped organize the demonstrations, was forced to flee the country.

The authorities did nothing when opposition meetings were attacked. When pro-Bani-Sadr hecklers disrupted a rally in Tuysirkan during a speech by Hashemi-Rafsanjani, however, six were sentenced to one to three years in prison and forty lashes for "conspirational support of the president." Finally, the IRP deployed its "partisans of the party of God," with their clubs, chains, and switchblade knives. The opposition parties lacked the means, the will, or the temperament to deal with the violence of the *hezbollahis.* The guerrilla organizations and the student movements, the Fadayan, the Mojahedin-e Khalq, and Paykar, often fought back; but the *hezbollahis* were brutal and unrestrained. Over a dozen young men and women were killed in street clashes in April and May in Tehran, Qazvin, Ramsar, Amol, Lahijan, and Bandar Abbas. Members of the IRP and the Raja'i government never unequivocally condemned this hooliganism. Abdol-Majid Ma'adikhah of the IRP central committee blamed the violence on the opposition politicians themselves who "acted in such a manner as to arouse the fury of the masses." Club wielding, he admitted, had "undesirable" effects, "but liberty for the plotters is much worse."[21] In this he echoed Khomaini, who set the tone of official reaction. In February, he was at last prevailed upon to issue a general and feeble condemnation of "club wielding." But he added: "The club of the pen and the club of the tongue is the worst of clubs, whose corruption is a hundred times greater than other clubs."[22]

The IRP, however, could not hope to have Bani-Sadr set aside without Khomaini's backing or agreement; Bani-Sadr could not hope to prevail, or even survive, without Khomaini's support. Both sides sought control of the streets and propaganda as a means of influencing Khomaini. In addition to the war of words and the war of the rallies, both sides also waged a war for Khomaini's ear. The IRP sought to impress on Khomaini the threatening nature of Bani-Sadr's collaboration with the forces of the left, the hostility of these "allies" to Islam, and what they perceived as the disruptive nature of Bani-Sadr's activities. Bani-Sadr, in turn, sought to depict himself as indispensible to the war effort and the health of the economy and as the popular choice of the masses. He attempted to influence the Imam through the agency of Ahmad Khomaini and bombarded both father and son with letters, memoranda, and dire warnings.

Khomaini's basic sympathies lay with the clerical party and with the revolutionary organizations ranged against the president; but he did not invariably support the IRP. He disapproved of IRP attempts to undermine the discipline of the armed forces. He had no desire to alienate the type of moderate and left-of-center "Islamic" political groups and intelligentsia that Bani-Sadr represented. The emotional ties between Khomaini and Bani-Sadr were complex. If the president looked to Khomaini as a spiritual father, the older man was attached to his younger disciple in ways that, at least for a time, overrode purely political considerations.

At times, Khomaini attempted to play a mediating role between the warring factions, urging moderation on both. At other moments, angered by the constant feuding, he threatened to dismiss all whom he had appointed to various positions. "Don't bite each other like snakes and scorpions," he told them. "Don't claw at one another."[23] Nevertheless, Khomaini gave Bani-Sadr considerable support. Following the December disturbances in Mashad, Isfahan, and Qom, he ordered the cancelation of a huge rally called for 19 December in the capital, at which a resolution demanding the dismissal of Bani-Sadr as commander-in-chief was to have been approved. Speaking to the Revolutionary Guard later that month, he urged cooperation between the fighting forces, an end to remarks disturbing to the military commanders, and support for Bani-Sadr's plea for a unified command. A few days later, noting that war "one day means victory, one day defeat, one day advance, one day withdrawal," he advised civilians not to interfere in military affairs "about which they know nothing," and implicitly criticized the attempts of Montazeri and members of Parliament to stir up the lower ranks against their officers. "It is the army that knows the arts of war, and in the army only the commanding officers," he said.[24] In February, he issued "a serious warning" to clerics in the courts, committees, and revolutionary organizations that "they should not interfere in areas outside their competence." He described such intervention as un-Islamic, a source of disorder, and an activity likely to alienate the people from their religious leaders.[25]*

Khomaini's support for Bani-Sadr, however, was not open ended, and the president's activities aroused grave misgivings in the Imam. Khomaini resented criticism of that part of the religious establishment with which he identified. He harbored strong animosity toward the opposition parties: the Fadayan because he regarded them as saboteurs and rick-burners, the Mojahedin because they had appropriated to themselves the authority to interpret Islamic doctrine; the NF because their hero, Mossadegh, provided a focus of loyalty to rival his own, the secular intelligentsia because they desired to drive the clerics out of politics. He was sensitive to any sign that people were rallying behind rival religious leaders.

Yet Bani-Sadr was attacking the institutions of the Islamic Republic and clerical leaders close to Khomaini. He appeared to be collaborating with the Mojahedin and making common cause with other opposition groups. Pro-Bani-Sadr and other opposition rallies had taken on an

*This formal message to mark the anniversary of the revolution was read publicly by Khomaini's son, Ahmad. Khomaini's formal messages during this period, delivered by Ahmad, often bore the imprint of Ahmad's and Bani-Sadr's ideas and went much further than did Khomaini himself, when speaking directly, in criticizing the religious community and the revolutionary organizations.

anticlerical, or at least anti-IRP, tone. Bani-Sadr had made overtures to Ayatollah Shirazi in Mashad; and Shirazi and Qomi were more outspoken in their criticism of IRP rule. All the signs pointed to an incipient coming together of the opposition forces. Meantime, the conflict between the president and the IRP was feeding unrest and disorder throughout the country.

Khomaini moved to nip these indications of resistance and opposition in the bud. He denounced the bazaar merchants who had organized in support of Qotbzadeh. He called the president and other government officials to him to denounce the press. "Why do you not stop these newspapers?" he asked. "Why do you not shut their mouths? Why do you not stop their pens?"[26] In December 1979, he had moved quickly to crush the swelling movement in Tabriz behind Ayatollah Shariat-madari. He now moved to squash the attempt to harness the prestige of the Mashad religious leaders against him. "I warn the clerics gathered at the seminary centers to desist from plotting," he said soon after Qomi and Shirazi had made statements critical of the regime. "If they continue, they will be summoned before the courts."[27]

An indication of Khomaini's uneasiness came in an interview with his grandson, Hosain, published in *Ettelaat* on 4 December. Like the other members of Khomaini's immediate household, Hosain had almost consistently and strongly supported the president. But he now spoke with a different voice:

> Today, those who have gathered under the umbrella of Bani-Sadr want to start acting against the Imam. They have made grave errors. The friends of Mr. Bani-Sadr are falling away. The clerical figures who had issued declarations supporting him for the presidency repent today. I myself was very active in his campaign for the presidency, but today I see that there is a big conspiracy against the Imam.[28]

In a subsequent gloss on the interview, Hosain adopted a more conciliatory tone. But he repeated advice that Bani-Sadr should not "cut himself off" from Khomaini. This early warning went unheeded. Bani-Sadr continued his quest for support and allies, his speechifying, and his polemics. He not only joined the critics of the government's budget and oil policies, he also harped on three issues embarrassing to the government and to officials close to Khomaini.

First, following a scandal in which European arms dealers in Paris disappeared with $56 million of Iranian money, Bani-Sadr continued to hint at corruption in Iran's arms purchases. The attempt by Beheshti and

Nabavi to hush up the deal lent credence to his charges. Second, Bani-Sadr refused to drop the issue of torture. Following the president's charge, Khomaini had appointed an investigative commission. But as anticipated, the commission concluded that the charges were unfounded; it had discovered only negligible instances of mistreatment of prisoners. But Bani-Sadr's office said it had submitted documents and photographs regarding 500 individual claims of torture, the Mojahedin several hundred more. A group of ninety-four lawyers and judges, in a letter published in *Mizan*, joined Bani-Sadr and the Mojahedin in charging that the commission had failed to investigate these cases.[29] Bani-Sadr helped confirm the public impression that the commission's report had been a whitewash. Finally, Bani-Sadr took up the cudgel against the IRP over the freeing of the American hostages.

"A Fruit Squeezed Dry of Juice"

The Iranian government began to negotiate in earnest over the release of the American hostages in September 1980. On 9 September, a Khomaini aide, Sadeq Tabataba'i, indicated to Washington through West German intermediaries Iran's readiness to reach a settlement. On 12 September, Khomaini set forth in a speech Iran's four conditions for freeing the hostages. The demand for an American apology for its past "crimes" in Iran, unacceptable to the United States, had been dropped. On 14 September, an American team, led by Warren Christopher, the deputy secretary of state, flew to West Germany to open talks with Tabataba'i, setting in motion the arduous process which resulted in the freeing of the hostages on 20 January 1981, Inauguration Day.[30]

Economic incentives played a role in the decision of Iran's clerics to settle. The government desired to gain access to Iran's frozen assets and to see trade sanctions lifted. The Iraqi invasion on 22 September lent urgency to these considerations. The death of the Shah in July permitted Iran to drop one demand, for a return of the ex-monarch, to which the United States could never agree. But the primary explanation for the decision to move toward a settlement lay in domestic politics. "The hostages," said Behzad Nabavi, Iran's chief negotiator, "are like a fruit from which all the juice has been squeezed out."[31] Most of the domestic aims of the radicals had been achieved. The public had been galvanized and mobilized against the foreign and domestic "enemies" of the revolution. The constitution of the Islamic Republic had been approved. The moderates were in retreat. The IRP was in firm control of Parliament and Raja'i had formed his government. The IRP, rather than Bani-Sadr, was in a position to negotiate a hostage settlement. This view was graphically put by the Majles deputy Mohammad Musavi-Khoeniha, the mentor of the "students of the Imam's line":

> We have reaped all the fruits of our undertaking. We defeated the attempt by the "liberals" to take control of the machinery of state. We forced Mr. Bazargan's government to resign. The tree of revolution has grown and gained in strength. We have demonstrated both to our own people and to international opinion that we have the weapons not only to resist but also to defeat the all-powerful United States, which believed it held Iran in the palm of its hand.[32]

Having decided to settle, the government in January rushed to conclude an agreement before the mandate of the Carter administration ran out because there was no desire to take up from the beginning the complex negotiating process with a new administration. Besides, there was considerable anxiety about what President Reagan, due to take office in January, might do once in the White House. Bani-Sadr had frequently spoken of the war-mongering inclinations of Republican administrations. Behzad Nabavi put it another way. Carter, he said, was just "a peanut farmer." But Reagan was a man who came on the scene "with a six-shooter, like a movie cowboy."

Some $11–12 billion in Iranian assets had been frozen by President Carter's order. Under the term of the agreement, these assets were unlocked; but the Iranian government agreed to repay around $5.1 billion in syndicated and nonsyndicated bank loans extended to Iran by consortia of American and foreign banks and to set aside another $1 billion in an escrow account to secure the hundreds of claims against Iran filed by American firms and citizens. The government thus gave up, at one stroke, $6 billion of its foreign exchange assets.[33] The question of the return of the Shah's wealth was dropped, buried in vague verbiage. The terms of the accords immediately came under sharp attack, primarily in Bani-Sadr's *Enqelab-e Eslami,* but also in *Mizan.*

In editorials, Bani-Sadr disavowed the agreement altogether. He said that by unnecessarily prolonging the crisis, the hard-liners had secured for Iran less favorable terms than were possible earlier. An American apology, he noted, had not been secured. The Shah's wealth had not been returned. Iran had ended up getting a negligible part of its assets in hard cash. The decision to repay Iran's outstanding bank loans in full was especially reprehensible, involving the repayment far before maturity of loans obtained at favorable interest rates. The governor of the Central Bank, Ali-Reza Nobari, published in *Enqelab-e Eslami* the full texts of his correspondence with the prime minister in this regard, providing detailed arguments why he considered the early repayment of the bank loans unnecessary and damaging to the country's balance of payments position. The newspaper also criticized the government's decision to entertain hundreds of legal suits against Iran, many of which Bani-Sadr and Nobari regarded as specious.

These criticisms did not fall on deaf ears. Among the educated classes there was a widespread conviction that Iran had concluded a financially disadvantageous agreement. Bani-Sadr's insistence on keeping alive the disputes over corruption, torture, and the hostage settlement gained him middle-class support. But it appears to have had two other consequences. It reinforced the determination of the IRP to seek Bani-Sadr's ouster from office; and it helped persuade Khomaini not to stand in the way of Bani-Sadr's fall.

For Bani-Sadr, the turning point in this unequal struggle came on 5 March. He was addressing a huge rally at Tehran University to mark the birthday of Mossadegh. Hecklers attempted to disrupt the meeting. They were seized by members of the audience, their pockets were emptied, and they were turned over to the police. Cards they were carrying indicated that almost all the sixty to seventy hecklers arrested were members of revolutionary and Islamic committees and various revolutionary organizations. The IRP, however, mobilized its propaganda machinery to turn the tables on the president in this potentially embarrassing affair.

The next day, Bani-Sadr was denounced in Friday prayers throughout the country for instigating violence against the Islamic Republic. Raja'i labeled the president a liar for attributing the disturbance to the supporters of the government. Khalkhali called for Bani-Sadr's dismissal and trial. A march was organized to demand the release of the rowdies arrested during Bani-Sadr's speech. Beheshti noted that many of those taken into custody had filed charges against Bani-Sadr and that "the president can be brought to trial like any other citizen." Having refused to look into numerous earlier instances of disorder at political meetings, the prosecutor-general, Musavi-Ardabili, now decided that an investigation of the 5 March incident would go forward and that the president might have to answer to charges before the supreme court. The clerical party moved quickly to press home its advantage against Bani-Sadr and his potential allies.

On 17 March, the trial opened in Tehran of Bazargan's former aide, Abbas Amir-Entezam. (Charged with treason, he was later sentenced to life imprisonment.) On 7 April, the newspaper of the Iran Freedom Movement, *Mizan,* was closed down and Reza Sadr, the publisher, a former minister and a close associate of Bazargan's, was arrested. Sadr was charged with slander, libel, and undermining national security. *Mizan's* chief crime appears to have been its persistence in criticizing the terms of the hostage settlement and Beheshti's involvement, as chief justice, in politics. Although *Mizan's* editor was soon released and the paper allowed, briefly, to resume publication, the attack on *Mizan* was also directed against Bazargan, who had been sharply critical of Beheshti's political activities.

A number of the president's aides were arrested. In May, guards seized Morteza Fazlinejad, from the president's office, and Esmail Nateqi, the foreign ministry's chief of consular affairs, for attempting to smuggle documents out of the building. The two men were apparently trying to collect evidence from the ministry's personnel files to use against the IRP. In June, Bani-Sadr's legal adviser, Manuchehr Mas'udi, who had put together evidence on torture cases and other complaints against the government, was arrested. He and thirteen others were charged with taking bribes, smuggling foreign exchange and persons out of the country, and supporting counterrevolution. On the excuse that official documents might be spirited out of the Central Bank, guards were placed at the doors of the bank and the governor, Ali-Reza Nobari, had each day to submit to a humiliating body search before leaving the building. In the provinces, representatives of the Office for the People's Cooperation with the President and of Bani-Sadr's newspaper were arrested or otherwise harassed. In Qom, Mashad, Hamadan, and other towns, headquarters of the cooperation office were attacked. In June, the minister of the interior declared the president's organization illegal and closed its offices.

In Parliament, Bani-Sadr found himself further shorn of his powers. A special allocation of $2.1 million for the president's office was dropped from the supplementary budget, forcing Bani-Sadr to appeal to the public for funds. (The Guardianship Council subsequently restored the cut.) A measure was approved permitting the prime minister to appoint caretakers to departments still lacking a minister, effectively giving Raja'i control over the foreign ministry. When Bani-Sadr refused to sign the bill into law, Parliament simply passed another law requiring the president to sign any measure approved by Parliament in five days and urgent measures in twenty-four hours. The Majles approved legislation to permit the prime minister, rather than the president, to appoint the representative of the executive branch to the council that supervised the broadcast media, thus denying Bani-Sadr any voice in running radio and television. Finally, the Majles approved a measure which in effect allowed the prime minister to name the governor of the Central Bank, the last important organization still in Bani-Sadr's hands. Nobari resigned on 10 June. The IRP's leaders were now ready to seek Bani-Sadr's ouster from office. For this, they required Khomaini's support.

"You Can Still Repent"

Even after the 5 March rally at Tehran University, Khomaini did not abandon Bani-Sadr. On the one hand, he allowed the investigation into the president's responsibility for the confrontation at the university to go forward and repeated himself the tenet that "no one stands above the law, even I." On the other hand, he continued to seek to bring the warring factions together, to give Bani-Sadr support, and to press the president first to break with his new-found allies, and second, to cease denouncing the institutions of the republic. He thus offered Bani-Sadr both stick and carrot, both threat and incentive.

On 15 March, Khomaini called the country's leaders to him in a last attempt at a reconciliation.[34] The participants at this meeting fell into three categories. Bani-Sadr came by himself. Representing the IRP and the government were party Secretary General and Chief Justice Beheshti, Majles Speaker Hashemi-Rafsanjani, Prime Minister Raja'i, former Defense Minister Khamene'i, and Prosecutor-General Musavi-Ardabili. The contrast was symbolic. Bani-Sadr held only the presidency; his rivals wielded authority over many powerful offices. Bani-Sadr, the loner, came by himself; his rivals, whatever their personal differences, came as a team. Two other participants fell between the two stools. Mehdi Bazargan, elder statesman and advocate of moderation, was cast in the role of mediator. Ahmad Khomaini was there as his father's aide. Both men tended in Bani-Sadr's favor. Khomaini himself, by turns conciliatory and deeply angry, now threatening to dismiss them all, now urging compromise, wished to know what the gentlemen proposed to do. "Do you intend to annihilate the Islamic Republic," he asked, ". . . to go on television and denounce one another like corrupt men?"[35]

The meeting grew bitterly acrimonious. Bani-Sadr reiterated his view of Raja'i, Beheshti, and the others as men lacking in intelligence, in principle, and in patriotism. He went further to declare all the institutions of the state, except his own presidency, to be illegitimate. Elections for Parliament had been fraudulent. The Raja'i government had been "imposed" on the president. The chief justice, the public prosecutor, and the entire supreme court had been appointed in a manner contrary to the constitution. The Council of Guardians was illegitimate because half its members had been picked by a Parliament and by a supreme court that were themselves illegal. The government, he concluded, should resign, Parliament and the other institutions should be dissolved and reconstituted. At the very least, the membership of the Guardianship Council should be entirely changed and his own authority as commander-in-chief should be formally recognized.

Beheshti and Rafsanjani took the view that cooperation with the president was impossible as long as Bani-Sadr refused to recognize the other institutions of the state and insisted, in Beheshti's words, on considering himself "the most luminous mind of the century, and all those who oppose him as devoid of intelligence and moral principles."[36] Rafsanjani demanded the president acknowledge the legitimacy of the other institutions of the republic, accept the limits on his authority set by the Guardianship Council, and, since he had lost popularity with the army and Revolutionary Guard, yield his position as commander-in-chief to a three-man council. Beheshti, more circumspect, held that, cooperation appearing impossible, one party to the dispute should withdraw and permit the other to run the country. Bazargan proposed that the president be confirmed as commander-in-chief, that the Guardianship Council be altered to reinforce its neutrality, and that a three-man committee be appointed to adjudicate differences between the president and his rivals.

Since no agreement could be reached, each participant was asked to submit his views in writing to Khomaini. The next day, the Imam issued a ten-point decree establishing guidelines for both sides. He banned all speeches, as well as newspaper articles and remarks contributing to friction, until the end of the war. He confirmed Bani-Sadr as commander-in-chief. Finally, he took up Bazargan's suggestion and set up a tripartite commission, one of whose members would be nominated by himself, one by Bani-Sadr, and one by "the other side." The committee would hear and help resolve differences and watch out for any violation by officials and newspapers of the ban on incendiary articles and statements. Khomaini named Mahdavi-Kani, the interior minister and a man who had taken a distance from the IRP, as his representative to the tripartite commission. The IRP named a member of its central committee and a Majles deputy, Mohammad Yazdi. Bani-Sadr selected Khomaini's son-in-law and his frequent supporter, Shahab ad-Din Eshraqi.

The 15 March meeting was similar in character and outcome to Khomaini's previous attempt at bringing about a reconciliation between the secular and clerical factions around him. In July 1979, when the Bazargan government and the Revolutionary Council were vying for supremacy, he had convened the leaders of the two sides at his home in Qom, where arrangements were agreed for closer coordination between the council and the cabinet. These arrangements only allowed the clerics of the Revolutionary Council further to encroach on the authority of the government. The guidelines announced by Khomaini after the 15 March meeting were no more effective in stemming the struggle between Bani-Sadr and the clerical party.

Bani-Sadr soon resumed his public campaign against his rivals. Blocked in Parliament, lacking influence in the cabinet, denied access to the broadcast media, unable to compete with the IRP's followers on the streets, he fell back on appealing to the public. Momentarily prevented by his undertaking from making speeches, he resorted to addressing letters to the tripartite commission and the prosecutor-general and having his newspaper publicize the contents in front-page stories. As already noted, he had the Central Bank governor make public his correspondence with the prime minister over the hostage settlement. He addressed the "nonpolitical" issue of the state of the country's economy and blamed conditions on the government. By early June, he was again making speeches. The IRP, in turn, fought with the president over ministerial appointments, harassed members of his staff, attacked his followers, and chipped at his powers through legislation. In May, as indicated earlier, Parliament passed the measure permitting the prime minister to name caretakers to departments lacking a minister.

Bani-Sadr's refusal to sign this measure into law, and his demand for a referendum to decide the issue between himself and his rivals, led

Khomaini to abandon any public pretense at neutrality in the struggle. On 27 May, in indirect but unmistakable terms, he attacked Bani-Sadr. "The nation," he said, "is hostile to the cult of personality." Anyone who refused to accept the sovereignty of Parliament and the decisions of the Guardianship Council, "is corrupt and must be prosecuted as a corrupter on earth." The discontented "can go back to Europe, the United States or wherever else they like."[37] That same day, the prosecutor-general asked the president to comply with the constitution and submit an accounting of his wealth. On 7 June *Enqelab-e Eslami, Mizan,* and three other newspapers were banned for publishing articles inimical to public order. Bani-Sadr, still defiant, announced he would make his views known through tracts and press conferences, distributed thousands of leaflets calling on the people to "resist the dictatorship they are trying to impose on you," and published his newspaper the next day in a four-page tabloid as *The Message of the President.*

Khomaini, however, turned the argument against Bani-Sadr. "The dictator," he said, "is the one who does not bow to the Majles, the laws of the Majles, the judicial authority." In words clearly directed at the president, he warned against using press and speeches to incite the populace, joining hands with other political groups, listening to the "corrupt persons who whisper in your ear," or planning strikes and demonstrations. "Today, to close the bazaar and to demonstrate is to defy the Prophet and to defy Islam," he stated. He pointedly noted that the Prophet would have severed the hand of his own son or daughter had they been guilty of theft. "The day I feel danger to the Islamic Republic, I will cut everybody's hand off," he threatened. "I will do to you what I did to Mohammad Reza [Shah]."[38]

Bani-Sadr responded in a letter dictated to Khomaini's nephew, Reza Pasandideh. The message was anything but contrite. The president told Khomaini he was "committing suicide" and leading the revolution to ruin by entrusting authority to his "power-hungry" enemies. He again demanded the dissolution and reconstitution of Parliament, the government, the High Judicial Council, and the Guardianship Council. Khomaini, Pasandideh told Bani-Sadr on 10 June, was so angered by this reply that he said he would no longer read Bani-Sadr's letters.[39] That same day, he dismissed the president as commander-in-chief of the armed forces. The army made no move in Bani-Sadr's favor, nor did Bani-Sadr ask it to. At a press conference the army chiefs praised Bani-Sadr as a faithful "soldier of Islam and Iran"; but they reaffirmed their loyalty to Khomaini and reiterated their determination to stay out of politics and to devote themselves to fighting the war with Iraq.

Bani-Sadr returned to the capital on 11 June, dejected but hoping desperately Khomaini would still declare in his favor, wavering between the inclination to resign and the inclination to resist, trying to gauge the public mood and to plan his next move with his advisers.[40] Already, fearing arrest, many of his aides had begun a semiunderground existence. Police stood guard outside the presidential palace to prevent an attack on the residence that served also as Bani-Sadr's office. On the night of 12–13 June, Bani-Sadr issued yet another "message to the people"; some time in the next two days, he went into hiding. In his message, Bani-Sadr defended his record, denied he had violated any laws, and credited to his own efforts the revival of the army. "At the moment when we were on the verge of annihilating the [Iraqi] aggressor, I was stabbed in the back." He claimed, not entirely accurately, that a political solution to the war with Iraq had been possible but was sabotaged by his domestic enemies. He was the victim of "a creeping coup d'état," while his rivals had betrayed the revolution, suppressed civil liberties, and pursued policies leading the country to economic and military ruin.[41]

Bani-Sadr also sent two further messages to Khomaini on 15 June in which he repeated his arguments regarding the unconstitutionality of the government and Parliament, urged the restoration of civil liberties, and pleaded for Khomaini's understanding and support: "However you behave, I will not violate my responsibility towards you. However angry you are, my honesty towards you will not be diminished. I think that your treatment of me is not fair. I have not had a bad thought towards you and the country I have served honestly."[42] Bani-Sadr now waited: for Khomaini to change his mind, for a popular movement in his favor.

Meantime, the closing of *Enqelab-e Eslami* and *Mizan*, the dismissal of Bani-Sadr as commander-in-chief, and the realization the IRP was fast tightening the noose around the opposition threw Tehran and provincial centers into turmoil. Gangs roamed the streets of the capital denouncing Bani-Sadr as "the Iranian Pinochet" and calling for the president's dismissal and death. Others called for the ouster of Beheshti. Following sporadic clashes between opposition and government forces, the Mojahedin called out tens of thousands of their supporters on 10 June for a demonstration at Revolution Square near Tehran University. They were confronted by the *hezbollahis*, who had been harangued outside Parliament by Hadi Ghaffari. "While Bani-Sadr lived in a gilded cage in Paris," Ghaffari told them, "we the disinherited of the earth, the real revolutionaries, rotted in the Shah's jails. While Bani-Sadr gave interviews to *Le Monde* and *Der Spiegel*, our jailors made us drink our urine and violated our sisters before our own eyes, to extract confessions from us."[43] The Mojahedin–*hezbollahi* clashes left several dead and hundreds injured.

The opposition attempted to mobilize its forces once again on 15 June, at a rally called by the National Front. The Front intended the meeting to serve as the focus for the middle classes, the bazaar, and the left wing. It distributed four million leaflets. For the first time, it attacked Khomaini directly as responsible for repression and a reign of terror. On the eve of the rally, the Mojahedin and the Ranjbaran, a Maoist group, declared their solidarity with Bani-Sadr. Barely two hours before the scheduled rally, however, Khomaini addressed the nation over the radio. He treated the protest meeting as "an invitation to uprising, an invitation to insurrection." He condemned the National Front as "apostates," poured scorn on their nationalism, and claimed, with some exaggeration, that up to the overthrow of the monarchy, its leaders had advised him to retain the Shah as a constitutional ruler. He focused a large part of his speech on the National Front's potential allies, particularly Bazargan's Iran Freedom Movement and Bani-Sadr himself. He demanded that the Iran Freedom Movement disassociate itself from the National Front within the hour if they wished to escape retribution. "Go to the radio today . . . and condemn the National Front announcement," he said. His attack on Bani-Sadr was equally uncompromising. He charged the president with standing against the constitution, defying Parliament, the Guardianship Council, and the tripartite commission, and with fueling faction in the country. "I want him now to go on television and announce his repentence and say he has been wrong in inviting the people to revolt."[44]

Khomaini's purpose was to arouse the mass of the people against the "ungodly" NF, to discredit the president, and, above all, to split the opposition and prevent the IFM, the bazaar, and the middle classes from joining the protest. In this, he was almost entirely successful. Bazargan hurried to the radio to dissociate the IFM from the NF rally. Bani-Sadr issued no statement of support. The bazaar did not close down. Instead, almost before Khomaini had finished speaking, the partisans of "the party of God," members of the Revolutionary Guard and committees, men and women from the wards of south Tehran organized by the IRP machine, poured into Ferdowsi Square, the designated meeting place for the rally. The large numbers of middle-class protesters and supporters of the NF who also showed up were cowed into virtual silence. There was no organized demonstration, no speeches, no march.

The focus of attention now shifted to Parliament, where support was growing for a move to impeach the president. According to the constitution, Khomaini could dismiss Bani-Sadr if the Majles declared him "incompetent." Already by 12 June, 120 deputies had signed a motion to have the president's competency debated on the floor of the house. On 13 June, however, after a meeting with Khomaini, Hashemi-Rafsanjani said it would be "preferable" for Bani-Sadr to remain president, provided he recognized the limitations the constitution placed on the president's authority. Khomaini confirmed that Bani-Sadr could remain in office. "Nothing new has happened," he said. "The president can carry on his duties as president."[45] But Bani-Sadr's defiant messages of 15 June, the NF call for a rally, and signs of collaboration between Bani-Sadr and the Mojahedin appear to have led Khomaini to change his mind. On 17 June, Hashemi-Rafsanjani, who had earlier blocked attempts in Parliament to take up the question of the president's fitness to serve, harshly criticized Bani-Sadr, allowed a vote on the motion to consider the president's competence, and scheduled the debate for the following week.

"Death to Bani-Sadr"

The debate over the fate of Bani-Sadr took place on 20 and 21 June in an atmosphere of violence and menace.[46] The arrest of Bani-Sadr's aides was already under way. Peaceful demonstrations in Bani-Sadr's favor were quickly dispersed. Throughout the two days, members of the Mojahedin, the minority Fadayan, and the Paykar movements, operating like shock troops in groups of 50 to 100, clashed in Tehran, Isfahan, Shiraz, Hamadan, and a dozen other cities with the *hezbollahis* and the Revolutionary Guard, attacked strategic targets, overturned buses, and set tires on fire. Dozens were killed and hundreds injured. On 18 June, the Mojahedin had in a declaration committed themselves to "revolutionary resistance in all its forms" and to exercising "revolutionary justice" against their attackers.[47] The government spokesman, Behzad

Nabavi, and Majles Speaker Hashemi-Rafsanjani treated this as a declaration of war against the government and sought increasingly to identify Bani-Sadr with the Mojahedin. "These people," said Hashemi-Rafsanjani, "have made war against God. They are oppressors. They have revolted against the Islamic Republic. They have shed blood."[48] Majles Deputy Sadeq Khalkhali said of the opposition on 21 June that "the revolutionary prosecutor and the revolutionary tribunals must today execute at least 50 of them . . . to display that we are men of war, will fight and will dig their graves right here in Tehran."[49] At dawn that morning, fifteen persons involved in street clashes had been executed at Evin prison; that night, another eight were sent before the firing squad. Outside the great, gray marble building which housed the Parliament on Imam Khomaini Avenue, a huge crowd, occasionally harangued by deputies or street orators, demanded Bani-Sadr's execution, cried out "Death to the liberals!" and intimidated opposition deputies as they made their way to the chamber.

The opposition in Parliament, which on the eve of Bani-Sadr's impeachment had 218 members,* in the best of times had been able to muster 40 to 45 votes against the IRP majority. A total of 45 deputies had abstained or voted against the Raja'i government in August 1980. Just 40 signed the petition condemning the *hezbollahi* club wielders. These same signatories accounted for all but three of the deputies who in February 1981 signed a petition implicitly critical of the terms of the hostage settlement. The pattern was repeated on 16 June, when 145 deputies voted for the motion to start impeachment proceedings and a handful against. During the two-day debate, and under threatening conditions, the number prepared to vote against Bani-Sadr grew. The number of his sympathizers remained constant at around 40, almost all of them the signatories of the earlier petitions critical of the government. However, the ranks of the sympathizers were diminished by the 20 to 25 deputies who, fearing arrest, absented themselves from the chamber and another dozen who attended the sessions but abstained on the critical ballot.[50]

Of the ten or so deputies who signed up to speak in Bani-Sadr's favor, four withdrew their names. Mohammad-Javad Hojjati-Kermani, a cleric who had supported Bani-Sadr, announced a change of position because of the president's defiance of Khomaini. "The Imam and the revolution

---

*Parliament normally has 270 members. But elections were not completed in some thirty constituencies; several other members were denied their seats; and a number resigned to take up cabinet posts and other positions.

are kneaded together," he said, "and to stand up against the Imam is to stand up against the revolution."[51] Two deputies who spoke for the president presented only a lukewarm and cautious defense. Only three deputies, none unqualified admirers of Bani-Sadr, with great courage, spoke in his favor or condemned unequivocally the impeachment proceedings: Ali-Akbar Mo'infar and Ezzatollah Sahabi, both of the IFM, and Salahaddin Bayani, a deputy from a Khorasan constituency.

Mo'infar began by referring to the reigning atmosphere of fear and terror. The opposition newspapers, he said, had been illegally suppressed. All the remaining newspapers, radio and television, and preachers at Friday prayers had joined hands in attacking the president. The crowd outside Parliament threatened any deputy speaking favorably of Bani-Sadr with "the severest retribution." No proper debate could be carried out under these conditions:

> It is not the constitution that regulates the country, but the law of violence, of the *hezbollahis* who beat at our gates. Your debate will not change the course of events. The verdict is already in and the victim already designated.[52]

Sahabi admitted that the president had acted with little wisdom, but noted that the opposition had deliberately egged him on and fueled the crisis. He knew the president could not continue in office even in the unlikely event the vote went in his favor; but he feared for the country when "demonstrations and marches, public turmoil and excitement, . . . incitement of the populace" was allowed to determine appointments, dismissals, and major decisions. "You gentlemen too will soon reach a dead end."[53]

The attack on Bani-Sadr was directed by the leading figures of the IRP, including Ali Khamene'i, later to become president, Ali-Akbar Velayati, later to become foreign minister, Musavi-Khoeniha, the mentor of the "students of the Imam's line," Mohammad Yazdi, the IRP's representative on the tripartite commission, and others. The president was charged with making common cause with the opposition, standing up to the Imam, lacking faith in the principle of *velayat-e faqih*, discrediting the revolutionary organizations, sowing faction in the Islamic Republic, and leaving Iran naked to foreign aggression as commander-in-chief of the armed forces. He was also accused of "haughtiness" and "insincerity," bringing shame on Iran in foreign eyes through his charges of torture, "presenting what is good as evil and what is evil as good," and attempting to "discredit Islam and reinforce nationalism."[54]

While the debate proceeded in the chamber, the crowd outside continued to demand the death of Bani-Sadr. At one time, Khalkhali went out to the balcony overlooking Imam Khomaini Avenue to be greeted enthusiastically. "Hang him," the crowd cried out, as Khalkhali grinned and put his fingers around his neck.[55] Mo'infar had hardly completed his remarks when the cry, "Death to Mo'infar!" rose from the street.

When the vote on the motion was finally taken, 177 deputies voted in favor of declaring the president incompetent and only one, Salahaddin Bayani, voted against. Thirteen other deputies remained in the chamber but abstained on the ballot. Another 20 to 25 deputies who, along with those who had abstained, had consistently criticized the IRP, absented themselves from the Majles on that final afternoon.

Following the ballot, Hashemi-Rafsanjani, Khalkhali, and Hadi Ghaffari emerged on the balcony of the Parliament building and listened to the great crowd below as it chanted, "Death to Bani-Sadr! Death to Bani-Sadr!" Rafsanjani addressed the crowd and, as if Bani-Sadr were already a thing of the past, concluded: "With your help, one of the greatest barriers to the continuation of the revolution has been eliminated. From this moment, Bani-Sadr is removed from the Islamic Republic. Switch your slogans to America."[56] The crowd, as one man, switched its slogans; and the cry of "Death to America!" echoed in the hot Tehran afternoon.

If the fall of the Bazargan government in November 1979 represented a serious setback for the moderate elements in the revolutionary coalition that had overthrown the Shah, the elimination of Bani-Sadr marked a crushing defeat for both the moderates and the left. Along with their scattered clerical allies, they had hoped to prevent the ascendancy of the IRP, the revolutionary organizations, and the theocratic idea implicit in the principle of the sovereignty of the jurists. In his struggle for control and then for survival, Bani-Sadr looked to three sources of support: to the army, whose cause he championed; to Khomaini, who he believed, to the last minute, would "revert" to the true ideals of the revolution, and embrace the president; and to the mass of the people, who he hoped would move in his favor. However, the army remained for Bani-Sadr only a potential source of strength; given his own temperament, Khomaini's prestige, and the army's bitter experience following the overthrow of the monarchy, there was never a serious possibility the armed forces would be deployed against the ruling government.

Khomaini in the end acquiesced in and even helped orchestrate the destruction of Bani-Sadr; but he arrived at this position only with some reluctance and in stages. Not until 27 May did he single out Bani-Sadr for condemnation; after dismissing him as commander-in-chief on 10 June, he remained willing to see him retain the presidency; as late as 13 June, he acted to block the move in Parliament to have the president declared incompetent, and he left the door open to Bani-Sadr to "repent." In all this, Khomaini was not being altruistic. He wished to avoid bringing discredit on the institution of the presidency, to prevent a further split in the revolutionary coalition, and to deny the opposition yet another ally. Three reasons explain Khomaini's decision to turn against the president.

First, the IRP succeeded, after the events of 5 March, in creating a powerful momentum for the president's impeachment: by mobilizing the street crowds and gangs; by showing the president to be helpless while they arrested his aides, closed down his offices, and deprived him of authority in Parliament; and by a massive propaganda campaign. Emboldened by Khomaini's silence in the face of such activities, the IRP leaders created a climate of crisis, silenced their critics, and overwhelmed the waverers. As they had used the hostage crisis to secure the destruction of the Bazargan government, so now once again they used the crisis of the presidency to force Khomaini's hand. Eventually members of Khomaini's household who had supported the president, were forced by this tide of events to adopt a neutral stance. Eshraqi, Bani-Sadr's representative on the tripartite council, abandoned him.

Second, Bani-Sadr himself did little to assuage Khomaini's qualms about the course of events. He continued to make speeches and to engage in polemics. He continued, in Khomaini's eyes, to obstruct the work of the government. He made it easy for the IRP to depict the president as the source of the turmoil and faction in the country. More seriously, he began to appeal over Khomaini's head to the people. His call for "resistance" came to appear more and more as a call to open rebellion. In early June, shortly before his dismissal as commander-in-chief, he addressed air force and army personnel at Shiraz and Tehran airports, again stressing "resistance." He continued to affirm his loyalty to Khomaini; but as president, he was in the impossible position of considering the institutions of the state to be illegitimate. He was in effect asking Khomaini to choose between himself and the clerics who had been associated with Khomaini for a lifetime, between the "regular" institutions of government and the revolutionary organizations. Khomaini's decision was a foregone conclusion. In every confrontation between the clerical and the secular parties, between the revolutionary organizations and state institutions, over the past two years, the Imam had invariably thrown his weight behind the clerics and the revolutionary organizations. Khomaini's personal inclinations aside, power, in the administration and on the streets, was overwhelmingly in the hands of the IRP forces.

Third, Khomaini came to believe that Bani-Sadr's defiance was part of or at least a focus for a larger conspiracy to replace the Islamic state with a secular government. He was made uneasy by Bani-Sadr's overtures to Ayatollah Shirazi, by the support extended to the president by the Iran Freedom Movement, and by signs that the opposition forces were banding together. Reports of contacts between the Mojahedin and Bani-Sadr were especially damaging to the president. Khomaini believed that the president had given the Mojahedin permission to rearm; he knew that contacts between the Mojahedin leader, Rajavi, and the president had increased. His alarm grew when the Mojahedin brought their forces into the streets in support of the president in early June. In messages sent to Bani-Sadr through Ahmad, Eshraqi, and others, he reverted to these issues: Bani-Sadr had contacted other religious leaders, he was attempting to incite the army, he had forged an alliance with the Mojahedin, he was gathering under his umbrella the opposition forces. "I did not know," he said of the opposition groups in his radio address of 16 June, "that they would unite, that they would come together in one place."[57] Thus, despite the president's expectations and hopes, Khomaini did not turn against the clerical party to take up the president's cause; the prodigal father did not return to the embrace of the faithful son.

The popular uprising for which Bani-Sadr hoped did not materialize either. The overthrow of Bani-Sadr convulsed the country. But the loose coalition of forces behind the president lacked the breadth and strength to prevent either his elimination or the victory of the IRP and its allies. The distribution of forces at Bani-Sadr's fall from power differed considerably from that which obtained at the fall of the monarchy.

By February 1979, the Shah had lost credibility and standing among large elements of the politically active population. In June 1981, Khomaini's prestige, though diminished, remained considerable among the urban masses and within the revolutionary organizations. On the eve of the fall of both the Shah and Bani-Sadr, the army opted to stay out of politics. But in February 1979, the neutrality of the army was essentially a decision to acquiesce in the seizure of power by Khomaini's forces. It was a decision against the established government and in favor of the opposition. In June 1981, the neutrality of the army was essentially a decision not to support Bani-Sadr. It was a decision for the established government and against the challengers. Moreover, while the discipline of the Shah's army had been greatly eroded on the streets and its loyalty was in doubt, the determination of Khomaini's Revolutionary Guard, the armed retainers of the revolutionary committees, and the *hezbollahis* to put down the incipient insurrection was never shaken; these groups in fact set the pace in the bloody repression.

The Shah was brought down by a broad coalition of forces: the urban masses, the middle classes, and the intelligentsia all joined the movement. The merchants shut down the bazaars, the civil servants shut down the government, public services, and the oil industry; strikes in these sectors led to a close-down of factories, and together, bazaar, civil servants, oil industry workers, and factory workers paralyzed the country. The loose coalition that came together against the IRP in 1981 enjoyed the broad sympathy of the middle classes and, through left-wing groups, of the student population. But this support was limited in degree, due to the government's resources and ruthlessness, the towering presence of Khomaini, the IRP's ability to mobilize the streets, and general weariness of upheaval. On the critical days of June, the bazaars remained open, the banks continued to operate, the civil servants remained on the sidelines, and the factory workers did not lay down their tools.

The attempt of the opposition to challenge the IRP and the government forces on the streets proved equally unsuccessful. The middle classes were never mentally or physically equipped to deal with the club-wielding gangs of the ruling party; and the guerrilla organizations, with their young followers, proved no match for the studied violence of the *hezbollahis*. The Mojahedin rally of 10 June and the National Front rally of 15 June, the show of force, respectively, by the radical left and the moderate center, both failed sufficiently to galvanize the public. The change of tactics by the Mojahedin, on 20 and 21 June, from massive confrontation to hit-and-run attacks also failed to shake the government. In June 1981, the opposition again suffered a massive defeat; and the ensuing bloody warfare between left-wing and government forces did not, in the three years that followed, greatly alter this verdict.

Chapter 7

The Economics
of Divine Harmony

THE REVOLUTION led to considerable disruption and to far-reaching changes in the structure of the Iranian economy. In the short term, industrial activity declined and there was a shift away from industry and toward trade and commerce. Various land distribution schemes proved abortive; yet the pattern of private ownership in agriculture was disturbed and agricultural production suffered. The central planning machinery broke down, and the Plan and Budget Organization (PBO) lost control over the expenditures of the ministries and government agencies. Some measures were adopted to ameliorate the lot of the poor and to spread economic opportunities. But these had only limited impact. More significantly, the government took over large sectors of the economy through nationalization and expropriation, including banking, insurance, major industry, large-scale agriculture and construction, and an important part of foreign trade. It also involved itself in the domestic distribution of goods. As a result, the economic role of the state was greatly swollen and that of the private sector greatly diminished by the revolution.

These developments occurred as a result of ideology and conscious design, pressure from the streets and the momentum of the revolution, internal disorder and foreign war, and because in the first three years following the revolution, the government's answer to problems of a deteriorating economy was further nationalization and government control.

Ideological Roots

The revolutionaries in Iran came to power with ideological baggage that implied an economic as well as a political transformation of society. The direction of this transformation was foreshadowed in the literature of left-wing political groups and, more importantly, in a growing literature on "Islamic economics," writings concerned with the economic goals and policies of an Islamic society. Several lay and clerical figures in the years before the revolution devoted books, or parts of books, to the subject of Islamic economics.[1] Three works were particularly influential, however: Mahmud Taleqani's *Eslam va Malekiyyat* (Islam and Property), Mohammad-Baqer Sadr's *Iqtisaduna* (Our Economics), and Abol-Hasan Bani-Sadr's *Eqtesad-e Towhidi* (The Economics of Divine Harmony).[2]

Despite differences in emphasis and approach, Taleqani, Sadr, and Bani-Sadr shared three aims in common. First, and similarly to other writers on Islamic economics, they wished to show that Islam, like capitalism and Marxism, had its own unique economic philosophy and its own answers to contemporary economic problems. Their work was an exercise in the rejection of "alien" ideologies and in the assertion of a distinct, Islamic identity. Both Taleqani and Sadr devoted chapters to a refutation of capitalism and Marxism. The books of all three are sprinkled with references to the superiority of the Islamic approach to economic questions.

Second, all three authors sought to depict Islam as a religion committed to social justice, the equitable distribution of wealth, and the cause of the deprived classes. Thus, they attempted to use Islam as an instrument for social and economic reform, and to suggest to a younger generation attracted to socialism or Marxism that Islam also could serve as a vehicle for social transformation. Third, they wished to prove that the economic system and doctrines they were advancing could be derived, systematically and in a manner acceptable to Islamic jurists, from the Koran and the authoritative texts on Islamic jurisprudence. They were contributors to the debate within the clerical community regarding the extent to which Islamic law and doctrine could be reinterpreted to allow for the more equitable distribution of wealth, tampering with property rights, and state regulation of the economy.

Mahmud Taleqani, the son of a politically active cleric, was born in Taleqan in northern Iran in 1911, completed his religious studies in Qom, and began to teach and preach in Tehran in 1939. He devoted the next forty years to various political causes, in association with politically minded religious leaders like Ayatollah Abol-Qasem Kashani and religiously minded political leaders like Mehdi Bazargan. He was active in preaching in support of Mossadegh and the oil nationalization movement in 1951–53. In association with other National Front figures, he helped found the National Resistance Movement in 1957; and in association with Mehdi Bazargan, he founded the Iran Freedom Movement (IFM) in 1961. In the 1970s he befriended the members of the Mojahedin-e Khalq, whose leaders looked to him as teacher and guide. Taleqani's political activities earned him several terms in exile and prison, the first time in 1940. Between 1964 and 1978, he spent nearly a decade in jail, in the sixties for his activities in the IFM, and in the seventies for his association with the Mojahedin.

Taleqani's greatest influence lay in his teaching of Koranic exegesis. As early as 1940, he established the *Kanun-e Eslami* (Islamic Society) and began semiclandestine classes in the Koran. These classes continued during the decades that followed, attracting large numbers of students, and inspiring many imitators. Taleqani taught two generations of young Iranians to regard the Koran as a living document, with a relevance to contemporary problems and a concern for social justice, and as a spur to political activism. Taleqani's association with Bazargan, which spanned four decades, began with these classes. Many of the prominent leaders in the revolutionary movement, including Ebrahim Yazdi and Mostafa Chamran, attended these classes. At least three founders of the Mojahedin-e Khalq were Taleqani's students. In subsequent years, secular political activitists, including the Mojahedin's ideologue, Ahmad Reza'i, the Mojahedin leaders, Mas'ud Rajavi and Musa Khiabani, and the first president of the Islamic Republic, Bani-Sadr, applied Taleqani's techniques to draw their own political lessons from the Koran.

In *Eslam va Malekiyyat*, Taleqani began with the proposition that God had made available, through the bounties of nature, sufficient resources to provide for the material well-being of all mankind. Each individual was free to exploit these resources to the extent of his needs and abilities. Each was free to cultivate unclaimed land, to work mines, to hunt, fish, and gather fuel and fodder. Islam, however, also sought to ensure each member of the community equal access to and a fair share of these resources. It did so by regulating economic transactions and activities, preferring the interests of the community to the interests of the individual, vesting in Islamic government the authority to enforce principles of equity, and requiring each Muslim to act justly. In developing these themes, Taleqani often simply reiterated traditional Islamic views as regarding, for example, the laws of inheritance or of contract. But his method was to read into these laws a strongly egalitarian intention, to seek to give practical economic application to the moral principles of Islam, to suggest that under Islam the unjust economic conditions prevailing in the Iran of his own day would be corrected in the interests of the poor, and to look to a vaguely defined Islamic state to institute economic and social justice.

Taleqani made no concerted attack on property. He acknowledged that private capital, which he defined as a form of "stored labor," played a legitimate and productive role. He praised the contribution of the merchant and the middleman to commercial life. He strongly defended the Islamic laws of inheritance. At times, he appeared to suggest that in order to create an equitable social order it would be sufficient to observe the Islamic ban on usury, hoarding, and monopoly, to collect the Islamic taxes on land *(kharaj)* and wealth *(khoms),* and the Islamic charitable contributions *(zakat* and *sadaqat),* and to enforce the Islamic laws of contract and inheritance. Yet he often gave these conventional observations an unconventional twist.

Islamic inheritance laws would seem to contravene Taleqani's assertion that in Islam only work establishes ownership rights; but he treated them as a praiseworthy incentive to productive enterprise (since men desire to guarantee the material well-being of their wives and offspring), and as a mechanism for distributing wealth (since rules specifically determine the division of the inheritance among family members). The Islamic laws of contract, which provide for sharecropping, tenancies, rentals, payment of workers on the bases of wages or piecework, and various forms of partnership would not seem to be inherently egalitarian; but Taleqani suggested that in Islam the worker himself may choose whether to work for wages, for a share in profits, or as a partner in the enterprise. Islamic taxes have traditionally not been onerous; but

Taleqani asserted that an Islamic government may levy the land tax at whatever level it deems necessary and use the proceeds to assist the peasantry. Agricultural land can be privately owned; but if left idle, Taleqani wrote, it must be distributed to the poor cultivators.

Confronted with laws and rulings that appeared to go against the grain of such an egalitarian interpretation, Taleqani appealed to the moral principles of Islam. The Koran, he noted, repeatedly enjoins equity and treats wealth not as an end in itself but as a means better to do God's will. Specific Islamic rulings regarding property, as other matters, must reflect these moral principles and cannot contravene them. If past Islamic rulings appeared sometimes to be tinged with a capitalist mentality, he wrote, this was due to the exigencies of the time and not to the spirit of Islam. Islamic rulings must, moreover, evolve to meet the needs of the time, and Islamic jurists and the Islamic ruler were responsible for deriving from these basic principles of equity the rules and laws to meet society's changing requirements.

More importantly, Taleqani argued that Islamic government, vested in the person of the imam, exists to establish equity and is authorized, in the public interest, to exercise supervision over the acquisition and disposal of property. The imam is authorized to limit the individual's freedom to engage in economic activity or to exploit natural resources which belong to the entire community. If an individual has more than his fair share of goods, his rights may be limited. The powers of the Islamic government in this regard were extensive, Taleqani suggested, going beyond even the express provisions of the law:

> . . . where the rights of the individual and those of society are in conflict, [Islamic government] is empowered to limit individual ownership to a greater degree than the law may authorise.[3]

Eslam va Malekiyyat is also an anguished cry in defense of "the hungry, barefoot, homeless and deprived," and against a capitalism which Taleqani invariably depicted as grasping and exploitative. He decried a system under which "the capitalists are free to suck the workers dry and then cast aside their empty shells without taking any responsibility."[4] Unlike the governments of his own day, he suggested, an Islamic government would not shut its eyes to "the withering scourges and piercing swords the kings and slaveholders aim at the bodies of slaves and peasants,"[5] or throw the power of the state behind exploitative landlords and capitalists.

Taleqani depicted as the Islamic ideal the community established by the Prophet at Medina, where the Prophet's companions from Medina and Mecca (*ansar* and *muhajirin*) shared equally in the material goods of society:

> In this exemplary city, a portion of the private wealth of the *Ansar* was given to the *Muhajirin,* and, except for a small portion of private fortunes, wealth was superintended by the state; apart from special allotments given to those participating in *jihad,* it was divided among all equally, to each according to his need. Individuals had no special distinctions; ruler and ruled were not set apart except in their capacities of governing and being governed. No noticeable difference existed in their houses and clothing.[6]

Mohammad Baqer Sadr was born in Iraq in 1930 to a prominent and learned Shi'a clerical family of Arab origin, whose members are to be found in Iran and Lebanon as well as Iraq. Sadr studied and then taught at the famous seminary at Najaf. He rapidly gained a wide following for his scholarship and the political relevance of his teaching. A prolific writer, he published a number of books and numerous pamphlets under the general rubric of *al-Madrasa al-Islamiyya* (The School of Islam) on Islamic government, the prophetic mission, interest-free banking, and aspects of Islamic history. His most important books are *Falsafatuna* (Our Philosophy) and *Iqtisaduna.* Sadr called for a social revolution against exploitation and injustice and for a government based on Islamic principles. In the 1970s he moved closer to Khomaini's view that sovereignty in such a government devolved on the Islamic jurists, as heirs to the mantle of the Prophet. He also came to be associated with *al-Da'wa al-Islamiyya* (The Call of Islam), a militant Shi'a movement founded in the 1960s, one of whose goals was to establish an Islamic government in the Shi'a regions of Iraq. Inspired by the Islamic Revolution in Iran, which he regarded as a model for other Islamic states, Sadr stepped up his pamphleteering and propaganda activities. He was executed for these activities by the Iraqi president, Saddam Hussein, in April 1980.

Four aspects of Sadr's work on Islamic economics make up its distinctive character. First, Sadr surrounded his economic theories with all the paraphernalia of both Western and Islamic scholarship. He consciously set out to elaborate, in the manner of an Adam Smith or a Marx, a complete economic system. He wrote with the model of standard Western or Marxist texts on economics in mind. He sought therefore to develop his case systematically, footnoted copiously, and took care to define, in Islamic terms, such key concepts as wages, profit, added value, structure, and superstructure. At the same time, he sought to root his arguments firmly in Islamic legal texts and opinions, cited a range of varying and often conflicting legal opinions, and presented reasons for preferring one opinion to another. His arguments were perhaps not always persuasive. Nevertheless, the grounding of *Iqtisaduna* in Islamic legal sources, the marshaling of evidence from recognized jurists, the method of argumentation itself, go a long way to explain the great influence Sadr's book came to exercise in the postrevolution period. His work served as a textbook for Iranian clerics seeking legal justification for egalitarian social policies and state intervention in the economy.

Second, Sadr developed further the idea that Islamic law places limitations on the acquisition and disposal of property. He was of course aware of the many ways in which property may be acquired legitimately, transacted, disposed of, and inherited in Islam. But he sought considerably to limit the concept of private property, and he so hedged it around with conditions as virtually to rule out any form of "absolute" ownership. He wrote that Islam provides for government, public, and private ownership, but defined private ownership in very narrow terms, as implying only a "priority right of use," "a special relationship between the individual and property which denies others the use of it."[7] He appealed to the history of the early Islamic conquests and the manner in which territories were added to the Islamic empire to argue that ultimate ownership in all but a very limited category of land was vested in the Islamic community; that individuals acquired rights of use, not property, over land; and that these rights could under a variety of circumstances lapse, be withdrawn, or revert to the community. He asserted that even where land is deemed to be private property, as for example in the case of the land owned by the early voluntary converts to Islam, such ownership remained conditional on continued cultivation and on the advancement of general good:

> Private ownership [of land] . . . is not absolute and is limited in duration, in the sense that if the owner fails to carry out his responsibilities in developing and cultivating the land, his rights lapse and he may no longer dispose of the land; for his action diminishes society's capacity to produce and results in the deprivation of others.[8]

By extension, Sadr suggested, similar conditions applied to the exploitation of other natural resources. Moreover, the Islamic ban on hoarding, waste, and overconsumption were to be taken literally. Violation of these principles, or the misuse of wealth, could also lead to a loss of ownership rights. Individual property could be limited by the need to maintain "social equilibrium" and to ensure each member of the community a decent standard of living.

Third, Sadr envisioned a major role for the state in economic activity, partly as an engine for economic development, partly as a means of limiting private enterprise. A state itself would undertake the major industrial and economic projects that in capitalist societies were carried out by private enterprise; large private concentrations of wealth simply would not exist.

> Private capital for the most part will lack the means and power to achieve in commerce and industry a size and strength that threatens the social equilibrium. . . . Private economic activity will remain within reasonable limits . . . and will not create class differences. As a result, the creation of large industrial enterprises will fall within the sphere, authority and activity of the government.[9]

Finally, Sadr found in the figure of the Islamic jurist, the *vali-ye amr* (Khomaini's *faqih*, Taleqani's imam), the mechanism through which programs of social reform could be carried out and attendant doctrinal problems overcome. Sadr vested the *vali-ye amr* with wide discretionary powers. Islam, he noted, designates all human acts according to a five-fold division, as religiously required, recommended, indifferent, reprehensible, or prohibited. He argued that the *vali-ye amr* could not tamper with those acts that were expressly required or specified, such as the performance of the five daily prayers or the observance of the fast; the *vali* could not suspend the Islamic laws on inheritance. The *vali* was also not authorized to permit what is expressly prohibited, such as usury or the consumption of alcohol. This was a sphere of "primary" religious rulings, where no flexibility obtained. However, there remained a whole intermediate category of actions whose performance was merely recommended, ill-advised, or regarded as neither inherently good or bad. Here, in what Sadr described as "the discretionary sphere of the law," the *vali-ye amr* enjoyed considerable authority and could issue "secondary" rulings to regulate human affairs.[10]

> The *vali-ye amr* has the authority, on the basis of a secondary ruling to prohibit or require any act or measure not expressly prohibited or required. Therefore any time he prohibits an indifferent act, that indifferent act is prohibited, and any time he recommends its implementation, it is required.[11]

Sadr suggested that a large part of the Islamic regulations relating to property and economic activity lay in the sphere of discretionary law and that the *vali*'s authority to rule on these "secondary" matters constituted the "dynamic element" in the law. It allowed the jurist, in his role as leader of the community, to regulate the relations between men, society, and material resources in keeping with advances in technology, the requirements of the time, and changing concepts of human needs. Thus, like Khomaini and Taleqani, Sadr vested the ultimate leadership of the Islamic community in the jurist. But he also reached back to earlier traditions to define a specific sphere of secondary rulings and discretionary law, where the jurist enjoyed extensive authority; and he identified the goal of social justice as a legitimate object of these discretionary powers.

Abol-Hasan Bani-Sadr drew heavily on the ideas of Taleqani and particularly of Mohammad-Baqer Sadr. But *Eqtesad-e Towhidi* represents in one important respect a departure from these earlier works. Bani-Sadr uncoupled Islamic economics from its Islamic moorings. He too quoted extensively from the Koran and Islamic sources to support his views. But Bani-Sadr conveys the impression not of a jurist grappling with the complicated doctrinal problems of interpreting Islam in the light of "socialist" theory, but of a layman drawing eclectically on Islamic texts to arrive at predetermined conclusions. At the same time, he offered not so much a systematic economic theory as a series of tenuously linked assertions, not so much practical prescriptions as a generalized picture of an ideal society. Absolute ownership, he argued, belongs only to God. Each man has the right only to the fruits of his own labor. No man may exploit another. Wealth acquired through domination or the exercise of force, for example through the power to set wages, is illegitimate. All economic relations that lead to inequality or to the concentration of wealth are unIslamic.

While each person is the master of his own work, the "surplus" earnings of each member of the community belongs to the society. By taking its share, society serves not only the interests of the community but the individual himself, for wealth leads to domination and domination corrupts the wielder of power. In Islam, all property will ultimately revert to its "natural state," and be commonly owned; each will place the fruits of his labor at the disposal of all and take only what he needs:

> According to the principle of *towhid* [divine harmony, divine unity] . . . the transfer of property is from the private to the public and social sphere. Thus all property, the conditions for whose transfer to public ownership exist, are transferred to this form of ownership.[12]

Like Taleqani and Mohammad-Baqer Sadr, Bani-Sadr envisioned a role for the imam in establishing social justice. But concerned to prevent the concentration of power in the hands of any central authority, he remained equivocal on this question. On the one hand, he depicted the imam as the "continuous repository of the consensus of the community," the administrator of the common property of both present and future generations, and the "executive representative of God."[13] On the other hand, in keeping with his theory of a "generalized imamate," he depicted common property rights as vested in some unspecified fashion in the community as a whole.

Bani-Sadr's economic views thus served as a kind of bridge between the ideas of those trained in Islamic jurisprudence and the ideologies of those, like the Mojahedin and the Fadayan, committed to radical economic policies. Bani-Sadr rejected the emphasis of the Mojahedin and the Fadayan on class and their use of dialectics as an analytical tool, believing that Islam's "harmonious" world view left no room for either. But he shared with the Mojahedin the technique of drawing on Islam to buttress political and economic views and with both groups the vision of a classless society, a commitment to the common ownership of property, a faith in the efficacy of autonomous, self-administrating economic units, and a belief in the overriding importance of freeing Iran from the domination of multinational corporations.

The writings of Bani-Sadr and Taleqani on Islamic economics, and even Sadr's intellectually more rigorous effort, left a host of unresolved problems, both of a doctrinal and a practical nature.[14] The complexity of these problems, and the political divisions they would engender, became apparent only much later. Here, it is sufficient to note that by the time of the revolution, these and similar works had played a significant role in undercutting the legitimacy of private property and in yoking Islam and the ideal of social justice to the same cart.

"They Have Destroyed Everything"

Having seized power, the revolutionaries were confronted with seemingly staggering economic problems. The treasury was nearly empty. The equivalent of $700 million remaining in the government's account with the Central Bank was used up in a few days to cover debts and shore up shaky institutions. The government had to resort to printing money and to borrowing from the Central Bank. Huge deficits were looming. The Shah's government, in a futile attempt to win support among civil servants in the fall of 1978, had granted increases in wages and benefits worth $3 billion a year. Months of strikes had reduced anticipated government revenues right across the line: from oil exports by $7 billion, from customs duties by over $1 billion, from cigarette sales by nearly $300 million. A $47 billion budget for 1979–80, drawn up before the fall of the monarchy, projected a deficit of over $15 billion.[15]

The banking system appeared to be near collapse. Anxious depositors had withdrawn funds from the banks on a massive scale, either to transfer to accounts abroad or to stuff in the proverbial mattresses at home. The flight of capital had begun in the months leading up to the revolution and continued after the overthrow of the Shah. In the five months between September 1978 and January 1979, the outflow of bank deposits topped $4 billion.[16] Many banks were unable to meet depositors' claims, were rationing out withdrawals among their customers, and were kept afloat only by infusions of credit from the Central Bank. The banks had also extended substantial loans to members of the royal family, contractors, industrialists, and businessmen who had already left the country, and to industries whose major shareholders were gone. There was little expectation that these loans would be repaid.

Foreign technicians had departed, leaving dozens of major government-financed projects—steel mills, petrochemical plants, copper works, wood-processing industries, power generation plants, nuclear reactors, and many road, port, and construction projects—half completed. Great cranes stood idle above unfinished office and apartment blocks. Lay-offs and closedowns had left 2.5 million men and women out of work, nearly 1 million of them construction workers employed by private contractors involved in government projects.[17] Many contractors, not paid by the government, were not paying their workers. The future of numerous projects was in any case in doubt.

On the factory floor, a near chaotic situation prevailed. Even financially sound industries were strapped for cash. Others, after months of stoppages, raw material shortages, and decline in markets were in serious difficulty. Some had been thoroughly squeezed by their departed owners. Most were heavily indebted to the banks. The large industries "are all bankrupt," Prime Minister Bazargan alleged. "The owners and shareholders have gone; they have taken the money and left us with a heritage of debts and difficulties."[18] Owners and managers who had remained behind were under siege. Middle-level employees and technicians in dozens of enterprises were leading a revolt against their superiors, whom they hoped to replace. Workers had organized councils and Islamic committees and were demanding higher wages and benefits. Some employees and workers were also pressing for a purge of "collaborators," a say in management, production, and sales, and the right to examine company books. In order to press their demands, workers sometimes took owners or managers hostage, expelled them from the factory, or had them arrested. The ministry of labor was besieged by complaints filed by both workers and management, locked in insoluble disputes.

Worker militancy was being encouraged by several outside elements. Activists from left-wing political groups such as the Fadayan and Paykar tried to organize workers and encourage them to take over their factories. The pressure from the political left for radical measures was considerable. Abol-Hasan Bani-Sadr, an "establishment" figure whose views were widely believed to reflect those of Khomaini, was addressing huge crowds of students and workers on Islamic economics. In the revolutionary courts and committees, there were invariably clerics and guardsmen ready to back militant workers against their employers. Khomaini himself continued to direct his powerful invective against the privileged classes.

The government of Mehdi Bazargan was thus buffeted by conflicting currents. It needed to restore order in the factories, start up production, reduce unemployment, and prevent the flight of capital and expertise. It also needed to respond to the expectation that the old order would be overturned in the interests of the underprivileged, that wealth would be distributed, that the dominant classes would be brought down and humiliated. Thus the prime minister castigated the "bloated capitalists," even while he urged workers to observe discipline and accept direction from employers and managers. Without a trace of irony, the minister of justice invited industrialists and businessmen to return from abroad, and promised them government protection, even while the government stood helplessly by as businessmen were carted off to jail and their enterprises were seized by revolutionary bodies.

The economic crisis was perhaps not as catastrophic as the revolutionaries claimed. Foreign exchange reserves stood at over $13 billion. Iran's foreign debt was small. With little effort, oil exports could bring revenues of over $20 billion annually. After a decade and a half of rapid development, the country was endowed with an extensive infrastructure of roads, ports, airports, communications networks, power-generating plants, and the foundations of a metallurgical industry. The private sector had built up a considerable capacity for the production of consumer durables and mass consumption goods. If many entrepreneurs had left the country, many remained behind. The country could draw on a rich pool of educated and experienced civil servants, economists, engineers, technicians, and managers. But it was the sense of turmoil and crisis that influenced and then overwhelmed government officials; and revolutionary leaders irresponsibly fed the impression of impending economic catastrophe. Bani-Sadr and left-wing political groups popularized the idea that the former regime had wrecked the economy. Khomaini took up this view. "They went," he said, "and left us a country in ruins." Ebrahim Yazdi echoed him. "They have destroyed everything," he asserted. "The country's economy is bankrupt. Agriculture is destroyed."[19] Such talk implied radical surgery.

Out of these conflicting cross-currents there emerged a series of officially sanctioned measures and unauthorized actions, of decrees issued by the government and the Revolutionary Council, and of ad hoc orders issued by local revolutionary courts and judges, that eventually saw the transfer of a sizable part of private industry and businesses to the control of the state.

Banking, Insurance, and Industry

The government took several immediate steps to ameliorate the situation and to permit private enterprises to resume operations. It authorized the payment of nearly $85 million in outstanding claims to contractors working for the government, and promised $200 million more. It provided $110 million for loans to allow industries to meet their payrolls and their raw material requirements. This sum, seemingly large, was hardly adequate. It established a fund of over $130 million for short-term loans to certain categories of unemployed wage earners.[20] Importers were granted deferred payment from some customs charges; and the government mandated a three- to six-month extension on overdue private sector promissory notes. More substantial measures soon followed.[21]

On 8 June, the Revolutionary Council nationalized the banking system. Twenty-seven privately owned banks, thirteen of them joint ventures with minority foreign share holdings, were affected. The prime minister and the director of the Plan and Budget Organization, Ali-Akbar Mo'infar, said the takeover was necessary in view of the huge foreign and domestic indebtedness of some of the banks, and in order to guard against bankruptcies, secure private deposits, and protect the "national interest," a reference to fears the private banks would be used to siphon off more money to accounts abroad. Mo'infar also described the nationalization as a first step toward creating a banking system in keeping with the Islamic ban on interest. The nationalized banks were subsequently merged with government-owned banks to create five specialized banking entities in the fields of commerce (two groups), agriculture, industries and mines, and housing and construction. Bank Saderat, one of the country's largest banks, with an extensive branch–banking network, was charged with providing provincial and regional banking services. Two large and financially sound government-owned commercial banks, Melli and Sepah, continued to operate as independent units, as did the much smaller Workers' Welfare Bank. The nationalization of the country's fifteen privately owned insurance companies followed on 25 June.

The government had already moved to appoint supervisors to such major private industrial enterprises as the Iran National automobile works in Tehran and the Shahriyar pipe and rolling mills complex at Ahwaz in the south. Once the government began to provide new funding for industrial enterprises, further state intervention became virtually inevitable. On 14 June the Revolutionary Council approved a measure, the Law for the Appointment of Managers, authorizing the government to appoint managers to all enterprises which had shut down, were deemed incapable of continuing operations, or whose owners were absent. Government-appointed managers began to appear at dozens of industrial and agricultural enterprises and construction and trading firms. These managers initially worked with managing boards composed of government representatives and representatives of employee committees who, in many instances, were in effective control of their enterprises. In due course, the rights of signature and financial control and the power to appoint boards of directors were transferred to government appointees. Even where enterprises were not eventually nationalized, effective control shifted to the state.

On 5 July, the Revolutionary Council approved the single most sweeping nationalization measure of the revolution. The Law for the Protection and Expansion of Iranian Industry provided for the nationalization of industries in three broad categories: (1) "heavy" industries, including metals, automobile assembly, chemicals, shipbuilding, aircraft manufacture, and mining; (2) industries owned by fifty specifically named individuals and one family, who had allegedly acquired their wealth illicitly through influence with the outgoing regime; and (3) industries in economic difficulty whose liabilities exceeded their net assets. Overnight, the Islamic Republic acquired ownership of the largest part of the country's private industry.

Among the industries nationalized were the huge Iran National automobile works, with 12,000 workers, and half-a-dozen other car and truck assembly plants; the Shahriyar pipe and rolling complex in the south; the Behshahr industrial group, with 13,500 employees; and pharmaceutical concerns, oil refineries, tire plants, and glass, brick, and tile factories. The government acquired a broad range of consumer goods industries. Among these was the Melli shoe and leather industrial empire, a complex of twenty-six factories, with 10,000 employees and a turnover in the year before the revolution of $450 million. Also nationalized were department stores, a supermarket chain, home furniture and carpet manufacturers, wine and soft drink manufacturing plants, vegetable oil industries, and producers of synthetic fibers, textiles, and clothing. The Iran–Polyacril synthetic fiber industry alone represented an investment of over $200 million; Hojabr Yazdani's livestock empire was producing 120,000 tons of lamb a year; the Karun sugar cane plant 100,000 tons of sugar annually.

The list of industrialists whose property had been expropriated was haphazard; it seemed to have been drawn up hastily. The criteria by which some were included and some excluded from the nationalization order were difficult to discern. A number of major industrialists did not have their property expropriated, but some of those whose names appeared on the list were not major owners of industry. One, Ali Hajj Tarkhani, was an industrialist but also an important figure in the bazaar who had contributed generously to the clerical cause.

In the weeks and months that followed, further legislation was approved to close loopholes in the law. The nationalization order was extended to cover shareholdings of brothers and sisters, as well as those of wives and children, of individuals whose assets had been taken over. In August 1980, Parliament authorized the government to decide the fate of small shareholders in nationalized and expropriated enterprises. These secondary shareholders also became subject to nationalization or saw their shares virtually written off as being of no value. Further measures led to the nationalization of specific areas of economic activity, for example of pharmaceutical industries, cold stores, warehousing, and trucking. The Law for the Appointment of Managers and the Law for the Protection and Expansion of Iranian Industry were in any case written broadly enough to allow the authorities almost unlimited freedom of action. The tempo of expropriations considerably slowed down in the second year of the revolution; but nationalizations and takeovers were occurring as late as mid-1982, as the government moved to clarify the status of industries, trading companies, or businesses, particularly in cases where it had already assumed management control, or where major shareholders had remained abroad. In 1982, the shares of absentee owners of a number of medium-sized industries that had escaped expropriation were taken over by the government. Numerous construction and engineering consulting firms were reorganized, with absentee owners losing their ownership rights.

A body of legislation was gradually developed, providing a "legal" framework for state takeover of business firms and enterprises. But often legislation was produced after the fact to justify property seizures that had already taken place. In July 1980, for example, the Revolutionary Council approved a bill implicitly recognizing and legalizing the expropriation of large agricultural enterprises that had already been seized by revolutionary organizations, the ministry of agriculture, or the courts.[22] Much expropriation took place in only a quasi-legal framework, or without any authorization in law. The Foundation for the Disinherited *(Bonyad-e Mostaz'afin)* was particularly active in such seizures.

The foundation was established in March 1979 to administer the expropriated property of members of the former royal family and "all persons who acquired wealth through relations with this family." Backed by its own gun-toting revolutionary guards and Islamic judges, and armed with another imprecisely worded law, the foundation went on the initiative and took over a large number of businesses, industries, agricultural enterprises, office and apartment blocs. Other property seizures were ordered by judges of the revolutionary courts, often acting on their own initiative, both in Tehran and the provinces. Such property was sometimes turned over to the Foundation for the Disinherited, sometimes to other revolutionary or government organizations, and sometimes retained and administered by local bodies. In the summer of 1979, Sadeq Khalkhali, acting on his authority as an Islamic judge, ordered the expropriation of the property of numerous individuals. Only some of the persons affected subsequently succeeded in having these orders canceled.

The zeal of revolutionary judges and organizations, worker and employee militancy, and financial and managerial difficulties, rather than government intent, explain the takeover of numerous industries not initially touched by the Law for the Appointment of Managers of 14 June and the nationalization decree of 5 July.[23] As already noted, the 5 July decree was not comprehensive in its coverage. In addition to a number of large industries, numerous small industries, employing a few dozen to a couple of hundred workers and considered of insufficient significance, were also left alone. Moreover, some government officials lost their enthusiasm for nationalization when they discovered such takeovers meant responsibility for labor unrest, bank debts, and the litigation initiated by foreign partners. An incomplete audit subsequently conducted by the Foundation for the Disinherited, for example, indicated that firms taken over by the foundation owed the banks over $1.2 billion. This did not include the liabilities of one businessman, Hojabr Yazdani, who alone left behind debts and accumulated interest exceeding several hundred million dollars.[24]

In some instances where employees seized control and ousted the former management, officials were inclined to look the other way as long as the new management was able to pay its way and maintain order. Within the revolutionary courts, committees, and organizations, some individuals connived at or acquiesced in unauthorized seizures; but others, after the first flush of takeovers, were more concerned with maintaining order and in any case disapproved of seizures initiated by workers and staff. However, other factors intervened to force the pace of takeovers; and while the general trend was toward state control of private industry, circumstances varied considerably from enterprise to enterprise.

The government, for example, did not nationalize Arj industries (consumer durables), or Minoo industries (biscuits and confectionery), both large and financially sound enterprises. However, at Arj, members of the founding family had left the country. Employees assumed management control and themselves invited the Foundation for the Disinherited to step in. At Minoo, the founder and major shareholder, Ali Khosrowshahi, continued for several months after the revolution to run his own factory. But a factory engineer organized the more militant workers and employees. Habibollah Payman, leader of the Islamic-leftist Jonbesh-e Mosalmanan-e Mobarez, came to the factory, addressed a workers' rally, and urged the workers to nationalize the plant. In due course, employees took Khosrowshahi hostage, held him for eight days, and demanded he surrender ownership, while several hundred members of the Revolutionary Guard, dispatched by the head of the Tehran revolutionary committees, Ayatollah Mahdavi-Kani, massed outside, threatening to break up the takeover by force. In the end, however, no collision took place. The militants won out, and the government assumed control of the factory.

In dozens of instances, owners who hoped to hold on to their enterprises were driven away by worker militancy, the inability or unwillingness to meet payrolls, and by deteriorating financial conditions. In some cases, hard-pressed owners welcomed a takeover by the authorities. In other instances, the government was forced to move in when employees took over the management and proved unable to run their enterprises or to remain financially solvent. At Jahan Chit, a large textile factory employing several thousand workers, on the other hand, employees took over from the old management and ran the plant successfully. But the government assumed control anyway.

Other industrial enterprises survived in the hands of their owners for many months because of strong finances, good labor relations, a tradition of religious philanthropy, and a workable arrangement with local clerical leaders. Yazdbaf, a large textile factory with two thousand employees in the city of Yazd, initially remained in the hands of its owners after the revolution, mainly because of a favorable local reputation as well as arrangements reached with Ayatollah Mohammad Sadduqi, the powerful clerical leader in the city. Under formal agreements, the entire production of the plant, valued at around $40 million annually, was turned over to a foundation Sadduqi had established. The foundation then acted as nominal "distributor" and marketed the textiles to retailers, earning the foundation $4 million a year. Such arrangements, based on a network of local relationships, secured for some enterprises the protection of influential individuals and permitted industries to survive and operate efficiently under volatile political conditions. Yazdbaf and similar enterprises did not often remain under the control of their owners. But they were not nationalized either. Having survived the first flush of expropriations, they came to constitute an intermediate category of industries that, in the absence of their major stockholders, continued to operate largely under their former managers and relatively free from government control. However, even large industrialists who survived the early expropriations and takeovers later also quit the country. "In the end, the game was not worth the candle, "explained one such industrialist, who successfully administered over ten family-owned factories and trading companies for a year after the revolution.

"The profits were good, even mind-boggling. But there was nothing you could do with the money; your every move was watched; and the harassment was constant."

Individual factories experienced waves of employee militancy and changes in management, often paralleling changes in the composition of those who controlled the government. As Bazargan was replaced by Bani-Sadr and Bani-Sadr outflanked by Mohammad Ali Raja'i and his IRP colleagues, so too at the factory level, management passed to more radical elements, or at least elements more in tune with the Islamic party. Leadership of the militant forces in manufacturing enterprises tended to come primarily from middle-level technical and managerial staff, and also from skilled workers. The workers, after the initial and politicized phase of plant takeovers, tended to be more concerned with the concrete questions of wages, benefits, and working conditions. Workers, for example, did not always welcome participation in management or in factory ownership. At the Qazvin glass factory, a worker was invited to sit on the board of directors, but he begged off when he found himself on the receiving end of worker dissatisfaction. At the Sassan bottling plant, workers rejected the offer of shares in the factory. They preferred secure wages. The desire for job and salary security explains the demand of many factory employees to have their plants nationalized.

At the end of 1982, when the nationalization and expropriation fever appeared to have abated, the Iran National Industries Organization, established to administer the nationalized industries, was in control of 500 to 600 industrial enterprises, with over 150,000 workers. Another 200 to 300 factories, some 100 construction companies (60 percent of them active and handling $2 billion worth of construction work), 150–200 commerical firms, 91 poultry, livestock, and agricultural enterprises, with a total of 90,000 employees, and over 1,000 buildings with 5,730 offices and apartments, were in the hands of the Foundation for the Disinherited.[25] The ministry of commerce had acquired responsibility for seventeen of the country's largest trading firms, involved in the importation of heavy machinery, construction equipment, motors, spare parts, and raw materials, and the bulk of the country's cold storage plants.[26] The ministry of finance and economic affairs had taken over the country's largest warehousing firms and, along with the ministry of commerce, was also in charge of eight of the largest trucking companies.

Only smaller industries remained in private hands. To cite some examples: the Minoo biscuit factory, with 6,000 workers, was nationalized; the Gorji biscuit factory, with 200 workers, remained under private ownership. The Behshahr vegetable oil company, with 35 percent of the market, was nationalized; The smaller Jahan and Naz-e Isfahan vegetable oil industries were not. The destruction of the old industrial elite created some new opportunities. Some of the smaller factories flourished, taking advantage of general shortages and the decline in the role of the large industrial enterprises. Small new entrepreneurs were able to move into the interstices created by the flight of the old industrial bourgeoisie. In 1982, the government itself adopted measures to widen ownership in engineering consulting firms and construction companies tendering for government contracts. But at the same time, a new privileged business elite emerged, utilizing links with powerful clerics and government officials close to the administration, and waxing rich on the control of import licenses, scarce resources, and land. The major impact of the revolutionary government's policies in the area of banking, insurance, industry, construction, and trade was not, therefore, to distribute wealth and economic opportunity more widely. It was, rather, to further fatten that already overfed leviathan—the government.

Housing and Urban Land

The revolutionary government was also hard pressed to provide housing for the urban poor. Many of those who had marched against the Shah were drawn from the badly housed population of the great urban centers. In mid-1977, a policeman was killed in a working-class district in south Tehran in the course of violent riots over housing policy. Not surprisingly, Khomaini accorded a high priority to the housing issue. "We will build homes for the poor all over Iran," he pledged in a major address on 1 March, just two weeks after the revolution.[27]

In the immediate postrevolution period, some housing shortages were eased by spontaneous action. Shantytown dwellers in Tehran and other urban centers, taking advantage of the breakdown in municipal controls, started a boom in do-it-yourself housing by building for themselves on lands lying just outside city limits and previously closed to construction. The more enterprising took over and built homes on private land within towns and cities. Members of the revolutionary committees routinely appropriated for their own use the homes of individuals they considered linked to the former regime.

However, housing problems quickly mounted. Rural migrants poured into urban centers, convinced that at the dawn of the revolutionary era the Imam would freely distribute land and housing to the deprived and deserving classes. In the prevailing uncertainty, private investment in large-scale housing construction virtually collapsed. For a long time after the revolution, the government remained incapable of planning and executing a sizable housing program. All this intensified pressures for more extreme measures.

A vociferous advocate of radical measures emerged from within the ranks of the clerical leaders in the person of Ayatollah Hadi Khosrowshahi, the director of the Housing Foundation. The foundation was established in June 1979, at Khomaini's behest, to provide housing for the poor through private contributions. But Khosrowshahi used the foundation as a platform to agitate for the seizure and distribution of private land and dwellings. He drew attention to the large number of apartments standing empty in Tehran. He wondered aloud why some families occupied multibedroomed houses while others were crowded into single rooms. He boasted he could solve the housing problem overnight if the government would only permit him to take over empty homes and apartment blocks, to exercise control over rents and real estate transactions, and to house several families in the city's large and wealthier dwellings. In preparation for such a step, young staffers from his organization for a while went around Tehran knocking on doors and noting down the number of residents and rooms in each dwelling. Khosrowshahi had the backing of elements within the IRP. His proposals were hugely popular among the urban masses, and they were echoed by left-wing groups. In the summer of 1979, militants from Paykar and the Fadayan led young men and women in the occupation of empty apartment buildings around Tehran University and of first-class hotels elsewhere in the capital, utilizing them as dormitories. The movement spread to provincial cities, and it was several weeks before the squatters were finally persuaded to leave.

Partly in response to such developments, in June 1979, the Revolutionary Council nationalized virtually all *mawat*,* or undeveloped, land in urban areas. The nationalization measure allowed each owner without a dwelling of his own to keep a maximum of 1,000 square meters of such land, and then only on condition he build on the land within a specified time limit. The nationalized land was to be made available for new housing construction, and a special office, the Urban Land

---

Mawat refers to land without a previous history of development. It is distinguished from *bayer* land which, even if currently unutilized, was at one time put to productive use.

Development Organization, was created to administer the nationalized land and arrange for its transfer to deserving families. Although considerable controversy subsequently arose regarding the implementation of the nationalization order, there was little wavering from the general thrust of the legislation. In April 1982, in a major extension of the measure, the nationalization order was expanded to cover all categories of unutilized urban land, including *bayer** holdings, that is, land with a previous history of development which may be currently unused. In this instance, some provision was made for the protection and compensation of owners at the instigation of the Guardianship Council. But the government, as a result of these measures, came into possession of substantial tracts of land lying around the major cities and large amounts of valuable land in urban centers. By early 1983, the government had taken over 20 million square meters of privately owned urban land; and another 200 million square meters was earmarked for nationalization.[28]

The government also attempted to deal, through legislation, with the severe housing shortage in Tehran and other major urban centers. Early in 1980, the Revolutionary Council approved legislation authorizing a newly created government agency, the Office for the Purchase and Transfer of Empty Dwellings, to buy or lease empty housing in designated urban centers for rent or resale to the public. The law implied a degree of consent by the owner for such transactions. As Khosrowshahi and his associates gained the upper hand in determining housing policy, the provisions of this measure were gradually extended. In April 1980, the Revolutionary Council authorized the government to utilize homes left empty without adequate cause to house shantytown dwellers. Two months later, it empowered the government to take over such dwellings and to rent them, with or without the consent of the owners. The regulatory zeal of the revolutionary authorities and the widespread impulse toward social engineering reached something of a climax in June 1980 when the government ruled that all real estate transactions would have to take place through the Office for the Purchase and Transfer of Empty Dwellings. Under the detailed provisions of the law, house owners in designated urban areas could sell only to this office; prospective buyers could purchase only from it. The office was, moreover, empowered to fix prices, to pay house owners partly in cash and partly in non-interest-bearing bonds, to take over and rent residences whose owners were unwilling to lease them at reasonable rates, and to confiscate homes whose owners were absent or could not be identified. To reduce migration to the large cities and prevent concentration of ownership or speculation in housing, the law also specified age, marital, and residence qualifications for prospective buyers, established a "point system" for assigning priorities to those applying to buy, and barred those already owning homes in urban centers from purchasing a second residence.

Despite these measures, or rather because of them, the housing situation remained greatly confused. Not all officials were eager to tamper with private housing, and the regulations on empty dwellings were not always enforced with zeal. The government, whatever its intentions, in any case lacked the means to exercise close control over real estate ownership and transactions. The regulations regarding the purchase and sale of housing required so extensive a degree of government involvement that they were virtually unenforceable. As one official remarked, "We cannot fulfill the function of 40,000 public notaries."[29] Individuals invariably found ways to circumvent regulations. Undeveloped urban land had been nationalized; but owners connived with land registry officials to backdate deeds, subdivide large holdings, and sell off their properties, thus necessitating additional legislation, this time to punish violators. Unauthorized housing transactions were theoretically banned; but Tehran residents bought and sold dwellings by exchanging semiformal documents. Khosrowshahi took over some housing and encouraged other "spontaneous" takeovers. But he was able to enforce regulations on vacant dwellings only sporadically. He repeatedly warned he would seize empty housing if owners did not voluntarily register with his office. But deadlines came and went, were extended, and continued to be ignored.

There was little coordination between government departments. The conflict between the advocates and opponents of radical seizures, between the proponents of "revolutionary" action and the spokesmen for orderly procedures, continued to bedevil housing policy. In the first year of the revolution, the Bank Melli granted nearly $1 billion in loans for home purchases, or three times the authorized amount,[30] sending real estate prices soaring. Such was the crush that the loan program had for a time to be suspended. The mayor of Tehran asserted that Khosrowshahi's uncontrolled parceling out of land and his ill-considered policies and statements were encouraging rural migration to urban centers, aggravating housing and building materials shortages, and increasing pressure on municipal services. Recipients of free land often built without municipal permission; and Khosrowshahi encouraged them to do so. The Housing Foundation director continued to draw migrants to the capital by promising to distribute land and the houses of the miscreant rich to the deprived classes, even when he had nothing to give away. When the Housing Foundation invited applications from those who needed housing, over 400,000 applications were filed within a few weeks.[31] This program too had to be suspended. At one stage, both the mayor of Tehran and the minister of housing handed in their resignations to protest Khosrowshahi's activities.

Eventually more moderate views prevailed and a degree of order was asserted over housing policy. Responsibility for the administration of nationalized land was gradually vested in the ministry of housing. The Housing Foundation itself was absorbed into the housing ministry. Khosrowshahi was eased out and sent to Rome as the Iranian ambassador to the Vatican. In June 1981, the more onerous and unenforceable regulations governing housing transactions were lifted. Under new legislation, prospective purchasers were still required to acquire permits and meet stiff qualifications, but the government permitted such transactions to take place without official intervention. The new law, by maintaining silence on the question of vacant housing, implicitly revoked the authority granted the authorities to take over such dwellings.

With the departure of Khosrowshahi, the Housing Foundation moved out of the limelight. Despite all the fanfare, its concrete achievements were limited. According to its own calculations, the foundation had distributed 12,000 plots of land to lower-income families in Tehran, and over 50,000 plots according to the calculations of Tehran municipality. The uncertainty over these figures was itself an indication of the confusion governing the foundation's activities. By early 1982, it had succeeded in acquiring 400 housing units by legal purchase, in constructing a further 7,576 small units, and in assisting private builders with the construction of 5,095 dwellings.[32] It had seized an indeterminate number of homes and apartments.

Khosrowshahi's impact on public attitudes and his contribution to the atmosphere of general disorder in the first year of the revolution, however, were considerably greater. He helped shape the early and radical housing and land legislation. His pronouncements contributed to the erosion of business confidence and the ever-present fears of expropriation experienced by the propertied classes. He was a leading advocate of the revolutionary seizure of private housing and of the idea, popular among the urban masses, that available housing should be used to house all and sundry, irrespective of ownership. By the end of 1981, the impulse in this direction had been blunted; but the idea itself did not die and continued to reappear in various guises.

At the end of five years of experimentation, mixed results also characterized the overall housing policy of the government. Primarily as a result of legislation, a very substantial amount of urban land was transferred from private hands to the public sector. Some of this land was in the early stages distributed among lower-income families; but beginning in 1983, the government appeared more committed to selling land to potential home owners, generally at prevailing market prices. In housing, five years of conflicting, ill-considered, and poorly administered policies had brought about some shifts, but no major improvement in housing patterns. A large amount of housing had been expropriated, either by legislation or the action of revolutionary organizations. Some of this was utilized to house lower-income families and war refugees, some to meet the needs of state-related organizations. An attempt to take over empty housing had proved abortive, and by 1983 government controls over housing transactions had been eased. But a cumbersome bureaucratic apparatus through which the government continued to involve itself in the sale and purchase of housing remained in place. There was a slow increment from year to year in housing starts and a shift toward the construction of more modest housing for lower-income families. Insofar as the unavailability of land had been the major impediment, the government's distribution of nationalized land proved a boost to the new construction. On the other hand, such construction as took place was the fruit of private efforts and often the result of a breakdown in municipal controls rather than of government planning and direction. The government itself launched no major housing program and proved unable to complete projects already under way when the revolution occurred. It was no more successful than its predecessor in stemming the flood of migrants from village to town or in meeting the demand for construction materials. As a result, land rent and housing costs soared; shortages remained severe; and for the mass of the people, housing remained inadequate and expensive.

Foreign and Domestic Trade

The merchant and bazaar classes had profited handsomely from the economic boom Iran experienced under the Shah in the 1970s. Many had amassed fortunes in these years. Yet the bazaar provided valuable support to the revolutionary movement. In the lead-up to the revolution, Hajj Manian, Hajj Taqi Tarkhani, Hajj Mehdi Araqi, and other leading Tehran merchants contributed generously to the clerical cause, helped organize the great protest march on the *id-e fetr* festival in Tehran in September 1978, and used their influence to keep the bazaar closed at the height of the anti-Shah demonstrations later that year. Hajj Kazem Tarkhani and another merchant, Aali-Nasab, represented the bazaar in the semiclandestine committee, formed in October 1978 with Khomaini's approval, to direct the revolutionary movement from Tehran and to coordinate activities with Khomaini's group in Paris.[33] Partly in recognition of these services, representatives of the bazaar were appointed after the revolution to supervise various organizations, including the Kayhan newspaper group and the Empress Farah Foundation. Some men from the bazaar sat on postrevolution economic supervisory committees.

The alliance between mosque and bazaar had historical roots. It was reinforced in the 1970s because, despite their newfound wealth, the bazaar classes harbored numerous grievances against the policies pursued by the Shah's government and also against the new industrial and entrepreneurial elite whose interests these policies helped to promote. Merchants resented the import licenses and privileges granted to court favorites. Although some of the new industrial families emerged from the bazaar and there existed economic links between industrialists and merchants, the two groups tended increasingly to inhabit different worlds. The bazaar merchants seemed relegated to secondary status by a government which emphasized industrialization and the "modern" sector of the economy; they sensed exclusion from a social world in which Western-educated government ministers and technocrats mixed easily with their counterparts in industry and banking. Moreover, by the mid-1970s, the major industrial families appeared to have developed a powerful grip over the economy by combining interests in industry with interests in banking, insurance, and trade. Several of the largest trading companies developed alongside major industrial enterprises.

These powerful industrial groups, along with dozens of lesser domestic industrialists, increasingly threatened the role of the traditional merchants. They were not only edging the bazaar merchants out of the wholesale trade; by establishing their own retail network and outlets, they were threatening the bazaar hold on the retail trade as well. Their price policies cut into the profit margins of the bazaar traders. The brunt of the government's 1976 campaign to control high prices and profiteering fell on the smaller merchants and traders, thousands of whom were fined, publicly humiliated, and in some instances jailed. The merchants had been lightly taxed, even by Iranian standards, under the Shah. Yet they found onerous government attempts, beginning in 1974, modestly to increase merchant and guild taxes. The government's well-intentioned but badly conceived attempt to control land speculation and soaring rents was regarded by the bazaar as yet another example of the government's arbitrary power and a threat to property.

In supporting revolution, the bazaar merchants were acting out of mixed motives. They resented their loss of status, competition from domestic industries, and what they perceived to be excessive concentration of economic power in the hands of a few. They were exercised to protect their wealth from government exactions and taxation, their freedom to set prices from government regulation, their property from the overzealous attention of what they saw as a predatory government. They attached little importance to the radical economic streak and hostility to wealth inherent in the ideology of elements in the Islamic movement. They could not conceive that in the eyes of the poor they too could appear as the privileged material beneficiaries of the Shah's economic policies. Rather, they believed that an Islamic government would protect property, free them from government restrictions and controls, provide them with greater business opportunities, and tax them more lightly. They hardly foresaw that private commerce, as well as industry, would be threatened by the revolutionary tide.

The revolutionary coalition contained politicians and clerics friendly to the bazaar. But it also contained elements who, if less hostile to commerce than to industry, were determined to bring foreign trade under government control, to regulate profits, and to pursue policies beneficial to the poorer classes. The fate of private trade and commerce in the postrevolution period reflects an unstable and shifting balance of forces between these two groups. The radicals in the Assembly of Experts had secured inclusion in the constitution of an article providing for a government monopoly over foreign trade. In May 1980, the Revolutionary Council, under pressure to implement this provision of the constitution, approved a measure which reflected the aspirations of the radicals but fell short of outright nationalization of foreign trade. The measure empowered the government to establish a government monopoly over those categories of goods where government controls were deemed desirable. Over the next year, the ministry of commerce announced government importation monopolies over several categories of goods, including wood, paper, metals, machinery, essential foods, and textiles. It established twelve procurement and distribution centers to handle both importation and the domestic distribution of these items.

The centers permitted private traders to import, but only under license, and required such importers to deliver 30 percent of each consignment to the government and to sell their products at specified margins of profit. Within a short time, some 40 percent of the import trade was passing through these centers. Government agencies attempted to distribute directly the goods over which they had established a monopoly. To control prices, the government also expanded the network of state-operated cooperative stores and involved itself more extensively in the domestic distribution of consumer goods. External events reinforced these trends. The assets freeze declared by President Carter in November 1979 denied Iran access to valuable foreign exchange holdings. The war with Iraq, as already noted, wrecked Iran's largest port, disrupted trade, interrupted oil exports, imposed heavy war costs, and helped deplete foreign exchange reserves. With the outbreak of hostilities, the government imposed rationing on essential items including sugar, meat, vegetable oil, and cloth. By the end of 1981, foreign exchange reserves had fallen so severely that further trade restrictions became necessary. Several agencies were now involved in the import, distribution, and pricing of goods and some wished to extend government controls even further. The *Bonyad-e Basij-e Eqtesadi* (Foundation for Economic Mobilization), a "revolutionary" body established following the outbreak of the Iran–Iraq war, proposed to create a network of wholesale and retail centers and to take over the domestic distribution of virtually all consumer goods.[34]

In the meantime, pressure mounted in Parliament for a complete nationalization of foreign trade. In March 1981, Parliament approved a resolution requiring the government to submit a bill for foreign trade nationalization within sixty days. A reluctant government finally did so and the bill was voted into law early in 1982, only to be struck down by the Council of Guardians. The council found the law to be in violation of constitutional and Islamic law and the dictates of common sense (see chapter 8). Nevertheless, even without nationalization, probably over 80 percent of all imports passed through government hands.[35]

As indicated by the veto of the foreign trade nationalization law, the extension of state control over the economy met with resistance. Opposition developed among three groups: the bazaar, the religious community, and the bureaucracy. The bazaar and the middle classes saw in these developments a threat to their own property and business interests. The bazaar-supported demonstrations in favor of Sadeq Qotb-zadeh in November 1980 were actuated in part by opposition to the government's economic policies. The bazaar merchants had strong allies among the clerical community, and a number of religious leaders were opposed to property takeovers and restrictions on private enterprise on doctrinal grounds. In March 1980, Ayatollah Qomi of Mashad had condemned the arbitrary nationalization and expropriation of private property.[36] Finally, pragmatic-minded officials in the bureaucracy were persuaded that the government lacked the capacity efficiently to fill the shoes of thousands of importers, wholesalers, shopkeepers, real estate agents, notaries, builders, entrepreneurs, and industrialists. The widening dispute over nationalization, expropriation, and state control of the economy was therefore only partly to be explained in terms of a struggle between the haves and the have-nots, the "conservatives" and the "revolutionaries." The dispute was more complex, involving disagreements over Islamic doctrine, over the importance of the rule of law and orderly administration, and over the capacity of the state, as against a mixed economy, to serve as the engine for economic development. The question of state versus private ownership was thus seen to have ramifications for a whole range of critical matters; it came to a head as a struggle over rural land distribution.

Chapter 8

The Struggle
Over Land

AGRICULTURAL LAND became the focus of violent confrontation, bitter struggle, and intense debate beginning virtually on the morning after the revolution. There were three reasons for this: economic, political, and doctrinal. First, nearly half the population lived on the land, many households still near subsistence level. Land also remained an important source of wealth. Some 200,000 families owned nearly half the arable land in the country.

Second, although they failed to understand its complexity, the land question exercised a powerful hold on the imagination of the intelligentsia and on the political movements of the center and the left. Land reform was the yardstick by which they would judge the revolutionary credentials of governments and their dedication to the masses. Third, land figured prominently in Islamic jurisprudence. There existed a large body of laws relating to land ownership, land grants, land taxes, sharecropping, and transactions in land and crops. This meant that government policy on land touched on intimate matters of Islamic law, and that while Islamic jurists might pass over in relative silence the national-ization of industries, for example, legislation on land would inevitably engage their attention and concern.

Under the monarchy, a major land reform program had been carried out.[1] The great estates were broken up, about half the arable land in the country was distributed, and nearly 2 million village families re-ceived land. A class of peasant proprietors emerged. However, 1.2 mil-lion agricultural laborers received no land at all. Among those who received land, over 70 percent received too little for basic subsistence. Land ownership remained concentrated. Of 2.5 million rural landhold-ers, 1 percent owned 21 percent of the land. Many of the larger landowners continued to work the land with agricultural workers or tenant farmers.

Moreover, in the late 1960s and 1970s, both government policy and the activities of agricultural entrepreneurs encouraged the reconsolida-tion of holdings and the commercialization of agriculture. While the smallest holdings grew more fragmented, the middle-sized and larger units (20 hectares and above) came to account for a larger share of the total land under cultivation. The government encouraged consolidation through its credit and loan policies, evicted some 60,000 peasants from villages to make room for huge agribusinesses (of over 5,000 hectares), established with foreign investment, and persuaded some 300,000 reluc-tant villagers to pool their land in large farm corporations and produc-tion cooperatives.[2] In villages near large cities, much land lay fallow, as urban investors bought up agricultural properties for speculative pur-poses. These developments aroused dissatisfaction among the poorest peasants.

On the eve of the revolution, the agricultural picture was thus a mixed one. There existed a state-sponsored sector of agribusinesses and farm corporations that was inefficient and unpopular; a growing commercial sector that was profitable and reasonably efficient; a lim-ited number of moderately well-off peasant proprietors; a large major-ity of subsistence-level farmers; and a mass of landless rural workers. Although the poorest families supplemented their income with work in urban centers or nearby industry and the villages also experienced the spillover effects of the economic boom of the 1970s, there was nevertheless a sharp contrast in the countryside between the rich and the poor, the commercial and the traditional cultivator; there existed a reservoir of resentment against the larger landowners and a great deal of land hunger. Not surprisingly, with the revolution and the breakdown of civil and police authority, land seizures began to take place in the countryside.

Phase I: February 1979–March 1980

The land seizures were initiated by three different groups: the revolutionary government and its organizations, the landlords, and the peasants. The confiscations ordered by the provisional government and the revolutionary courts in Tehran and major cities covered agricultural as well as urban-based property. In the countryside, revolutionary committees and local courts seized the land of locally prominent individuals whom they considered in some fashion reprehensible. The Foundation for the Disinherited was responsible for many such takeovers. The activities of these official and semiofficial bodies spread the revolutionary temper, eroded respect for private property, and encouraged land seizures by others.

In parts of Khorasan, and in areas where semitribal forms of social organization persisted, such as Kurdistan, Fars, and Baluchistan, khans and landlords sought in the general disorder to reclaim lands they had lost under the Shah's land reform. Elsewhere, landlords laid claim to disputed properties or pasturelands lying in the public domain. Seizures by peasants occurred in virtually every major province and in villages and districts throughout the country.

The impetus was sometimes provided by outside organizers, sometimes by young village activists politicized by their experience in urban centers, sometimes even by middle-level peasant proprietors eager to increase their holdings. But the most common participants in seizures, and in demands for the distribution of land, were the landless and land-poor peasants. According to one sampling, over 80 percent of the village participants in these movements were peasants who owned under 5 hectares or no land at all.[3] They were spurred on by the breakdown of authority and the absence of landlords, the availability of tracts of fallow land, and Khomaini's call on the farmers to plant extensively in the first year of the Islamic Republic. The sense of deprivation, and the expectation that an Islamic regime must do something to alleviate it, was also widespread. One peasant from the village of Khairabad in Torbat Jam remarked:

We continue to struggle day and night for a piece of bread. If we all speak of an Islamic Republic, then we must all be equal. Everyone who toils and suffers must also have a living. At least, things should not be such that we die of hunger, while others are bursting with satiation.[4]

There was a basic pattern to the land seizures with many local variations.[5] The most intense activity occurred in Gonbad and Gorgan, on the Turkoman plain. This is an area of cotton and wheat cultivation. The farms were extensive, the agriculture mechanized, the owners absentee, and the land worked by agricultural workers. Subsistence farms existed alongside the large estates; and many local farmers worked their own land and hired themselves and members of their family out as wage laborers to the large landowners. Following the revolution, the Turkomans, encouraged by activists from the Fadayan guerrilla movement, organized village and regional councils, set up two Turkoman people's organizations, seized the farm machinery on the great estates, and began to cultivate the land on a communal basis.

In the Hamadan district, in western Iran, villagers took over mechanized farms and distributed the land equally between every man, woman, and child. The courts eventually ruled against them, but in many instances they remained in possession of the land by preventing the landlords from returning to their villages. In Bam, in the east, cultivators who had abandoned their tenancies to work in nearby brick kilns returned, joined hands with landless and land-poor villagers, took over the fallow land belonging to the landlords, and started planting. In Samirom, in the south, a semitribal area, villagers took over land belonging to the khans and then petitioned the government to keep the khans in prison so they could hold onto the land.

In Qaljaq, near Shirvan, in the northeast, some villagers, though not all, agreed to seize land they considered to be theirs by right, and to distribute it equally among themselves. "Those who do not march in step with the people," they warned, "and did not participate in liberating usurped land will have no claim to ownership; no share will accrue to them."[6] For the rest, the villagers petitioned the government, appealed to their religious leaders, marched on provincial centers, and staged sit-ins at government offices.

These activities did not go unresisted by the landowners.[7] They armed retainers and used them to threaten the villagers. They drove their herds onto disputed land planted by the villagers and used tractors to plow up villagers' crops. Often, they were able to utilize prerevolutionary local networks of authority and their influence with the local gendarmerie, clerics, and courts to retain their lands.

Clashes between villagers and landlords occurred in numerous villages, but only on the Turkoman plain was the violence extensive. Here, the villagers were well-organized and had access to arms; the land question became intertwined with a demand by the Turkomans for local autonomy; and the Fadayan played an important role in politicizing and radicalizing the villagers. In February 1980, four Turkoman leaders were kidnapped and murdered. There was a general uprising; units of the Revolutionary Guard and the army moved into towns with tanks and heavy arms. As many as 100 persons were killed.

Elsewhere, farmers and agents of landlords fought each other with stones, clubs, and chains. Here and there, during a village clash, shots would ring out. In Dasht-e Arzhan in December 1979, one villager was killed and thirty-eight injured. In Qaljaq two men and one woman were killed.

The reaction of the authorities to these developments tended to vary from locality to locality.[8] In Qasemabad and Azizabad, two villages in the Bam-Kerman region, the Revolutionary Guard helped the villagers seize land and distribute it among the landless farmers. In the villages of Ruh-Kandi and Baba-Kandi near Ardabil, the local branch of the Crusade for Reconstruction acquiesced in property seizures and reached an agreement with the villagers to split the harvest on the confiscated properties. In Khuzestan, the Revolutionary Guards office issued a proclamation warning "feudal elements" that land belonged only to the tiller, and that ownership established under the monarchy was valueless. They encouraged the villagers to take over the fallow land from large landlords and promised to support them in any physical confrontations with the landowners.

However, in the Turkoman areas, the Revolutionary Guards participated in expelling villagers from lands they had occupied. In Izdeh, Mazandaran, the local branch of the Crusade for Reconstruction opposed peasant seizures. Local authorities repeatedly called in gendarmes to arrest peasants who were involved in illegal seizures. Local and religious judges often tended to side with the landowners. In Azizabad, a religious judge told the villagers who had been brought before him: "Since you usurped the land, I must either exile you or cut your hands off."[9] In another village in the same district, a religious judge told peasants that it was unlawful for them to farm land they had irrigated by diverting the landlord's water. A cleric sent to adjudicate a dispute between landlords and villagers in Banesh, in Fars, remarked while holding out his prayer beads: "Just as these prayer beads belong to me, the lands belong to their owners. You have no right to trespass on them."[10]

On the other hand, Ayatollah Abdol-Hosain Dastghaib, head of the Shiraz revolutionary court, accused the minister of agriculture and the committees he was appointing to adjudicate landlord–peasant disputes of invariably siding with the landlords and sending villagers to jail.[11] The Gorgan revolutionary prosecutor called for the distribution of the great estates to the villagers.

During this period, local revolutionary and governmental organizations acted with little consistency because of the persistence of former patterns of authority; because, strictly speaking, the landlords held the deeds and it was the peasants who were seizing land; and because no clear direction had come from Tehran. Khomaini himself remained silent on the land issue; and the Bazargan government emphasized the need to restore order. The government had a healthy respect for private property; it considered the commercial farmers not as cruel oppressors but as successful entrepreneurs. It feared that rural disorder would lead to a fall in food production. Moreover, the government greatly underestimated the extent of land hunger in the villages, and the impact of revolutionary rhetoric regarding land, both on the villagers and on the urban population. It urged farmers to exercise "revolutionary patience" and wait for government measures. "This revolutionary patience," remarked a farmer in Khairabad, "is killing us."[12]

Finally, in September 1979, the provisional government secured the approval of the Revolutionary Council for a Law for the Transfer and Revival of Land.[13] The law, however, was limited in scope. It envisioned the distribution of arable land already held by the government or which had been confiscated from members of the former regime, of which there was not a great deal, and of *mawat*, or barren land, which few wanted anyway. Although it empowered the government in the future to set upper limits on land ownership, it basically left the private sector untouched. The law provided that land left uncultivated would revert to the state. But it allowed owners of barren land two years, and of fallow arable land three to five years to bring their holdings under cultivation.

Otherwise, the underlying assumption of the law, as officials explained, was that a land reform program had already been carried out in the country; that mechanization and commercialization of agriculture by the private sector were desirable; and that the government could best improve productivity by providing loans and services and encouraging better techniques and increased cultivation. The law failed to end illegal seizures or to quell the turmoil in the countryside.

Phase II: April–November 1980

By the early spring of 1980, however, conditions had altered dramatically. The moderate Bazargan government had resigned, a victim of the American hostage crisis; men more committed to radical economic policies were in power. The Revolutionary Council began to consider a new land reform measure within days of Bazargan's resignation. The minister of agriculture had been replaced; Reza Esfahani, the new undersecretary for land affairs at the ministry, who was to become closely identified with the next land reform law, was an advocate of radical land distribution. The constitution had been approved, and the articles on social and economic justice provided a legal justification for a more extensive land reform.

These articles guaranteed each Iranian the tools and fruit of his own labor and a decent standard of living; they banned illegally acquired wealth, the economic exploitation of others, and hoarding and monopoly. Beheshti, who in the Revolutionary Council pressed for the breakup of large holdings, was inclined to give these constitutional principles a broad application. Once these articles were implemented, he said, "The problem of housing—even small [ownership], let alone large —will not arise. . . . There will no longer be an owner of a large or even a small factory."[14] In agriculture, grounds for sharecropping or leasing arrangements simply would not exist, he said, since each person would own the tools of his own labor.

Between November and March, the Revolutionary Council wrestled with a new bill on land distribution. It approved one version of the bill early in March, which would have broken up all but the smallest estates and would have paid no compensation to owners, then revised it to meet a flood of objections. In April 1980, the Revolutionary Council finally approved and announced a new law. As a precaution, Khomaini asked three leading jurists, Beheshti, Montazeri, and Meshgini, to review it from an Islamic perspective. They also gave it their stamp of approval.

The law provided for a sweeping land distribution.[15] It limited landowners who directly cultivated their land to three times the acreage that in each district was considered sufficient for the maintenance of one peasant family. Absentee landowners who had no other source of income were limited to twice this amount. Since seven hectares was regarded as an average subsistence holding, this implied the breakup of the middle-sized and even small enterprises. Provisions for the compensation of landlords subject to distribution were vague; and landowners were in any case to be compensated only after their debts to the government and their outstanding religious dues—also vaguely defined—had been deducted. These provisions for compensation, the exemption of livestock enterprises, and the allowance made for absentee owners were the only concessions to critics of the first draft of the bill. The law also provided that mechanized farms would be retained as units and transferred to groups of farmers on a cooperative basis.

Land was to be distributed, in order of priority, to landless and land-poor peasants, and to high-school and agricultural college graduates, civil servants, and others ready to take up farming. Despite the shortage of land, government officials in 1979–82 continued to hope agriculture would absorb unemployed graduates and lessen the burden on the overstaffed civil service and the overcrowded cities. A central staff was established in Tehran to oversee the land reform program. Actual distribution in the villages was to be carried out by seven-man local "land transfer committees," made up of representatives of government agencies, revolutionary organizations, the religious judge of the district, and local villagers.

The seven-man committees were vested with considerable powers. They were authorized to determine the local upper limit on landholding, to designate the properties subject to distribution, and to determine who was to receive land. The committees very quickly began their work. Some thirty-two committees, fielding hundreds of agents, were established. They carried out surveys of villages, took over land, transferred the land to local farmers, and provided uncultivated land to graduates for new enterprises. Where disputes over land arose and could not be settled, they took the initiative in leasing the disputed land to the peasants under rental or crop-sharing arrangements until land ownership could be finally determined. The Crusade for Reconstruction, whose representatives sat on the land transfer committees, provided extension services, seeds, loans, and the like.

The land distribution work, however, was not everywhere an orderly affair. "Reza Esfahani's law" had been under discussion since December 1979. It had aroused a great deal of excitement in the villages and had elicited statements of support around the country. Already in December, unauthorized seizures by semiofficial committees and revolutionary organizations were reported from a string of northern districts where the left was active: Gonbad, Shahsavar, Nowshahr, Ramsar, and Chalus. When the law was approved, revolutionary organizations in a number of localities formed land transfer committees and began to distribute land before instructions arrived from Tehran. Furthermore, the adoption by the Tehran authorities of a clearer attitude on the land questions had a galvanizing effect on local officials. The local clerics and members of the Reconstruction Crusade and the Revolutionary Guard became strong supporters of land distribution. The land transfer committees everywhere saw themselves as champions of the cause of the local peasantry.

The law was worded with sufficient vagueness to allow land transfer committees unusual scope for interpretation. Many committees appear to have acted arbitrarily, to have exceeded their mandates, and to have tampered with smaller, efficient enterprises. Moreover, unofficial committees continued in some areas to seize and distribute land. The work of the land distribution committees was subsequently criticized by clerics close to the government, including Ali-Akbar Hashemi-Rafsanjani and Ali-Akbar Nateq-Nuri.[16]

A number of government economists and planners were critical of the law because they felt it would break up efficient, mechanized farms and because the manner of its implementation was causing a drop in production. But the serious opposition to land distribution came from two groups: landowners and prominent clerics.

The landowners were numerous and vocal.[17] Many of the most active were middle-level commercial farmers. Taking advantage of a law passed by the Revolutionary Council in April 1979 for the establishment of "agricultural councils," they organized themselves in Tehran and the provinces. They used these councils to lobby with parliamentary deputies, ministers, and religious leaders. They issued declarations, printed articles, and gave interviews to the press. They secured *fatvas* (formal legal opinions) against land distribution from clerical leaders and sent their agents into the villages to tell the peasants the land seizures were unIslamic. In Hamadan, landlords circulated an older *fatva* by Khomaini, declaring it religiously unlawful to usurp the land of another. The Tehran agricultural council issued an open letter to

Khomaini declaring that the new bill violated Islamic law, would encourage fratricide, and would undermine agricultural production. Agricultural councils in Hamadan, Gonbad, and Mazandaran sent telegrams of protest to the government.

The provincial agricultural councils—all landowner-dominated organizations—sent representatives to a preliminary conference in Tehran in March 1980 and to national conferences at the capital in May and September. At the May conference the participants adopted a resolution stating that "the denial of ownership and the violation of property rights of the people is not in accordance with any of the principles of Islam, the *fatvas* of the great *faqih* [Khomaini] and the leading ulama, or the constitution."[18] At the September conference, the participants proposed an alternate land reform law that left private property untouched. Support for the landowners came from bazaar merchants for whom land reform seemed the cutting edge of a broader attack on other forms of property.

More serious for the government was the opposition to the measure by a number of the leading Islamic jurists. They voiced their criticisms in legal opinions, in *responsa* to questions put to them by members of the public, and in sermons from the pulpit.[19] Ayatollah Golpaygani issued a statement declaring the law to be in violation of Islamic tenets. Ayatollah Sadeq Ruhani, speaking against the measure from the pulpit of the New Mosque in Qom, commented adversely on the measure in reply to a question posed to him by landless agricultural workers from Gorgan; he also addressed a telegram to the president telling him the land distribution measure violated both Islam and the constitution and instructing him to rescind it. Ayatollahs Mahallati, Qomi, and Shirazi also criticized the measure.

The Society of the Seminary Teachers at Qom, a group considered close to Khomaini, issued a declaration warning against bills "damaging to the interests of the oppressed . . . which appear in the dress of Islam," and said the land reform measure would lead to "the ruin of the cultivated lands."[20] Moreover, the majority of the jurists on the Guardianship Council, all Khomaini appointees, were known to have strong reservations about the law. Some of these religious authorities no doubt had close links with the bazaar community and with landlords. But they were motivated primarily by the growing disorder and lawlessness in the country and what they considered as disregard for Islamic principles.

These clerics saw little justification for the takeover of fallow lands, no matter how long they had been left uncultivated. They found unpersuasive the argument that the public good overrode the specific dictates of the law, as they understood it. Ayatollah Ruhani, one of the most outspoken critics of the law, said guilt on other grounds did not justify the confiscation of a man's property. Only property unlawfully acquired could be reclaimed and returned to its rightful owners; even here, in other words, property could not be distributed among all-comers. "Otherwise," he said, "even if an individual has committed a thousand crimes, his property goes to his heirs."[21]

Khomaini himself appears to have been disturbed by reports that the land transfer committees were exceeding their authority and taking property to which the law gave them no right. He also appears to have entertained doctrinal reservations about the law. "The Imam," Beheshti explained afterwards, "did not object to the general outlines of the project; but he did not approve the details either."[22] On 12 November, he ordered the suspension of the articles of the law dealing with private property.

The suspension of these articles did not end the agitation over land distribution. The hopes of the villagers, once ignited, could not be easily extinguished. They issued petitions, sent delegations to Tehran, and pressed their Majles representatives on the land question. The newspaper *Kayhan* reported it had received dozens of petitions, some "several meters long" and bearing hundreds of signatures, calling for a resumption of land distribution. A delegation of Turkomans and Zabolis arrived from Gorgan and appealed directly to Khomaini to permit the suspended clauses of the law to be enforced. In newspaper interviews, a significant number of Majles deputies, many from rural districts, called for a takeover of the large estates. The deputy from Bojnurd, for example, asserted that to acquiesce in the continuation of the large landholdings was to acquiesce in "poverty, hunger and death for the great mass of toiling cultivators."[23]

In declarations and interviews, members of the Crusade for Reconstruction and land transfer committees in Fars, Isfahan, Hamadan, Arak, Gorgan, Kerman, and a dozen other centers dwelt on the exploitative nature of the large landlords, depicted in graphic terms the hardships borne by the land-poor peasants, and extolled the benefits of the land distribution.[24] The religious judge on the Kermanshahan land transfer committee ridiculed the attempts of landlords to justify their landholdings on the basis of Islamic law. "The Islam that fires the hearts of the feudal elements," he said, "is an American Islam."[25] The Crusade for

Reconstruction sponsored a television series featuring two Khorasan villages. The series, focusing on the big landlords, was entitled "The Leeches," and depicted, according to one commentator, "the suffering of lacking one's daily bread, lacking enough land to cultivate, lacking four walls in which to spend the night . . . and, on the other hand, the leech-like landlords, who have sucked dry the blood of the suffering villagers."[26]

Moreover, the havoc caused on the countryside by the implementation of the land reform law was not alleviated by its suspension. On the contrary, uncertainty over the government's intentions regarding the ultimate disposal of the land, and the disputes over ownership that flared up everywhere, interfered with cultivation and caused a sometimes catastrophic drop in production. Reports by agricultural officials from the provinces invariably emphasized that production would not recover until these disputes were resolved and the question of land ownership clarified.

A decision was all the more urgent because the vexing question of private property appeared to the authorities to lie at the heart of other major problems facing the government and to constitute the principal barrier to their resolution. The government felt unable to deal with the severe shortage of urban housing, the steeply rising prices of urban real estate, the high price of basic commodities, and such practices as hoarding and profiteering, without tampering with private property and the freedom of trade. Yet there were fundamental doctrinal objections to legislating in these areas.

Phase III: The Doctrinal Dispute

The search for a way out of this impasse led in October 1981 to an important exchange of letters between Hashemi-Rafsanjani, as speaker of the Majles, and Khomaini. The exchange itself arose out of consultations on the property question held by Rafsanjani and his associates with Khomaini. As Rafsanjani later explained, land reform, urban land, and housing, and the prices of goods were critical issues. Yet Parliament and the government lacked the authority to act on these matters. "This is an area for the exercise of the authority of the *faqih*. The *faqih* is the guardian [of the community] exercising his authority in situations where over-riding necessity requires extraordinary decisions to be taken." Such situations of "necessity" arose, he said, where the common good or the social order were at stake, or where Islamic requirements could not be otherwise realized.*[27]

Hashemi-Rafsanjani explained the dilemma facing Parliament to Khomaini in person. Then, clearly by prearrangement, he did so in writing. Khomaini replied in a terse, carefully worded but elusive letter. He said that Majles could itself "enact and implement" legislation, in situations of necessity, where action or inaction threatened the vital interests of the community, or when "wickedness and corruption" might result. He set two conditions, however: that the laws Parliament approved be temporary in nature and remain in effect only as long as the emergency for which they were designed continued; and (with an eye to the excesses committed under the land distribution program) that provision be made for punishment of officials who exceeded their authority.

In his letter to Rafsanjani, Khomaini nowhere referred to the concept of *velayat*, to the vice-regency of the jurist, to his own authority as *faqih*, or to the delegation of such authority to Parliament. The previous year, when the new land-reform bill measure was first under discussion, he had left it to three other jurists, Beheshti, Montazeri, and Meshgini, to determine whether the law violated Islamic principles. He now, in effect, again avoided taking a public stand. He left it to Parliament to decide on land distribution and other property matters and to determine whether a critical situation existed, requiring special legislation.

Rafsanjani, however, was much more specific in the two major statements he made to explain the significance of the exchange of letters. He interpreted the Imam's directive as a means by which Khomaini delegated part of his authority to Parliament, empowering the Majles to exercise *velayat*, to identify situations in which the interests of the community required special laws, and to provide the necessary legislative remedies. He described the exercise of these special powers as lying within the sphere of "secondary rulings," which Mohammad-Baqer Sadr in *Iqtisaduna* had described as the "discretionary sphere" of the law. Rafsanjani, in fact, closely followed the argument developed by Sadr regarding the broad discretionary powers of the *vali-ye amr*, or *faqih*, in utilizing secondary rulings to dispose of private property in the interests of the community.[28]

In the early stages of land reform, Beheshti too had drawn on Sadr

---

*In the debate on land reform, the terms *haraj*, *'osr*, and *zarurat* were frequently used to depict an extreme predicament, straitened circumstances, or crisis conditions. I have throughout translated these terms as "overriding necessity."

to justify the takeover of private land. He formulated a case that was later echoed by Rafsanjani. Beheshti acknowledged that private property, in certain forms, was recognized by Islam:

> But private and individual property, even if it were to be accepted in the case of land, does not imply that the *vali-ye amr* may also not dispose of it. In other words, private and individual property exists in harmony and not conflict with the vice-regency and the priority rights of the *vali*. [29]

Beheshti asserted, furthermore, that in dealing with private property, the determination of the general interest "belongs to the *vali-ye amr* alone. In this matter, he cannot be subject to the opinion of others."[30] This was an argument designed to dispose of the objections to land distribution raised by other leading jurists. Finally, he somewhat inconsistently argued that because the *vali* may lack the opportunity directly to supervise and judge all matters, he may consult with those whose judgment he trusts, or even delegate the final decision to them.

In the elaboration of Sadr's theory, two new elements thus appear: the concept of "overriding necessity," and the idea that the *faqih*'s authority may be delegated. Rafsanjani justified the controversial land reform measure and later bills dealing with urban land and other forms of property as necessary temporary measures, designed to remedy conditions damaging to the community. Like Beheshti, he justified Khomaini's decision to delegate such matters to others by referring to the complexity of modern government, the inability of any single individual to master all subjects, and the need to consult experts. He explained, in his rambling style:

> Everyone knows that in today's complex world, the determination of advantages and evils by one man is not possible. These require special training. They require experience. They require a knowledge of politics, a knowledge of history. . . . What should we do about water? What should we do about land? What should we do about monopolies?[31]

Hence the Khomaini directive to Parliament. The members of the Majles, Rafsanjani said, possessed the necessary Islamic knowledge and expertise to deal with these complex matters themselves, or they could consult outside experts.

Although Rafsanjani triumphantly announced that Khomaini's directive "will resolve the problems faced by the parliament and the government," no breakthrough occurred. Following the Khomaini–Rafsanjani exchange, two bills were tabled before Parliament. The first, prepared by the ministry of agriculture, was an amended version of the suspended law and made only two concessions to the critics of that measure. It strengthened provisions for compensation of dispossessed landowners and it allowed owners of fallow land liable to distribution a grace period in which to cultivate their farms themselves.[32]

The second bill, more conservative in intent, was tabled by sixteen deputies.[33] The bill is interesting because it is modeled on Khomaini's views on the land question. Khomaini had frequently stated that most landlords could be dispossessed because they had acquired their lands illegally, had amassed wealth by oppressing the peasants, and had failed to pay their Islamic dues and taxes.[34]

The sixteen sponsors of the bills sought to make this assumption the basis for a land distribution program. They also sought through legislation to stabilize the situation in the countryside and to give existing landowners a measure of security. The bill set no upper limits on land ownership. But it called for an investigation into the manner of acquisition of all properties above a certain size, for the confiscation of lands illegally acquired, and for the full payment by all landlords of their Islamic dues and taxes. Delinquent landlords would have to settle in full (going back over an unspecified number of years) or lose their lands.

A curious confusion of aims characterized the bill. Ahmad Tavakkoli, one of the sponsors, argued both that the bill would restore respect for legally acquired private property and that it would lead to a breakup of the big estates. Asserting that the average landlord was seriously delinquent in paying his religious dues, he predicted that under the law "even if [the landlord] gave up all his goods and lands, he would still be indebted. . . . There will be left a very small number [of landlords] who did not usurp the land, are not guilty of oppression and excesses, and who always paid the religious dues on their income."[35]

Both these bills languished in Parliament. The Majles did not finally approve a land reform measure until a year later, in December 1982.[36] The new law represented a triumph for the advocates of Islamic orthodoxy. It retained the previously established upper limits on landholdings (two and three times the size of an average family farm) for absentee landlords and landowners actively engaged in agriculture. But it required owners merely to lease the excess to the local peasants under sharecropping, rental, or partnership arrangements. The impact of even this provision was strictly limited, for the law allowed landowners to give priority in leasing land to their own children.

The law exempted dairy, livestock, and mechanized farms. It eased requirements for absentee landlords. It allowed holders of fallow land one year in which to cultivate the land themselves. In certain instances it raised the maximum holding to up to four times the size of an average family farm. The law, in other words, did not aim at distribution of land but at ensuring more extensive leasing under forms of contract (sharecropping, rental, and partnerships) acceptable under Islamic law. According to one calculation, after provision is made for various exemptions under the law, only 1 to 2 million hectares would have been affected, and these would have been leased, rather than distributed to villagers.[37]

Even this fairly conservative measure was vetoed by the Council of Guardians in January 1983 for violating Islamic and constitutional principles. Such was the denouément, after four years of debate and struggle, over the land question.

In the villages and in the countryside, the abortive land reform program left its mark in three areas. In terms of land distribution, the impact of the program was limited. During eight months of activity and until the partial suspension of the land reform law in November 1980, the land transfer committees distributed to villagers 150,000 hectares of barren land and 35,000 hectares of arable land; they also leased to villagers on a temporary basis 850,000 hectares of disputed land. The committees returned to their original owners deeds to 515,000 hectares of land the farmers were cultivating in common in the agricultural corporations and production cooperatives established under the former regime. Finally, the committees transferred 60,000 hectares of barren land to government organizations for distribution among graduates and other potential farmers.[38]

Of these transfers, those relating to *mawat*, or wasteland, can be largely ignored. Without substantial loans, irrigation, and support services, most of this acreage was of little practical value. No breakdown is available of the 850,000 hectares of disputed land leased to villagers. It can be assumed that lease agreements were for the most part signed with those already working the land as tenants and agricultural workers, and that farmers generally obtained better terms than were available from the landowners. On the farm corporations and production cooperatives, a large number of farmers achieved a long-term aspiration, receiving title to what had been their own land; this was perhaps an important change in status. Only 35,000 hectares of land, most of it confiscated from landlords, was actually distributed. Villagers had not in every instance gained final deed to this land when the land reform program was suspended.

The second legacy of land reform was confusion and uncertainty. The doctrinal and constitutional disputes over land and property remained unresolved. Because of unauthorized seizures, laws approved and then struck down, distribution programs begun and then suspended, very large amounts of land remained in dispute between landowners and villagers, private citizens and the government. Villagers who received land, often without title deed, could not be certain they would be permitted to keep it. Landowners who emerged with their holdings intact, remained vulnerable to a renewed attempt at land distribution. Although the land distribution program had been halted, the position of the large and middle-level landowners had been greatly eroded.

Finally, the government emerged from the land agitation with its presence in the villages and the countryside greatly enhanced. The revolutionary government retained control of the majority of the agribusinesses and agricultural projects launched under the monarchy. The Foundation for the Disinherited came into possession of 100,000 hectares of agricultural land confiscated from members of the former regime. Government and revolutionary organization officials came to administer hundreds of thousands of hectares of disputed land.

Members of the Crusade for Reconstruction and the land transfer committees joined the agricultural officials of the old bureaucracy as extension agents, land distribution officials, and loan administrators across the countryside, active in many aspects of village life. By January 1980, the land transfer central staff had already established 25,000 Islamic committees to operate under its supervision in the villages. The inclination of these revolutionary organizations, and of the revolutionary government itself, was toward the greater regulation of village agriculture. Each of the land reform measures approved during this period gave government representatives extensive authority to dictate which crops were to be planted by land and loan recipients and to intervene in the agricultural decisions of individual farmers.

Economic Thermidor?

Reverberations from the controversy over land were felt not only in the villages. The dispute also left its mark on constitutional doctrine, on the balance of forces in the government, and on economic policy in general. Each of these results deserves more detailed attention.

First, the struggle over land witnessed the most ambitious and concerted effort in the first five years of the revolution to apply the doctrine of the vice-regency of the jurist as an instrument for social revolution. Advocates of land reform, as well as the takeover of urban land and housing and the nationalization of foreign trade, hoped to invoke Khomaini's authority as *faqih* to carry out what they considered to be an extensive program for the distribution of wealth. This effort did not succeed.

In the case of land distribution, advocates drew on writers on Islamic economics to argue that in Islam land ultimately belongs to God alone, that property is always "limited and conditional," that Islam abhors the exploitation of man by man, and that the concentration of wealth and the landlord–tenant relationship are by nature exploitative. Others focused on the allegedly illicit manner in which the large estates had been acquired, or on the nonpayment of religious dues by the landlords over many years.

This approach, however, came to grief against Islamic texts and traditions supportive of private property, inherited wealth, and freedom to engage in economic activity and in contractual arrangements, such as sharecropping, rentals, and wage labor, common in Iranian agriculture. Advocates of land reform and the distribution of wealth therefore sought increasingly in the doctrine of *velayat-e faqih,* and the jurist's discretionary powers, the mechanism through which to achieve their ends.

Critics, however, questioned the legitimacy of the extensive powers claimed for Khomaini under this doctrine. If willing to concede such powers to the *faqih,* they rejected the idea that this authority could be delegated. They continued to challenge the claim that conditions of "overriding necessity" existed, requiring the exercise of these special powers. They noted that, however great the need for emergency measures, the transfer of title to property hardly constituted a "temporary" remedy.

Khomaini's position on land reform and other legislation touching on property remained equivocal. He allowed land distribution to go ahead, until opposition persuaded him to suspend the measure. He embraced the concept of a sphere of secondary rulings, where the jurist could exercise special authority. But he refrained from publicly endorsing land reform, or any other controversial measures touching on private property, a fact which the opposition emphasized. He refrained from exercising the authority claimed for him on property questions; and he never explained how the conflict between property rights and the general interest might be resolved.

Khomaini may have feared seriously splitting the clerical community. Most of the senior ayatollahs, including Ayatollah Golpaygani, Khomaini's senior in age and a man whose support Khomaini valued, were opposed to the takeover of private land. Khomaini himself may have been uncomfortable with the manner in which the doctrine of the *faqih*'s discretionary powers had been elaborated in relation to property. On this one issue, the jurist in him appears to have dictated caution and hesitation. His equivocation weakened the advocates and emboldened the opponents of land distribution.

Second, the controversy over land and property saw the emergence of the Council of Guardians as an institution of considerable influence in the new constitutional order. The council, established in the summer of 1980, played only a minor role in the great political and constitutional controversies of the Bani-Sadr presidency. The decisions it handed down, beginning in mid-1982, regarding a cluster of legislation relating to private property and private trade, however, had the effect of turning the council into a major source of policy.

In May 1982, the Guardianship Council struck down the Foreign Trade Nationalization Law. In the fall, it forced Parliament to revise the bill on urban land (the bill had been previously approved only by the Revolutionary Council), giving more protection to private owners, requiring them to be compensated for expropriated land, and limiting the government's freedom to take over such property. In January 1983, it rejected the new land reform law in its entirety. That same month it vetoed a new statute, the Law for the Expropriation of the Property of Fugitives.[39] The law would have permitted the government to take over the property of any Iranian living abroad who did not return to Iran within two months.

While the particulars differed from case to case, the council rejected these laws on broadly similar grounds. It objected to the laws on land reform, urban land, and foreign trade nationalization for interfering with the rights of property and the freedom of trade; for claiming the existence of conditions of overriding necessity where none existed; for encroaching on the sphere of "primary rulings"; and for seeking for these laws a universal or general application, where only a limited application was permissible or necessary. The council, for example, ruled that the government could not claim a blanket foreign trade monopoly; it could control the import or export only of specific items, where necessary. It ruled that the government could not apply the urban land law indiscriminately to all cities; it could do so only in those cities where the housing shortage was critical and could be resolved only through the buying up of private property.

In the case of the foreign trade nationalization and the land reform laws, the council also objected that these statutes gave the government excessive power to interfere in agriculture and foreign trade. On the law on the expropriation of the property of "fugitives," the council ruled that absence from the country does not constitute guilt, and that the government must prove guilt on a case-by-case basis.

In the space of a few months, the Guardianship Council thus articulated an economic position at variance with that advanced by the advocates of "Islamic economics," and established the council as a countervailing force to the government and Parliament. In this controversy, Khomaini, after some hesitation, threw his weight behind the Council of Guardians.

When he received members of Parliament in January 1983, he advised them to "take care you so express matters, you so vote on matters, that they are not rejected by the Council of Guardians." His great fear, he said, was that the people, "who do not understand these matters," finding the leaders split on issues of religious doctrine, would begin to question the Islamic nature of the state:

> If the people see that those whom they sent to the Majles, and whom they believe to be religious, repeatedly vote in a manner that the Council of Guardians rejects because of conflict with Islam, they will begin to feel doubt. . . . On that day a calamity will befall us. . . . On that day, our funeral dirge must be sung.[40]

Third, the cluster of decisions handed down by the Guardianship Council beginning in the second half of 1982 marked the reversal of the trend toward increasingly radical economic policies and the beginnings of a thermidor, at least in the economic field. The council's decisions reflected a broader reaction against the earlier confiscations and nationalizations; the excesses of the land-transfer committees and revolutionary organizations; and the impact of these activities on agricultural and industrial production, investment, trade, and public confidence. In both the economic and political fields, this reaction culminated in Khomaini's eight-point decree of December 1982. The reaction, as already suggested, was fueled by doctrinal anxieties, property interests, alarm at the continuing disorder, and purely pragmatic considerations.

Government administrators, in particular, came to feel that extremist policies were seriously damaging the economy; and they concluded that the government could not efficiently manage the nationalized and confiscated enterprises. The decisions of the Council of Guardians were mirrored in changes in government policy. Officials in 1983 began to offer to return the nationalized enterprises to their former owners, to invite entrepreneurs and specialists living abroad to return to the country, to assure private businessmen their investments would be secure, to seek improved trade relations with the West, and to show a renewed interest in Western technology.

These developments, however, left unresolved the problem that had exercised the attention of leaders and opposition, clerics and lay intellectuals, ever since the fall of the monarchy: how was the goal of social and economic justice that the revolution had promised to be achieved? In advocating strategies, the revolutionaries had tended to divide broadly into two camps. The Bazargan government believed that the best hope for the improvement of the lot of the disadvantaged classes lay in general economic prosperity. It viewed the private entrepreneur not as a barrier but as an engine for economic growth. It emphasized a mixed economy, investment by both government and the private sector, and a strategy of broad-based economic development. This implied a continuation of the economic strategies pursued under the Shah, but with less emphasis on grandiose projects, and more on social justice and probity in government.

The radicals, on the other hand, saw the concentration of wealth in private hands as a barrier to both economic development and social justice. In the spreading turmoil, moreover, they despaired of being able to alleviate the housing shortage through the construction of new housing, unemployment through increased economic activity, and poverty through the general spread of prosperity. They emphasized instead a strategy of distributing existing wealth—housing, land, and other forms of income—and also state ownership and government control of the economy.

The radicals had come to power believing that Islam would smooth the way for policies of distributive justice; they attempted to fashion out of the doctrines of Sadr and others the weapons for an assault on private property. But Islamic jurists showed that Islam was a sword that cut both ways. If it was possible to marshal up from broad Islamic principles arguments for social justice, it was also possible to mine Islamic jurisprudence for arguments in defense of private property. The injection of Islam into the debate on property and social justice therefore proved a highly complicating factor; and by 1983, at both the doctrinal and the practical levels, this debate was at a stalemate.

In January 1983, when Hashemi-Rafsanjani took members of Parliament to meet with Khomaini, he again appealed to the Imam for guidance on this vexing matter. Khomaini in October 1981 had in effect empowered the Majles to pass legislation on pressing economic and social matters on the basis of *zarurat,* or overriding necessity. But this had not resolved matters, as the Guardianship Council continued to veto bills, or parts of bills, approved under this rubric by rejecting the claim of the Majles that conditions of overriding necessity existed. Khomaini, Hashemi-Rafsanjani now said, should assist Parliament to turn Iran's Islamic Republic into a "model for the world" and to disprove the claim that "the heavenly religions cannot serve as a basis for the social life of the people."[41] Khomaini on this occasion suggested that the determination of overriding necessity by the Majles would appear more persuasive if relevant bills were approved by a two-thirds majority. The "two-thirds principle," as it came to be known, was applied by the Majles to various bills over the next several years. But the Guardianship Council continued to dispute with the Majles the authority to determine the existence of conditions of overriding necessity. The two-thirds principle could thus be applied only with circumspection, and it failed to provide an effective means of resolving the doctrinal impasse.

Chapter 9

Terror and Consolidation

IN THE THREE YEARS that followed the overthrow of Bani-Sadr, the Khomaini regime beat back an attempt at armed rebellion by left-wing guerrillas, neutralized or eliminated other opposition groups, contained the Kurdish rebellion, and consolidated its hold on the country. Khomaini settled a struggle between the extremists and the moderates in the ruling party in favor of the moderate elements. This led to a slackening of revolutionary terror and allowed the government to devote attention to rebuilding the economy and strengthening institutions.

The government also found the means successfully to prosecute the war with Iraq and to pursue a foreign policy based on militant Islam, nationalism, regional ambitions, and the slogan of "neither East nor West." This in practice meant attempting to export revolution to the Persian Gulf states, maintaining distance from both great powers, and seeking friends and trade partners in the third world and in Europe.

After his impeachment Bani-Sadr remained in hiding for a month, staying first with friends, then with the Mojahedin leader, Mas'ud

Rajavi. During a series of discussions, the informal alliance between the two men became a formal pact. On 29 July, Rajavi and Bani-Sadr secretly flew to Paris. At the French capital, they announced the formation of a National Council of Resistance (NCR), launched a campaign to overthrow Khomaini, and formed the nucleus of a provisional government to take charge once Khomaini was overthrown. Bani-Sadr was to be president and Rajavi to head the provisional government.

The charter of the NCR was almost identical to the program the Mojahedin had espoused in Iran. It reflected special concern for the interests of the lower middle class—minor civil servants, shopkeepers, artisans, small merchants—and a slightly more moderate position on private property. The charter promised respect for individual liberties, except for persons identified with the Shah's or Khomaini's regime; special rights for the ethnic minorities, particularly the Kurds; land to the farmers who would, however, be encouraged to consolidate their holdings in collective farms; housing, education, and health services, jobs and low-interest loans to farmers, workers, and lower-rank civil servants; equality for women; decision making based on elected and consultative councils; and a "democratic" army, in which the rank and file would be consulted on decisions and selection of officers.

The charter also promised respect for private property and capital, as long as private wealth was not excessive and as long as economic activity did not contribute to "dependence," was not "harmful" to society, and was "nationalistic" rather than "comprador" in character. It pledged protection for the small farmers, artisans, and shopkeepers who would be taxed only with their own consent.[1]

The Kurdish Democratic Party (KDP), at its fifth congress, in December 1981, voted to join the NCR, although differences between the KDP and the NCR remained. The other Kurdish rebel group, Komaleh, decided against joining. The leader of the National Democratic Front (NDF), Matin-Daftari, joined the exiles in Paris in December and announced the adherence of the NDF to the National Resistance Council (NCR). Smaller groups also joined. This made the NCR the largest and most formidable of the exile opposition organizations.

The real struggle for power, however, was being waged on the streets of Tehran. Finding the door to constitutional opposition closed, the Mojahedin and other leftist movements undertook to overthrow the Islamic Republic by force.

Crushing the Opposition

On 28 June 1981, a powerful bomb ripped through the central headquarters of the Islamic Republic Party (IRP), where a meeting of party
leaders was in progress. The bomb killed the secretary general, Mohammad Beheshti, four cabinet ministers, six ministerial undersecretaries,
twenty-seven parliamentary deputies, and several other party and government officials. On 30 August, a bomb exploded at the prime minister's offices, where the government's special security committee was
meeting. It killed Mohammad-Ali Raja'i, who had replaced Bani-Sadr
as president; Mohammad-Javad Bahonar, the new prime minister and
IRP chief; and Hushang Dastgerdi, the chief of the national police. A
week later, a bomb took the life of the revolutionary prosecutor-general, Ali Qoddusi.

In this same period, and in the weeks and months that followed,
assassins killed the Friday prayer leaders in key cities, including Tabriz,
Kerman, Shiraz, Yazd, and Kermanshah. Khomaini's personal appointees, these men constituted parts of the chain of command through
which Khomaini's writ was exercised in the provinces. The Friday
prayer leaders in Tehran and Rasht barely escaped assassination.

Assassins also killed the governor-general of Gilan province; the war-
den of the much-feared Evin prison; the IRP ideologue, Hasan Ayat;
revolutionary court judges in several cities; and other Majles deputies.
As security was tightened around key officials, assassins struck at minor
officials, members of the revolutionary organizations, and the Revolutionary Guard. Hundreds of officials, and large numbers of guardsmen,
were eventually killed in these attacks.

The pattern of assassinations was in keeping with the three-phase
strategy the Mojahedin had outlined for the overthrow of the regime:
first, destabilization, elimination of key figures, and the exposure of the
regime's vulnerability; second, direct confrontation, demonstrations,
and strikes to mobilize the people; and finally, a mass uprising to bring
down the government. In September, the Mojahedin launched what
was presumably the second phase of this plan. They sent their followers
into the streets of Tehran, in groups of 100 to 200, to distribute leaflets,
shout anti-Khomaini slogans, and initiate protest marches which they
expected the people to join. They backed these shock troops with guerrillas, who provided a protective shield and engaged the Revolutionary
Guard in shooting matches. Several days of street engagements cul-

minated on 27 September with a major confrontation, in which the Mojahedin used machine guns and rocket-propelled grenade launchers against the Revolutionary Guard, upturned buses, and set a gas station on fire. Although street clashes continued, the mass demonstrations for which the Mojahedin hoped did not materialize.

The Fadayan (minority faction), the Paykar, and other left-wing groups also went underground and took up arms against the Islamic Republic. In Bandar Abbas and Abadan, in Isfahan and Kermanshah, in Rasht and Tabriz, guerrillas and revolutionaries, the gun-bearing children of the Iranian revolution, fought and killed one another. In July 1981, adherents of the *Ettehadiyyeh-ye Kommunist-ha* (Union of Communists), a Maoist group that believed in rural-based rather than urban-based guerrilla war, emerged from their secret camps in the forests of Mazandaran and tried to seize control of the Caspian town of Amol. At least seventy guerrillas and guards were killed in the ensuing clashes.

The bombing of the IRP headquarters and of the prime minister's offices, along with the first rush of assassinations, shook the government to its foundations. For a moment it appeared that the leaders of the country would be systematically eliminated. The death of Beheshti was a particularly serious blow. Moreover, it appeared as if the opposition could strike at will and had penetrated the innermost sanctums of the government. For example, the authorities had traced the 30 August bomb, placed in a booby-trapped briefcase which was set before the prime minister, to Mas'ud Kashmiri, an aide to the special security committee. Kashmiri, who had disappeared and was now thought to be a member or a sympathizer of the Mojahedin, had received security clearance to work at the highest levels of military counterintelligence. He had served in J-2, or army counterintelligence, was then assigned to review confidential files in the air force, and in his last assignment had access to confidential files in the prime minister's office.[2]

The government responded by ruthlessly suppressing street demonstrations, by raiding the "safe houses" of the left-wing organizations, and by mass arrests and executions. The executions began immediately after Bani-Sadr's impeachment and intensified after the bombing attacks on the IRP headquarters and the prime minister's offices. Driven by fear, determined to crush the incipient rebellion, the authorities visited a terrible vengeance on their challengers. Executions of fifty a day became routine. Some 149 persons were executed on 19 September alone, 110 on a single day a week later.

The executions, primarily aimed at the left-wing opposition, were indiscriminate. Among those killed were two prominent bazaar merchants, Baha'is, and royalists already long in jail. Sa'id Soltanpour, the left-wing poet, was taken out of his cell and shot. In September 1981, a thirteen-year-old girl, Fatemeh Mesbah, and her fifteen-year-old sister were sent before the firing squad. Families of the executed often received mutilated bodies; mistreatment of prisoners became widespread at Evin prison in Tehran, where Asadollah Lajvardi, a shopkeeper turned revolutionary prosecutor, and Mohammad Mohammadi-Gilani, a cleric and chief of the Tehran revolutionary court, held sway. The provincial revolutionary courts proved themselves apt pupils of the Tehran model.

Little attempt was made in the early months to disguise the executions. On the contrary, the emphasis was on setting an example. In Kerman in September 1981, two members of the Mojahedin were publicly hanged; the arch of one of the city's bridges served as their scaffold. When students at the Tehran high school expressed sympathy with their purged instructors, four of the teachers were shot in the school yard, in view of the children.[3] It was the size and strength of the opposition that fed the government's fears. "We cannot practice forgiveness or leniency," the revolutionary prosecutor-general, Hosain Musavi-Tabrizi, said, "when faced with so many people."[4]

Revolutionary court officials manufactured a rough Islamic justice to support their actions. Even twelve-year-olds could be shot for participating in armed demonstrations, Lajvardi said. "The age does not matter." Musavi-Tabrizi announced that henceforth demonstrators would be "tried in the streets"; and Mohammadi-Gilani remarked that "Islam does not allow wounded rebels to be hospitalized. They should be finished off."[5] The executions were, in fact, the result of deliberate policy and a high-level government decision. In a circular to the revolutionary courts, the High Judicial Council had ordered the death penalty for "active members" of the guerrilla groups.[6]

The terror continued at high pitch for eighteen months. The number who lost their lives will probably never be known with certainty. Amnesty International documented 2,946 executions in the twelve months following Bani-Sadr's impeachment.[7] In a list compiled the following year, the Mojahedin claimed 7,746 persons had lost their lives through execution, in street battles, or under torture in the short period from June 1981 to September 1983. Of those whose manner of death, party affiliation, and age could be determined, 85 percent died by execution. Nearly 90 percent were affiliated to the Mojahedin. Most of the rest were affiliated to the Fadayan, Paykar, and the Kurdish Democratic Party; a number came from a clutch of small left-wing organizations. The average age of those killed was twenty-four; over 50 percent were either high-school or college students.[8]

The post-Bani-Sadr terror had far-reaching consequences for the opposition movement and the government. First, the guerrilla groups emerged from two years of armed struggle with their ranks decimated, their printing presses and weapons in government hands, their organizational networks ruptured, and their leaders eliminated. The Paykar chief and his deputy, and the leading figures of the Fadayan movement, were arrested or killed in confrontations in 1981 and 1982. Several of the smaller guerrilla movements were for all practical purposes annihilated. In August 1982, one year after the dramatic raid on Amol, 100 members of the *Ettehadiyyeh-ye Kommunist-ha* were captured. Twenty-two were subsequently sentenced to death, most of the others to prison terms.

The Mojahedin survived, thanks to their numerical and organizational superiority and their tactical and doctrinal flexibility. Hashemi-Rafsanjani said later that the authorities had seized from them "enough safe houses to make up a city . . . enough arms to equip several divisions."[9] Nevertheless, the Mojahedin lost their second-in-command, Musa Khiabani, several field commanders and key leaders, and thousands of their followers.

Second, the results expected by the left from the strategy of urban armed struggle were not realized. The Mojahedin and other guerrilla organizations believed they could ignite through armed warfare a second rebellion—this time against Khomaini himself. However, the Revolutionary Guard held firm. The government did not collapse. The "masses," whether out of fear, despair, or indifference did not rise up against the state. The sharp drop in guerrilla activities in 1983 was a consequence both of the losses that these organizations had suffered and also of their uncertainty as to the effectiveness of further urban guerrilla activities. Many Fadayan and Mojahedin, in fact, abandoned urban guerrilla activity to join the Kurds in the mountains of northwest Iran, where the fitful fire of the Kurdish rebellion continued to smolder.

Third, while two years of violent struggle initially reinforced the extremist elements in the ruling party, enshrined terror as a legitimate tool of government, and led to the erosion of public support for the regime, the Islamic government, ironically, emerged from the experience more firmly in control of the country.

The government acted to crush not only the guerrilla organizations but other opponents of the Islamic Republic as well. It uncovered several royalist and what it described as "nationalist" plots against the state, sometimes involving elements in the armed forces. Eleven other officers involved in the 1981 "Operation Red Alert," at the air base at Hamadan, were sent before the firing squad.

In April 1982, Sadeq Qotbzadeh was arrested on charges of plotting with military officers and clerics to bomb Khomaini's home and to overthrow the state. Qotbzadeh denied any intentions on Khomaini's life and claimed he had sought to change the government, not to overthrow the Islamic Republic. He also implicated Ayatollah Shariatmadari, who he claimed had been informed of the plan and promised funds and his blessings if the scheme succeeded.[10]

Qotbzadeh, Khomaini's ardent promoter during the long years of exile, his aide and confidante in Paris, his foreign minister in Tehran, was executed. Shariatmadari's son-in-law, who served as intermediary between Qotbzadeh and the Ayatollah, was sentenced to a prison term. A propaganda campaign was mounted to discredit Shariatmadari himself. Doctored documents were produced to suggest that in negotiations with the Shah's government in 1978, Shariatmadari had approved of martial law and had described himself as an opponent of Khomaini.

Shariatmadari's Center for Islamic Study and Publications in Qom was shut down. He was placed under house arrest. In Parliament and from the pulpit, younger clerics accused him of treason. He was denounced by members of the influential Society of the Qom Seminary Teachers; at their behest, in a move virtually without precedent, he was declared to have been stripped of his title as a *marja'-e taqlid*, or source of emulation. No voice was raised against this treatment of an eminent religious leader. Whereas in December 1979, the people of Tabriz rose in rebellion in Shariatmadari's name, in the fear-ridden atmosphere of 1982 these events were passed over in silence in his constituency.

In June 1982, a contingent of the Revolutionary Guard pursued and finally caught Khosrow Qashqa'i, who had been leading his tribesmen in a minor rebellion in the province of Fars. Qashqa'i was tried and hanged on 1 October in a public square in Firuzabad, the administrative center of the Qashqa'i tribal country.

The Kurdish rebels proved more intractable. The Kurds operated in mountain country and the Kurdish Democratic Party (KDP) enjoyed considerable support in the major towns, such as Mahabad, Sardasht, Bukan, and Piranshahr. The Kurds were receiving arms and support from the government of Iraq. The rebels straddled areas of the frontier, and hampered the war effort against Baghdad. The adherence of the KDP to the NCR was a cause of concern to the Iranian government. The KDP leader, Qasemlu, moved easily from Kurdistan, through Iraq or Turkey, to Paris and back, as did members of other rebel groups, linking the opposition at home and abroad. Mojahedin and Fadayan were receiving valuable training fighting alongside the Kurds. Both the KDP and the Mojahedin broadcast antigovernment news and programs from small transmitters in Kurdish territory.

A campaign against the Kurds was already under way when Bani-Sadr was impeached. With the fall of Bukan to government forces in November 1981, the government came to control all the major towns, although the Kurds had the freedom of the roads and held important smaller centers like Miraveh. The government launched a new offensive in the spring of 1982. In the fall, the commander of the ground forces, Sayyad Shirazi, led a combined force of army and Revolutionary Guard units against the rebels. It was the largest force to be massed against the Kurds. Although the KDP and Komaleh patched up differences to set up a joint command, government forces succeeded in securing the strategic Sardasht–Piranshahr road. The Kurds lost territory and part of their radio transmitting equipment. Kurdish resistance persisted, but on a reduced scale.[11]

"The Vengeance of God"

The assassination of IRP and government leaders brought new faces to the fore in the party and the government. Following the death of Raja'i and Bahonar, Khomaini named the minister of interior and chief of the Tehran revolutionary committees, Mohammed-Reza Mahdavi-Kani, as interim prime minister. Mahdavi-Kani was a moderate. The Association of the Combatant Clerics of Tehran which he headed competed with the IRP for power, and he aspired to the presidency. However, Ali Khamene'i, the IRP candidate, was elected president in the elections held in October 1981. Mahdavi-Kani was passed over as prime minister, a post which went to Mir-Hosain Musavi, the editor of the IRP party newspaper, *Jomhuri-ye Eslami*. In August, Mahdavi-Kani was replaced as interior minister by another cleric and IRP member, Ali-Akbar

Nateq-Nuri. Mahdavi-Kani's appointees were replaced by IRP men in provincial governments, sometimes down to the township and district levels. In this way the IRP consolidated its hold on the administrative apparatus.

The rise of Ali Khamene'i, who also became secretary-general of the IRP, and the changes that occurred in the cabinet, did not in the short run greatly influence the course of policy. The war waged against the left played a far more immediate role in determining the character of the post-Bani-Sadr government. The terror enhanced the influence of the extremist and anarchic elements in the ruling coalition; and it intensified efforts to impose ideological conformity and to Islamize the society.

The role and importance of the Revolutionary Guard and the revolutionary committees grew. In effect they became the protective shield standing between the clerics and those who would destroy them. They gathered the intelligence through which left-wing cells were discovered. In the process, they secured once again freedom for the full expression of their lawless inclinations. They entered homes at will, harassed members of households, and made unauthorized arrests. When they could not find the person they sought, they took away other members of the family. Believing guerrillas to lie behind every door, they attacked private homes and shot innocent people.

Guards of the *Gasht-e Thar Allah,* or the "Mobile Units of God's Vengeance," toured the cities in cars, machine guns in hand, seeking out suspicious-looking characters. The courts resumed property confiscation on a large scale. In December 1981, Khomaini issued orders to the courts to end unlawful arrests and imprisonment, unwarranted confiscation of property, and the freezing of bank accounts. He named a cleric to check on allegations against the Revolutionary Guard and another cleric to review the activities of the courts. But the directive was ignored and Khomaini did not pursue it.

Khomaini's remarks to the judicial authorities and the courts in August of the following year inadvertently advertised the lawlessness of these bodies. He urged the courts to exercise care lest they "imprison one of the disinherited [thinking him to be] an oppressor and, God forbid, put him to death." He urged the Revolutionary Guard to make sure a house was a guerrilla hideout before shooting it up, "lest they enter a home to come upon women and children and, before they realize what is what, some of the children are killed or wounded."[12]

The stubborn persistence of the resistance movement transformed the inclination to root out ideological nonconformity into an obsession and infected virtually every area of public life. Khomaini urged parents to turn in their misguided children, students to report on their classmates and teachers, and Islamic committees in factories and offices to purge their fellow employees. Khomaini noted with satisfaction that if the Shah had to rely on a secret police, the Islamic Republic could call on a nation of thirty-six million informers.

The Ideological-Political Bureau in the armed forces, run by clerics and charged with ensuring ideological conformity among the troops, maintained 2,000 secret agents to watch out for and report on "suspicious movements" in the barracks. Some 270 clerics of the bureau served in the role of political commissars. They led communal prayers and delivered sermons at military bases, saw to the ideological instruction of the troops, and vetoed applicants to the Officers Staff College to prevent the admission of those with leftist political ideas. Ideological-political bureaus also operated in the national police and gendarmerie.[13]

When the universities began to reopen in 1982, students were subjected to similar tests of political loyalty; those with left-wing leanings were refused admission. The imposition of loyalty tests and of Islamic and ideological criteria in public employment, became widespread. Applicants to a three-year program to train university instructors, for example, were required to be practicing Muslims and to declare their loyalty to the Islamic Republic, the revolution, and the doctrine of the vice-regency of the *faqih*. Non-Muslims were required to refrain from behavior "offensive to Muslims," and were excluded from all fields of study except accounting and foreign languages.[14]

The Law for the Renewal of Manpower Resources in Ministries and Government Offices, approved in 1981, had been intended to curb the excesses of the ubiquitous purge committees. Fresh committees (now called "manpower renewal" rather than "purge" committees) were formed under the new law, however. They usurped the authority of the ministers and departmental chiefs and launched a new wave of expulsions from the civil service. Thousands of teachers were among those who were dismissed. "Placement committees" *(komiteh-ha-ye gozinesh)* materialized in government departments and state-owned enterprises. They assumed responsibility for checking on the ideological credentials of job applicants, examined applicants on arcane points of Islamic faith, impugned the reputation of employees with "revelations," quizzed wives of employees on the private life and religious conduct of their husbands, and expelled civil servants from jobs.

Further measures were introduced to Islamize the judiciary. In May 1982, Parliament approved the Law on the Conditions for the Selection of Judges. The law reserved judgeships to the *mojtaheds*, or the seminary-trained experts in Islamic law, alone. It permitted secular judges to hear cases only if they were proficient in Islamic law, and only as long as there were insufficient *mojtaheds* to go around. Secular judges were otherwise to be transferred to advisory and clerical posts, to be retired or to be dismissed. The chief justice estimated that 50 percent of the existing civil judges would have to be sacked.

In August, Khomaini forced the issue on the highly complex and controversial problem of Islamizing the country's law codes. He instructed the courts to "throw out" all non-Islamic laws and to base their decisions on Islamic regulations alone. This fed the turmoil in the courts, since Islamic rulings on many issues were not clear. Special panels of jurists had to be established to respond to the queries of lower-level judges. Khomaini's ruling, however, galvanized Parliament to approve bills for the Islamization of the penal, civil, and procedural law codes and led a reluctant Council of Guardians, after some changes had been made in the penal law, to give them its imprimatur. The new codes meant that the canonically specified Islamic punishments *(hadd)*, for example the cutting off of hands for theft and stoning for adultery, the law of talion *(qasas)*—an eye for an eye, a life for a life—and the law of blood money *(diyat)* would have to be imposed by the courts.[15]

In the fall, Mehdi Bazargan addressed an open letter to Majles Speaker Hashemi-Rafsanjani, accusing the government of creating an "atmosphere of terror, fear, revenge and national disintegration." He then asked, "What has the ruling elite done in nearly four years, besides bringing death and destruction, packing the prisons and the cemeteries in every city, creating long queues, shortages, high prices, unemployment, poverty, homeless people, repetitious slogans and a dark future?"[16] This had become a widely shared sentiment.

Khomaini's December Decree

The wave of extremism and terror peaked, and then in late 1982 it began to wane. By then, the back of the opposition movement had been broken. The thirst for bloodletting, as in the 1979 cycle, had spent itself. Moreover, support for the regime among the middle classes and even the urban masses—Khomaini's natural constituency—had been further eroded; a deep revulsion set in against the routine killing of the young.

The turnout for the election held late in the year for the Assembly of Experts, which was to select Khomaini's successor, was unusually low. Constant purges were crippling the civil service. Educated Iranians continued to leave the country. Uncertainty and turmoil were adversely affecting business confidence and economic activity.

Pragmatists in the ruling coalition were able in December 1982 to persuade Khomaini to issue an eight-point declaration, aimed at curbing the worst excesses of the revolutionary organizations. The declaration banned the Revolutionary Guard and committees from entering homes, making arrests, conducting searches and interrogations, and confiscating property without legal authorization. It also banned the revolutionary bodies from tapping telephones, delving into the political and religious beliefs of job applicants, spying on Iranians in the privacy of their homes, and dismissing civil servants on flimsy evidence. It urged the courts to act with circumspection, so that the people should feel that "under the protection of the laws of Islamic justice, their life, property and honor are secure."[17]

A high-ranking Central Staff to Follow Up the Imam's Decree, chaired by the prime minister and the chief justice, was established to enforce Khomaini's instructions, to look into the activities of the revolutionary organizations, and to hear citizens' complaints. Subcommittees toured the provinces to hear grievances. Khomaini made a dozen speeches over the next few weeks stressing the need to end revolutionary excesses. "We should no longer say, we are in a revolutionary situation," he remarked. "No. Now is the time of calm. It is a time for people to be secure in all things, to put their capital to work."[18] In a second decree, Khomaini dissolved the notorious "placement committees" and ordered new, more reliable committees to be established.[19] Ministers, Friday prayer leaders, parliamentary deputies, the press, and the mass media pushed the new line.

The impact of the new decree was palpable. The harassment of citizens not involved in politics was eased. The tempo of executions declined. Property confiscations grew more restrained. Curbs were placed on the activities of the purge and placement committees. Travel restrictions were partially lifted. Long-discussed controls over the two revolutionary bodies were given form. The revolutionary committees were placed under the minister of interior; a separate ministry was created for the Revolutionary Guard. This brought both organizations into the cabinet, made them answerable to the Parliament for their budgets and programs, and allowed the interior minister to define jurisdictions between the committees, the national police, and the gendarmerie. Officials of the Shah's government, who had been languishing in prison for over three years, began to be released—in a slow trickle.

Khomaini's December 1982 decree marked a shift away from the prevailing policies of the previous eighteen months. But the exact nature of this shift needs to be understood. The revolutionary organizations were reined in; but there was no sweeping attack on their authority. A few officials, including the revolutionary prosecutor of Qom, were dismissed; but none of the architects of the terror or its worst excesses were touched. The Imam's follow-up committee acted on some of the 300,000 complaints received from citizens; but it referred the bulk of these complaints back to the judiciary and to government and revolutionary organizations for action. In late May, after five months' work, the follow-up committee was dissolved to allow the ministers and other officials on the body to devote themselves to their executive duties, and its responsibilities were transferred to the judiciary. It was an indication that the task of follow-up had become a routine matter and had lost its urgency. The attempt by a few officials to use Khomaini's decree to neutralize the revolutionary organizations, and by the middle classes to reverse the trend toward Islamization, was quickly squelched.

The Revolutionary Guard stoutly defended its record. The chief justice and the prosecutor-general rejected suggestions that there had been abuses in the administration of justice. Khomaini himself remained restrained in his criticism of these organizations. For four years the regime had based its power on an unruly but highly effective network of revolutionary organizations. Khomaini was not about to permit the ax to be taken to the pillars of this edifice. The prime minister, an advocate of curbs on the revolutionary organizations, took cognizance of Khomaini's attitude. He remarked in May: "Those who imagine the era of the [revolutionary] organizations is over and there is no longer any need for them should know that as long as the Islamic revolution bears aloft the banner of divine unity and preserves its Islamic character, the revolutionary organizations will remain and enjoy the people's support."[20]

The most important effect of the December decree was to curb the brutalities of the Revolutionary Guard, committees, and courts, to create an environment in which citizens would sense a measure of security and resume economic activity, and to establish conditions in which the government could pursue its administrative goals. In another of the pendulum swings between extremism and retrenchment which had characterized the revolution, the pragmatists had emerged on top.

The decree thus helped confirm and consolidate trends noticeable even during the period of the terror and to mark the emergence to political influence of those among the clerics and in the cabinet who desired to get on with the business of rebuilding the economy; devoting attention to such matters as industry, agriculture, housing, domestic distribution, and supply; repairing Iran's relations with Western Europe; and attracting back to the country and the government businessmen and the educated classes. Much of the impulse came from the technocrats of the cabinet and the government: the prime minister, Mir-Hosain Musavi, the director of the Plan and Budget Organization, Taqi Banki, the governor of the Central Bank, Mohsen Nurbakhsh, and the minister of heavy industry, Behzad Nabavi. But these men received support from powerful clerics, such as Hashemi-Rafsanjani, who had inherited a pragmatic streak from his mentor, Beheshti, and had Khomaini's ear. Clerics like Interior Minister Nateq-Nuri did not have to be "moderates" to wish to control the revolutionary committees and to be able to manage the departments under their jurisdiction.

The earliest indications of a returning, if limited, pragmatism, at least in oil and economic policy, emerged during the economic crisis that confronted the government in late 1981. Due to the government's insistence on maintaining high oil prices during a world oil glut and a reputation for unreliability among customers, Iran's oil exports had fallen to under 700,000 barrels a day, or nearly one-third the level necessary to meet the country's foreign exchange requirements. Due to careless foreign exchange management, the high cost of the war, and the terms of the hostage settlement, Iran's reserves had reportedly fallen to under $1 billion, or barely enough to meet one-month's import needs.

The government reacted to this crisis in two ways. First, the Central Bank severely curtailed imports, eventually cutting the import bill by 25 percent. Second, in February 1982 the National Iranian Oil Company cut oil prices by $5 per barrel and launched an aggressive marketing campaign. Iran gave price discounts under the table and exchanged oil for goods in barter deals with third world countries. In the Organization of Petroleum Exporting Countries (OPEC), Iran continued to press for higher production quotas for itself and production cutbacks for Saudi Arabia. But at the OPEC conference Iran surprised other participants by reversing its high-price policy, agreeing to a reduction of official prices, and working more closely with other members.

This was accompanied by an energetic campaign to improve trade ties and win friends abroad, and to resume work on major projects which required foreign technical expertise. The government overcame ideological scruples to expand trade with neighboring countries, particularly Pakistan and Turkey. With Turkey alone, a goods-for-oil agreement worth $1 billion was worked out. It expanded trade with other third world countries, including Brazil and India. It invited Japanese, Italian, German, and other foreign firms back to undertake a number of projects, including a second steel mill at Isfahan, the completion of the Sarcheshmeh copper works, expansion of the Shiraz petrochemical plant, oil-well maintenance, and electric power generation projects.

By mid-1982, technocrats in the cabinet were able to speak out with increasing confidence. They tended to emphasize planning, technical expertise, management skills, and fiscal responsibility. They attributed the country's economic ills, if only by implication, to revolutionary excesses, or at least to haste in dismantling the old order. They made a case for economic development. Ahmad Tavakkoli, the labor minister, criticized the middlemen and distributors who handled basic consumer goods under the monarchy. But he blamed shortages of consumer goods in the Islamic Republic on the dismantling of the old distribution system before the new one was in place.

Nabavi, a former radical transformed into a pragmatist by the realities of office, said in an interview that plant managers appointed after the revolution "have faith but little skill." He noted that Iran had lost "many opportunities" by breaking ties with the industrial countries. He treated the purge of prerevolution managers as a regrettable necessity, decried the lack of economic planning, defended private ownership, and spoke caustically of the achievements of the state-controlled economies of the communist states. Hashemi-Rafsanjani urged exiles to return home: "They can return to Iran," he said. "The people are prepared to forgive their past. We have great plans for building the country, and we need you."[21]

This new mood of pragmatism did not imply political liberalization, a deemphasis on Islamic orthodoxy, or greater tolerance for political opposition. The instruments of repression remained firmly in place. The revolutionary organizations continued to play a key role in decision making and in the administration of the country. The propensity toward extremism was blunted but not eradicated. Rather, the new mood suggested a desire by the religious leaders to restore economic and administrative order and a readiness on their part to allow the technocrats to look after the economy, while the clerics retained power, controlled politics, saw after ideology, and made the basic decisions. At the same time, the leaders of the Islamic Republic developed a foreign policy that was both more self-confident and more intent on exporting Islamic and revolutionary ideology.

Iraq: Exporting Revolution

The war with Iraq and its ramifications in the Persian Gulf remained the primary focus of Iran's foreign policy. While battling its domestic opponents, moving to replace officials lost through assassination, and grappling with a severe economic crisis, the government, astonishingly, found the resources successfully to pursue the war.

After a lull of several months in the fighting, in September 1981 Iranian forces broke the seige of Abadan. In March of the following year, they pushed back Iraqi forces across a wide front in the Dezful area, farther north. In May, a turning point, they routed the Iraqi army and recaptured the port of Khorramshahr. Smaller victories followed. When these campaigns began, Iraq held 4,126 square miles of Iranian territory. By the end of the year, less than 200 square miles remained in Iraqi hands.

For four weeks following the Khorramshahr campaign, hawks and doves in the inner circle of the Iranian government argued over the advantages of carrying the war across the frontier into Iraqi territory. Hashemi-Rafsanjani declared that Iran would not be "adventurous." On the other hand, Colonel Sayyad Shirazi, the young officer who had risen rapidly in the ranks as a result of the revolution and was the architect of the successful offensives against Iraq, said Iran would "continue the war until Saddam falls and we can pray in Karbala." (Karbala is one of Shi'ism's holiest shrine cities.)

Khomaini resolved this debate on 21 June in a statement calling for the overthrow of Saddam Hussein. He appears to have glimpsed the possibility of installing an Islamic regime, allied to Iran, in Baghdad and making this the nucleus of a string of Islamic states throughout the Gulf region. If Saddam is overthrown, he said, the Iraqi people will establish an Islamic government, and "if Iran and Iraq unite and link up with one another, the other, smaller nations of the region will join them as well."[22]

In July, Iranian forces crossed into Iraq in a massive assault on Basra and suffered heavy casualties. Subsequent offensives were also halted by the Iraqis. Iranian attempts to breach Iraqi lines along the northern and central portions of the 340-mile front in October and November, failed to yield dramatic gains.

Nevertheless, the prospects for peace remained dim. Iran demanded the complete evacuation of Iranian territory, the payment by Iraq of reparations, the return to their homes of an estimated 120,000 refugees of Iranian origin expelled from Iraq by the Baghdad authorities, and the "punishment" or overthrow of Saddam Hussein and his Baath regime. The first three of these conditions did not pose a major stumbling block; the fourth did, and Khomaini refused to abandon it. In August 1983, he again squelched talk of a settlement of the war: "The Islamic government of Iran cannot sit at the peace table with a government that has no faith in Islam and in humanity," he said. "Islam does not allow peace between us and him [Saddam], between a Muslim and an infidel."[23]

The Iranian government arranged for the formation in Tehran of the Supreme Council of the Islamic Revolution of Iraq, under the leadership of Mohammad-Baqer Hakim. Hakim, living in exile in Iran, was the son of Ayatollah Mohsen Hakim and a member of one of the leading Shi'a clerical families in Iraq. He declared the primary aim of the council to be the overthrow of the Baath and the establishment of an Islamic government in Iraq. Iranian officials referred to Hakim as the leader of Iraq's future Islamic state; and when in a new offensive in February 1983, Iranian forces secured a small sector of Iraqi territory at the northern end of the front, this was treated as the first base of operations inside Iraq of the supreme council of Iraq's Islamic revolution.

Iraq was not the only target of Iranian efforts to export revolution, or at least to export Khomaini's brand of a militant, politicized Islam. Iran was active in a number of Islamic countries. The regime, however, concentrated on the Persian Gulf states and on Lebanon, focused on the Shi'a communities in these countries, and used as its instruments the army and Revolutionary Guard, propaganda and propagandists, money and subversion. From the early weeks of the revolution, there emerged clerics and ideological schools committed to an activist foreign policy.

The preamble to the constitution refers to the "ideological mission" of the army and the Revolutionary Guard to "extend the sovereignty of God's law throughout the world." The constitution commits the government to strive for the political, cultural, and economic unity of the Islamic world.[24] Khomaini often spoke of Islam as a potent weapon for the overthrow of tyrants and for ridding the Islamic world of Israel, the great powers, and other alien influences. Ayatollah Hosain-Ali Montazeri emerged as the spokesman for the group in the IRP and among the religious leaders who advocated a foreign policy geared to the promotion of a revolutionary Islam.

Iranian officials also claimed for Khomaini, as *faqih,* leadership over Shi'as outside Iran's frontiers and indeed over Muslims everywhere. Following Iranian victories in the Iran–Iraq war in the spring of 1982, President Ali Khamene'i remarked:

> The future government of Iraq should be an Islamic and a popular one. The policy of *velayat-e faqih* will be Iraq's future policy, and the leader of the Islamic nation is Imam Khomaini. There is no difference between the two nations of Iran and Iraq in accepting the Imam as the leader, and following the Imam and his line. Government and state officials are limited to international borders, but the Imam is not limited by geographical frontiers.[25]

Khomaini regarded the annual *hajj* pilgrimage to Mecca as an appropriate vehicle for Islamic propaganda. He rejected the notion that the *hajj* should be kept free from politics. He appointed Mohammad Musavi-Khoeniha, the militant cleric who had served as mentor to the "students of the Imam's line," as the head of Iran's *hajj* organization. In the fall of 1982, an activist core among Iran's 100,000 pilgrims clashed with Saudi police when they staged marches, displayed Khomaini's portrait, and shouted slogans against Israel and America. Musavi-Khoeniha and a number of other Iranians were expelled from Saudi Arabia as a result.

In the following year, Khomaini urged the Iranian pilgrims to treat the *hajj* as an occasion for an "Islamic uprising" and to make it "a vibrant *hajj,* a crushing *hajj,* a *hajj* that condemns the criminal Soviet Union and the criminal America."[26] Ayatollah Montazeri had meantime called on the Islamic nations to take over the administration of the holy sanctuaries in Mecca and Medina. He called the Saudis "a bunch of pleasure-seekers and mercenaries" and asked, "How long must Satan rule in the house of God."[27] On the eve of the 1983 pilgrimage, when the Saudis sought to impose restrictions on the Iranian pilgrims, Musavi-Khoeniha repeated this theme. "If a bunch of Saudi rulers should be able to dictate policies for the *hajj,*" he said, "then we must ask if the government of Saudi Arabia is qualified to administer the holy sanctuaries."[28]

Iran established a Permanent Committee for the *Hajj* to emphasize the political significance of the pilgrimage. It also established the World Congress of Friday Prayer Leaders. At the first international conference in Tehran, in December 1982, President Khamene'i called on Friday prayer leaders from forty countries to turn their mosques into "prayer, political, cultural and military bases" and to "prepare the ground for the creation of Islamic governments in all countries."[29]

There were indications that Iran was prepared to finance subversion in the Gulf sheikhdoms. In December 1981 the government of Bahrain arrested seventy-three persons for plotting to overthrow the government. The well-armed plotters, fifty-eight Bahrainis, eleven Saudis, one Omani, and one Kuwaiti, all Shi'as, were said to have been trained and motivated by Iran.

Iran was also active in Lebanon. Following the Israeli invasion of Lebanon in the summer of 1982, Iran sent a contingent of 300 to 500 Revolutionary Guard, by way of Syria, to assist in the war against Israel. An apparently reluctant Syria allowed the guards to install themselves at Baalbek. The Iranians immediately established a propaganda office, proselytzed among the inhabitants in favor of a Khomaini-type Islamic state, and pressured the local women to wear the Islamic headdress. In November, the Shi'as in Baalbek seized control of the town to protest the policies of the then Lebanese president, Bashir Gemayel. They described themselves as followers of Khomaini. The Iranian government denied any responsibility for their activities, but the Revolutionary Guard contingent reportedly inspired the uprising.

The Iranian government supplied funds to the Amal movement, the predominant Shi'a organization in Lebanon. Iranian officials, including Majles Speaker Hashemi-Rafsanjani, encouraged the organization to adopt more militant policies. Iran was perhaps behind the emergence of a breakaway, strongly pro-Khomaini group, the Islamic Amal led by a Lebanese Shi'a, Hosain Musavi. The organization established its headquarters in Baalbek.

It was reported to be responsible for the bombing of the American embassy in Beirut in April 1982 and for the October 1983 car-bomb attacks against three buildings in Lebanon housing respectively, American, French, and Israeli military personnel. The bombings cost nearly 300 lives. American Secretary of Defense Caspar Weinberger accused Syria and the Iranians of involvement in the bombing attacks; and the Lebanese government suspended diplomatic relations with Iran, closed the Iranian embassy in Beirut, and asked for the withdrawal of Iranian fighting men from Lebanese soil.

On a smaller scale, Iran was accused of stirring up or offering assistance to Muslim communities in the Philippines and Malaysia. The Iranian example appears to have inspired Shi'a communities in Pakistan and Turkey, in Saudi Arabia and North Yemen, to demand greater rights.[30]

The Islamic Republic brought a number of assets to its campaign to export its militancy to Islamic communities in other countries. The Iranian revolution and Khomaini's leadership excited Shi'a communities everywhere and the urban masses in the Arab world. Iran could draw on a large pool of preachers, lay propagandists, and the Revolutionary Guard to serve as the vehicles for the message of the Iranian revolution. Oil money allowed Iran to finance its own operations and to sponsor activities by indigenous Islamic groups.

On the other hand, the Iranian revolution has lost some of its allure with widespread executions and evidence of internal divisions. Khomaini's successor is unlikely to exercise an equal degree of magnetism on Muslims in other countries. Iran's strongly Shi'a character stirs up hostility among Sunni Muslims. Iran's desire for working relations with other Muslim states and in OPEC acts as a restraint on Iranian extremism. Thus, pragmatism has often got the better of ideology.

Iran did not permit Sunni–Shi'a sectarian clashes in Karachi to stand in the way of continued good relations with Pakistan; nor did it allow Turkey's secular character or membership in NATO to stand in the way of substantial trade exchanges with that country. Iran–Saudi relations remained strained; but Iran maintained good relations with the United Arab Emirates and, beginning in 1982, worked fairly smoothly with other OPEC states. Iran, nevertheless, retained the capacity to stir up mischief in other Muslim countries, particularly where sizable Shi'a communities exist.

The USA and the USSR

The release of the American hostages in January 1981 did not lead to an abatement of the fierce anti-American rhetoric emanating from Tehran. On the contrary, Iranian officials blamed the Iraqi invasion on American instigation. Iranians, Khomaini said, should "cut off the hand of America which has emerged from Saddam's sleeve." Cartoons routinely depicted Iraqi aircraft raining down bombs, marked with American (and Israeli) flags, on Iranian cities.

Official propaganda depicted the Mojahedin as American agents; deputies in Parliament accused Bazargan of being "in the American line." The Saudis were frequently described as "American mercenaries." Khomaini continued to project an overwhelming personal animosity toward the United States. Anti-Americanism was an integral component of revolutionary rhetoric and ideology, public opinion was powerfully aroused on the issue, and there appeared to be little likelihood of improved relations.

However, hostility toward the United States did not, in the longer run, rebound to the Soviet Union's advantage.[31] In the first two years following the revolution, the Soviet Union appeared to enjoy a favored status in Tehran. It took Khomaini several months, and then only at the urging of Bani-Sadr, to remark disapprovingly of the Soviet presence in Afghanistan.

As noted earlier, Iran came to rely more heavily on a Soviet ally, North Korea, for arms, on Soviet trade and transit routes, and on imports from the socialist bloc countries, as a result of the war with Iraq. The Soviet bloc accounted for 15 percent of Iranian imports in 1981 as against 5 percent before the revolution. Some 21 percent of Iranian imports moved through Soviet ports and transit routes in 1981 as against 6 percent in the prerevolution period. Soviet technicians continued to work on the second-phase expansion of the Isfahan steel mill, railway electrification, and silo and electric power plant construction. These were carryovers of projects agreed upon before the revolution.

In a dispute over prices, the Iranian government interrupted the supply of natural gas to the Soviet Union shortly after the revolution. Gas shipments were not resumed. In 1980, the Iranian government closed down the Russian consulate at Rasht and reduced the size of the Soviet mission in Tehran. These appeared to be minor irritants in an otherwise smooth relationship.

However, Iranian–Soviet relations deteriorated rapidly in 1982. Iranian officials grew increasingly critical of the Soviet presence in Afghanistan. In February, during celebrations to mark the anniversary of the revolution, marchers on parade briefly trampled on the Russian flag (trampling on the American flag was routine practice on such occasions). The Iranians directed Islamic propaganda at the Muslim population in southern Russia from a new transmitter erected near the Soviet frontier. When a delegation of Shi'a religious leaders from the Caucasus visited Iran, Iranian clerics lectured them on the mistreatment of Muslims in the Soviet Union. Iran sent only a low-level delegation to Brezhnev's funeral. In December, Afghan refugees were permitted to demonstrate in front of the Soviet embassy in Tehran.

There were a number of reasons for the change in Iranian attitudes.

Officials appear to have grown alarmed over the implications of the Soviet military presence in Afghanistan. Within the inner circle of the IRP and the government, the influence of elements who favored close relations with the USSR declined. Possibly as a result of the war with Iraq, both nationalist and Islamic sentiments were reinforced; there emerged an almost fierce determination to stay free of entanglements with both East and West. Anti-Russian sentiment was heightened by Soviet attitudes to the course of the revolution and to the Iran–Iraq war.

The Russians in turn grew critical of what they saw as the increasingly conservative and anti-Soviet course of the revolution, of restrictions placed on Tudeh party activity, and of the Iranian tendency to equate Russian with American imperialism. Pavel Demchenko, writing in *Pravda* in March 1982, said Soviet-Iranian relations were characterized by "both positive and negative aspects." While economic cooperation was "not going badly," he noted, "unfortunately this cannot be said about other spheres of Soviet Iranian relations, which have suffered casualties in the past two or three years."[32] The Soviets were also irritated by Iran's refusal to settle the war with Iraq. In the fall of 1982, they resumed arms deliveries to Iraq, which had been suspended at the start of the war. Soviet missiles were subsequently used to attack residential areas in Dezful, further fueling Iranian resentment.

The major casualty of the deteriorating relations with the Soviet Union was the Tudeh party. The Tudeh had been tolerated because of its unstinting support for Khomaini; but after June 1981, it did not escape the general political repression. Its party newspaper was closed in June and other party publications were suspended in the following year. The party found it difficult to engage in open political activity. Government officials in 1982 openly criticized the party. Hashemi-Rafsanjani said the Tudeh and their allies, the majority Fadayan, "are inspired from abroad; they are practically Russians."[33] Foreign Minister Ali-Akbar Velayati described members of the party as "impudent" for seeking to appropriate the revolution to their own ends and warned that the communists seek to visit on Iran a calamity "like the calamity which the communists brought down on the Muslim people of Afghanistan."[34]

The traditional animosity felt by the clerics toward Marxist groups intensified during the struggle against the Mojahedin and other guerrilla organizations. The Tudeh had collaborated with the IRP in undermining first Bazargan, then Bani-Sadr. They supported the suppression of the Mojahedin. The IRP welcomed this support; but with the elimination of the IRP's rivals, the Tudeh themselves became dispensible. In June 1982, Vladimir Kuzichkin, a Soviet diplomat who had served as vice-consul in Tehran, defected to Britain. He reportedly provided information on 400 Soviet agents operating in Iran, which the British passed on to the Iranian authorities. Such information could have precipitated the decision to crack down on the Tudeh.

In February 1983, the government arrested Nureddin Kianuri, the secretary-general of the party, members of the Tudeh central committee, and other party leaders. The party was proscribed and its remaining offices shut down. Well over one thousand party members were arrested and other members were ordered to present themselves to the public prosecutor or risk arrest. In April, eighteen Soviet diplomats were expelled in connection with the charges brought against the Tudeh. The Tudeh leaders were brought on television that same month and, in a performance reminiscent of the Stalinist show trials of the 1930s, Kianuri confessed to "espionage, deceit and treason."

He declared the party guilty of spying for the Soviet Union, working to infiltrate government organizations, seeking to overthrow the Islamic Republic, and acting in other ways in violation of Khomaini's express instructions and against the interests of the state. Other party members described the Tudeh as a washed-up force in Iran. Lest the lesson be lost on the television audience, Kianuri urged the country's youth to beware of leftist tendencies, "since this is the mother of all treason, the source of all treasonable acts."[35]

The Soviet reaction to these developments was surprisingly subdued. Moscow denied charges directed at the Soviet Union, criticized the arrest of members of the Tudeh party, and blamed "reactionaries" in the government for these precipitate actions. However, there was no attempt to disrupt trade, interrupt projects, or withdraw technicians working in Iran.

The government, meantime, developed relations with third world countries, espoused third world causes, and was active as a member of the nonaligned group of countries, gave verbal support to a broad spectrum of national liberation movements, and joined Syria and the other countries of the "steadfastness front" in adopting an uncompromising stand against the state of Israel. Along with the strong anti-American and anti-Soviet tone of official propaganda, it was a foreign policy that appeared to have a large degree of domestic appeal.

Chapter 10

A House Divided

THE CONSOLIDATION of power did not, in the post-1984 period, end divisions and conflicts within the ruling coalition. The men around Khomaini had succeeded in eliminating their political rivals. But they remained divided among themselves on major issues of policy and over the manner in which Islamic law was to be applied to governing the country. The central government could not always control its own officers, and the revolutionary organizations remained only imperfectly integrated into the governmental structure. War and economic problems deepened divisions within the leadership.

Opposition at Home

A deteriorating economy, a seemingly endless war, the government's inability to protect the cities against Iraqi aerial bombings (which were resumed in March 1985), and the constant harassment by the numerous guardians of public morality fed general dissatisfaction. On 10 April 1985, antigovernment demonstrations broke out in the 13th Aban district of Tehran. Demonstrations spread quickly to other parts of the city and to other cities in the country.

These demonstrations were the first popular manifestations of unrest in many years. Everywhere, the protests involved ordinary people, and they took on both an antigovernment and an antiwar character. The government responded in a predictable manner. It arrested several hundred demonstrators; denounced the protests as the work of the radical, left-wing opposition; and organized counterdemonstrations of its own. Over several days, the *hezbollahis,* the club wielders of the Party of God, roamed the streets of Tehran, on foot and on motorcycles, harassing men and women for improper dress and appearance. The authorities made no attempt to control them. Alarmed at the pervading air of disorder, President Khamene'i, on 23 April 1985, called for an end to *hezbollahi* activity. The antigovernment protests also died down, but the sharp, sudden explosion in April provided a glimpse of the antiwar sentiment and a simmering resentment, even in urban, working-class areas, against the government.

Few political channels for the articulation of grievances remained. Of the opposition groups and parties, only the Iran Freedom Movement, led by the former Prime Minister Mehdi Bazargan, survived the ruthless repression of 1981–83, and the movement was tolerated as long as it maintained a low level of activity. Bazargan continued to speak out against the violation of civil liberties, the clerical monopolization of power, and the spreading financial corruption. He issued public declarations and open letters to the authorities, published books, and gave on-the-record interviews to the foreign press when possible. A member of the Majles until the spring of 1984, he occasionally spoke from the floor of the house. The Iran Freedom Movement itself pursued a range of party activities.

But the Freedom Movement's position was precarious. As already noted, party headquarters were attacked in 1983, when Bazargan tried to organize a meeting to discuss the forthcoming parliamentary elections. Two party officials, also members of Parliament, were physically assaulted on the floor of the house. Bazargan and his colleagues, citing the absence of freedom, decided not to contest seats in the 1984 parliamentary elections. After the term of the first Majles ended in 1984, the Iran Freedom Movement as well was excluded from Parliament. A letter Bazargan addressed to Khomaini in August on the issues of political freedom and government mismanagement of the country went unanswered. In 1985, on the eve of celebrations to mark the sixth anniversary of the revolution, Bazargan issued a declaration calling for a return to the rule of law and warning that "the nation may be approaching the point of explosion."[1] On 6 February, under the eye of the Tehran public prosecutor, bands of *hezbollahis* attacked and wrecked the Freedom Movement offices. The party newspaper was shut down. This became the pattern. The Freedom Movement would, for a while, enjoy limited freedom to issue declarations or publish books. Club wielders were on hand whenever the movement attempted to broaden its political activities.

Bazargan aroused official ire by his criticism of political conditions and by his forthright antiwar position. He believed Iraq, as the aggressor, must accept responsibility for the war and pay Iran reparations. And he also believed the killing must stop. While Khomaini rejected negotiations with Baghdad and insisted on the overthrow of Saddam Hussein, Bazargan argued for direct negotiations, a "just and honorable" peace, and the principle of noninterference, leaving the Iraqi people to determine their own internal affairs. The war was damaging to Iran, he said, and Iran lacked religious justification once the enemy had been expelled from Iranian territory.[2]

Both the antiwar and the prowar positions were articulated in Islamic terms. Bazargan's stand received indirect support from a number of clerics who held either that Islam sanctioned self-defense, not aggressive war, against other Muslims, or that *jihad,* or holy war, to spread the faith could not be declared in the absence of the Hidden Imam. Ayatollah Qomi-Tabataba'i publicly and repeatedly condemned the war and implicitly denied it religious sanction by stating that no martyrdom could be earned by death in this enterprise. In April 1985, Bazargan and sixty other members of the Iran Freedom Movement and the National Front addressed a letter to the United Nations secretary general, urging him to negotiate a peaceful settlement of the conflict. In August 1986, in an open letter to Khomaini, he described the government's slogan of "war, war until victory" as a formula for "war, war until self-annihilation."[3]

Bazargan was attacked, though not by name, in sermons by leading officials. Khomaini himself condemned those, at home and abroad, "who want us at any price to make peace with Saddam Hussein."[4] He took the view that Saddam Hussein was not a true Muslim; that he intended to destroy not only Iran but also Islam; that the war was therefore defensive; and that it was a religious imperative for Muslims to fight it. "When it becomes necessary, one should draw the sword and fight against the enemies of Islam," he said, even if those enemies professed themselves to be Muslims. "If Islam instructs [the believer] to fight against Muslims, he will fight against them; if Islam instructs him to fight against the infidels, he will do so."[5]

The war issue reinforced Bazargan's difficulties with the authorities. Bazargan was not permitted to stand as a candidate in the presidential elections in the summer of 1985. For a moment, his candidacy had appeared to be a possibility. Some in the clerical leadership, notably Ayatollah Montazeri, argued that Bazargan should be allowed to run. But fear that his antiwar stand would prove popular, that he would win a substantial bloc of votes, that his candidacy would prove divisive, and that his campaign would elicit a violent reaction from the radical right prevailed. The Guardianship Council vetoed his candidacy, and Khomaini did not intercede.

Bazargan's politics were moderate; his piety was not in question. He had never publicly wavered in his loyalty to Khomaini, the revolution, and the constitution. But he was perceived as a threat to the ruling clerics precisely because he appeared to offer an Islam without repression and regimentation. His book, *The Revolution in Two Movements,* had sold 100,000 copies. He enjoyed support among the middle classes and the technocracy. The ban on his candidacy extinguished the hope, entertained by Bazargan and others, that political change might be effected through the ballot box. Bazargan himself appeared to draw such a conclusion. In an unusually strong open letter and interviews on the eve of the presidential election, he denounced the violation of freedoms granted by the constitution and described the elections themselves as lacking in legitimacy. To vote in the elections, he said, was to sign "the warrant for the enslavement of the nation."[6]

When the Iran Freedom Movement attempted to resume political activity in April 1986, the gathering was attacked, and participants were taken outside the city and beaten. That same month, Bazargan joined former members of the National Front to form the Society for the Defense, Freedom, and National Sovereignty of the Iranian People, which also campaigned against the suppression of civil rights. In May 1988, eight members of the Freedom Movement and the new society were again arrested and not released for several weeks. In another open letter to Khomaini, Bazargan noted in October that the impossibility of legitimate political opposition would lend credence to those who argued for violent resistance and overthrow of the state. Khomaini, he said, was paving the way for "unbelief, internal dictatorship, despotism and foreign domination."[7]

The government also displayed little tolerance for nonpolitical but autonomous professional organizations. In June 1986, it submitted a bill to the Majles to permit the government to name an overwhelming majority of the members on the governing board of the Medical Association, the primary body representing and regulating the affairs of the country's physicians. The officers of the Medical Association had been elected by the association's own members. In July, the prime minister dissolved the governing board and the local boards of the Medical Association throughout the country. When the doctors went on strike, club wielders attacked their clinics. Officers of the association were arrested and sentenced to terms of exile in the provinces. Earlier, the government had dissolved the Lawyers' Association. In 1987, it transferred the authority to issue permits to businessmen who wished to engage in the import-export trade, a prerogative that had always been in the hands of the business community itself, from the Tehran Chamber of Commerce to the commerce ministry.

Radical opposition groups operating underground maintained a low level of terrorist activities. Bombs occasionally went off on busy Tehran streets and, in one instance, during Friday prayers at Tehran University. Low-level assassinations occurred, but the scale of such activities was small in 1984 when compared to previous years. In 1986, the Mojahedin-e Khalq were expelled from France and moved their headquarters and operations to Iraq. Identification with the Baghdad regime damaged the organization's standing inside the country. The Iranian government's repressive apparatus was, in any case, reorganized and reinforced. In 1984, the security organization was upgraded to a ministry, the Ministry of Intelligence and Security Affairs, headed by Mohammad Mohammadi-Rayshahri, the former judge of the military revolutionary court. Although the number of executions reported by Amnesty International, 115 in 1986 and 158 in 1987, was lower than in previous years, widespread arrests of political activists continued.[8]

There was some diminution in the harassment of ordinary citizens, but little improvement occurred in the harsh treatment of political prisoners or in the nightmare world of Evin prison. Ayatollah Hosain-Ali Montazeri, who sought some softening of the worst features of Evin, succeeded in October 1984 in securing the removal of the notorious Tehran revolutionary prosecutor, Asadollah Lajvardi. Conditions at Evin, however, did not markedly improve under Lajvardi's successor. Amnesty International continued to report widespread mistreatment of political prisoners.

The Economy

The government's economic problems were exacerbated by the war with Iraq, an inflated and inefficient government sector, the erosion of private sector confidence, the drop in both private and public sector investment, and a steep decline in oil revenues. By 1983–84, the war and war-related activities were absorbing almost one-third of the budget.[9] The war drained away foreign exchange, manpower, and scarce resources. Iraqi attacks on tanker and merchant shipping, and damage inflicted by aerial bombing on the Khark terminal, disrupted oil exports, raised the price of shipping insurance, and forced Iran to offer substantial discounts on oil prices. To add to this problem, oil exports were adversely affected by falling prices and a slack world market.

Oil revenues, which in 1983–84 were $3.7 billion below projected earnings, fell $6 billion below projections in 1984–85. Oil income declined from over $20 billion in 1983 to under $6 billion in 1986–87, a particularly difficult year. The result was an erratic, alternating pattern of short-interval economic expansion and retrenchment. The government permitted imports to rise rapidly in 1983–84, imposed import restrictions when faced with a foreign exchange crisis early in 1984, allowed imports to increase again in the latter part of the year, and reverted to much sharper import restrictions and severe cutbacks in domestic spending in 1985. The allocation for industrial raw material imports, which stood at $4 billion in 1983–84, was cut to $2.4 billion in the following year and to $2 billion in 1985–86.

Foreign exchange difficulties mirrored problems in other sectors of the economy. In its industrial policy, the government concentrated on those major projects in steel, copper, petrochemicals, electric power generation, port, railway, and road development, and auto assembly that it had inherited from the previous regime. Virtually no new large industrial projects were initiated during the first decade of the revolution. The government, rather, sought to complete projects already underway or those for which blueprints had already been drawn up. Progress, however, was hampered by the war, shortages of foreign exchange, weak planning, and the absence of trained personnel.

The large nationalized sector was inefficient and operated at a loss. The Foundation for the Disinherited, responsible for hundreds of confiscated industries, farms, apartments, and office blocs, estimated in 1984 that it had real earnings equivalent to around $2 billion and expenses of $4 billion a year. By 1984, the 500 to 600 nationalized industries under the control of the Iran National Industries Organization had piled up liabilities far in excess of total assets.

Large investments in the rural areas and improved prices for agricultural products helped raise rural incomes, but the substantial allocations in the early years of the revolution to encourage small private ventures were inefficiently managed and proved wasteful. The Central Bank reported in 1983, for example, that out of 4,045 small industrial and agricultural ventures funded at the cost of hundreds of millions of dollars, 1,232 failed and had to be written off. The revolutionary organizations did not keep proper books and were not subjected to a careful audit; it was often impossible to say how they spent their money. Only superficial control was exercised over the substantial allocations for arms purchases provided to the military and the Revolutionary Guard.

As a result, a huge state apparatus emerged to oversee rationing; import of essential goods; and allocation, distribution, and pricing of scarce commodities. This helped guarantee subsidized prices for bread, tea, sugar, and other staples. But controls were cumbersome and distorted prices. Shortages were common and corruption in the handling of scarce goods and commodities became widespread.

Tax laws were revised to increase taxation on high-income groups and on property holders. Yet, the tax-collecting machinery remained inefficient. The government consistently ran large budget deficits, which it financed by borrowing from the Central Bank. Levels of inflation remained high. Beginning in 1983, the Majles sought to impose a degree of financial discipline on the government, and the government itself cut back substantially on spending. Nevertheless, deficits continued because revenues were inadequate to meet expenditures. The ratio between development and current expenditure shifted sharply toward current spending, and investments declined.

The Conflict over Social Justice

The poor performance of the economy and the inability of the government to provide adequately for the many or to prevent the excessive enrichment of the few reopened the earlier debate on the fundamental economic policies and orientation of the Islamic Republic.

There were those who blamed inflation, low productivity, and persistent shortages on the government's mismanagement of the economy and the wasteful habits of the bureaucracy. They believed that the private sector was more efficient and a better agent of economic growth. They also believed that uncertainty and the constant fear of nationalization or property confiscation had undermined business confidence and undercut the propensity of the private sector to invest. They argued that the private sector should be given freer rein and that stronger safeguards for property should be provided through legislation.

If the government was demonstrably wasteful and inefficient, then the private sector, when left to itself, appeared recklessly committed to optimum gain and to hoarding and profiteering. Others saw the solution to the country's economic problems to lie in a greater degree of control and direct government involvement in the distribution of wealth. They favored nationalization of foreign trade, government involvement in the distribution of goods, land reform, price controls, and a large government-sponsored housing program.

Both groups were amply represented in the government, in the Majles, and among the senior clerics. Lines could not always be drawn sharply, but Montazeri emerged as a spokesman for the bazaar and the private sector. In the Majles, there were many deputies who favored a narrow interpretation of Islamic law and opposed excessive interference with the private sector. At the other extreme were a group of deputies who favored radical policies of distributive justice, limits on private wealth, and further nationalization of private sector enterprises. In the cabinet, there were also ministers committed to such policies. Between the two groups, but to the left of the center, stood a group led by Ali-Akbar Hashemi-Rafsanjani. He believed in strong government controls over economic activity and in measures, such as land distribution, to ameliorate the lot of the poor. Rafsanjani, however, was not unwaveringly hostile to the private sector.

Both the radicals and those who favored less drastic measures chafed at the Guardianship Council's strict interpretation of Islamic doctrine and its propensity to veto much of the legislation that touched on private property. The radicals grew impatient with the unwillingness of the "moderates" to push ahead with extreme measures.

The debate between these various groups grew acrimonious in the winter of 1983–84. The government came under attack; leaflets critical of the Guardianship Council were circulated. The debate continued into the spring when the new Majles, which included a larger contingent of deputies of a radical temper, was elected. Khomaini, always sensitive to dissension among his followers and to criticism of the clerics he favored, personally intervened in this quarrel. On several occasions, he warned against attempts to weaken the government. He continued to support the government when Parliament convened in May, thus preventing any move from the floor to replace the prime minister. In his message to the opening session of the new Majles, he echoed Rafsanjani's emphasis on the need for legislation to help the deprived, working, and salaried classes. Khomaini also warned that legislation should not deviate "the slightest" from Islam, "for not only is voting against God's laws itself a sin, but also the honorable Guardianship Council will certainly reject [such laws]."[10] Although he subsequently chided the Guardianship Council for obstructing the work of the government, Khomaini's support for the Council remained strong. In September, he advised the cabinet to allow the bazaar merchants to participate more fully in economic activity: "If you do that, capital which they may have held back will come to the bazaar and the banks, people will be assisted in their activities, they will feel secure, and those who believe that the Islamic Republic does not want to work for the people will realize that it does."[11]

Khomaini's intervention did not resolve the issue of the relationship between the private and public sectors or the underlying question of how social justice is to be achieved under an Islamic republic. The proponents of private enterprise and state control, private property and distributive justice, and narrow and broad interpretations of Islamic law confronted one another over virtually every major piece of economic legislation. The Majles and the Guardianship Council repeatedly found themselves at loggerheads over primacy in the interpretation of the constitution and Islamic law.

The parties to this debate were often representing the interests of different constituencies and social groups, although not exclusively. The debate over social justice tended increasingly to turn into a dispute over whether the government or the private sector should control the economy. Both sides appealed to Islamic law and tradition. Since Khomaini tended to speak on behalf of one side then of the other, the result was zigzagging policies, perpetual uncertainty, and a great deal of ideological confusion.

The balance of forces—now in favor of one group, now another—was reflected in the shifting course of legislation during 1984–86. The Guardianship Council beat back attempts to revive laws for the nationalization of foreign trade and vetoed a bill for the regulation of domestic trade and goods distribution. The new foreign trade bill would have allowed the government to take control, over a four-year period, of the import of all essential goods, pharmaceuticals, raw materials, and consumer goods. Extension of state control over the economy seemed to advance inexorably anyway. The government found ways, primarily through regulations relating to the allocation of foreign exchange, to concentrate 80 to 90 percent of foreign trade in its own hands. It resorted to administrative measures to expand its control over the domestic distribution of goods.

The Majles was also able to secure Guardianship Council approval in 1984 for a law to implement Article 49 of the constitution, which made all wealth obtained in a manner violating Islamic principles subject to confiscation. In October 1986, after revisions to meet the objections of the Guardianship Council, it also secured confirmation for a limited land reform bill.

The law on Article 49 of the constitution reflected the inclinations of the Majles radicals. It was so broadly and loosely worded as to ensure a renewed attack on private property. It made the property of virtually every high official, military officer, diplomat, and member of Parliament under the former regime liable to investigation and, when appropriate, to confiscation. Shareholders in expropriated enterprises, multinational companies, and "American, British or Israeli firms," officers of major former-regime contracting and engineering firms, "Freemasons," and those with links to "international spy agencies" were also affected.[12] Depending on how the law was interpreted, several categories of post-revolution officeholders might be subject to investigation. Prosecutor General Mohammed Musavi-Khoeniha used the law to begin once again the confiscation of private companies and enterprises. But counsels in the government remained divided, and Khoeniha was soon stopped. Takeover of private property, however, did not end; the law on Article 49 of the constitution was only erratically implemented.

The land reform law of October 1986 transferred ownership of so-called temporary cultivation agricultural land from the owners to the cultivators actually working the land. Temporary cultivation was the term assigned to land that had been seized by peasants and revolutionary organizations in the immediate aftermath of the revolution and whose status had remained undetermined and in dispute. Uncertainty over ultimate ownership had led to the neglect of the land, its irrigation networks and wells. Hoping to stem this deterioration, the Majles voted to turn over the land to the actual cultivators and to compensate owners who could prove title. About 700,000 to 750,000 hectares of land were to be distributed to around 120,000 cultivators. Between 5,000 and 5,600 landowners were to be dispossessed.[13] The temporary cultivation law, actuated primarily by practical considerations, received strong support from the advocates of distributive justice. Yet it fell far short of the earlier, more sweeping, plans for land distribution and, in the end, settled the status of a limited amount of disputed land. It was one of the few measures on which the Majles and the Guardianship Council could agree—but even then with some difficulty.

Khomaini's January 1988 Rulings

By mid-1987, the Majles and the Guardianship Council were deadlocked over a new series of laws. In the government and the Majles, a sense of paralysis and immobility was once again pervasive. The Guardianship Council had vetoed laws to extend state control over forests, pastures, and undeveloped urban land as well as laws that would have permitted the state to extend its control over the domestic distribution of goods, either through the agency of the ministry of commerce or through the agency of mixed state and private sector distributors' cooperatives. It had objected to a law for the punishment of hoarding and profiteering. It had struck down a new labor law providing for minimum wage guidelines, collective bargaining, maternity leave, and employer contributions to workers' insurance. Such provisions were standard in the labor laws under the monarchy, but the Guardianship Council now ruled that Islamic law did not permit the state to intervene and impose conditions in contracts between consenting adults.

In June 1987, Hashemi-Rafsanjani again took deputies of the Majles and a number of clerical leaders to a meeting with Khomaini. In very much the same language he had employed during a similar session with Khomaini in January 1983 (see chapter 8), Rafsanjani appealed to Khomaini to help the Majles and the Guardianship Council out of their impasse.[14] Khomaini was noncommittal. Six months later, he abandoned his seemingly neutral stance. Early in December, he responded to a query from the minister of labor by ruling that the state could intervene in contracts between private parties and set requirements for those making use of public facilities.[15] This was made clear two weeks later by Hashemi-Rafsanjani: the government could require employers to implement regulations on minimum wages, maternity leave, and workmen's compensation as stipulated in the abortive labor law and restrict access to state-supplied services and facilities such as electricity, water, roads, and ports for noncompliance.[16] The Guardianship Council, expressing fears that this would be interpreted to mean that legal contracts could be voided and activities Islam permitted could be banned or made obligatory, sought a clarification from Khomaini. With no further explanation, he reaffirmed the position that he had already taken.[17]

A month later, Khomaini elaborated further on his ruling. In an important letter to President Khamene'i, dated 6 January 1988, Khomaini articulated an unusually broad—even unlimited—definition of the powers of the Islamic state. Such a state, he said, derives its authority from the "absolute vice-regency entrusted by God to the Prophet," and, like the Prophet's government, exercises power by divine sanction. In the interests of the community, Islam, and the country, he said, an Islamic government "can unilaterally revoke any lawful agreements it concluded with the people . . . prevent any matter, whether religious or secular." It can void contracts and forms of commercial transactions deemed permissible and binding under canon law. Moreover, Khomaini did not restrict the powers of the Islamic state to matters of "secondary" importance under Islamic law. In the wider interests of the community, he said, an Islamic government can even suspend the exercise of the five pillars of the faith, including fasting, prayer, and the pilgrimage to Mecca, whose performance is required of every Muslim. The Islamic state, he suggested, exercised "other, greater" powers, which he would not now touch upon.[18]

The advocates of distributive justice and expanded state control over the economy treated Khomaini's January ruling as a broad mandate for the government to push ahead with stalled legislation. Prime Minister Musavi described Khomaini's remarks as a "clarification of ambiguities" and a green light to proceed with legislation in dispute between the Majles and the Guardianship Council.[19] Majles Speaker Rafsanjani echoed this view. He and Montazeri argued that a ruling *(hukm)* by Khomaini on broad matters of social and economic policy was binding on everyone, including other Islamic jurists.[20] Clerics scrambled to declare their agreement with Khomaini's interpretation of Islamic law. The country's Friday prayer leaders hastily convened a seminar in order to do so.[21] The secretary general of the Guardianship Council met

Khomaini to affirm that the council, too, considered itself bound by the leader's ruling.[22]

Khomaini's January ruling represented yet another effort to grapple with a question that had troubled Iran's leaders since the revolution: Where, in an Islamic state, does ultimate authority lie when deciding on fundamental issues of public policy? His ruling was an argument, from Islamic law, for virtually unrestricted state authority to regulate the affairs of the community. The context of his ruling gave it added weight. Khomaini spoke in the midst of a debate on governmental regulation and in response to a sermon by President Khamene'i that argued for strict adherence to the constitution and for limits on state authority.[23]

Khomaini's ruling, however, did not prove the breakthrough on deadlocked legislation that its supporters had anticipated. The items of legislation in dispute between the Guardianship Council and the Majles were not in themselves innovative or revolutionary. Under the Shah, similar legislation on labor, land reform, hoarding, or eminent domain was routinely enacted. Khomaini's ruling, however, defined the powers of the Islamic state in unusually broad terms. By stipulating *maslahat,* the interests of the community, as a basis for legislation, he was turning to a principle that had been associated with Sunni rather than Shi'ite jurisprudence. (This might explain the accusation of "Wahhabism"— the form of Sunni Islam practiced in Saudi Arabia—that was later directed at the advocates of basing legislation on this principle.) The ruling was therefore innovative and controversial, and among clerical leaders there was less unanimity than suggested by the chorus of approval that greeted it. A few months earlier, the spokesman for the Guardianship Council, Ayatollah Mohammad Imami-Kashani, had expressed the council's strong reservations regarding legislation that the Majles had approved under the rubric of "overriding necessity." He again reserved for the council the authority to determine, on a case-by-case basis, whether in fact conditions of overriding necessity existed.[24] Not long after Khomaini's ruling, the secretary of the Guardianship Council, Ayatollah Lotfollah Safi, quietly resigned.

Even before the January ruling, Khomaini had in a few, rare instances personally intervened to decide doctrinal disputes. He, for example, ruled in favor of the state in the case of ownership of *anfal* (mines, natural resources, undeveloped or waste land lying outside settled areas, and unclaimed property). He permitted a commission, headed by Montazeri, to establish uniform punishments for comparable crimes (the traditional view was that each Islamic judge could determine punishments at his own discretion). He ruled that the state could impose taxes and dues other than those canonically specified.

In other statements, he had again emphasized the need for governmental action in favor of the less privileged classes. In a long message to Iranians undertaking the 1987 *hajj* pilgrimage to Mecca he had reminded the government that "the interests of the disinherited take priority over the interests of the dwellers of great houses and the wealthy."[25] This was immediately dubbed the "Charter of the Revolution" by the advocates of state intervention, who sought to use it to justify measures, such as land takeovers, that touched on property rights. On the eve of the parliamentary elections of April 1988, Khomaini urged voters to elect deputies devoted to "the Islam of the barefoot people, the Islam of the deprived and the meek," and to reject candidates favoring "capitalist Islam, the Islam of the arrogant . . . in other words, American-style Islam."[26]

In the year or so following the January ruling, Khomaini reasserted his stand regarding the powers of the Islamic state. But, as was often the case in the past, he avoided taking a position on specific items of legislation, relegating this decision to others. In February 1988, he appointed a new thirteen-man commission, the awkwardly named Assembly for Discerning the Interests of the System of the Islamic Republic *(Majma'-e Tashkhis-e Maslahat-e Nezam-e Jomhuri-ye Islami)* to mediate differences between the Guardianship Council and the Majles. The new commission was composed of the six jurists on the Guardianship Council and six representatives of the three branches of government (the speaker of the Majles, the chief justice, the prosecutor-general, the president, the prime minister, and the minister directly concerned with the legislation under consideration). The thirteenth member, Hojjat ol-Islam Mohammad-Reza Tavassoli, was to serve as Khomaini's personal representative.

The precise role of the Assembly for Discerning the Interests of the System was not clearly defined in Khomaini's letter of appointment. Khomaini apparently wished the Majles and the Guardianship Council to continue to attempt to resolve their own differences, and the new body initially acted with circumspection. It did not take up the laws at issue between the legislature and the council. It spent several weeks discussing its own role. Thereafter, the members of the new body appear to have determined that Khomaini had given them a mandate to issue decrees that could be enforced as law, whenever they deemed the interests of the community to require their intervention. The new body issued several such decrees of which two constituted major items of legislation. The assembly approved a decree that sharply increased punishments for trafficking in narcotics. The assembly also began deliberations (the regulations were not promulgated until early 1989) on a second decree imposing stiff punishments for hoarding, profiteering, trade malpractices, bribery, and official corruption. Whatever Khomaini's original intention, the Assembly for Discerning the Interests of the System had become a vehicle for legislation, a means for bypassing the Majles and the Guardianship Council altogether. (Such a decree-issuing role for the new body was implicit in remarks made by President Khamene'i as early as February 1988.)[27]

In November 1988, over 100 Majles deputies warned Khomaini in a letter that the new body was encroaching on the prerogatives of the Majles and taking on legislative functions. Khomaini responded in December in a letter to the members of the Assembly for Discerning the Interests of the System. He said that the decree-issuing functions of the assembly, necessitated by conditions of war, need no longer be exercised now that the fighting had ended (a cease-fire in the Iran-Iraq war had come into effect in July). The decrees already issued would remain in force, and the assembly should complete work on measures it already had under consideration. Otherwise, no measure should be considered by the assembly, he said, before it had been taken up by the Majles and the Guardianship Council.

Khomaini thus, once again, circumscribed the functions of the new body. But, at the same time, he issued a "fatherly reminder" to the members of the Guardianship Council. He returned to themes that he had been articulating over the past year. The government, he said, was faced with major domestic and foreign problems. "Seminarian debates in the theological schools . . . not only cannot solve these problems but they lead us to stalemate." The Guardianship Council must guard against violations of Islam, but it should not act so that, "God forbid, Islam . . . may be accused of inability to administer [the affairs of] this world" and appear unable to deal with complex economic, social, and political issues.[28]

By the end of 1988, the central issue with which Iran's clerics had grappled for nearly a decade remained unresolved. Khomaini in the course of the year had articulated a powerful claim for state authority and for an approach to jurisprudence committed to the resolution of present-day problems. There was, however, no consensus among the ruling clerics as how best this might be done. The establishment of the Assembly for Discerning the Interests of the System was an attempt to resolve the differences that had emerged within the ruling coalition by means of an *ad hoc* body. But as Khomaini suggested in his remarks addressed to the members of the Guardianship Council, the recourse to such extraparliamentary bodies could lead to a violation of the constitution. The issues raised by Khomaini's January ruling and the legislative problems his ruling sought to address continued to command the attention of Iran's leaders. These issues also dominated the 1988 parliamentary elections.

The 1988 Elections

During the 1987 debates on the state and social justice, a majority in the Majles and the cabinet as well as Majles Speaker Hashemi-Rafsanjani and Prime Minister Musavi were generally on the same side. It was Rafsanjani who had urged Khomaini in June 1987 to indicate a way in which the Majles and the government could act on urgent issues facing the country. He had taken a similar position in 1981 and 1983. Rafsanjani, however, was never as strong an advocate of state control as the prime minister, and he did not share Musavi's basic hostility to the private sector. By the second half of 1988, Hashemi-Rafsanjani and Musavi had drawn farther apart. Rafsanjani's support for private sector participation in the economy and Musavi's for the extension of state control both grew more pronounced. Rafsanjani had the support of President Khamene'i, while Musavi strengthened his position by an alliance with Khomaini's son, Ahmad, who was growing in influence, and with such powerful clerics as Prosecutor-General Musavi-Khoeniha and Interior Minister Mohtashami. Khomaini remained a strong supporter of Rafsanjani. But as indicated by Khomaini's 1987 *hajj* message, on social justice issues he was also inclined to listen to Prime Minister Musavi and his allies. The newspaper *Resalat,* published by Ayatollah Azari-Qomi, spoke for conservative clerics who stood closest to the Guardianship Council in defending property rights and a narrow interpretation of Islamic law and the constitution.

Just before the election, a split occurred within the Association of the Combatant Clerics of Tehran, the umbrella organization of the capital's clerics. Under the leadership of the deputy speaker of the Majles, Hojjat ol-Islam Mehdi Karrubi, and with Khomaini's endorsement, clerics with more radical inclinations on economic and political issues broke away to form their own organization. The hand of the radicals was also strengthened by Mohtashami's control over the interior ministry and, therefore, over the election process, vetoing of candidates, balloting, and vote-counting.

The elections turned out to be not so much a contest between radicals and conservatives, interventionists and libertarians (although it was fought on these political distinctions as well), but a contest between the radicals, represented by the prime minister, the Karrubi group, Mohtashami and Ahmad Khomaini, and the supporters of Rafsanjani. Even here, the lines were not always sharply drawn, and some slates, in Tehran, for example, were endorsed by organizations associated with both groups. Balloting for the 270 Majles seats was held in two stages during April and May. Although the economic radicals improved their position, the results were not clear-cut. Many of the candidates associated with the Karrubi group won seats. A number of well-known, conservative clerics were defeated. In the provinces, several candidates assisted by the interior minister were elected. But Rafsanjani, followed by Karrubi, again received the highest number of votes in Tehran. Several of Rafsanjani's protégés were also elected. Around 160 of the deputies were new faces, evidence that younger, upwardly mobile men were making their way up through service in the revolutionary organizations and provincial offices. But many of these newly elected deputies were unknown quantities. Moreover, when Musavi presented his cabinet to the Majles for confirmation, the voting pattern did not suggest domination of the new Majles by the radicals.

The Majles deputies made known their dissatisfaction with Iranian reverses in the Iran-Iraq war and talk of a negotiated settlement to the conflict by rejecting the Revolutionary Guard Minister Mohsen Rafiqdust. Furthermore, ministers identified with more centrist policies received the highest number of votes, while several ministers identified with radical policies, including Mohtashami and Heavy Industries Minister Nabavi, were confirmed with only small majorities.

The balance of forces in the Majles was not quickly put to the test. By the time the new legislature convened in late May, Iran had already suffered two stunning setbacks in the war, and missiles and bombs were raining down on the capital. War and foreign policy were again at the center of attention.

Chapter 11

Foreign Policy:

1984–1988

THE WAR WITH IRAQ remained Iran's primary foreign policy concern. Nevertheless, Iranian officials could not ignore the country's greatly straitened circumstances. Iran was diplomatically isolated and enjoyed little international support. It was experiencing difficulty securing arms. Better relations with other Persian Gulf states were necessary if Iran was to have any influence in OPEC or wean these countries away from Iraq. Beginning in 1984, the government made a concerted effort to improve relations with the outside world. These efforts yielded fruit. But Iran's new diplomatic initiatives were complicated by its war aims, its ambitions in Lebanon, the activities of its clients abroad, and its own hard-liners at home. The powerful pull of ideology competed with pragmatism in shaping foreign policy. Factions within the ruling coalition who regarded accommodation with the West and a less militant stand abroad as a sellout of the revolution sought to derail Iran's new diplomatic initiative. This initiative thus could not be pursued with any consistency. Subject to repeated setbacks, it became a major issue in domestic politics.

Khomaini's "Open Window" Policy

Iran's desire for improved relations with the international community was reflected in 1984 in a spate of visits abroad by the foreign minister and the Speaker of the Majles, Hashjemi-Rafsanjani, who began to play an increasingly important role in shaping foreign policy. Criticism of these visits led in October 1984 to a direct intervention by Khomaini himself. In widely publicized remarks, Khomaini attributed such criticism to Iran's enemies. He noted that the Prophet had sent emissaries to all parts of the world and that for Iran not to do so now would mean "defeat, annihilation, and burial." He did not even rule out relations with the United States, on the condition that America ended its hostility toward Iran and its domineering approach to the region.[1] This came to be known as Khomaini's "open window" diplomacy.

Iran's diplomatic initiative was intensified in the wake of Iraq's air offensive and bombing of urban population centers in early 1985. In April, the Iranian government, for the first time, had good words to say for the United Nations and welcomed the mediation of the secretary general, not to negotiate an end to the war, as many thought, but to arrange for a halt to Iraqi bombing and Iraq's use of chemical weapons. The Iranian government continued to express displeasure at the financial assistance the Gulf states were providing Iraq, but the anti-Saudi rhetoric was considerably toned down. Although committed to hold the line on oil prices, Iran acquiesced in March 1985 to a price reduction voted by OPEC and refrained from the usual recriminations against Saudi Arabia and the other price-cutters. The following year, in a concession to Iran, Saudi Arabia abandoned its high-production policy, and Iran was able to agree with other OPEC states on a common formula for production cutbacks and quotas.

The government sought to distance itself from terrorist acts in the Gulf states. It blamed bombings in Saudi Arabia and Kuwait and the 1985 assassination attempt on the ruler of Kuwait on enemies intent on undermining Iran's relations with its Arab "brothers." When in December 1984, pro-Iranian hijackers diverted a Kuwaiti airliner to Tehran airport to secure the release of political prisoners in Kuwait, officials, after what appeared to be an internal debate between hard-liners and more pragmatic elements, condemned the hijacking and secured the release of the hostages. Again, when American citizens aboard a hijacked TWA passenger aircraft were held hostage in Beirut in June 1985,

Iran expressed sympathy for the hijackers' aims, but condemned their method and disassociated itself from what Hashemi-Rafsanjani described as an act of terrorism. Iran used its influence with its protégés in Lebanon to get the American hostages released. In May 1985, the Saudi foreign minister became the first high-ranking Saudi official since the revolution to visit Iran; he was cordially received.

Earlier, Musavi-Khoeniha, the radical cleric who on Khomaini's orders had organized political demonstrations among Iranians making the annual *hajj* pilgrimage to the holy places in Mecca and Medina, and whose annual visits the Saudi government did not welcome, was removed from his post as head of the *hajj* organization. The Khoeniha affair reflected the conflicting currents that shaped Iranian foreign policy. Stung by foreign press comments that had interpreted Khoeniha's removal as a signal he was out of favor and a sign of growing moderation in Tehran, Khomaini named Khoeniha to the powerful post of prosecutor-general. He denied any change in the policy of utilizing the *hajj* for political purposes. For good measure, the new *hajj* chief led thousands of Iranian pilgrims in anti-American and anti-Soviet demonstrations during the 1985 pilgrimage—but these were less disruptive than in previous years.

The government also sought to cement ties with its two immediate neighbors, Turkey and Pakistan. Iran increased bilateral trade with both countries. In January 1985, the Regional Cooperation for Development, a tripartite organization for economic cooperation between Iran, Turkey, and Pakistan established under the Shah but allowed to lapse after the revolution, was revived and its economic committees reconstituted. The name, however, was changed to avoid the suggestion that there was merit to any of the previous regime's foreign policy initiatives.

A more activist policy was also pursued in Europe. The West German foreign minister was told during a visit to Tehran in 1984 that Iran wished to expand ties with European states. A less confrontational attitude was adopted toward France, which along with the Soviet Union was Iraq's chief arms supplier. Officials seemed inclined to use trade incentives rather than invectives to secure a French agreement to three primary Iranian demands.

France, however, refused the Iranian demand that it either end arms deliveries to Iraq or adopt a position of "neutrality" in the war and thus sell Iran arms as well. But the French were eager for Iranian assistance in securing the release of French hostages in Lebanon and for a share of Iran's lucrative import market. Negotiations over many months in the second half of 1986 led to a partial satisfaction of Iran's two other demands. In June, the French expelled Mas'ud Rajavi and hundreds of members of the Mojahedin-e Khalq, the most important (and, to Tehran, the most threatening) of the Iranian opposition groups based in Paris. Rajavi moved to Iraq, where he set up headquarters under the aegis of Saddam Hussein. In December, France acceded to Iran's other long-standing demand and agreed to repay a $1 billion loan Iran had extended to the French company Eurodif in 1975. An initial installment of $300 million was immediately repaid. Two French hostages in Lebanon were released in June, two more in November, and a fifth in December.

In addition, Iranian diplomats and officials visited or hosted representatives from a wide range of countries in Asia, Africa, and East Europe during 1984 and 1985. Both the Japanese and Chinese foreign ministers went to Iran in 1984, and Hashemi-Rafsanjani paid official visits to both countries later in July 1985. Such visits, rare in the early years of the revolution, became routine. In cultivating China, Iran was developing a new and ultimately important source of arms supplies.

The United States and the Soviet Union remained the targets of vehement, persistent propaganda. The propaganda was a means of asserting Iranian independence from the superpowers and making good the slogan of "Neither East nor West." Hostility to the United States was woven into the very mythology of the revolution and was fueled by American support for Iraq, conservative Arab states, and Israel; by the U.S. presence in Lebanon and the Persian Gulf; and by the Reagan administration's identification of Iran as an agent of international terrorism. Even here, there was a shift. In what came to be known as the Iran-Contra affair, Iran in 1985–86 entered a secret arms relationship with the United States.

Relations with the Soviet Union continued to be strained by the Soviet supply of arms to Iraq and the Soviet presence in Afghanistan. The Soviets resented Iranian criticism of their role in Afghanistan, Iranian assistance to the Afghan resistance, and the routine coupling of the Soviet Union with the United States in Iranian revolutionary slogans. In 1983, a Soviet commentator writing in *Literaturnaya gazeta* characterized the regime as "a unique type of Islamic despotism"; denounced the slogan "Neither East nor West" as "politically bankrupt"; and charged Iran's rulers with deliberately exacerbating relations with the Soviet Union.[2] By early 1985, relations had so deteriorated that Radio Moscow accused the Iranian government of being involved in "another war," this time against Afghanistan, and of training dozens of "merce-naries" for "armed intervention" and "aggression" in Afghanistan.[3]

Partly due to its increasing difficulties in the war with Iraq, the Iranian government in 1985 took steps to improve relations with Moscow. It dispatched a high-ranking foreign ministry official to Moscow at the height of Iraqi aerial bombing in the spring of 1985. It announced readi-ness to reactivate the Iran-Soviet economic commission. Although Mos-cow continued to criticize Iran harshly for its anti-Soviet propaganda and its policy toward Afghanistan, the Iranian prime minister described Iran-Soviet relations in May as "outstanding" and looked to expanding economic ties.[4] During a visit to Moscow in the following year, the Iranian oil minister raised the possibility of a resumption of Iranian gas deliveries to the Soviet Union. In December 1986, the Iran-Soviet eco-nomic commission met for the first time in six years to discuss resump-tion of Iranian gas deliveries to the USSR and Soviet assistance in the areas of steel production, electric power generation, refinery construc-tion, and railway electrification and construction. These discussions were continued in August 1987, when Soviet Deputy Foreign Minister Yuli Vorontsov became the highest ranking Soviet official to visit Iran since the revolution.

The "Radical" Strain in Foreign Policy

"Open window" diplomacy and the pragmatism it implied, however, continued to compete with a radical strain in Iranian foreign policy. If Rafsanjani emerged as the advocate of a pragmatic diplomacy, there were important factions in Iran committed to the pursuit of the vague but powerfully emotive slogans of the Iranian upheaval, such as "Nei-ther East nor West," the export of the Islamic revolution, support for liberation movements abroad, support for the world's disinherited, and confrontation with the imperialist powers. Iran had invested heavily in support of radical Shi'ite movements in Lebanon. It could not afford to abandon its alliance with its two Arab allies, Syria and Libya.

In 1985, Iran, Syria, and Libya moved to coordinate their foreign policies more closely. The foreign ministers of the three countries met in Tehran in June and in Damascus in August. They agreed to form an informal alliance to confront "Zionism, imperialism, and Arab reaction," and to make common cause against Iraq, the Camp David accords, and peace negotiations with Israel. The Iranian foreign minister described the initiative as necessitated by the developing Washington-Cairo-Amman axis.

Some consultation also took place on security affairs. Mohsen Rafiq-dust, the Iranian minister of the Revolutionary Guard, was in Syria and Libya for discussions during 1985. In June, Iran and Libya announced their agreement to form an "international Islamic revolutionary league" and also to establish an "army of Jerusalem" to liberate Palestine.[5] Although Iran was grateful to Libya for supplying arms at critical moments in the Iran-Iraq war and the two countries shared similar positions on a number of foreign policy questions, the Iranian-Libyan connection remained of secondary importance to Iran in comparison to its strategic relationship with Syria.

For Iran, continued Syrian support against Iraq was vital. The Islamic Republic increasingly aligned its policies on questions relating to Israel with those of Syria. It pursued its interests in Lebanon with an eye to Syrian sensitivities. The Syrians valued the alliance with Iran because of the enmity they felt toward Iraq.[6] For Syria, there were material incentives as well. Syria in 1982 had shut the pipeline that carried Iraqi oil through Syria to Mediterranean ports. Iran, in turn, provided Syria with non-interest bearing loans, oil at discounted prices, and around one million tons of additional oil each year as an outright gift. By early 1987, the Syrian debt to Iran was reported to exceed $2 billion.[7]

The links with Syria facilitated Iran's activities in Lebanon. With its large and dissatisfied Shi'ite community, Lebanon appeared ripe for Islamic revolutionary propaganda. Moreover, the family, scholarly, and political ties between Iranian and Lebanese Shi'ite clerics predated the revolution. These ties were expanded after the establishment of the Islamic Republic. As noted, Iran supported Islamic Amal, a radical breakaway group that vied with the larger and more moderate Amal movement for influence among Lebanon's Shi'ites. It also supported Hezbollah (not to be confused with the *hezbollahis* in Iran), the loose alliance of Shi'ite groups committed to the expulsion of both Israel and the United Nations peace-keeping force from Lebanon. Iran used the several hundred Revolutionary Guard soldiers stationed in Baalbek to train Shi'ite militiamen and to spread the message of the Iranian revolution. Among Shi'ite clerics in villages in the south where Khomaini had a following, they encouraged the idea that Lebanon, too, should establish an Islamic government.

Iran cultivated Lebanese Shi'ite clerics such as Shaikh Muhammad Hosain Fadlallah and Shaikh Sobhi al-Tofaili in Beirut. Desiring to appeal across sectarian lines and to press its claim to speak not just for Shi'ites but for all Muslims, Iran also cultivated Sunni clerics, such as Shaikh Sa'id Sha'ban in Tripoli. Fadlallah, Sha'ban, and other Lebanese clerics were regular visitors to Iran. The Iranians expanded their influence by establishing religious schools and providing medical, social, and welfare services. The Imam Khomaini hospital in Baalbek ministered to the local population.[8]

Iranian activity in Lebanon was thought to be directed from the Iranian embassy in Damascus. Until the mid-1980s, the ambassador was Ali-Akbar Mohtashami, a man close to Khomaini. He later served in Iran as minister of interior. Another Iranian group active in Lebanon was the unit in the Revolutionary Guard responsible for the support of liberation movements abroad. This unit was run by Mehdi Hashemi, who was related to Ayatollah Montazeri by marriage. (For further discussion on Hashemi, see chapter 12.)

Iranian activity in Lebanon was a potential source of friction in Iranian-Syrian relations. Although dividing lines could not always be sharply drawn, Syrian support for Nabih Berri's Amal movement and Iranian support for Islamic Amal and the Hezbollah meant the two countries were generally backing competitors for supremacy among Lebanon's Shi'ites. In the second half of 1986, Hezbollah partisans, perhaps with Iranian encouragement, intensified attacks in the south against the Israeli-backed South Lebanon Army, inviting Israeli retaliation. Yet Syria had no wish for others to force its hand on a confrontation with Israel. When Syria sent 7,000 troops into Lebanon in February 1987 and entered Beirut to stop infighting between Lebanese factions, the Syrian forces clashed with Hezbollah and killed some twenty-three members of the Hezbollah militia. Iranian diplomats had to persuade Hezbollah to back off. Severe fighting broke out between Hezbollah and Amal for control of south Beirut in May 1988, and it was with difficulty that Iran and Syria were able to patch up a cease-fire.

Relations with Syria also became a factor in factional conflict in Iran. Groups in Iran committed to Hezbollah, including the Mehdi Hashemi group, were hostile to Syria and to the Iran-Syria alliance. In addition, remarks by President Asad in September 1986 were interpreted to mean Syria favored a negotiated settlement to the Iran-Iraq war. These remarks came at a particularly sensitive time, when elements in the Iranian leadership and in the opposition were seeking to persuade Khomaini to consider a nonmilitary solution to the war or at least to modify Iran's war aims. In October 1986, armed men thought to be associated with Mehdi Hashemi kidnapped the Syrian *chargé d'affaires* in Tehran and held him for twenty-four hours. Hashemi and several of his colleagues were arrested soon afterward.[9]

The importance of the Iranian-Syrian relationship to both countries meant that these frictions were generally overcome. The Iranians sought to keep their clients in Lebanon on a tight leash where Syria was concerned. Although Iranian oil shipments to Syria were interrupted in June 1986, ostensibly due to the unpaid Syrian debt, deliveries were soon resumed and the debt rescheduled. A secret meeting between Asad and Iraq's Saddam Hussein in April 1987, arranged by King Hussein of Jordan, did not go well and did not materially affect Iranian-Syrian relations. Syria went along with a resolution agreed at the Arab summit in November 1987 that criticized Iran for remaining in occupied Iraqi territory and refusing to comply with the July 1987 UN Security Council call for a cease-fire. But Asad was soon denouncing the resolution and again speaking of Iran as the victim of aggression.

The kidnapping of the Syrian *chargé d'affaires* was one indication that the Iranian government could not always control radical elements with its own ruling coalition. There were numerous others. Iran officially condemned the bombings in Kuwait in 1984 and 1985, but encouragement or direct involvement of elements in Iran could not be ruled out. During the *hajj* pilgrimage in 1986, the Saudi authorities arrested over 100 Iranians on charges of trying to smuggle weapons and explosives into the country. The complicity of factions in Iran, possibly those associated with Mehdi Hashemi, was later indirectly confirmed by Iranian authorities.[10]

The influence of the hard-liners on foreign policy was increasingly evident in 1987. This reflected the fallout from revelations in late 1986 that Rafsanjani and other officials had been secretly buying weapons from the United States, the frustrations felt at the reversal of Iran's fortunes in the war, and the appearance of American warships in the Gulf in the spring of 1987. Iranian complicity was suspected in bombings of Kuwaiti oil installations on the eve of the Islamic conference, which met in Kuwait in January 1987 despite Iranian objections. Evidence that became available in the following year suggests that Iranian officials, and probably Interior Minister Mohtashami, permitted another hijacked Kuwaiti aircraft to land in Mashad, in northeastern Iran, in August 1987.[11] After what appeared to be a debate between factions in the Iranian government, saner counsels prevailed and the aircraft was sent on its way.

Hard-liners in Tehran also played a role in disrupting relations with England and France. When an Iranian consular officer in Manchester was arrested in May 1987 on a shoplifting charge, the second-ranking British diplomat in Tehran was abducted by armed men and severely beaten when he resisted arrest. The incident led to the withdrawal of British diplomats from Tehran and to the departure of Iranian diplomats from London. The British also closed down the Iranian office in London that handled Iranian arms purchases in Europe. This was a setback to Iran's war effort. In June, Iran refused a French demand to question a member of the Iranian embassy staff, Vahid Gorji, in connection with a series of bombings that had taken place in Paris in 1986. Gorji did not enjoy diplomatic immunity. When French authorities surrounded the Iranian embassy in Paris, where Gorji had taken up residence to avoid arrest, armed guards from the interior ministry surrounded the French embassy in Tehran and refused to permit embassy staff and families to leave the embassy or the country. This affair led to a rupture in diplomatic relations with France. In both these incidents, elements in the leadership in Tehran appear to have either deliberately set out to disrupt relations with England and France or to have insisted on a policy of confrontation that inevitably undermined months of careful diplomacy.

Khomaini's position also hardened. By August, the Iraqis had intensified the tanker war and the "war of the cities," and the United States had begun to escort reflagged Kuwaiti tankers in the Gulf. Khomaini once again called on Iran's 150,000 pilgrims to Mecca to use the *hajj* to demonstrate against America and the Soviet Union and to "disavow the infidel." Inept handling of the demonstrations in Mecca by the authorities led to riots and shooting by Saudi police. More than 400 died, some 270 of them Iranians. (Saudi Arabia subsequently insisted Iran limit the number of its pilgrims to 45,000 or 50,000. When Iran refused, mutual recriminations followed, and the Saudis broke diplomatic relations. No Iranians made the *hajj* pilgrimage in 1988 or 1989.)

The War

Internal factionalism over the course of Iran's foreign policy was played out against the background of the Iran-Iraq war. Khomaini insisted on continuing the war until Saddam Hussein was overthrown. Up to 1986, few in the ruling coalition were inclined to question his war aims.

Iran's offensive in the summer of 1982 failed to break Iraqi defenses. Offensives across the central and northern sectors of the front in 1983 and in the south in the spring of 1984 secured slices of its own territory held by Iraq and chunks of Iraqi territory, notably the strategic area around Hajj Omran in the central sector in Kurdistan and the Majnoon Islands, the site of a large but undeveloped oil field, in the south.

Iran's primary objective was to cut the Baghdad–Basra highway and to isolate Basra and the nearby Shi'ite holy cities from the rest of the country. This objective was not achieved in the 1983 offensive. Iran's long-announced "final push" was repeatedly anticipated throughout 1984 but never materialized. Iranian forces launched another offensive toward Basra in the following year. They succeeded in taking a sector of the Baghdad–Basra highway, but could not hold it due to the lack of air cover and logistical support. Iran's February 1986 offensive, however, resulted in a major defeat for the Iraqis. Iranian forces captured the Fao Peninsula; subsequent efforts by crack Iraqi units to dislodge them failed. The Iranians continued to display initiative and intelligent military planning but were paying a heavy price. The 1985 offensive cost Iran upward of 20,000 lives, and the capture of Fao proved costly as well.

Iraq enjoyed air superiority, enhanced by the acquisition of new aircraft and missiles from France and the Soviet Union. Beginning in April 1984, Saddam Hussein utilized this newfound capacity to renew the tanker war and to attack the Khark Island oil terminal and shipping to and from Iranian ports. By September 1985, 140 ships had been hit, the vast majority by Iraq. Attacks on Iranian oil installations continued, with some interruptions, into the following year. In March 1985, Iraq began indiscriminate bombing of Iranian cities. Tehran received the brunt of Iraqi bombing. Iran retaliated with ground-to-ground Scud missiles aimed at targets in Baghdad, but its supply was limited and no more than a dozen missiles were fired.

The bombing of cities was intended by Iraq to terrorize the civilian population. In the war at sea, Iraq hoped to cut off Iran's lifeline by damaging its oil-exporting and revenue-earning capacity and by raising the risk of a wider conflagration to increase international pressure for an end to the conflict. Iraq succeeded in doing considerable, but not irreparable, damage to Iran's oil installations. It also succeeded, but again to a limited degree, in heightening international awareness of the danger that the war would spread. The United States pledged to keep the Straits of Hormuz open, stationed a naval force outside the Gulf, and resumed diplomatic relations with Iraq in 1984. It lent Saudi Arabia AWACS, early warning aircraft, and stepped up consultations with its European allies on Gulf security. Saudi Arabia and Kuwait acted to coordinate defense efforts. In June 1984, Saudi interceptors, guided by American-manned AWACS ground installations, shot down two Iranian fighter planes. Iran did not attempt to tangle with Saudi aircraft again.

Iran had promised for some time a "final offensive" that would decide the fate of the war or a decisive victory that would allow it to end the conflict. In January 1987, Iran launched Operation Karbala V, its largest, best-prepared, and longest-sustained offensive in five years.[12] Iran once again gained territory; its forces pushed nearer the town of Basra. But Iraqi defenses in the south were by now formidable. After five weeks of fighting, it was clear that the offensive had failed to achieve its major objective.

The limited success of Karbala V appeared to mark a shift in Iranian tactics and perhaps even its war aims. Iran no longer spoke of one major "final offensive" but of several limited ones. The commander of the Revolutionary Guard even spoke of opening a new front by training popular forces inside Iraq. Rafsanjani suggested in a sermon that Iran no longer insisted on seeing an Islamic government established at Baghdad. As long as Saddam Hussein and the Baath did not rule Iraq, he said, Iran would accept any popular government, "even a pro-American one," if that is what the Iraqi people want.[13]

Iran-Contra and Its Repercussions

Iran's January 1987 offensive had been facilitated not only by arms Iran secured from China, North Korea, and other suppliers, but also by substantial arms deliveries from the United States in 1985–86. The clandestine sale of American arms to Iran was initially suggested to the Reagan administration by the Israelis. The administration found the idea attractive as a means of establishing contact with elements in the Iranian leadership, checking potential Soviet influence in Iran in the post-Khomaini period, and securing the release of American hostages in Lebanon. The dealings with Iran, however, remained primarily an arms-for-hostages swap. In addition, as the arms sales progressed, they generated substantial profits, which White House officials were able to divert to the support of the Contra rebels in Nicaragua. Since Congress had refused to vote funds for military aid to the Contras, this proved to be a further incentive for the arms deliveries.

Only a small number of officials, in addition to President Reagan, were kept informed on the American side about the arms transfers. Secretary of State George Shultz and Secretary of Defense Caspar Weinberger opposed the arms sales but were overruled. The chief U.S. managers of the arms-for-hostages arrangement were National Security Advisor Robert McFarlane, his successor to the post, John Poindexter, National Security Council staff member Lieutenant Colonel Oliver North, and CIA Chief William Casey.

Between August 1985 and October 1986, over 2,000 TOW antitank missiles and various parts for Hawk antiaircraft missile systems were delivered to Iran in seven highly secret shipments. One of these shipments, flown to the Iranian capital in May 1986, was accompanied to Tehran by McFarlane, North, other White House and CIA officials, and Amiram Nir, an aide to Israeli Prime Minister Shimon Peres. Three American hostages in Lebanon were released, one in September 1985 and one each in July and November 1986, as a result of these arms deliveries.

Initially, the Americans and the Israelis dealt with the Iranians primarily through the intermediary of an Iranian arms merchant, Manuchehr Qorbanifar. The arms sales also led to more direct contacts and discussions. When McFarlane was in Tehran in May 1986, he and his team held talks with a number of middle-ranking Iranian officials that included Mohammad-Ali Hadi Najafabadi, the deputy chairman of the Majles foreign affairs committee, and an Iranian intelligence officer identified as Manuchehr Kangarloo. Kangarloo was Qorbanifar's main contact in Iran. During their discussions with McFarlane, the Iranian team reported to and was guided by senior Iranian officials. In August 1986, after a "second channel" had been opened to the Iranians, American representatives met in Brussels with a relative of Hashemi-Rafsanjani, the speaker of the Iranian Majles. This relative was probably Rafsanjani's nephew, Ali Hashemi-Bahremani. Contact was also established with Sadeq Tabataba'i, a brother-in-law of Khomaini's son, Ahmad. Tabataba'i had been involved in the negotiations that in 1980 led to the release of the American hostages then being held in Iran. Ali Hashemi-Bahremani held discussions with American officials in Washington in September and again, on two separate occasions, in Frankfurt in October. In these discussions, the Iranians focused primarily on securing arms and intelligence information from the United States. But they also suggested establishing a joint United States-Iranian commission to discuss a wider range of issues. In proposing this, the Iranians were no doubt encouraged by unauthorized statements by North that expressed support by the Reagan administration for an end to the Iran-Iraq war on terms favorable to Iran. "We . . . recognize that Saddam Husain must go," North told the Iranians in Frankfurt.[14] The Iranians appeared interested in a continuing, if limited, dialogue with the United States. Iranian foreign ministry sources were discreetly and circumspectly relaying the same message to Washington through friendly, third-party governments.[15]

The arms deal came to light on 3 November 1986, when a Beirut weekly, *al-Shira'a,* published a somewhat garbled account of the McFarlane trip to Iran. On 4 November in a speech before a large audience in Tehran, Rafsanjani confirmed that McFarlane and four other Americans had been in Iran. The story created an uproar in the United States, and the repercussions continued to be felt over the following year as details of the arms-for-hostages deal and the diversion of funds to the Contras emerged in newspaper accounts, in congressional hearings, and in the report of the Tower Commission—the special review board appointed by the President. In Iran, a similar uproar did not materialize. Khomaini silenced potential critics and quashed demands in the Majles for a full accounting by the government. Nevertheless, the revelation of secret dealings with the United States had important consequences for Iran.

Iran's dealings with the United States took place with Khomaini's knowledge and involved several key leaders. Even after the story broke, the Iranians attempted to keep alive the arms-for-hostages arrangement. In a number of statements in November and December, Rafsanjani repeated the offer of Iranian assistance for the release of American hostages in exchange for American arms and access to Iranian funds frozen in the United States. The United States-Iran arms-for-hostages relationship could not be continued once it became public. It proved immensely controversial in the United States and was potentially an explosive issue in Iran as well. Many in the leadership who knew of the dealings with the United States were strongly opposed; others had been kept in the dark. Only Khomaini's intervention prevented a damaging attack on Rafsanjani and others involved.

In fact, oblique references to the arms deals had first surfaced in leaflets distributed in Tehran around 15–16 October, at the same time or immediately following the arrest of Mehdi Hashemi.[16] The leaflets were probably attributable to Hashemi's followers.[17] Documents later made public in the Tower Report suggest that the Iranians had great difficulty in persuading their Lebanese allies to release the American hostages. Three Americans were released in the course of the arms sales but three other Americans were taken hostage in September 1986. It is apparent that elements in Tehran or Iran's clients in Lebanon had deliberately set out to sabotage the United States-Iran exchanges.

In the aftermath of the Iran-Contra revelations, the United States moved decisively to prevent further arms deliveries to Iran. It made a concerted effort to secure support for a United Nations Security Council resolution calling for an end to the Iran-Iraq war. To reassure the Arab states of the Persian Gulf, the United States agreed to reflag Kuwaiti tankers in March 1987. All three measures worked to Iran's disadvantage.

The Reflagging and Its Consequences

In the second half of 1986, Iraq had greatly increased its attacks on Iranian oil installations and Iranian tanker traffic. These attacks were far more effective than similar attacks in 1984 and 1985. Iraqi aircraft succeeded in virtually closing down Iran's oil-exporting terminal at Khark and disrupted tanker traffic that Iran was diverting to export terminals at Sirri and Larak farther down the Gulf. Iraq struck at refineries in Tabriz, Tehran, and Isfahan. By October, Iranian oil exports were reported at half the previous year's level of 1.4 million barrels a day. The government once again introduced gas rationing. With brief interruptions, Iraqi attacks on Iranian shipping and oil installations continued into 1987 and 1988.

In January 1987, during Iran's Karbala V offensive, Iraq also resumed the "war of the cities," bombing Iranian urban centers. After a lull in August, Iraq intensified its aerial assault of Iranian cities. As missile attacks continued into 1988, a terrified populace fled Tehran in the hundreds of thousands for safety in the provinces.

Since the government was virtually powerless to prevent these missile attacks and lacked means to retaliate at the same level of intensity, Iran began to attack neutral targets, particularly Kuwaiti ships in the Persian Gulf. The Kuwaitis reacted by asking the United States and the Soviet Union for protection. The initial U.S. response was noncommittal. But when the Soviets arranged to lease three tankers to Kuwait, the United States agreed to reflag and provide escorts for Kuwaiti tankers. A large fleet of American battleships and aircraft carriers moved into the Indian Ocean and the Persian Gulf. The first Kuwaiti tankers under an American flag sailed through the Gulf in July 1987. Subsequently, French, British, Italian, Soviet, and other European governments sent naval escorts into the Gulf. The reflagging had major consequences for Iran. It tipped the balance in the war against the Islamic Republic, brought Iran into direct conflict with the United States, and strengthened the hand of hard-liners in Tehran who argued for a policy of confrontation.

During the first half of 1987, the pace of the "war of the cities" and the tanker war was determined by Iraq, not Iran. Iran's capacity to retaliate for attacks on its urban centers was limited. Iran also consistently took the position that the tanker war could end if Iraqi attacks on Iranian shipping stopped. When American naval forces moved into the Gulf in the summer, Iran was initially careful to avoid a direct confrontation. The Iranians, however, had laid mines in the Gulf. During the first escort mission in July, the Kuwaiti tanker *Bridgeton* was hit and was damaged by a mine. In subsequent weeks, the ships of other countries were damaged by mines as well. In addition, three direct military confrontations took place between Iran and the United States. On 21 September, American forces sighted the Iranian frigate *Iran Ajr* laying mines off the coast of Bahrain. The *Iran Ajr* was attacked, four members of the crew were killed, twenty-six were taken into custody. The ship itself was destroyed and the crew released. On 17 October, an Iranian missile struck and severely damaged the reflagged Kuwaiti tanker *Sea Isle City*. The United States retaliated by destroying the Iranian Rostam oil drilling platform in the Persian Gulf; the Iranians responded by a missile attack on a floating oil platform in Kuwait waters. On 18 April 1988, the United States destroyed two other Iranian oil platforms, Nasr and Sassan, and responded to Iranian naval activity by sinking or crippling six Iranian vessels.

Several factors explain these clashes. The *Iran Ajr* mine-laying incident in September bore the imprint of the hard-liners. It occurred the night before Iranian President Khamene'i was due to address the UN General Assembly. He was expected to make a conciliatory speech and to suggest greater Iranian receptivity to a United Nations-sponsored cease-fire. The attack on the *Iran Ajr* led him to adopt a more uncompromising stance. Moreover, restraint at sea and a more flexible attitude in the United Nations (where the security council had approved a cease-fire resolution little to Iran's liking) had won Iran no international support. Iraqi use of poison gas against Iranian forces had been met with relative silence by the international community. Iranian cities were being bombed. The government was thus under considerable pressure to react. As already noted, a hardening of the Iranian position was already evident in the rupture of diplomatic relations with France, the near rupture of relations with England earlier in 1987, and the Mecca riots in August. Finally, the United States had already begun providing Iraq with military intelligence; in 1988, it may have carried such cooperation a step further. The U.S. attack on Iranian platforms and vessels in April coincided with a major Iraqi offensive at Fao. This diversion may not have been entirely fortuitous. Both the war and the diplomatic equation had turned decidedly in Iraq's favor.

Drinking the Poison Cup

On 20 July 1987, largely through American efforts, the United Nations Security Council adopted Resolution 598, calling on both Iran and Iraq to observe an immediate cease-fire and simultaneously to withdraw their troops to international borders. The resolution, coupling a cease-fire with a troop withdrawal, seemed calculated to elicit an Iranian rejection.[18] Iran at this juncture occupied large slices of Iraqi territory and was unlikely to give up the leverage this afforded in future negotiations. A last-minute attempt to modify the resolution so that a troop withdrawal would *follow* a cease-fire was met with opposition in Baghdad and Washington. The United States, in the meantime, had prepared a second security council resolution, also directed against Iran, calling for sanctions against the belligerent party that refused to abide by the cease-fire.

Iran, however, was no longer unalterably opposed to a cease-fire or to a negotiated end to the war. In the summer of 1986, senior officials and clerics had privately urged Khomaini to explore nonmilitary options for ending the war.[19] Although Khomaini turned a deaf ear to these pleas, by 1987 public dissatisfaction with the war was widespread and the economy was suffering. Despite Iranian military successes, it had become clear, at least to some in the leadership, that the war was not winnable on the terms set down by Khomaini. The 1987 offensive, the largest and best-sustained Iranian effort in five years, had failed. The massing of arms for these offensives proved increasingly difficult. The U.S. naval presence in the Gulf provided a protective umbrella under which Iraq could attack Iranian shipping with impunity. The missile attacks on Tehran were affecting civilian morale.

Iran did not accept Resolution 598, but it did not reject it either. Rather, it sought to modify the resolution in two ways: first, to provide for a United Nations commission to convene at the same time the cease-fire went into effect and to identify the country responsible for initiating the conflict (Iran always assumed Iraq would be labeled the aggressor); second, to have the commission set a timetable for troop withdrawal subsequent to the cease-fire and the commission's report. In late 1987 and early 1988, Iran seemed to secure some support, even among the Arab states of the Gulf, for a modified schedule for the implementation of Resolution 598. The Soviet Union, moreover, refused to agree to a second resolution imposing sanctions on Iran. Iraq continued to resist any modification of 598. In the end, however, the cease-fire issue was decided not in diplomatic exchanges but on the battlefield.

On 18 April, simultaneous with the United States-Iranian naval engagements at sea, Iraq launched a massive offensive against Iranian positions on the Fao Peninsula and retook the territory it had lost to Iran fifteen months earlier. In May, the Iraqis succeeded in expelling the Iranians from the region around Basra and in the Fish Lake area. On 25 June, Iraqi forces recaptured the Majnoon Islands, thus expelling the Iranians from the last important piece of their territory in Iranian hands. Further advances over the next few weeks left the Iraqis in control of Iranian territory as well. Iran now suffered another shock. On 3 July, the American warship *Vincennes* mistook an Iranian civilian airbus for an F-14 fighter and destroyed it. All 290 passengers and crew were killed; all but 40 were Iranians. The airbus was on a regularly scheduled flight between Bandar Abbas and Dubai, flying in its assigned corridor and emitting commercial aircraft signals. The United States admitted its error and proffered an unofficial apology, but not in a manner Iran considered commensurate with the size of the tragedy. Iranian officials denounced the downing of the aircraft as a "barbaric massacre" but made no move to retaliate. The incident reinforced Iran's sense of helplessness before a superior American force and the country's international isolation.

Iraqi missile attacks on Iranian cities and urban centers, which resumed in February, had continued unabated. Some 100 missiles fell on Tehran in a five-week period. In March, the Iraqis used poison gas to kill hundreds and perhaps thousands of their own Kurdish citizens in the village of Halabja, which had been taken by Iranian forces. The United Nations subsequently condemned the use of chemical weapons, but failed to identify Iraq as the country responsible. The Iraqis used chemical weapons again in their Fao and Shalamcheh offensives, a factor that may have contributed to the defeat and demoralization of Iranian forces. The collapse of Iranian resistance was attributable not only to Iraqi superiority in equipment, but also to the government's decision to entertain the idea of a cease-fire. The Revolutionary Guard proved unwilling to continue fighting once the long-articulated purpose of the war—the overthrow of Saddam Hussein and the establishment of an Islamic government at Baghdad—appeared to have been abandoned.

Iran's military setbacks led to a series of crisis meetings among high-ranking Iranian clerics and military and civilian officials. A report was submitted to Khomaini on Iran's military condition and capabilities. On 17 July, a council of the leading men of the state was called to hear Khomaini's views and to decide on a course of action. On 18 July, almost exactly one year after the security council adopted Resolution 598, the Iranian foreign minister informed the United Nations secretary general that Iran was accepting the cease-fire proposal.[20] The attempt to suggest a collective decision by the Iranian leadership notwithstanding, the ultimate decision to end the war was Khomaini's own. On 21 July, he delivered his famous "cup of poison" address to the people. Although the acceptance of the cease-fire was "a very bitter and tragic" decision, he said, "at this juncture I regard it to be in the best interests of the revolution and the [Islamic Republic]." The decision, he noted, "is more lethal to me than poison . . . I made a pact with you to fight to the last drop of blood and the last breath. I abandoned whatever I said before only for the sake of His blessing and satisfaction."[21]

Chapter 12

The End of the Khomaini Decade

THE END OF THE IRAN-IRAQ war was greeted with universal relief. It permitted the government to turn its attention to the long-neglected economic and social problems and to the task of repairing war-ravaged cities and industries. The Iranian government, which failed to end the war when it might have dictated terms for peace, had some explaining to do to its people. Hundreds of thousands of demobilized fighters had to be reintegrated into the economy. The task of postwar reconstruction appeared immense, and the debate on postwar reconstruction strategy revealed deep divisions within the leadership. Iran's slow emergence from diplomatic isolation was once again disrupted by external events, the play of personalities, and the exigencies of revolutionary and Islamic ideology. These problems were exacerbated by a crisis over the succession and the constitutional structure of the state.

The Wages of Peace

Iran's acceptance of Resolution 598 did not bring an immediate end to hostilities. The cease-fire did not take effect until 20 August, and while arrangements were being negotiated through the auspices of the United Nations secretary general, Iraq made further incursions into Iran. In July, the Iraqis permitted the Mojahedin-e Khalq to send troops and armored units they had been training in Iraq across the border. The Mojahedin were able to penetrate as far as Islamabad, twenty miles into Iran. Although the rebel troops were eventually routed, their rapid advance was another sign of disarray in the Iranian camp and of the bewilderment Khomaini's about-face had generated in the ranks of the Revolutionary Guard.

The cease-fire did not please those in the government, the Majles, and the revolutionary organizations who believed the war could still be fought and won. They blamed Hashemi-Rafsanjani for persuading Khomaini to end hostilities and directed their anger toward him. Khomaini's public endorsement of the cease-fire resolution was necessary to silence them. There was also widespread criticism of the government among the general public for having ended the war far too late. Bazargan, after all, had been publicly denigrated for arguing, as early as 1982 and more urgently after 1985, when Iran was in a much stronger position, for a negotiated end to the conflict. Government spokesmen, including Rafsanjani and Khamene'i, looked for ways to justify the cease-fire. The international community, they said, would now see that Iraq, and not Iran, was the war-mongering, aggressor state. Iran could have prevailed, but as the U.S. and international naval presence in the Persian Gulf and the destruction of the Iranian passenger plane had shown, the entire international community had ranged itself against Iran. These explanations were not very convincing. Forgotten were the demands for the overthrow of Saddam Hussein and the slogan of "war, war until victory." In the end, Iran's leaders justified the cease-fire decision by identifying it with Khomaini and his superior wisdom. "The Imam accepted the cease-fire," President Khamene'i remarked. "The decision was beyond our authority. It was the leader's responsibility."[1] Montazeri remarked that Khomaini was acting in the interests of Islam, the revolution, and the country when he called for resistance in the past. "And now, if he, for some reason, invited the nation to accept the cease-fire, that too is in the interests of Islam, the revolution, and the country."[2]

Frustration over a war that ended badly was expressed in a reversion to political repression and a renewed emphasis on moral rectitude. The government claimed that members of the Mojahedin-e Khalq inside Iran, including former political prisoners who had been given amnesty and freed, had linked up with the Mojahedin invading force in July. Other members of the organization still in prison had found ways of assisting their colleagues. These allegations of collaboration became the excuse for a renewed wave of executions. Well over 1,000 and as many as 1,700 members of opposition groups were executed in a six-month period beginning in July. These included some members of the Mojahedin captured with the invading force, but also hundreds of members of other organizations (the Tudeh and the Fadayan) who were still in prison or who were arrested in their homes, at work, and on the street. Another 900 persons were executed between January and July of the following year as the new drug-trafficking law came into effect.[3]

The end of the war coincided with criticism of inefficiencies in the judiciary. Khomaini had ordered the chief justice to speed up the judicial process. Chief Justice Musavi-Ardabili reported in a Friday sermon in January that cases that used to drag through the courts for years were now decided in a matter of days. In case of a crime "just one telephone call" was sufficient to ensure that justice was served. In a rape and murder case, which had been before the courts for a year, he reported, "a verdict was issued immediately—within twenty-four hours. Four were executed, two hands were cut off, three others were given seven to nine years in prison."[4] To placate demobilized Revolutionary Guardsmen angered at clerics close to the government who had been leading less-than-austere lives while the fighters were at the front, the government in November announced the execution of six "pseudo-clerics," including three members of the Majles who had been found guilty on morals charges. In another show of moral rectitude, the Tehran revolutionary committees razed homes and shops in two working-class districts in Tehran—a former red-light district and a shantytown—claiming they had become centers of corruption and prostitution.

The Debate on Postwar Reconstruction

The end of the war presented an opportunity to begin the task of rebuilding the towns, cities, industries, and oil installations devastated by the war; housing the war refugees; and providing welfare for war victims and their families. Both the government's five-year plan and its budget for 1989–90 foresaw the resumption of work on refineries and on petrochemical, steel, construction materials, motor vehicle, and consumer goods plants slated for expansion and construction.

Sharp differences, however, emerged within the leadership on what roles the domestic private sector and foreign capital and expertise were allowed in this endeavor. Prime Minister Musavi held the view that Iran should rely on its own resources, emphasize self-sufficiency, and draw on the revolutionary energies of the people. He believed the people were prepared for more self-sacrifice in order to retain their independence. Iran's experience in the past with the great powers should also be a lesson for the future: "Whenever you shake hands with the foreigners . . . be careful that your fingers are not grabbed and left in the foreigners' hands," he said. Foreigners were ready to invest in Iran, he contended, only to defeat the revolution, exploit Iran's resources, and dominate the country. They "are using the pretext of reconstruction . . . in order to make us dependent."[5] Musavi was also opposed to permitting a wider scope to the private sector. This would lead to monopoly and exploitation, he said.

President Khamene'i described this vision of a self-sufficient Iran— making everything itself and totally independent of foreign suppliers— as "the Molotov cocktail mentality."[6] He and Hashemi-Rafsanjani argued that domestic resources would not suffice, and that the postwar reconstruction effort could not be accomplished reasonably quickly without foreign assistance. "We cannot prolong the issue of reconstruction for 100 years," Khamene'i remarked. While self-sufficiency remained the goal, "the resources obtained from others are a prelude to self-sufficiency."[7] Rafsanjani argued that the people could not be asked to sacrifice and do without material necessities forever. Islam was about construction and good management, as well as "martyr-seeking, crusade, and self-sacrifice." Iranian businessmen lacked expertise in certain fields, he argued, and private businessmen and investors could contribute their capital, energies, and talent to the reconstruction effort. He decried the "frozen mentalities" of those who cried out that the principles of the revolution were being abandoned every time Iran wished to utilize a foreign expert or a foreign company. There was a "middle way," he said, between opening the doors wide to unrestricted foreign investment and shutting foreign investment out entirely.[8]

Both sides in this debate appealed to Khomaini. In August, he appointed the heads of the three branches of government (Khamene'i, Hashemi-Rafsanjani, and Musavi-Ardabili) and the prime minister to a committee to determine long-range development policy. Disagreements persisted, and disputes broke out over the committee's mandate and the degree of control it could exercise over the Plan and Budget Ministry, the country's chief planning and budgeting body. In October, the members of the committee appealed to Khomaini to define their mandate more precisely. In his reply, Khomaini repeated many of the themes dear to the prime minister: the importance of economic independence, agricultural self-sufficiency, welfare for the victims of the war, mobilization of popular energies, and continued expenditures for military preparedness.[9] This was the thrust of other statements by Khomaini during this period and in the spirit of his 1987 *hajj* message.

Although he left the determination of long-term reconstruction policy in the hands of the four-man committee, he issued instructions that the private sector should be allowed a role in the reconstruction effort. He was also persuaded by Rafsanjani to permit businessmen able to provide their own foreign exchange to import a limited range of goods and to sell them, free from government price controls. Khomaini was thus on both sides of the reconstruction issue. His rhetoric remained close to that of the prime minister, but in practice he allowed the Rafsanjani-Khamene'i camp to provide a limited role for foreign investments and the domestic private sector in the postwar economy. When the 1989–90 budget was presented to the Majles, it contained provision for the use of $3.8 billion in new foreign credits for industrial expansion.

Moreover, Khomaini allowed Hashemi-Rafsanjani to mend fences in Europe. Rafsanjani argued that during the war Iran needlessly made enemies and lost international support. Under his direction, the foreign ministry now moved to repair Iran's relations with a half-a-dozen countries. By the summer, diplomatic relations were resumed with England and France. Rafsanjani and members of the foreign ministry dropped hints that they desired a dialogue with the United States as well. A stream of foreign visitors, including the French and West German foreign ministers, went to Iran to discuss industrial projects and technology transfers. There continued to be resistance against this process within the government and the clerical leadership. Mohtashami, responding to a question on the prospects for improved U.S.-Iran relations, remarked that "a wolf is a wolf even in sheep's clothing."[10] Musavi-Ardabili regretted that during the early wave of nationalization a law had not been passed altogether forbidding foreign companies from returning to

Iran. Nevertheless, by the end of the year, Rafsanjani's diplomatic initiative seemed firmly in place.

The Rushdie Affair

In February 1989, Khomaini wrecked months of careful fence-mending by Hashemi-Rafsanjani by injecting Iran into the Salman Rushdie affair. Rushdie's novel, *Satanic Verses,* published in England in November 1988, contained material offensive to Muslims. Muslim communities in London, India, and Pakistan protested the publication of the book. In Pakistan, demonstrators were killed in clashes with the police. The book had gone almost unnoticed in Iran until these protests came to Khomaini's attention. He could not keep silent on an issue of moment to Muslims. Moreover, eight months after Iran had accepted a cease-fire with Iraq there was no sign of the support the government had anticipated in its difficult negotiations with the Baghdad regime, fueling Khomaini's anger at the West. On 14 February, Khomaini issued a decree that declared Rushdie (and those of his publishers aware of the contents of his book) "sentenced to death." He called on Muslims "to execute them quickly, wherever they find them, so that no one will dare insult the Islamic sanctities."[11] Once Khomaini had taken his stand, other Iranian leaders had little choice but to follow suit. Rafsanjani confirmed the ruling. Khamene'i remarked that "the arrow has already been fired and is travelling towards its target."[12] Montazeri condemned Rushdie, although significantly, some thought, without repeating the death sentence. Those in the ruling coalition opposed to a rapprochement with the West seized on the Rushdie book, as had Khomaini, as evidence that the West remained inveterately hostile to Islam and that good relations with the West were not feasible.

The call for the murder of a writer and the citizen of another country caused an international outrage. The European Community jointly agreed to withdraw their ambassadors from Iran. Iran's relations with West European countries rapidly deteriorated. The Majles voted to break diplomatic relations with England altogether. Discussions on industrial projects with West Germany, France, and other countries were suspended. Once again, months of patient fence-mending in foreign policy had come to nothing.

The Dismissal of Montazeri

Six weeks after pronouncing his "death sentence" against Rushdie, Khomaini dropped another bombshell. On March 28, he dismissed Ayatollah Montazeri as his successor designate. In a letter ostensibly accepting Montazeri's "resignation," he remarked that the supreme leadership of the Islamic Republic "is a difficult, heavy, and august responsibility which requires strength beyond your capacity."[13]

Montazeri had been selected as Khomaini's successor in 1985 by the Assembly of Experts (not to be confused with the Assembly of Experts that wrote the constitution), a body constitutionally designated to make such a selection. Even before that date, and following a 1983 session of the Assembly of Experts, when no selection was formally announced, Montazeri was widely assumed to be the likely successor. Ahmad Khomaini, speaking of his father's preference, declared Montazeri as the most suitable successor.[14] Khomaini delegated important functions to him, especially in the judicial sphere. Montazeri routinely received domestic and foreign delegations and gave his views on national issues. The press referred to him as *ayatollah-e ozma,* one of the few grand ayatollahs. After 1985, he served not only as the successor designate, but as Khomaini's deputy *(qa'em maqam),* and performed a number of public functions in this capacity. In the early years of the revolution, Montazeri gained a reputation as one of the radicals, who favored the revolutionary organizations, egalitarian economic policies, and export of the revolution. He appeared to have retained a radical streak on foreign policy questions, but on domestic policy his views underwent a sea change. He became a champion of the private sector and the bazaar and repeatedly urged a larger share for private businesses in the economy. He called for a general amnesty to attract home the thousands of educated Iranians who had left the country after the revolution. He spoke out for better treatment of political prisoners. Occasionally, he urged greater freedom for the press and for political activity.

Friction between Khomaini and Montazeri first developed in 1985–86 over the case of Mehdi Hashemi.[15] Hashemi, the brother of Montazeri's son-in-law, Hadi, was a controversial figure. Before the revolution, he was implicated in the murder of a cleric in a dispute over religious doctrine and political ideology. After the revolution, he was associated with Montazeri's son, Mohammad, who used to make his way about Tehran with his own armed retainers. Hashemi took over this armed contingent when Mohammad died. He used the influence afforded by Montazeri's patronage and his position as the head of the liberation movements unit in the Revolutionary Guard to pursue his own agenda at home, in Lebanon, and other areas of foreign policy. If the charges brought against him in 1986 are accurate, he was implicated in one or more murders after the revolution, sought to instigate units of the Revolutionary Guard against their headquarters in Isfahan, opposed the policies pursued by Rafsanjani and others at home and abroad, and distributed clandestine leaflets under the name of fictitious organizations attacking various officials. In October 1986, shortly following the abduction of the Syrian *chargé d'affaires* in Tehran and a few weeks before the Iran-Contra story broke, he was arrested on orders of the Ministry of Intelligence and Security Affairs along with a number of his colleagues. Khomaini had personally endorsed the arrest order. Hashemi was charged with various crimes against the security of the state; nearly a year later, he was tried and executed.

According to an account later given by Ahmad Khomaini, the elder Khomaini had urged Montazeri as early as 1985 to dissociate himself from Hashemi, but Montazeri refused. When Hashemi was arrested then charged and executed, Montazeri continued to defend him. Montazeri was sufficiently angered by Hashemi's arrest that he asked to be excused from his political responsibilities and refused to resume these when urged to do so. Of all this, there was little public knowledge at the time. Montazeri's reputation was damaged by Hashemi's arrest and the later revelations about his activities. Yet, Montazeri continued to be treated as the successor-designate by men close to Khomaini, such as Rafsanjani. In private letters to Khomaini, whose contents became public only much later, Montazeri, however, was highly critical of political conditions. He protested the treatment of political prisoners: "the crimes of your Intelligence [and Security Affairs Ministry] and your prisons," he wrote Khomaini on one occasion, "are far worse than those of the Shah and his Savak." He also suggested Khomaini had lost touch with public opinion. "I anticipated that in time your excellency would be cut off from your well-wishers, but I did not think this would occur so soon."[16]

In the postwar period, Montazeri went public with these criticisms. He said Iran had become known in the world only for executions. He criticized press censorship and said even his own remarks did not find their way into print. In an interview early in February, he said that the revolution had produced "more slogans than action" and that it had violated many of its own principles. He suggested that competent men were being passed over for public office; that Khomaini, as *faqih,* was not consulting with others sufficiently; and that an honest exchange of opinion would not be possible without freedom of expression. The regime, he said, had been guilty of "injustice [and] denial of people's rights."[17] In calling for broader political participation, Montazeri had in mind the Iran Freedom Movement. He was known to meet with Bazargan and other members of the movement from time to time. He also received members of other opposition political parties at his home. The minister of health under Bazargan, Kazem Sami, was his personal physician. (Sami was assassinated in his clinic in November; his assailants were not apprehended.)

As officials assessed the record of the first decade of the revolution, there appeared a general propensity to rake over the mistakes of the past. Rafsanjani and Musavi-Ardabili both said that the war with Iraq had gone on too long for Iran's good. Musavi-Ardabili even suggested that Iran had allowed the American hostage crisis to go on too long. Between February and March 1989, Khomaini brought this discussion to a sudden end. In a message to the clerics on 22 February, he sharply attacked those who saw Khomaini's claims for the authority of the state as a form of Sunni Islam. He asserted jurisprudential tradition was on his side. He also attacked "pseudo-clerics" and said that he would never allow the government to fall into the hands of the liberals. Critics of the war, he said, were demeaning "the martyrdom, the self-sacrifice" of their fighting men. He decried the view that reasonable behavior on Iran's part would cause East and West to respect Islam and Muslims. He rejected charges that the government had been poorly managed by the clerics. And in an echo of remarks he would repeat when accepting Montazeri's resignation, he said that in a world of deceit and danger, a real jurist and leader needed "shrewdness and intelligence" to manage and safeguard a great Islamic state.[18] Khomaini's message of 22 February was not exclusively aimed at Montazeri; it addressed many of the questions that Montazeri was raising. It was an indication that Khomaini would not tolerate any further criticism of major policies of the past and that, despite his acquiescence in Rafsanjani's diplomacy, he still regarded the West with deep and unwavering suspicion.

The New Constitutional Order

The dismissal of Montazeri created a mini–constitutional crisis. Khomaini's own clerical lieutenants lacked the necessary qualifications under the terms of the constitution to succeed Khomaini. Senior clerics who were qualified were too old and lacked desirable revolutionary credentials. Succession by a council of jurists was possible under the terms of the constitution, but this still required clerics who were qualified; besides, the option of a supreme leadership exercised by a council had been rejected in the past as cumbersome and unworkable.

Before the dismissal of Montazeri, there had already been a discussion on the desirability of amending the constitution to deal with problems encountered in the first decade of the Islamic Republic. The succession problem made revising the constitution an urgent matter, if only to appoint a successor to Khomaini of less eminent scholarly standing. On 24 April, declaring revision to the constitution "an unavoidable necessity," Khomaini named twenty of the leading officials and clerics of the regime to a new council charged with revising the constitution. He invited the Majles to name an additional five members. The new body convened almost immediately and by mid-July had completed its work. It produced a revised constitution that reflected the lessons Iran's leaders believed they had learned from the first decade of rule. The 1979 constitution was characterized by a reaction against royal autocracy and by a determination to distribute authority, which was often divided among individuals or vested in councils (except for the wide powers granted to Khomaini). The 1989 constitution represented a reaction to this experience. It provided for greater centralization and concentration of authority. The revised constitution also reflected the concern of Iran's clerics to establish a mechanism or source of authority by which broad policy lines could be established and divisive debate on crucial policy choices avoided.

Iran's leaders blamed the immobility of the government and their inability to reach decisions partly on the fragmentation of executive authority between the president and the prime minister. The prime minister's post was therefore abolished in favor of the president, who remained the chief executive. All powers previously vested in the prime minister, including the authority to name the cabinet, devolved to the president. While individual ministers required the confirmation of the Majles and could be removed on a vote of no-confidence, the president (except in the case of impeachment for gross violations), unlike the prime minister under the old constitution, was not liable to a no-confidence vote. The president was specifically given authority over budgeting and planning affairs (Prime Minister Musavi had lost this authority in turf struggles in 1988).

Iran's leaders believed that the disorder in the judiciary stemmed from the fact that judicial authority was wielded by a five-member Supreme Judicial Council. The constitution was amended to concentrate judicial authority in a single individual, the chief judicial official. As in the past, this officer was required to be an Islamic jurist. He was empowered to name all senior judicial officials including the prosecutor-general, who under the old constitution was named by the supreme leader.

The constituent assembly also downgraded the qualifications required of the *faqih,* or supreme leader, so that clerics who lacked Khomaini's high scholarly standing could be appointed to the office. Under the 1979 constitution, the *faqih,* or supreme jurist, was required to be a *marja',* a source of emulation or guide for Shi'ites in matters of religious practice and other affairs. The revised constitution only required that the supreme jurist be a *mojtahed,* a cleric with sufficient learning to issue rulings on matters of Islamic law. Moreover, while the 1979 constitution permitted supreme leadership to be exercised by a council of three or five senior jurists, under the revised constitution the supreme leadership could be exercised only by a single individual. The 1979 constitution specified that the supreme leader would in the first instance be appointed (as was Khomaini) on the basis of national consensus. Only if no such consensus emerged would the Assembly of Experts be convened to select the *faqih.* The revised constitution vested the authority to select the supreme jurist exclusively in the Assembly of Experts. At the same time, the authority of the supreme leader was enhanced. In addition to the extensive powers granted him under the 1979 constitution, the *faqih* was also empowered to set the general policies of the Islamic Republic and to decide issues "which cannot be resolved in ordinary ways." This vaguely defined and open-ended authority was clearly designed to cut through the impasse over issues of trade, investment, social justice, and general economic policy experienced over the previous decade. The supreme leader was also given the authority to appoint the director of the broadcasting services (supervised by a council representing the three branches of government under the 1979 constitution) and the members of the Assembly for Discerning the Interests of the System of the Islamic Republic. Direction of the broadcasting services was thus transferred from a council to a single individual. Under the revised constitution, the Assembly for Discerning the Interests of the System became a permanent institution of the new order. In addition to mediating differences between the Majles and the Council of Guardians, the assembly was to serve in an advisory capacity on major policy issues to the supreme leader and to perform other vaguely defined duties. The entire membership was to be appointed by the supreme leader. Finally, the revised constitution established a Supreme Security Council, headed by the president, to deal with matters of both internal and external security, including the duties formerly performed by the Supreme Defense Council.

These constitutional changes represented a triumph for Hashemi-Rafsanjani, who was widely expected to be elected the new president with greatly enhanced powers, and a defeat for Prime Minister Musavi, who tried to resist the abolition of the prime minister's post. The overwhelming majority in the constituent assembly was in favor of the new arrangements.

Khomaini died on 3 June 1989, before the assembly could complete its work. He was buried two days later in an immense outpouring of national grief. The transition was smooth, and the Assembly of Experts quickly convened and named President Khamene'i as Khomaini's successor. On 28 July, the proposed constitutional amendments were approved in a national referendum and Rafsanjani was elected the new president. The Khomaini decade was over; the post-Khomaini period had begun.

Conclusion

MILLIONS OF frenzied Iranians greeted Khomaini when he returned in triumph to Iran in February 1979 to claim the revolution he had set in motion. Frenzied millions mourned his passing a decade later, snatching at the shroud that covered him for a memento, a shred, of his supposed sanctity. For ten years, Khomaini dominated Iran. He made possible the clerical domination of the Iranian state. The chief officers of the state served at his discretion. On major issues of policy, he was the final arbiter. Khomaini came to power with a vision. He wished to create an Islamic state modeled on the community the Prophet established in seventh-century Arabia, a community based on Islamic law and ruled by the clerics. He did not originate the concept that the clerics, as heirs to the mantle of the Prophet, have a mandate to rule. But the idea of the Islamic jurist, as the regent of the Prophet, empowered to decide issues of public life was, until his time, only an idea. He articulated and elaborated it with great force and turned it into reality.

He wielded immense power by virtue of his personality, the aura

A part of this conclusion first appeared in "What Khomeini Did," *New York Review of Books,* 20 July 1989.

attached to him as the architect of the revolution, the authority vested in him by the constitution, and the deference with which the increasingly sycophantic clerics and officials of the Islamic Republic treated him. Senior clerics continued to elaborate on the theory of Khomaini's authority as supreme jurist until this authority seemed virtually limitless. He ruled, it was alleged, by divine mandate. The legitimacy of Parliament and its laws, of the constitution, and of the Islamic state itself, it was argued, derived from his "permission." By implication, he could withdraw his sanction for the Islamic Republic whenever he saw fit.

Such exaggerated claims on Khomaini's behalf were extended to the international sphere. His lieutenants claimed that his spiritual leadership encompassed not only Iran's Shi'ites but the worldwide Muslim community. "The hope of the world's disinherited" was one of the many honorifics with which he was addressed. Khomaini took his role as spiritual leader of the Muslim world seriously. It was in this capacity that he addressed a message in January 1989 to Soviet leader Mikhael Gorbachev, urging him to eschew the false gods of both communism and capitalism and to return to God, read the Koran, and study the Islamic philosophers and mystics. As the defender of the Muslim community against the supposed insults and blasphemous content of *The Satanic Verses*, Khomaini condemned Salman Rushdie to death. He addressed his last will and testament not only to the people of Iran but "to all the Muslim nations and the oppressed of the world."

He believed the Islamic revolution in Iran could become the model for revolutions elsewhere in the Islamic world and directed his efforts against what he saw as the autocratic rulers at home and the exploitative, innately anti-Islamic West. To this end he employed a highly emotive rhetoric. He used the *hajj,* the great annual pilgrimage of Muslims to Mecca, for similar purposes. In Lebanon and elsewhere, he permitted his lieutenants to use violence, as well as propaganda and money, to extend the reach of the Iranian revolution. Like Nasser in the Arab world, Khomaini had a powerful impact on Muslim communities outside his own country. Protesters as far away as Lebanon and the Philippines have borne aloft his picture. But, like Nasser's, his was always an impossibly ambitious vision. Iran under Khomaini lacked the means for such a role and drained resources needed at home for these foreign adventures. Moreover, Khomaini and Shi'ite Iran were unlikely candidates for leadership of the worldwide Muslim community, which is largely Sunni and greatly diverse. Iran's international Islamic role was already waning in the last year of Khomaini's life and, except in a general way, is unlikely to survive him.

Revolutionary Change

At home, however, major transformations took place as a result of the revolution. The old ruling elite of the court and the bureaucracy was eliminated through execution, purge, forced retirement, and self-imposed exile. In the bazaar, the old merchant families were edged out by new men with connections to the clerics in the government. Even within the clerical community, younger, middle-rank clerics hungry for power and ready to espouse a revolutionary ideology elbowed out the old clerical families to dominate the new regime. The Pahlavi elite was replaced by a new ruling elite of clerics associated, even before the revolution, with Khomaini and with the anti-Shah resistance, and by upwardly mobile young men who rose rapidly through revolutionary activity and service in the revolutionary organizations to positions of great prominence.

Mohammad-Ali Raja'i was a street peddler and school teacher before he became prime minister. Mohammad Gharazi was a member of the Saltanatabad revolutionary committee in Tehran before he became governor-general of Khuzestan, then minister for oil. Va'ez Tabassi, the head of the revolutionary committee in Mashad, became the Keeper of the Shrine of Imam Reza, the richest and most important religious endowment in the country. Abbas Zamani (Abu-Sharif), the PLO-trained Islamic guerrilla, became commander of the Revolutionary Guard, then ambassador to Pakistan. Ahmad Azizi, one of the leaders of the "students of the Imam's line," was appointed political undersecretary of the ministry for foreign affairs. Behzad Nabavi, one of the organizers of the Mojahedin of the Islamic Republic, became an assistant to Prime Minister Raja'i, organized the food rationing program, and was appointed minister of heavy industry. Several members of these revolutionary bodies were elected to the Majles and went from the legislature to cabinet offices. In 1983 two officers of the Revolutionary Guard became ministers of commerce and labor. Two other revolutionary committee members became the ministers of agriculture and housing. By the end of the decade, the new ruling elite had consolidated its hold on the state, but there still remained opportunity for upward mobility. Nearly half the deputies elected to the 1988 Majles were new faces.

Rapid upward mobility was also characteristic of the military organizations. Following the rapid turnover in command posts in the early months of the revolution, military commanders were recruited almost invariably from among junior officers. Sayyad Shirazi, appointed commander of the ground forces, caught Khomaini's eye because of his harsh suppression of the Kurdish rebellion. Most of the commanders of the Revolutionary Guard rose from humble and poor backgrounds.

Nowhere was the transformation of elites more striking than in the clerical community. Clerics like Musavi-Ardabili and Mohammadi-Rayshahri were running mosques, preaching in small towns, tending to local parishes, or teaching in religious seminaries before, almost overnight, they found themselves administering ministries and holding the highest offices in the land. Ali Khamene'i was a middle-rank cleric in the provincial capital of Mashad when the revolutionary upheaval carried him to the presidency and then the supreme leadership of the Islamic Republic. Hashemi-Rafsanjani, another minor cleric involved in the clerical opposition, dealt in real estate in Qom before the revolution made him one of the half-dozen most powerful men in Iran. Mohtashami served in a minor capacity in Khomaini's household in Najaf, before the revolution propelled him to an ambassadorship in Damascus, then the influential post of interior minister.

A second major transformation occurred in the ownership of property and wealth. The transfer of wealth was not so much a transfer from the rich to the poor as from the private to the public sector. The state took over all major industries, insurance, and banking; seized private land and housing; established control over foreign trade; and interfered in the domestic distribution of goods. In the process it created a huge bureaucracy to manage the nationalized industries and the state trading companies and to oversee pricing and food rationing operations. Attempts to roll back this cumbersome system of state controls following the end of the Iran-Iraq war met with very limited success.

The extension of the role of the state was not limited to the economy. A third major result of the revolution was the extension of the tentacles of the state into virtually every sphere of public and even private life. Under the Islamic Republic, the state has attempted to dictate the standards of public morality—from women's dress to the music to which the public may listen. The government insisted, on and off, on ideological conformity, for example, by subjecting applicants to universities or to the civil service to loyalty tests. As in other third world upheavals, the revolution thus produced a swollen state and a diminished private sector. The tendency toward extension of state authority and bureaucratic control was already evident under the Pahlavi monarchy. But the revolution greatly accelerated this process.

Finally, the revolution transformed the constitutional structure of the state. Other Middle Eastern societies have aspired to the ideal of an Islamic government; in Iran, uniquely, the clerics came to power and have governed Iran. Clerical domination of the state was written into the constitution and largely realized in practice. The clerics controlled the chief offices of the state. They dominated the judiciary, the revolutionary organizations, the state security apparatus, and until 1988, the Majles as well. They formulated state ideology, watched over the technocrats who ran the ministries, decided the issues of peace and war, and determined the laws. Islam (variously interpreted) became the criteria for judging the legitimacy of legislation and state institutions.

Bureaucrats, Clerics, and Dissenters

The revolutionaries came into possession of a state apparatus and bureaucracy with strong administrative traditions and capabilities. They caused considerable upheaval in the state bureaucracy, but the bureaucratic structure remained in place. The bureaucrats kept the machinery of government going in the early days of the revolution; they ensured that the mail was delivered, electric power was generated, taxes were collected. Gradually they taught the newcomers to manage the balance of payments, to write budgets, to keep the national accounts, and to negotiate foreign trade agreements. In due course, the natural conservatism of the bureaucracy and its insistence on regulations and procedures acted as a check on the more impractical inclinations of the revolutionaries; as the new men took over the state apparatus, many of them became advocates of orderly rather than "revolutionary" action.

Alongside the state apparatus, the regime created an array of new organizations. These revolutionary organizations not only duplicated or usurped functions of the existing bureaucracy, they also constituted a formidable machinery of patronage, mass mobilization, ideological education, and repression. By the end of the decade, the revolutionary organizations were institutionalized and generally integrated into the state structure, but only imperfectly. The revolutionary organizations continued to be governed by their own free-swinging revolutionary culture. Different traditions governed the organization, the behavior and self-image of the regular army and the Revolutionary Guard, the police, and the revolutionary committees. The central government managed, by the end of the decade, to eliminate or to assert control over semi-autonomous groups; the arrest of Mehdi Hashemi in 1986 signaled the assertion of central government authority. However, as indicated by the example of Interior Minister Mohtashami, powerful clerics holding major office were able to mobilize public support and could still pursue an independent agenda.

Because central authority remained imperfect and the leadership divided and because of the structure of Iran's clerical establishment and Khomaini's leadership style, there continued to be room for a large degree of elite politics. The Majles, for example, was not a representative or democratic body. Elections were tampered with, and opposition candidates prevented from running for seats. Some issues could be raised in the legislature only at considerable risk. Nevertheless, debate on a wide number of issues remained vigorous. Government, Guardianship Council, and Majles acted as checks on one another. Differences within the leadership on some issues of economic and even foreign policy were fairly openly articulated. However, this did not imply an open political system. Khomaini silenced clerical leaders who challenged his authority. His lieutenants and followers eliminated or silenced the political groups and leaders of the original revolutionary coalition—Mojahedin, Fadayan, Tudeh, National Front, and the Iran Freedom Movement. There remained very little tolerance for dissent. Groups like the Freedom Movement could barely operate openly. Club-wielding *hezbollahis* were always on hand to break up meetings of tolerated, but disliked, opposition groups. An element of thuggery was never far below the surface of the political process. As the mass executions in 1988–89 indicated, the regime was always prepared to revert to violent repression of the opposition. The dissatisfied elements—the professional and middle classes, parts of the bazaar, Westernized intelligentsia, and dissenting clerical leaders—were cowed into silence rather than accommodated.

Leadership Divisions

While more pragmatic elements gained in influence, the powerful and highly emotive slogans of the revolution, such as "Neither East nor West" and "Islam of the barefoot" (as opposed to "American Islam" and the Islam of the rich), continued to exercise a powerful influence on elements within the clerical leadership, the government, and the important constituencies in society at large. The revolution was institutionalized but revolutionary ideology, often articulated in the vocabulary of Islam, continued to shape policy and political culture.

This made for conflicting policies both abroad and at home. Attempts to normalize relations with the outside world after 1984 repeatedly failed as a result of the activities of hard-liners within the leadership; Khomaini's own inveterate hostility to the West; Iran's support for radical elements in Lebanon; and attitudes, born out of the revolution, regarding Iran's international mission. At home, deep disagreements surfaced within the leadership over the definition of Islam and the revolution and the implications of this for social and economic policy. But Khomaini's lieutenants remained uncomfortable with the kind of bargaining, compromise, coalition building, and search for parliamentary majorities that were necessary if interest groups and factions in the leadership could coexist. They therefore looked to Khomaini to serve as the final source of authority and to make the difficult policy decisions. Khomaini, however, was well aware his lieutenants were of many minds regarding these major policy issues; he knew the senior clerics were divided on the application of Islamic law to the large and small questions of governing the country. He listened to one faction, then to the other.

Khomaini spoke both in favor of state control of the economy and in defense of the private sector. He made extraordinary claims for the authority of the Islamic state then retreated from such an extreme formulation. Repeatedly, he endorsed normalization of relations with the West, yet personally undermined these initiatives or stood by as radicals in the leadership did so with impunity. He bequeathed to his heirs a legacy of fierce animosity to the West, a militant assertion of Iran's Islamic identity, a conviction that only through religion can Muslims end the humiliation and exploitation of their societies by the West, and a belief that Islam can successfully be applied to the problems of governing modern societies. However, he provided no specific guidance to his heirs for running the state or deciding the issues that have persistently divided the leadership.

The constitutional amendments approved in 1989 were designed primarily to overcome these divisions. These amendments strengthened the authority of the supreme leader, the president, and the chief of the judiciary and explicitly gave the supreme leader the authority to determine the fundamental policies of the Islamic Republic (which Khomaini exercised in any case, by virtue of his own unique position). It seemed unlikely that divisions that could not be resolved during Khomaini's lifetime could be overcome by leaders lacking his immense prestige and authority. The constitutional amendments permitted the appointment of a cleric of less eminent scholarly standing to the position of supreme leader, but they also implied a separation between the office of senior *marja'* and the *faqih* and therefore a separation between the spiritual and political leadership of the community. This possibility was not foreseen by the constitution's framers. For a decade Iran's clerical leaders had insisted that the legitimacy of the state derived from divine mandate granted not only to the community of Islamic jurists but specifically to the supreme jurist of the age, in light of his superior learning, grace, and sanctity. Thus the post-Khomaini period seems likely to be characterized not only by leadership by clerics of diminished scholarly authority but also by a diminution of the basis of legitimacy on which the Islamic Republic was founded.

NOTES

Chapter 1: The Collapse of the Old Order

1. See especially, Ervand Abrahamian, *Iran Between Two Revolutions* (Princeton, N.J.: Princeton University Press, 1982), 426–29; and Marvin Zonis, "Iran: A Theory of Revolution from the Accounts of the Revolution," *World Politics* (July 1983): 586–606.
2. Zonis, 600.

Chapter 2: Khomaini: The "Idol Smasher"

1. For a biography of Khomaini, see *Zendegi-nameh-ye Imam Khomaini* (The Life of Imam Khomaini), 2 vols. (Tehran: 12 Moharram Publications, 1357 (1978)). This biography (hereafter *Zendegi-nameh*) appeared in Iran in various clandestine editions and under slightly varying titles. See also, Mohammad Razi, *Asar al-Hojjat ya Tarikh va Dayerat al-Mo'aref-e Howzeh-ye Elimyyeh-ye Qom* (History and Encyclopedia of the Qom Seminary), 2 vols. (Qom, Iran: Borqe'i Publications 1373–74 (1953–55), 2: 44–45 (hereafter *Asar al-Hojjat*).
2. Razi, *Asar al-Hojjat*, 45.
3. *Time*, 16 July 1979, p. 25.
4. Ibid.
5. For the following summary, see Ruhollah Khomaini, *Kashf ol-Asrar* (no date or place of publication), especially 179–221.
6. Ibid., 186.
7. *Zendegi-nameh*, 1: 157.
8. *Zendegi-nameh*, 1: 65–66.
9. Ibid., 67.
10. Ibid., 81–82. This quotation has been telescoped from a longer passage.
11. Ibid., 104.
12. Ibid., 98.
13. Ibid., 99.
14. Ibid., 157–58.
15. For these passages, see: ibid., 173; and *Khomaini va Jonbesh* (Khomaini and the Movement) (n.p.: 12 Moharram Publications: 1352 [1973]), 3, 54, and 185.
16. *Khomaini va Jonbesh*, 4.
17. Ibid., 6–7.
18. Naser Hariri, *Mosahebeh ba Tarikh Sazan-e Iran* (Interviews with the History Makers of Iran) (Tehran, 1358 [1979]), 10–11.
19. These declarations appear in *Zendegi-nameh*, vol. 2. The July declaration, 69–72; the August declaration, 93–96; and the March 1964 declaration, 97–99.

20. Hariri, *Mosahebeh ba Tarikh Sazan*, 64.

21. *Zendegi-nameh*, 2: 71–72, 95–96, and 98–99, for lists of signatories.

22. Ibid., 142.

23. *Khomaini va Jonbesh*, 24.

24. Ibid., 19; *Zendegi-nameh*, 2: 174.

25. The text of Khomaini's declaration, from which the following quotations are taken, is in *Khomaini va Jonbesh*, 30–31.

26. In addition to *Khomaini va Jonbesh*, cited above, Khomaini's declarations during the period of exile can be found in *Collection of Speeches, Position Papers by Ayatollah Ruhollah Khomaini* (Arlington, Va.: Joint Publication and Research Service [JPRS], 1979); *Payam-e Pishva dar Sal-e Enqelab* (The Message of the Leader in the Year of Revolution) (Qom: Fajr Publications, n.d.); *Ava-ye Enqelab: Khotbeh-ha-ye Tarikhi va Enqelabi-ye Imam Khomaini* (The Voice of Revolution: Imam Khomaini's Historic and Revolutionary Sermons) (Qom: 12 Moharram Publications, 1399 [1979]); Muslim Student Societies in America, Europe, and Canada (M.S.S.), *Neda-ye Haqq: Majmu'eh-i az Payamha, Mosahebeh-ha va Sokhranrani-ha-ye Imam Khomaini dar Paris* (The Voice of Truth: A Collection of the Messages, Interviews, and Speeches by Imam Khomaini in Paris) (Solon, Ohio: M.S.S., Dey 1357 [1979]); and *Islam and Revolution, Writings and Declarations of Imam Khomeini*, trans. Hamid Algar (Berkeley, Calif.: Mizan Press, 1981).

27. JPRS, *Collection of Speeches*, 20; I have slightly revised the translation, in keeping with the Persian original.

28. *Khomaini va Jonbesh*, 59.

29. Ibid., 56–57; *Farmudeh-ha-ye Imam dar Bareh-ye Falastin* (The Imam's Statements Regarding Palestine) (1393 [1978]), 90, 95–96.

30. Imam Khomaini, *Velayat-e Faqih: Hukumat-e Eslami* [The Vice-Regency of the Jurist: Islamic Government] (Tehran, 1357 [1978]). This book appeared in numerous clandestine editions in 1978–79.

31. Ibid., 60.

32. Ibid., 63.

33. Ibid., 41.

34. Ibid., 158.

35. Ibid., 157.

36. For brief biographies of these clerical leaders, see *Echo of Iran: Dawn of Islamic Revolution* (Tehran: Ministry of Islamic Guidance, n.d.), as follows: Beheshti, 176–83; Bahonar, 244–45; Mohammad Mofattah, 390.

37. For a brief biography of Ali Khamene'i, see, *Shahed*, Aban 1360 (November 1981): 10–13.

38. A biography of Mohammad-Reza Mahdavi-Kani is in *Shahed*, Mehr 1360 (October 1981): 18–25.

39. A biography of Ayatollah Sa'idi is in *Echo of Iran: Dawn of Islamic Revolution*, 138–39.

40. A biography of Hosain Ghaffari is in *Echo of Iran*, 398–401.

41. Mohammad Beheshti, cited in *Shahed*, Mordad 1360 (August 1981): 11.

42. Hariri, *Mosahebeh ba Tarikh Sazan*, 70.

43. *Payam-e Pishva*, 24.

44. Ibid., 93; *Neda-ye Haqq*, 428.

45. *Payam-e Pishva*, 116; *Neda-ye Haqq*, 427.

46. *Payam-e Pishva*, 70.

47. Ibid., 24.

48. Ibid., 20.

49. Mehdi Bazargan, *Showra-ye Enqelab va Dowlat-e Movaqqat* (The Revolutionary Council and the Provisional Government) (Tehran: Iran Freedom Movement, 1361 [1982]), 19–20.

50. *Payam-e Pishva*, 33.

51. From a leaflet in the author's possession, quoting a Khomaini interview with the BBC.

52. *Neda-ye Haqq*, 92–93.

53. *Khabarnameh* (Newsletter of the National Front, Tehran, 14 Aban 1357 [5 November 1978]).

54. Bazargan, *Showra-ye Enqelab va Dowlat-e Movaqqat*, 22.

55. Beheshti, cited in *Echo of Iran: Dawn of Islamic Revolution*, 182.

56. Bazargan, *Showra-ye Enqelab va Dowlat-e Movaqqat*, 23–25.

Chapter 3: Bazargan: A Knife Without the Blade

1. For a brief biography of Mehdi Bazargan, see Iran Freedom Movement, *Haft-e Esfand* (7 Esfand) (Tehran: Iran Freedom Movement, 1360 [1981], 67–86.

2. Mehdi Bazargan, *Moshkelat va Masa'el-e Avvalin Sal-e Enqelab* (Difficulties and Problems of the First Year of the Revolution) (Tehran: Iran Freedom Movement, 1361 [1982], 86.

3. Mehdi Bazargan, *Showra-ye Enqelab va Dowlat-e Movaqqat* (The Revolutionary Council and the Provisional Government) (Tehran: Iran Freedom Movement, 1361 [1982], 27.

4. Bazargan, *Moshkelat va Masa'el*, 74.

5. On the composition of the cabinet, see: Bazargan, *Showra-ye Enqelab va Dowlat-e Movaqqat*, 35–40.

6. Bazargan, *Moshkelat va Masa'el*, 90.

7. *International Herald Tribune*, 8 May 1979; Abol Hassan Bani-Sadr, *L'Espérance trahie*, (Paris: Papyrus Editions, 1982) 99.

8. Bazargan, *Moshkelat va Masa'el*, 131 and 93.

9. *Kayhan*, 26 Farvardin 1358 (15 April 1979).

10. Naser Hariri, *Mosahebeh ba Tarikh Sazan-e Iran* (Interviews with the History Makers of Iran) (Tehran: 1358 [1979]), 73.

11. *Kayhan*, 17 Esfand 1357 (8 March 1979).

12. *Kayhan*, 30 Farvardin 1358 (19 April 1979).

13. Amnesty International documented 438 executions up to 12 August 1979 and at least 120 more executions in the period 13 August to 14 September 1979, seven weeks before the fall of the Bazargan government. See Amnesty International, *Law and Human Rights in the Islamic Republic of Iran* (London: Amnesty International, 1980), 170, 189–94.

14. Text in *Kayhan*, 16 Farvardin 1358 (5 April 1979); English summary in Amnesty International, *Law and Human Rights*, 43–51.

15. Bani-Sadr, *L'Espérance trahie*, 55.

16. On the extraordinary courts, see account in Amnesty International, *Law and Human Rights*, 123–27.

17. Text in *Ettelaat*, 20 Tir 1358 (11 July 1979); English summary in Amnesty International, *Law and Human Rights*, 31–32.

18. *Le Monde*, 15 May 1979.

19. Ahmad Azari-Qomi: *Le Monde*, 18 May 1979; Sadeq Khalkhali: *Ettelaat*, 24 Ordibehesht 1358 (14 May 1979).

20. *Kayhan*, 14 and 23 Farvardin 1358 (3 and 12 April 1979).

21. Amnesty International, *Law and Human Rights*, 52.

22. Bazargan, *Showra-ye Enqelab va Dowlat-e Movaqqat*, 24–25.

23. Ibid., 30.

24. Ibid., 28.

Chapter 4: The Debate on the Constitution

1. *Ayandegan*, 25 Dey 1357 (15 January 1979).

2. *Ayandegan*, 26 Dey 1357 (16 January 1979).

3. *Ayandegan*, 25–26 Dey 1357 (15–16 January 1979).

4. *Guardian*, 2 March 1979.

5. *Enqelab-e Eslami*, 1 Shahrivar 1358 (23 August 1979).

6. Abol Hassan Bani-Sadr, *L'Espérance trahie* (Paris: Papyrus Editions, 1982), p. 70.

7. *Ayandegan*, 30 Khordad 1358 (21 June 1979). The National Front's critique of the draft constitution is in *Ayandegan*, 11 Mordad 1358 (2 August 1979).

8. *Ayandegan*, 18 Tir 1358 (9 July 1979).

9. The resolutions of the Seminar on the People's Expectations from the Constitution in *Ayandegan*, 18 Tir 1358 (9 July 1979).

10. Comments on the draft constitution by the Mojahedin in *Ettelaat*, 10 Mordad 1358 (1 August 1979); by the Fadayan in *Ayandegan*, 6 Mordad 1358 (28 July 1979).

11. *Ayandegan*, 6 Mordad, 1358 (28 July 1979).

12. Ezz ed-Din Hosaini: *Ayandegan*, 30 Khordad 1358 (20 June 1979); Shubayr Khaqani: *Ayandegan*, 20 Khordad 1358 (10 June 1979); United Muslims of Kurdistan: *Kayhan*, 16 Tir 1358 (7 July 1979).

13. *Ayandegan*, 2 Tir 1358 (23 June 1979).

14. The resolutions of the Congress of the Muslim Critics of the Constitution are in *Ayandegan*, 24 Tir 1358 (15 July 1979); Hosain-Ali Montazeri's detailed commentary on the draft constitution is in *Jomhuri-ye Eslami*, 24 Tir 1358 (15 July 1979). For other examples of the "Islamic" perspective on the draft constitution, see Gholam-Hosain Reza-Nejat, "An Examination of the Draft Constitution from the Perspective of Islamic Law," *Ayandegan*, 12 Tir 1358 (3 July 1979); Shaikh Mohammad Reza Ja'fari et al., "Review of the Draft Constitution," *Jomhuri-ye Eslami*, 16 Tir 1358 (7 July 1979); and Ayatollah Esma'il Mar'ashi-Najafi, *Kayhan* 18 Tir 1358 (9 July 1979).

15. Gholam-Hosain Reza-Nejat: *Ayandegan*, 12 Tir 1358 (3 July 1979).

16. Abbas Mo'aref: *Jomhuri-ye Eslami*, 16 Tir 1358 (7 July 1979).

17. Hasan Ayat: *Ayandegan*, 14 Tir 1358 (5 July 1979).

18. Reza-Nejat: *Ayandegan*, 12 Tir 1358 (3 July 1979).

19. *Mojahed*, 14 Aban 1358 (5 November 1979).

20. *Enqelab-e Eslami*, 28 Mordad 1358 (19 August 1979).

21. *Enqelab-e Eslami*, 30 Mordad 1358 (21 August 1979).

22. *Enqelab-e Eslami*, 28 Shahrivar 1358 (19 September 1979).

23. *Constitution of the Islamic Republic of Iran*, trans. Hamid Algar (Berkeley, Calif.: Mizan Press, 1980), 29.

24. *Enqelab-e Eslami*, 10 Shahrivar 1358 (1 September 1979).

25. *Enqelab-e Eslami*, 22 Shahrivar 1358 (13 September 1979).

26. *Enqelab-e Eslami*, 19 Mehr 1358 (11 October 1979).

27. Ibid.

28. Ibid.

29. *Ettelaat*, 28 Shahrivar 1358 (19 September 1979). For the IRP's response, see *Ettelaat*, 29 Shahrivar 1358.

30. *Enqelab-e Eslami*, 22 Mehr 1358 (13 September 1979).

31. *Enqelab-e Eslami*, 30 Mordad 1358 (21 August 1979).

32. *Enqelab-e Eslami*, 21 Mehr 1358 (13 October 1979).

33. *Enqelab-e Eslami*, 18 Mehr 1358 (10 October 1979).

34. Ibid.

35. See *Guardian*, 6 November 1979. After his arrest, Abbas Amir-Entezam gave the Tehran revolutionary tribunal a detailed account of these events. See *Ettelaat*, 9 Tir 1359 (30 June 1980).

36. *International Herald Tribune*, 24 October 1979.

37. The debates on the clauses of the constitution relating to individual rights appeared in the 29 Shahrivar–4 Mehr 1358 (20–26 September 1979) issues of *Enqelab-e Eslami*.

38. Mohammad Anvari: *Enqelab-e Eslami*, 2 Mehr 1358 (24 September 1979).

39. Hosain-Ali Montazeri: Abdol-Rahim Rabbani-Shirazi: *Enqelab-e Eslami*, 1 Mehr 1358; Ali Meshgini: *Enqelab-e Eslami*, 2 Mehr 1358 (23–24 September 1979).

40. *Enqelab-e Eslami*, 2 Mehr 1358 (24 September 1979).

41. *Enqelab-e Eslami*, 4 Mehr 1358 (26 September 1979).
42. Ibid.
43. Statements by Abol-Hasan Bani-Sadr in *Enqelab-e Eslami*, 1–2 Mehr 1358 (23–24 September 1979).
44. *Enqelab-e Eslami*, 1 Mehr 1358 (23 September 1979).

Chapter 5: Bani-Sadr: The "Devoted Son" as President

1. Bani-Sadr, *L'Espérance trahie* (Paris: Papyrus Editions, 1982), 40.
2. Abol-Hasan Bani-Sadr, *Usul-e Payeh va Zavabet-e Hukumat-e Eslami* (*Hukumat-e Eslami* hereafter) (The Basic Principles and Criteria of Islamic Government) (n.p., n.d.), 51.
3. These views are summarized from *Hukumat-e Eslami*. For the relevant quotations, see: army, 62–63; clothing, 65; mosque network, 63; role of the imam, 45, 17; the generalized imamate, 12.
4. Bani-Sadr, *Hukumat-e Eslami*, 27, 53.
5. Bani-Sadr, *L'Espérance trahie*, 67.
6. Mehdi Bazargan, *Showra-ye Enqelab va Dowlat-e Movaqqat*, (The Revolutionary Council and the Provisional Government) (Tehran: Iran Freedom Movement, 1361 [1982]), 31.
7. Bani-Sadr, *L'Espérance trahie*, 65.
8. *Le Monde*, 27–28 January 1980. Bani-Sadr's program and policies are outlined in statements and interviews cited in *Le Monde*, 27–28, 29 January and 12 February 1980; *Bamdad*, 7–10 Bahman 1358 (27–30 January 1980); *Kayhan*, 16 Bahman 1358 (5 February 1980); and *Ettelaat*, 27 Bahman 1358 (16 February 1980).
9. *Ettelaat*, 27 Bahman 1358 (16 February 1980).
10. Aii Khameme'i: *Kayhan*, 13 Bahman 1358 (2 February 1980); Mohammad Beheshti: *Bamdad*, 11 Bahman 1358 (31 January 1980); and *Le Monde*, 2 February 1980.
11. *Bamdad*, 10 Bahman 1358 (30 January 1980).
12. An English translation of Khomaini's New Year address appears in *Merip Reports*, June 1980.
13. *Bamdad*, 20 Esfand 1358 (10 March 1980).
14. *Ettelaat*, 21 Bahman 1358 (10 February 1980).
15. Ibid.
16. Ali Meshgini and Hosain-Ali Montazeri: *Bamdad*, 5 Esfand 1358 (24 February 1980); Mohammadi-Gilani: *Bamdad*, 16 Farvardin 1359 (5 April 1980); Qoddusi: *Bamdad*, 23 Farvardin 1359 (12 April 1980).
17. *Bamdad*, 24 Ordibehesht 1359 (14 May 1980).
18. Letter from Amnesty International to the author, 6 July 1982.
19. *Iran Times*, 26 September 1980.
20. *Bamdad*, 8 Tir 1359 (29 June 1980).
21. For overall figures, Sadeq Qotbzadeh (source): *Iran Times*, 29 August 1980; Mohammad-Ali Raja'i, *Iran Times*, 19 September 1980; Valiollah Fallahi, *Iran Times*, 1 August 1980.
22. *Bamdad*, 14 Tir 1359 (5 July 1980).
23. Sadeq Tababata'i: *Iran Times*, 19 September 1980; Hosain-Ali Montazeri: *Iran Times*, 29 August 1980; figures based on reports in *Iran Times*.
24. By February 1980, according to Defense Minister Mostafa Chamran and Chief of Staff Valiollah Fallahi, between 7,000 and 8,000 military men had been purged or designated for dismissal. (Chamran: *Kayhan*, 21 Bahman 1358 [10 February 1980], and Fallahi: *Ettelaat*, 23 Bahman 1358 [12 February 1980]). But by July 1980, some four weeks after the beginning of the new wave of purges, Fallahi cited a figure of 10,000 for those dismissed from the armed forces (*Iran Times*, 1 August 1980); and following the outbreak of hostilities with Iraq in September, Bani-Sadr remarked that 12,000 men had been purged from the military. Cited in William F. Hickman, *Ravaged and Reborn: The Iranian Army, 1982* (Washington, D.C.: Brookings Institution, 1982), 14.

This would suggest that between 2,000 and 4,000 were dismissed in the purges of the summer of 1980.

25. On the reaction of the Mojahedin to the seizure of the American embassy and the abortive April 1980 rescue attempt, see *Mojahed,* 21 and 28 Aban (12 and 19 November 1979), 4 Dey (25 December 1979), and 9 Bahman 1358 (29 January 1980); 14 and 20 Farvardin (3 and 9 April 1980), and 17, 21–22 Ordibehesht 1359 (7, 11, and 12 May 1980). On the reaction of the Fadayan see *Kar,* 22 Esfand 1358 (13 March 1980); 13 and 21 Farvardin (2 and 10 April 1980), and 17 Ordibehesht 1359 (7 May 1980. These are only a sample of the numerous articles attacking the United States and the "liberals" in Iran who would compromise with America that characterized the attitude of both groups on the hostage issue.

26. Bani-Sadr, *L'Espérance trahie,* 248.

27. Tabulated from reports on the trials in the Iranian press.

28. *Bamdad,* 24 Tir 1359 (15 July 1980).

29. *Ettelaat,* 23 Tir 1359 (14 July 1980).

30. Mehdi Bazargan, *Moshkelat va Masa'el-e Avvalin Sal-e Enqelab* (Difficulties and Problems of the First Year of the Revolution) (Tehran: Iran Freedom Movement, 1361, [1982]), 30, 280.

31. Bani-Sadr, *L'Espérance trahie,* 122.

32. Mas'ud Rajavi, *Tabyin-e Jahan: Qava'ed va Mafhum-e Takamol* (The World Made Manifest: The Meaning and Meaning of Evolution), 2 vols. (Long Beach, Calif.: Moslem Students Society, 1980), 2:16.

33. *Kayhan,* 30 Farvardin 1359 (19 April 1980).

34. *Mojahed,* 3 Tir 1359 (24 June 1980) and 13 Khordad 1359 (3 June 1980).

35. Cited in *Mojahed* 18 Farvardin 1362 (7 April 1983).

Chapter 6: The Destruction of Bani-Sadr

1. Details on the background to the war can be found in S. Bakhash, *The Politics of Oil and Revolution in Iran* (Washington, D.C.: Brookings Institution, 1982), and in Bakhash, "Why the War Will Get Worse," *New York Review of Books,* 20 November 1981.

2. *Iran Times,* 12 December 1981.

3. The summary that follows is based on various diary entries in this period.

4. *Iran Times,* 28 November 1980.

5. *Financial Times,* 17 March 1981.

6. *New York Times,* 5 January 1980.

7. *Enqelab-e Eslami,* 14 Aban 1359 (5 November 1980).

8. *Jomhuri-ye Eslami,* 19 Aban 1359 (10 November 1980).

9. *Iran Times,* 30 January 1981.

10. *Enqelab-e Eslami,* 20 Aban 1359 (11 November 1980).

11. *Iran Times,* 19 December 1980.

12. *Iran Times,* 9 January 1981.

13. *Iran Times,* 20 February 1981.

14. *Iran Times,* 30 January 1981.

15. *Enqelab-e Eslami,* 27 Bahman 1359 (16 February 1981).

16. *Financial Times,* 19 February 1981.

17. Hajj Seyyed Javadi's letter, *As Seda-ye Pa-ye Fashism ta Ghul-e Fashism,* (From the Sound of the Feet of Fascism to the Monster of Fascism), appeared in the form of a pamphlet (Tehran: Kushesh Publications, 1359 [1981]).

18. *Iran Times,* 17 July 1981.

19. *Iran Times,* 17 April 1981.

20. Ibid.

21. *Ettelaat,* 2 Esfand 1359 (21 February 1981).

22. *Iran Times,* 27 February 1981.

23. *Kayhan*, 16 Bahman 1359 (5 February 1981).

24. *Iran Times*, 23 January 1981.

25. *Kayhan*, 23 Bahman 1359 (12 February 1981).

26. *Iran Times*, 21 November 1980.

27. *Iran Times*, 17 April 1981.

28. *Ettelaat*, 13 Azar 1359 (4 December 1980).

29. *Iran Times*, 16 January 1981.

30. Several good accounts of the hostage crisis and the negotiations that led to its resolution have appeared. See, Jimmy Carter, *Keeping Faith* (New York: Bantam Books, 1982; Zbigniew Brzezinski, *Power and Principle: Memoirs of the National Security Advisor 1977–1981*; (New York: Farrar, Straus & Giroux, 1983); Hamilton Jordan, *Crisis: The Last Year of the Carter Presidency*, (New York: G. P. Putnam, 1982); Cyrus Vance, *Hard Choices: Critical Years in America's Foreign Policy* (New York: Simon & Schuster, 1983); and Pierre Salinger, *America Held Hostage: The Secret Negotiations* (New York: G. P. Putnam, 1981).

31. *Kayhan*, 28 Dey 1359 (15 January 1981).

32. *New York Times*, "Week in Review," 2 November 1981.

33. Robert Carswell, "Economic Sanctions and the Iran Experience," *Foreign Affairs* 60 (Winter 1981–82), 254–56.

34. The meeting is described in Abol Hassan Bani-Sadr, *L'Espérance trahie* (Paris: Papyrus Editions, 1982) 260–66.

35. Ibid., 261.

36. Ibid., 264.

37. *Enqelab-e Eslami*, 7 Khordad 1360 (28 May 1981).

38. *Kayhan*, 19 Khordad 1360 (9 June 1981).

39. Bani-Sadr, *L'Espérance trahie*, 34–35.

40. Bani-Sadr describes the final days of his administration in *L'Espérance trahie*, 27–48. I have also drawn on Eric Rouleau's graphic reports in *Le Monde*, 6, 13–17, and 21–23 June 1981.

41. *Le Monde*, 14–15 June 1981.

42. *New York Times*, 16 June 1981.

43. *Le Monde*, 16 June 1981.

44. *Kayhan*, 26 Khordad 1960 (16 June 1981).

45. *Financial Times*, 15 June 1980.

46. Speeches made in favor and against Bani-Sadr's impeachment appear in *Kayhan*, 30–31 Khordad and 1–2 Tir 1360 (20–23 June 1981).

47. *Kayhan*, 31 Khordad 1360 (21 June 1981).

48. Ibid., 1 Tir 1360 (22 June 1981).

49. Ibid.

50. A list of the deputies who absented themselves from the Majles on 20–21 June 1981 is given in *Kayhan*, 21–22 June.

51. *Kayhan*, 1 Tir 1360 (22 June 1981).

52. *Le Monde*, 21–22 June 1981.

53. *Kayhan*, 31 Khordad 1360 (21 June 1981).

54. See especially speech by Ali-Akbar Velayati, *Kayhan*, 31 Khordad 1360 (21 June 1981).

55. *Le Monde*, 21–22 June 1981.

56. *New York Times*, 22 June 1981.

57. *Kayhan*, 19 Khordad 1360 (9 June 1981).

Chapter 7: The Economics of Divine Harmony

1. See, for example: Ali Tehrani, *Eqtesad-e Eslami* (Islamic Economics), (Mashad, Iran: Khorasan Press, 1353 [1974]); Musa Sadr, *Eqtesad dar Maktab-e Eslam* (Economics According to Islam), trans. from Arabic by Ali Hojjati-Kermani. (Tehran: Entesharat

Press, 1350 [1971]); and Habibollah Payman, *Bardashti dar bareh-ye Malekiyyat va Sarmayeh az Didgah-e Eslam* (Reflections on Property and Capital from the Perspective of Islam) (Tehran: n.d.).

2. Mahmud Taleqani, *Eslam va Malekiyyat,* 4th ed. (Tehran: Entesharat Press 1344 [1965]). For an English trans., by R. Campbell, of the important chapters, see, Taleghani, *Society and Economics in Islam.* (Berkeley, Calif.: Mizan Press, 1982). Mohammad-Baqer Sadr, *Iqtisaduna* (Beirut: 1961). In Persian, *Eqtesad-e Ma* (Our Economics), vol. 1, trans. Mohammad-Kazem Musavi (n.p.: Borhan Press, 1971); vol. 2, trans. Abdol-Ali Espahbodi (Tehran: Borhan Press, 1357 [1978]). Abol-Hasan Bani-Sadr, *Eqtesad-e Towhidi* (n.p. 1978).

3. Taleghani, *Society and Economics,* 28.

4. Ibid., 46.

5. Ibid., 52.

6. Ibid., 58.

7. Sadr, *Eqtesad-e Ma,* 2: 63n.

8. Ibid., 101–2.

9. Ibid., 341.

10. Sadr develops this thesis in *Eqtesad-e Ma,* 1: 362–63 and 2: 344–94. For an earlier formulation by Shi'a scholars of the concept of discretionary authority, see Hossein Modarressi Tabataba'i, *Kharaj in Islamic Law* (London, 1983), 84.

11. Sadr, *Eqtesad-e Ma,* 2:348.

12. Bani-Sadr, *Eqtesad-e Towhidi,* 282.

13. Ibid, 297.

14. See the analysis by Homa Katouzian, "Shi'ism and Islamic Economics: Sadr and Bani Sadr," in Nikkie R. Keddie, ed., *Religion and Politics in Iran* (New Haven: Yale University Press, 1983), 145–65.

15. For these figures see Mehdi Bazargan, *Moshkelat va Masa'el-e Avvalin Sal-e Enqelab* (Difficulties and Problems of the First Year of the Revolution) (Tehran: Iran Freedom Movement, 1361 [1982]), 97, 158, 102.

16. Bank Markazi-ye Iran, *Gozaresh-e Eqtesadi va Taraznameh-ye Sal-e 1357* (Central Bank of Iran, Annual Report and Balance Sheet for 1978–79). (Tehran: Central Bank of Iran, 1358 [1979]), 58.

17. Bazargan, *Moshkelat va Masa'el,* 119–20 and 122.

18. Ibid, 101 and 102.

19. *Kayhan,* 12 Esfand and 3 Esfand, 1357 (3 March and 22 February 1979).

20. Bazargan, *Moshkelat va Masa'el,* 122–23 and 202.

21. Test of the decrees and laws cited in this chapter can be found in the *Ruznameh-ye Rasmi: Dadgostari-ye Jomhuri-ye Eslami-ye Iran, Majmu'eh-ye Qavanin* (Official Gazette: Judiciary of the Islamic Republic of Iran, Collection of Laws). (Tehran: Ministry of Justice, 1358, 1359, and 1360 [1979–80, 1980–81, and 1981–82]).

22. Ibid, 1359 (1980–81), 331–34.

23. The discussion on Iranian industry that follows is based on personal observation and interviews with Iranian industrialists and businessmen.

24. Mehdi Tabataba'i of the Foundation for the Disinherited in *Kayhan* (weekly air edition), 18 Khordad 1362 (8 June 1983).

25. For these figures *Kayhan International,* 7 February 1982; Ali-Akbar Hashemi-Rafsanjani in Ettelaat, 1 Aban 1361 (23 October 1982); deputy managing director of the National Industries Organization in *Kayhan,* 9 Esfand 1361 (28 February 1983); and "Iran's Traders Replace Slogans with Realism," *Financial Times,* 3 May 1983. The *Financial Times* correspondent gives a much higher figure (400–500) for factories taken over by the foundation.

26. Minister of Commerce Asgar-Owladi in *Ruznameh-ye Rasmi: Mashruh-e Mozakerat-e Majles-e Showra-ye Eslami* (Official Gazette: Parliamentary Proceedings). (Tehran: Ministry of Justice, 7 Dey 1361 [28 December 1982]).

27. *Kayhan,* 12 Esfand 1357 (3 March 1979).

28. *Iran Times,* 20 May 1983.

29. *Enqelab-e Eslami,* 13 Ordibehesht 1360 (3 May 1981).

30. *Bamdad,* 21 Esfand 1358 (12 March 1980).

31. *Enqelab-e Eslami,* 13 Ordibehesht 1360 (3 May 1981).

32. *Bamdad*, 18 Farvardin 1359 (7 April 1980); *Enqelab-e Eslami*, 13 Ordibehesht 1360 (3 May 1981); *Enqelab-e Eslami dar Hejrat*, 17 May 1983.

33. Bazargan, *Showra-ye Enqelab va Dowlat-e Movaqqat*, 14, 16, and 23.

34. *Enqelab-e Eslami*, 21 Ordibehesht 1360 (11 May 1981).

35. According to the minister of commerce (see comments in *Iran Times*, 27 May 1983) just over 60 percent of the import trade—for example, in 1982–83—was in government hands. But this figure does not appear to include the substantial imports of the revolutionary organizations, such as the Foundation for the Disinherited, or of industries taken over by the government but not formally nationalized. The 80 percent figure is a conservative estimate of the government's share of the import trade.

36. *Bamdad*, 20 Esfand 1358 (10 March 1980).

Chapter 8: The Struggle Over Land

1. On land reform under the monarchy see: A. K. S. Lambton, *The Persian Land Reform, 1962–1966* (London: Oxford University Press, 1969). For a later, more pessimistic assessment: Eric J. Hooglund, *Land and Revolution in Iran, 1960–1980* (Austin: University of Texas Press, 1982). For an assessment of the impact of land reform in this period that contrasts sharply with Hooglund's conclusions, see the limited study by Hossein Mahdavy, "Tahavvolat-e Si Saleh-ye Yek Deh dar Dasht-e Qazvin" (Changes over Thirty Years in One Village on the Qazvin Plain), in *Masa'el-e Arzi va Dehqani* (Problems of Land and Peasants). (Tehran: Agah Publications, 1361 [1982]), 50–74.

2. Hooglund, *Land and Revolution in Iran*, 85–87; and Ashraf, "Dehqanan Zamin va Enqelab" (Peasant, Land, and Revolution), in *Masa'el-e Arzi va Dehqani* (cited above), 14. The Ashraf article (hereafter "Ashraf"), is the best study so far published on the postrevolution land question.

3. Ashraf, 28.

4. *Mojahed*, 18 Khordad 1359 (8 June 1980).

5. Accounts of land disputes in the Turkoman region in 1979–80 can be found in *Bamdad*, 29 Aban 1358 (20 November 1979); *Mojahed*, 4–5 Khordad 1359 (25–26 May 1980); *Kayhan*, 26 Farvardin 1360 (15 April 1981); and *Kar International*, March, July–August, and September 1981. For examples of peasant-initiated seizures in the period March–July 1979 in villages around such districts as Hamadan, Qa'emshahr, and Sari, Bam, and Kerman, Torbat Jam, Samirom, the Banesh district of Fars, and Shirvan, see, *Enqelab-e Eslami*, 23–25 Esfand, 1359 (12–14 February 1981); and *Mojahed*, 1 Ordibehesht; 12, 18, 19, and 25 Khordad; and 2 Tir 1359 (21 March; 2, 8, 9, and 15 June; and 23 June 1980).

6. *Mojahed*, 2 Tir 1359 (23 June 1980).

7. The accounts of peasant seizures cited above also contain accounts of landlord reaction. For other examples of landlord activity in the Biza and Dasht-e Arzhan districts of Fars, the Kiakola district of Mazandaran, and the Banesh district of Fars, see *Mojahed*, 26 Azar, 4 and 18 Dey 1358 (17 and 25 December 1979; and 8 January 1980); 3 and 9 Ordibehesht 1359 (23 and 29 April 1980); and 10 and 25 Khordad 1359 (31 May and 15 June 1980).

8. For the examples of official reaction cited below, see issues of *Mojahed*, as follows: Qasemabad and Azizabad, 5 Tir 1359 (26 June 1980); Ruh-Kandi and Baba-Kandi, 21 Ordibehesht 1359 (11 May 1980); Revolutionary Guards, 4 Dey 1358 (25 December 1959); Izdeh, 5 Tir 1359 (26 June 1980); Banesh, 25 Khordad 1359 (15 June 1980).

9. *Mojahed*, 12 Khordad, 1359 (2 June 1980).

10. *Mojahed*, 25 Khordad 1359 (15 June 1980).

11. *Kayhan*, 3 Mehr 1358 (25 September 1979).

12. *Mojahed*, 12 Khordad 1359 (2 June 1980).

13. Text in *Ettelaat*, 12 Mehr 1358 (4 October 1979); Ashraf, 420–27.

14. *Kayhan,* 10 Azar 1358 (1 December 1979).

15. Text in Ashraf, 434–37.

16. Ali-Akbar Hashemi-Rafsanjani, *Kayhan,* 2 Aban 1360 (24 October 1981); Ali-Akbar Nateq-Nuri, *Kayhan,* 24 Khordad 1360 (14 June 1981).

17. For a summary of landlord activities, see Ashraf, 37–39.

18. Cited in Ashraf, 38.

19. For clerical opposition to the land reform law see Ashraf, 36–37; article by M. Beheshtipur in *Ettelaat,* 20 Farvardin 1359 (9 April 1980); survey of land distribution program in *Enqelab-e Eslami,* 21 Ordibehesht 1360 (11 May 1981). Views of Ayatollahs Shirazi and Ruhani appear in *Bamdad,* 16 Esfand 1358 (6 March 1980), and of Ayatollah Qomi in *Bamdad,* 20 Esfand 1358 (10 March 1980).

20. Cited in survey of land distribution in *Enqelab-e Eslami,* 21 Ordibehesht 1360 (11 May 1981).

21. *Bamdad,* 16 Esfand 1358 (6 March 1980).

22. Cited in *Enqelab-e Eslami,* 21 Ordibehesht 1360 (11 May 1981).

23. Mostafa Tabrizi in *Kayhan,* 10 Esfand 1359 (1 March 1981). *Kayhan* conducted a series of interviews with Majles deputies. With few exceptions, they questioned the legitimacy of large landlordism and called for implementation of the land distribution program. See, for example, interviews with deputies from Khodabandeh, Zarand, Abadan, Gonbad, and Saveh in the issues of 9 Esfand 1359 and 11 Farvardin, 3 Khordad, 14 Khordad, 29 Tir, and 7 Shahrivar 1360 (between March and August 1981).

24. See, for example, reports and remarks by members of the seven-man committees between February and July 1981, from the following districts: Kurdistan (*Kayhan,* 3 Esfand 1359), Gorgan, Gonbad, and Isfahan (*Kayhan,* 21 Esfand 1359), Semnan and Shahrud (*Kayhan,* 2 Khordad 1359), Arak (*Kayhan,* 21 Tir 1360), Jiroft (*Kayhan,* 20 Tir 1360), and Kermanshahan (*Kayhan,* 31 Tir 360).

25. *Kayhan,* 31 Tir 1360 (22 July 1981).

26. *Kayhan,* 30 Mehr 1360 (22 October 1981).

27. *Kayhan,* 20 Mehr 1360 (12 October 1981). Hashemi-Rafsanjani had broached the subject in a radio interview two months earlier. He remarked that Islam permits a legitimate government to set limits and conditions on the accumulation and disposal of property and to exercise this authority in keeping with social conditions. He added: "This government is reserved to the *velayat-e faqih.* In truth, the legal heirs to the exercise of the Godly vice-regency, within a limit, are the jurists who, with the assistance of experts in each field, determine the limits to property and the conditions and manner of exercising [property rights]." (*Kayhan,* 3 Shahrivar 1360) (25 August 1981).

28. The text of the letters exchanged between Khomaini and Hashemi-Rafsanjani as well as Rafsanjani's comments on the significance of Khomaini's remarks appear in *Kayhan,* 20 Mehr 1360 (12 October 1981). The same issue carries comments by the chief justice, Musavi-Ardabili, and of a member of the Guardianship Council, Yusef Sane'i. Sane'i, adopting a position similar to Rafsanjani's, added that once the *faqih* issues an order, it must be obeyed. "Disobedience to him is disobedience to a [religious] requirement and an obligation due to the government, and the violator must be punished in the same way as the violator of God's primary laws."

Ayatollah Montazeri explained that "on the basis of the principle of *velayat,* the Imam can where necessary and in order to preserve the interests of society make decisions regarding the property of individuals. . . . and private property will thus always be used in the public interest." *Kayhan,* 27 Mehr 1360 (19 October 1981).

Hashemi-Rafsanjani devoted his Friday prayer sermon that week to the jurist's powers to dispose of private property in the public interest. See *Kayhan* 2 Aban 1360 (24 October 1981).

29. Mohammad Beheshti's earlier remarks were reprinted in *Kayhan,* 2 Mehr 1360 (24 September 1981).

30. Ibid.

31. *Kayhan,* 2 Aban 1360 (24 October 1981).

32. Text in Ashraf, 449–53.

33. Text in *Kayhan,* 11 Aban 1360 (2 November 1981); and Ashraf, 453–57.

34. See remarks by Tavakkoli in *Kayhan,* 14 Aban 1360 (5 November 1981), and by Ali Tehrani in *Enqelab-e Eslami,* 6 and 8 Azar 1359 (27 and 29 November 1980).

35. *Kayhan,* 14 Aban 1360 (5 November 1981).

36. Text in *Ettelaat,* 8 Dey 1361 (29 December 1982).

37. Ashraf, 43–44.

38. Ashraf, 33, on the basis of the report of the seven-man committee's central staff on eight months of operations. For slightly different figures, see *Kayhan,* 13 Dey 1359 (3 January 1981).

39. For the Guardianship Council's explanations for the vetoes see: on the trade nationalization law, *Ettelaat,* 6 Azar 1361 (27 November 1982); on the land reform law, *Kayhan,* 29 Dey 1361 (19 January 1983); on the urban land law, *Kayhan,* 10 Esfand 1360 (29 February 1982); and on the property of "fugitives," *Iran Times,* 28 January 1983.

40. *Kayhan,* 5 Bahman 1361 (25 January 1983).

41. *Kayhan,* 5 Bahman 1361 (25 January 1983).

Chapter 9: Terror and Consolidation

1. *Platform of the Provisional Government of the Democratic Islamic Republic of Iran* (Long Beach, Calif.: Muslim Students Society, 1981).

2. *Iran Times,* 3 September 1982. (See exchange between Majles deputy Reza Zavvare'i and Minister of Justice M. Asghari.)

3. "Le témoinage d'un opposant iranien," *Le Monde,* 20 February 1982.

4. *Iran Times,* 25 September 1981.

5. Both quotations in *Iran Times,* 25 September 1981.

6. Mohammad Mo'men, cited in *Iran Times,* 8 October 1982.

7. Letter from Amnesty International to author, 6 July 1982.

8. *Asami va Moshakhkhesat-e Bakhshi (7,746 tan) az Shohada-ye Enqelab-e Novin-e Iran* (The Names and Characteristics of Part [7,746 persons] of the Martyrs of the New Iranian Revolution), *Mojahed,* 17 Shahrivar 1362 (8 September 1983). The list did not include 140 Baha'is executed since the revolution. The Mojahedin were able to determine the age of 3,223, the educational level of 3,600, the political affiliation of 6,230, and the manner of death of 5,987 of those listed. Mojahedin figures, however, should be treated with caution.

9. *Iran Times,* 3 September 1982.

10. *Iran Times,* 23 April and 27 August 1982.

11. On the Kurds, see: Eric Rouleau, "La guerre 'secrete' du Kurdistan iranien," *Le Monde,* 12 and 13 December 1980; "The Clergy Have Confiscated the Revolution" (interview with Abdol-Rahman Qasemlu), *Merip Reports,* July–August 1981; "La longue lutte de Kurdes d'Iran, *Le Monde,* 13 and 14 August 1983; "A Dictatorship under the Name of Islam" (interview with Ezz ed-Din Hosaini), *Merip Reports,* March–April 1983.

12. *Ettelaat,* 18 Mordad 1361 (9 August 1982).

13. Gholam-Reza Safa'i, director of the army Ideological–Political Bureau, cited in *Iran Times,* 16 April 1982.

14. Advertisement in *Ettelaat,* 11 Mordad 1361 (2 August 1982).

15. Texts of these laws appear in the *Ruznameh-ye Rasmi* (Official Gazette) as follows: Law on the Conditions for the Selection of Judges, 12 Ordibehesht 1361 (2 May 1982); Amendment to the Penal Procedures Law, 11 Mehr 1361 (3 October 1982); Law on *Hudud* and *Qasas,* 4 Aban and 15 Aban 1361 (26 October and 6 November 1982); Law on Islamic Punishments, 25 Aban 1361 (16 November 1981); Law on *Diyat,* 18 Dey 1361 (8 January 1982); and Amendments to the Civil Law, 21 Esfand 1361 (12 March 1983).

16. *New York Times,* 21 November 1982.

17. Text of decree in *Iran Times*, 7 January 1982.

18. *Ettelaat*, 2 Dey 1361 (24 December 1982).

19. Text of decree in *Iran Times*, 14 January 1983.

20. *Kayhan* (airmail weekly), 1 June 1983.

21. Nabavi in *Iran Times*, 8 October 1982; Hashemi-Rafsanjani in *Iran Times*, 5 November 1982.

22. *Kayhan*, 1 Tir 1361 (22 June 1982); *Iran Times*, 25 June 1982.

23. *Kayhan* (airmail weekly), 31 August 1983.

24. *Constitution of the Islamic Republic of Iran* (trans. H. Algar), 22 and 31.

25. Summary of World Broadcasts, Monitoring Report, ME 6992/i, 31 March 1982. I am grateful to Christine Helms for calling this quotation to my attention.

26. *Kayhan* (airmail weekly), 24 August 1983.

27. Foreign Broadcast Information Service (FBIS), 10 October 1982, cited by Elaine Sciolino, "Iran's Durable Revolution," *Foreign Affairs* (vol. 61, no. 4, 1983), 910.

28. *Kayhan* (airmail weekly), 10 August 1983.

29. *Iran Times*, 7 January 1983.

30. For a brief survey of the impact of the Iranian revolution on Shi'a and other Muslim communities, and of Iranian activity among these communities in various countries: Daniel Pipes, *In the Path of God: Islam and Political Power* (New York: Basic Books, 1983), 323–28.

31. On Soviet-Iranian relations, see three articles by Muriel Atkin: "The Kremlin and Khomeini," *The Washington Quarterly* (Spring 1981); "Soviet Relations with the Islamic Republic," *SAIS Review* (Winter–Spring 1983); and "Moscow's Disenchantment with Iran," *Survey* 27, no. 118–19 (1983): 247–60. For a somewhat different perspective, see Shahram Chubin, "The Soviet Union and Iran," *Foreign Affairs* (vol. 61, no. 4, 1983), 921–49.

32. *Pravda*, 9 March 1982, and *New York Times*, 10 March 1982.

33. *Iran Times*, 26 March 1982.

34. *Iran Times*, 10 December 1982.

35. Text of Kianuri's statement in *Iran Times*, 6 May 1983.

Chapter 10: A House Divided

1. See translation, "Appeal to the Iranian People," *London Times*, 14 February 1985.

2. Bazargan issued numerous statements on the war, the most carefully argued in the fall of 1986. See *Nameh-ye Sargoshadeh-ye Nehzat-e Azadi be Ayatollah Khomaini* (Open Letter from the Freedom Movement to Ayatollah Khomaini), Shahrivar 1365 (August-September 1986). The document was printed and distributed by the Iran Freedom Movement.

3. Ibid.

4. "Iran dans le piège de guerre," *Le Monde*, 16 March 1985.

5. Foreign Broadcasting Information Service (FBIS), South Asia, 5 April 1985, I1.

6. *Iran Times*, 6 September 1985.

7. English translation circulated by the Liberation Movement of Iran and Maktab, Houston, Texas, November 1988.

8. Amnesty International, *Annual Report 1987* (London: Amnesty International Publications, 1987), 340; and *Annual Report 1988* (London: Amnesty International Publications, 1988), 234.

9. For a more modest assessment of the costs of the war, see Patrick Clawson, "Islamic Iran's Economic Politics and Prospects," *Middle East Journal* (vol. 42, no. 3, Summer 1988), 371–88.

10. *Kayhan* (airmail weekly), 6 June 1984.

11. *Kayhan* (airmail weekly), 5 September 1984, 10.

12. Text of law in *Ruznameh-ye Rasmi* (Official Gazette), 2 Mehr 1363 (24 September 1984), 1–2.

13. The temporary cultivation law is discussed in detail in Shaul Bakhash, "The Politics of Land, Law and Social Justice in Iran," *Middle East Journal* (vol. 43, no. 2, Spring 1989), 186–201.

14. *Kayhan,* 13 Khordad 1366 (3 June 1987), 2.

15. FBIS, Near East and South Asia (FBIS/NESA), 8 December 1987, 50–51.

16. FBIS/NESA, 28 December 1987, 60.

17. *Kayhan,* 3 Dey 1366 (24 December 1987), 18. For an English translation of Khomaini's remarks, see FBIS/NESA, 24 December 1987, 36.

18. Khomaini's reply to Khamene'i is printed in *Kayhan,* 17 Dey 1366 (7 January 1988), 18. An English translation is in FBIS/NESA, 7 January 1988, 49–50.

19. *Kayhan,* 20 Dey 1366 (10 January 1988), 1–2.

20. Montazeri in *Kayhan,* 19 Dey 1366 (9 January 1988), 2; an English translation is in FBIS/NESA, 11 January 1988, 74–75. Hashemi-Rafsanjani in *Kayhan,* 17 Dey 1366 (7 January 1988), 2. A more complete version of his remarks is in FBIS/NESA, 7 January 1988, 15. Also relevant are Rafsanjani's Friday sermon in *Kayhan,* 26 Dey 1366 (16 January 1988), 3 and 13; and FBIS/NESA, 19 January 1988, 71–75. For Rafsanjani on the powers of Khomaini as *faqih,* see FBIS/NESA, 28 December 1987, esp. 60–62.

21. The resolutions of the Friday prayer leaders' seminar are in *Kayhan,* 30 Dey 1366 (20 January 1988), 2.

22. *Kayhan,* 24 Dey 1366 (14 January 1988), 18.

23. Khamene'i's sermon is in FBIS/NESA, 14 December 1987, 58–62.

24. *Kayhan,* 14 Khordad 1366 (4 June 1987), 2; and *Kayhan,* 19 Khordad 1366 (9 June 1987), 18.

25. The *hajj* message was published as an independent pamphlet. See *Payam-e Tarikhi-ye Imam be Za'erin-e Bayt-e Haram* (The Message of the Imam to the Pilgrims to the Holy Precincts), Tehran, 1 Dhu al-Hijja 1407 (28 July 1987), 22.

26. FBIS/NESA, 31 March 1988, 48.

27. See sermon by Khamene'i in FBIS/NESA, 29 February 1988, 67–68.

28. FBIS/NESA, 3 January 1989, 45. I have slightly amended the translation in keeping with the Persian original.

Chapter 11: Foreign Policy: 1984–1988

1. Foreign Broadcasting Information Service (FBIS), South Asia, 30 October 1984, I1–2.

2. R. Ul'ianovski, "Moral Principles in Politics and Politics in the Sphere of Morals," *Literaturnaya gazeta,* 22 June 1983, 10.

3. FBIS, USSR International Affairs, 28 March 1985, H2.

4. FBIS, South Asia, 13 May 1985, I2.

5. *Congressional Record,* United States Senate, 27 June 1985, S9048.

6. For a more detailed discussion of Syria's alliance with Iran, see Patrick Seale, *Asad: The Struggle for the Middle East* (Berkeley and Los Angeles: University of California Press, 1989), 349–64.

7. Nora Boustany, "Syria's Economic Crisis Seen Straining Links with Iran," *Washington Post,* 17 July 1987.

8. For a description of Iranian activities in Lebanon, see Nora Boustany, "Iran Uses Void in Lebanon to Expand Network of Ties," *Washington Post,* 19 July 1987.

9. On the factional infighting that preceded the kidnapping of the Syrian *chargé d'affaires,* see Jean Gueyras, "La guerre de succession s'aggrave en Iran," *Le Monde,* 25 October 1986, and *L'Express,* 24 October 1986, 12–13.

10. There is a reference to this incident in part one of the letter from Ahmad Khomaini to Ayatollah Montazeri, reprinted in *Resalat,* 25 Ordibehesht 1368 (15 May 1989), 4; and also an oblique reference in the letter written by Prime Minister Musavi to President Khamene'i, cited in Patrick Tyler, "Correspondence Reveals High-Level Rift in Iran," *Washington Post,* 11 November 1988, A17.

11. An oblique reference to this incident is contained in the letter written by Prime

Minister Musavi to President Khamene'i. See Patrick Tyler, "Correspondence Reveals High-Level Rift in Iran," *Washington Post,* 11 November 1988, A17.

12. For a detailed account of the war and cease-fire negotiations in 1987–88, see Gary Sick, "Slouching Towards Settlement: The Internationalization of the Iran-Iraq War, 1987–88," in Nikkie Keddie and Mark Gasiorowski, eds., *Iran, the United States and the Soviet Union: The Fateful Triangle* (New Haven: Yale University Press, 1990), forthcoming.

13. Cited in Jean Gueyras, "La guerre de succession s'aggrave en Iran," *Le Monde,* 25 October 1986.

14. *Report of the President's Special Review Board* (hereafter Tower Report) (Washington, D.C.: U.S. Government Printing Office), 26 February 1987, III–18.

15. See North's memo to Poindexter of 10 July 1986, and references to third-country initiatives in North memo to Poindexter of 2 September 1986, both in Tower Report, B–136–37 and B–150.

16. The Iranians mentioned these leaflets in their discussions with North and other members of the American team at Frankfurt on 26–29 October. See Tower Report, III–18.

17. Patrick Seale, however, asserts that it was the Syrians who leaked the story of the McFarlane visit to *al-Shira'a,* thus sabotaging the U.S.-Iran arms-for-hostages arrangements. See *Asad,* 489–90.

18. This point is persuasively argued by Gary Sick, "Slouching Towards Settlement: The Internationalization of the Iran-Iraq War."

19. A reference to the delegations from the cabinet and the Society of the Qom Seminary Teachers that had urged such a course on Khomaini in the summer of 1986 is in the "Open Letter to Ayatollah Khomaini," dated August-September 1986, written to Khomaini by Mehdi Bazargan. According to Bazargan, Khomaini told the cabinet ministers they could step down if they felt themselves not up to the task of continuing the war. He reportedly told the Qom seminary instructors: "Do not speak of peace and the end of the war as long as I am alive. After that, do whatever you want." The Bazargan pamphlet was printed and circulated as a separate document by the Iran Freedom Movement. See *Nameh-ye Sargoshadeh-ye Nehzat-e Azadi be Ayatollah Khomaini* (Open Letter from the Freedom Movement to Ayatollah Khomaini), Shahrivar 1365 (September-October 1986).

20. A description of these events was given by Rafsanjani. See the account of his press conference of 19 July in FBIS, Near East and South Asia, 19 July 1988, 63–66.

21. FBIS, Near East and South Asia, 21 July 1988, 49–50.

Chapter 12: The End of the Khomaini Decade

1. Foreign Broadcasting Information Service, Near East and South Asia (FBIS/NESA), 7 December 1988, 34.

2. FBIS/NESA, 25 July 1988, 48.

3. For these figures, see *Iran: Over 900 Executions Announced in Five Months* (London: Amnesty International), June 1989.

4. See David Hirst, "Radicals Again in the Ascendant in Iran," *The Guardian Weekly,* 26 February 1989; and FBIS/NESA, 23 January 1989, 53.

5. FBIS/NESA, 26 August 1988, 42. See also Musavi's remarks in FBIS/NESA, 22 August 1988, 61, and 23 August 1988, 64.

6. FBIS/NESA, 29 August 1988, 58.

7. FBIS/NESA, 11 October 1988, 59–61.

8. FBIS/NESA, 1 August 1988, 55–60, and 13 October 1988, 45–51.

9. FBIS/NESA, 4 October 1988, 46–48.

10. FBIS/NESA, 7 December 1988, 57.

11. FBIS/NESA, 14 February 1989, 43.

12. FBIS/NESA, 23 February 1989, 51.

13. FBIS/NESA, 29 March 1989, 39.

14. On the early background to Montazeri's succession, see Shahrough Akhavi, "Elite Factionalism in the Islamic Republic of Iran," *Middle East Journal* (vol. 41, no. 2, Spring 1987), esp. 194–98.

15. This account of Mehdi Hashemi's activities and the Khomaini-Montazeri quarrel is based on material in a long letter, dated 29 April 1989, that Ahmad Khomaini wrote to Montazeri after the latter's dismissal. The account is biased and one-sided, but contains useful information. For a text of the letter, see *Resalat*, 25, 26, 27 Ordibehesht 1368 (15, 16, 17 May 1989) (hereafter called Ahmad Khomaini's letter). An English translation appears in FBIS/NESA, 6 July 1989, 37–59.

16. Ahmad Khomaini's letter, *Resalat*, 27 Ordibehesht 1368 (17 May 1989), 3; and 26 Ordibehesht 1368 (16 May 1989), 10.

17. *Kayhan Havai*, 8 February 1989, 11; an English translation is in FBIS/NESA, 3 March 1989, 66–69.

18. FBIS/NESA, 23 February 1989, 44–49.

INDEX

Index

Index